50

FABULOUS PLANNED RETIREMENT COMMUNITIES FOR ACTIVE ADULTS

A Comprehensive Directory of Outstanding
Master-Planned Residential Developments

By

Bob Greenwald

CAREER PRESS
3 Tice Road
P.O. Box 687
Franklin Lakes, NJ 07417
1-800-CAREER-1
201-848-0310 (NJ and outside U.S.)
Fax: 201-848-1727

**50 FABULOUS PLANNED RETIREMENT COMMUNITIES
FOR ACTIVE ADULTS**
Cover design by JenMar Graphics Corp.
Cover photo courtesy of Robson Communities, Sun Lakes, AZ
Printed in the U.S.A. by Book-mart Press

To order this title, please call toll-free 1-800-CAREER-1 (NJ and Canada:
201-848-0310) to order using VISA or MasterCard, or for further
information on books from Career Press.

Library of Congress Cataloging-in-Publication Data

Greenwald, Robert, 1923-
    50 fabulous planned retirement communities for active adults : a
comprehensive directory of outstanding master-planned residential
developments / by Robert Greenwald.
      p.   cm.
    Includes index.
    ISBN 1-56414-347-3 (pbk.)
    1. Retirement communities--United States--Directories.   2. Planned
communities--United States--Directories.   I. Title.
    HQ1063.2.U6G74   1998
307.3'36'08696--dc21   97-45742
                                                                   CIP

ACKNOWLEDGMENTS

Few authors write a book without inspiration and encouragement from others. Through months of research, travel, and contemplation, my wife Pat was a constant mainstay and patient companion. The investment of time and energy was such as to make me something less than an accessible and attentive husband. A wordsmith in her own right, she contributed routinely and substantially to my work in progress. Moreover, my self-imposed regimen for 10 months of long hours and preoccupied weekends provided ample demonstration of her devotion to our partnership.

My son, David, who was born with uncommon language skills, put his discriminating pencil to paper in my behalf in a show of syntax surgery. It was one of those rare opportunities for him to contest the old adage, "father knows best," not the first time he has been so inclined.

A special word of thanks goes to Frances Bell, humanities division manager of the Dallas Public Library. She graciously applied her insights and editing skills to initial text drafts, much to the improvement of the final product.

Perhaps most deserving of my gratitude are the marketing and management officials from each of our 50 profiled communities. They had to cope with what must have seemed like an endless questionnaire designed to provide detailed information in formulating the profiles. One of my earliest contacts among them was Gary L. Newman, executive vice president of Cooper Communities, Inc., who endorsed my proposal with enthusiasm and gave spark to my determination to see the project through.

I am indebted to all of you.

CONTENTS

INTRODUCTION

My wife, Pat, and I have spent much time in recent years researching retirement communities around the country and making on-site visits in search of just the combination of features and environmental conditions that would best meet our particular life style and relocation objectives. It has been a formidable task to find sources of information that would help us sensibly and methodically plan our investigation.

Frequently, in the course of our travels, we would arrive at our destination only to find that at least one critical element among our priority considerations was missing. Sometimes it was the size, cost, design, or configuration of housing units available. Other times, the planned activities agenda, access to shopping, leisure and cultural attractions, scheduled airline service, or recreational amenities fell short of expectations. Convenient access to shopping, leisure and cultural attractions, or scheduled airline service, were also notable influences in our evaluations. Climatic characteristics were of prime importance, yet typically could not readily be determined in advance for a particular geographic location (often because the site was not close enough to an official weather reporting station for conditions there to be reliably assessed).

Such priorities and preferences vary widely from one family to another. Surveys have demonstrated convincingly, however, that most relocating retirees find that certain features for a target destination are high among their most important criteria. In broadest terms, for the great majority, they center on location, affordability, and environmental appeal.

It is these fundamentals and their tangent influences that this directory addresses. It is our purpose to help you explore a retirement relocation by providing you with reliable and comprehensive background documentation to screen and narrow choices so that fewer personal visits to selected communities will be necessary in making final evaluations. With this information, you can devise a more practical plan.

There are few more important questions most of us will face in our later years than where those years should be spent. Finding the answer is a quest deserving of a full measure of inquiry and preparation.

There is considerable evidence to suggest that land developers, builders, and real estate investors are showing increasing interest in this emerging retirement sector of the housing industry. Some of the earliest pioneers in this field broke ground in the 60s. More recently, especially during the past decade, there has been a growing number of newcomers to the scene. Among them are companies with well-established credentials in the residential construction industry. They have come to recognize, as had their forerunners years before, the explosive demand for this new kind of alternative residential planning and development.

While every effort has been made to ensure the reliability of the information presented in this publication, the author cannot guarantee the accuracy of statements or data contained herein. Most information on each listing is supplied by sources from within the community featured. In some instances, conditions and the basis for data citations change. It is always a good idea to obtain the latest information directly from the communities in which you're interested. Errors or omissions brought to the attention of the author and satisfactorily verified will be corrected in future editions.

A PHENOMENON OF THE TIMES

During the past three decades, there has been significant economic stimulation among land developers and home builders resulting from the dramatic changes occurring in the retirement marketplace.

With the advent of extended longevity, sustained good health, and increased economic independence among growing numbers of elders, has come a new paradigm of consumer appetite and a new outlook on aging. More and more people are arriving at the zenith of their lives, free of career and family responsibilities, relatively secure in their financial condition, ready to escape to a life style that was earlier beyond their reach. And now, as the century draws to a close, a new retirement influence is beginning to emerge—the baby boomer.

The prospect of finally getting to enjoy the fruits of long years of earning a livelihood has proved invigorating, to say the least. Trading an alarm clock and congested rush hour freeways for a laid-back routine in a pristine hideaway can intoxicate the imagination.

This same age revolution has affected many facets of business and community life. Financial institutions have spawned new investment instruments. Health care and insurance providers scramble to serve a dominating new market niche. Makers of everything from hearing aids to bathroom fixtures reexamine product lines and sales strategies. Churches, local and state governments, hospitals and life care facilities, and an endless number of community and charitable nonprofits that depend to one degree or another on volunteer resources, are tasting and enjoying the fruits of this unprecedented leisure class.

WHAT IS A MASTER-PLANNED RETIREMENT COMMUNITY?

It is estimated that there are more than 3,000 age-restricted, adult-only communities nationwide. They vary widely in the types of living environments offered to retired residents. Some emphasize different levels of on-site health care and daily living assistance. Others are targeted primarily at mature adults who are in relatively good health and who need no ongoing caregiver assistance. These are retirees who seek a quality of life that is represented by the features of a leisure-oriented planned community.

There are thousands more communities that are *primarily* for adults only, but have no age restrictions and may have a significant number of younger families in residence. This directory is devoted to a combination of the two latter groups.

For purposes of presenting the information found on these pages, we define our community model as a residential development *exclusively or primarily for active adults*, with the following additional key characteristics as criteria for inclusion.

Mandatory requirements:

♦ Age-restricted eligibility policy whereby *at least one member of the family is 50 years of age or older with no children under the age of 18* living permanently in the community.

Or

♦ No age restrictions, but *not less than an estimated 60 percent* of the total population is in retirement or semiretirement status (do not commute to full-time employment).

♦ A year-round permanent population of no fewer than 150 households (with only occasional exceptions), in most cases situated on at least 100 and up to 20,000 or more acres, of sufficient size to support a program of activities appropriate to the interests of active retirees.

Optional/desirable features:

♦ A resort or recreational environment that offers an extensive variety of activity choices for residents.

♦ Time share units and/or short-term rentals.

♦ Broad selection of housing styles and price ranges (new construction and/or resale), as well as rental options.

♦ A self-contained community where all or most daily living conveniences are found within or immediately adjacent to the development property.

♦ A gated perimeter, controlled access to residential areas.

♦ Preservation of natural environment.

Excluded from this directory are:

♦ Communities that are *primarily or exclusively* centered on congregate or assisted living services (fee-based housing, personal/daily living assistance, congregate meals, scheduled transportation).

♦ Communities that cater *primarily or exclusively* to on-site continuing health care needs of residents who can progress from one level of care to a more supportive level as changing needs and conditions require.

♦ Resort, recreational, or other master-planned communities that cater *primarily* to families with young children and that do not operate a significant program geared to active adult retirees.

RETIREMENT RELOCATION INFLUENCES/DECISIONS

Retirement status in today's society is drawn from many circumstances. Corporate reorganization has resulted in departure from the work force of many productive and relatively young employees at all levels of responsibility. Often, the victim of downsizing has not adequately prepared for the trauma of such an event. For reasons of age, economic conditions, outdated qualifications, or other factors, retirement or semiretirement may be the only alternative. There are those too, of course, who welcome the external forces that may push them prematurely into a career-ending decision that would not otherwise have been made. For those looking for new life style fields to plow, the prospect of moving to a new location can be appealing. One can enjoy the luxury of choosing a place that has the best combination of opportunities and resources to meet particular individual needs and inclinations.

The retirement decision often rests firmly on the question of what activity will replace the preretirement life style. Leisure attractions such as golf, fishing, travel, hobbies, gardening, and such are enough to satisfy some people. Others require more. The fact is that in today's world of personal computers, enhanced communication, and access to resources, the opportunities for exploring new horizons of creativity and productiveness are boundless. Few who are willing to generate initiatives are disappointed in their quest for challenges.

Like most crossroads to greater reward in life, there can be a downside to pulling up stakes. Those who come to retirement and the attractions of a new beginning often have to face the reality of leaving valued friendships, long-held institutional ties, and familiar surroundings. Change is not something to which our species tends to take kindly. A retirement relocation can be especially difficult for those who have had a relatively stable background of long-term residence in a single town or city or neighborhood. Sometimes it's a matter of uprooting from a place that has been home for the better part of a lifetime.

On the other hand, moving to an adult-oriented retirement community offers any number of attractions that can make such a transition more inviting and less daunting. One of the greatest appeals is the fact that virtually all new friends and neighbors at the destination community are likely to have experienced the very same departure trauma.

They too probably left behind cherished relationships, familiar surroundings, and maybe even important family ties. They weighed the consequences and made their decision. So you, following along a parallel path, can expect to be greeted by others who have been through a very similar experience.

It is quite a different scenario than when moving to a new town or city in a traditional setting where many of your new neighbors and others you meet are well-ensconced in long-nurtured relationships. In too many instances in that circumstance, newcomers find few shortcuts to establishing compatible friendships and satisfying connections.

A retirement community, by its very nature, offers opportunities to fast-forward the assimilation process. The mechanisms for social interaction and the common denominator of shared experience accelerate the pace of inclusion. For those whose lives have been marked by frequent moves because of job transfers, military mobility, or other circumstances there is, of course, likely to be far less apprehension than among those unaccustomed to residential transplant. Such a background generally provides conditioning to relocation long before facing a retirement decision to pack up and move.

Then there is the excitement of entering a new life style, until now only visualized or dreamed about. Maybe you have longed for a more temperate climate or a back deck overlooking an idyllic vista of nature's bounty. Some of us yearn merely to escape a polluted environment or the noise and congestion of too many people too closely crowded together.

Most of all, though, we are social creatures who, as we get along in life, find our greatest joys in shared interests and stimulating relationships that emerge from a wider range of human contact. Self-centered career objectives and absorbing family responsibilities are no longer the focus of our lives. The new age of active retirement offers an assortment of opportunities to cultivate interests, talents, and satisfactions never before recognized.

Retirees who plan to make travel an important part of their lives will assign greater weight to commercial airport access. If chronic medical problems are part of the mix of concerns, then obviously it is of particular importance that related health care resources are readily available. Those whose incomes dictate careful budgeting are likely to pay closer attention to cost-of-living variables: comparative tax burdens, housing, food and utility costs, availability of public transportation, etc. To many, the nature and convenience of opportunities for social interaction and recreation are near the top in order of importance. The parts of the country where children and grandchildren are currently living is a tempting consideration, but is too unpredictable in this highly mobile world, most would agree, to unduly influence the choice of a retirement relocation.

For some who yearn to escape the big city, issues of crime and pollution can be powerful incentives in making the destination area decision. Important, too, is convenience to retail shopping, especially for routine daily necessities found at full-service grocery markets, drug stores, beauty/barber shops, cleaners, and such.

There is one piece of advice that can be found in almost any book written about retirement relocation: Do your homework! Careful research pays handsome dividends. It is well to remember that while promotion materials (brochures, videos, and the like) can be very useful sources of information, they may also have more than their share of hype. There is no substitute for *an on-site visit over a reasonably extended period of time.* Being there makes one-on-one exchanges possible with residents who are more than likely willing to share their candid opinions about the pros and cons of life in their community. If you feel you're close to deciding on a particular community, a longer term rental before purchasing could prove to be the best insurance against a flawed or hasty decision.

Most adult communities welcome prospective residents to sample the life style and environment. Some offer attractive lodging options to accommodate such arrangements. It becomes a matter of practicality in terms of costs and time availability that in order to heed the advice for a trial living scenario, it is necessary to screen choices down to a few. It is precisely to help with that process of narrowing the field to the most promising prospects that this directory is dedicated.

There is one concluding observation that bears on the search for an ideal place to retire. It is that perfection is elusive. Pursue it and you are likely to meet with disappointment. The ideal defies definition because it has different meaning to different people. That's why it is important that you decide for yourself where your priorities lie. Your own needs and preferences must dictate your strategy in finding the best formula for a hospitable relocation.

DIRECTORY RATIONALE AND FORMAT

This book is written primarily for those who are near or already in retirement and who are inclined to explore relocation as a possible option. In order to pursue such inclinations, one question looms large—*where to look?*

Because people's values, desires, and intentions vary so widely, we have resisted the temptation to rate the overall comparative "living appeal" of one place over another. We recognize that one family's Shangri-La can be another's discard. Given that reality, we have attempted to focus on those elements that are likely to appeal to the greater majority of those who may consult this directory.

We have, for example, chosen to limit our community selections to locations in 14 states in the southeast, middle south, southwest, and Pacific coast. That decision was based, in part, on the assumption that a great majority of retirement relocation prospects seek scenic enchantment coupled with relatively moderate climates where they can, to some degree, escape cold weather-related discomforts. The states included are:

Alabama	Colorado	Oregon	Virginia
Arizona	Florida	South Carolina	Washington
Arkansas	Maryland	Tennessee	
California	North Carolina	Texas	

By and large, these states are known for exceptional environmental appeal and outdoor recreational attractions. Rivers, lakes, the seashore, woodlands, mountains, and other natural amenities are typical panoramic features. They have within their borders a variety of tourist attractions. With some exceptions, these states offer below-average costs of living and many boast outstanding medical and cultural assets. Most of them are not highly urbanized.

Parenthetically, a note of clarification is in order. Clearly, there are many master-planned retirement-oriented communities, in these selected states and elsewhere, that meet the criteria we have established for inclusion but do not appear on these pages. Some we simply have been unable to uncover in our research. Some we contacted did not respond to our survey questionnaire because they were no longer actively marketing their communities, or for other reasons. Several failed to return the necessary information in time to make the publishing deadline.

It should also be pointed out that the information presented in this directory is subject to change. The cost of living in some places is prone to fluctuation. Tax rates can change from one year to the next. The best way to be sure you have accurate, up-to-date information is to contact the sources we have provided and, perhaps later, to visit the site yourself.

Communities are listed first by state in alphabetical order, then by name. Information for each profile was collected through distribution of a comprehensive questionnaire sent to communities identified through extensive research. Each entry is divided into a basic information summary and specific topical subsections:

1. Why (name of community)?
2. Who's In Charge?
3. The Weather Report
4. Home Sweet Home
5. Money Matters
6. Take Good Care of Yourself
7. Places to Go, Things to Do
8. Safe and Secure
9. Let's Go Shopping

The following subsections should enable the reader to evaluate information presented under some of the foregoing headings. These comments represent an effort to underscore once again the infinite range of variables that play on retirement relocation decisions.

WHY (NAME OF COMMUNITY)?

Every community has its own distinctive appeal. This section sums up the benefits and attractions unique to each, from world-class golf courses to award-winning home design and construction.

WHO'S IN CHARGE?

In a growing number of instances, active adult retirement communities are governed under the supervision of property owners' associations. Typically, they function much like a municipal government in miniature. In early stages of site evolution, the developer may retain control over all or most of the final decision-making process, especially with regard to budgeting and financial commitments. Gradually (usually over a period of years), more and more authority and responsibility may be turned over to the residents until they have full, collective ownership of common land and facilities and responsibility for policy formulation, program operations, and property upkeep, among other obligations.

In order to accomplish that goal, of course, the owners' association must build a sound financial foundation. That is achieved primarily through the development of a system of assessments and user fees paid by residents for the various benefits and services they enjoy (golf courses, swimming pools, fitness/exercise facilities, etc.). Needless to say, such costs to the owners vary widely.

It is of prime importance in evaluating a community for its appeal to your relocation objectives to examine the nature and structure of the management mechanism. Certainly the cost of membership in the association, the charges that are optional and mandatory, and a general appraisal of value received, are among critical considerations. Past quarterly or annual reports, financial statements, meeting minutes, newsletters, and the bylaws or other guidelines under which the organization functions (covering such matters as leader-ship selection, conditions of volunteer or paid service, financial planning/budgeting, determination of fees/assessments, safeguarding property values, etc.) are also of great importance.

Other crucial factors are the reputation and track record of the developer and the history of the self-governing body. The development of a master-planned adult community requires enormous capital outlay and superior management resources. It is of considerable importance to find out how long it has been since the project was established and to examine the results of marketing efforts to date. How long has the sponsoring company (usually the developer) been involved with active adult or retirement housing? Is the community run by the residents themselves? How long has it taken to reach 60 or 80 percent occupancy? What facilities are completed (golf course, swimming pools, club house, retail center, etc.)? The answers to such questions will provide useful insights into the pace of progress in reaching the community's proclaimed objectives.

THE WEATHER REPORT

The desire to live in a better climate is one of the most compelling reasons retirees consider relocation. But when it comes to the weather, there is no universal perfection. Individual differences about what conditions make for optimal comfort are too dissimilar. So it comes down to finding the climate that best suits *you*.

As we grow older, the extremes of weather can become formidable. Many grandfathers can still wield a snow shovel, but there comes a time when, even if we are able, we are unwilling. Much more threatening than a loss of stamina or motivation is the reality that climate severity actually may have a deleterious effect on our health and well-being. Medical researchers have found that unstable weather conditions can even adversely affect certain drug therapies.

Those with coronary conditions tend to do better in climates where ex-treme temperatures are avoided. Arthritics and people with other skeletal difficulties find more comfort in warmer climes. The desert southwest has long been a haven for those who suffer from hay fever, asthma, or other respiratory/allergenic ailments and for whom low humidity is very desirable. The combi-nation of high humidity and high temperature is stressful even to the healthiest among us.

Some older people can readily adapt to oppressive heat or bone-chilling cold. Many more have difficulty in coping. There are those who suffer few, if any, ill effects but are aware of a certain imbalance in their bodies with their surroundings. There is evidence to suggest that more of us can withstand heat extremes more readily than we can cold. But we know that as we age, there are changes in our physiology that tend to limit our capacities to absorb any kind of environmental punishment.

When it comes to measuring personal comfort when temperatures are excessively high, however, *humidity* is a central influence. The amount of moisture in the air affects the body's capacity to cool itself through its natural process of evaporation. The greater the moisture content (water vapor) in the air, the more difficult it is to sustain evaporation and avoid discomfort. When the humidity level drops too low, on the other hand, there can be other equally undesirable consequences (dry sinuses, sore throat, skin and/or eye irritation, etc.). Humidity is a product of temperature (the same humidity can be comfortable at one temperature and not at another) and is also influenced significantly by the time of day at which it is measured. Different people react differently to the very same humidity conditions, depending on such factors as age, state of health, exertion, and conditioning to past climatic experience.

There also is a man-made influence on the weather that should not be overlooked. If you are in or very near a large urban population, there are all sorts of heating sources with which to contend other than the sun. Exhaust, concrete and asphalt streets, large commercial buildings, and industrial emissions all conspire to raise daytime temperatures, and to make matters worse, their induced heat clings to the lower atmosphere at night in a pollution haze that reduces the cooling effect that otherwise normally comes with darkness.

So where in the United States is the ideal climate? The answer is as variable as individual needs and preferences. No matter where one turns, it seems, there are offsetting balances. Southern California has long been heralded for its near-perfect weather. That may be appealing unless you are among those who consider a four-season rotation essential to your meteorological tastes (to say nothing of any aversion to earthquakes and air pollution). There are those who tout the Pacific Northwest for its relatively mild year-round temperatures. But the enjoyment of that benefit is surely tempered by the marine climate that keeps a significant portion of the year in a state of overcast skies and persistent rainfall. Hawaii, you say? Maybe so. That is if you can afford the real estate prices, handle the isolation from the mainland, and are not apt to become saturated with the sameness of a tropical weather forecast.

A final note about weather temperatures. *Year-round averages* are misleading and of little value. The same moderate average can be found for two locations where one has consistently mild climate and the other great seasonal extremes. It is the daily *high and low averages* for a given month or other period of time that provide meaningful temperature data.

HOME SWEET HOME

What is the shape, size, and style of your retirement dream home? What would best suit your needs and desires? Excess space usually means excessive cost in initial outlay as well as ongoing expense (taxes, utilities, maintenance, etc.). A smaller lot may make more sense, also reducing the time and expense associated with caring for sprawling lawns and elaborate landscaping.

In general, there are as many types of communities as there are housing needs and preferences; some consist of only manufactured homes, while others have mostly apartments and/or condominiums. If you are exclusively interested in the purchase of a site-built single family detached home, then clearly these choices can be eliminated from your list of prospective inspection visits. More often than not, however, the larger master-planned developments provide a variety of housing styles from which to choose.

If you are among those who bought homes in the 60s or 70s and managed to pay off a relatively modest 20- or 30-year mortgage, you are in an enviable position. Chances are you can use your equity to buy a retirement spread at a considerably lower figure and have a nice cash surplus to spend on other things.

Another question looms large in the home buying decision. To build or not to build? On the face of it, there are obvious advantages to building over buying an existing home. You can please every desire in creating a "perfect" floor plan. Lot selection, color schemes, appliance options, exterior features, storage capacity, etc., are subject to your every fancy. Your dream of a picture-perfect setting is pretty much limited only by the condition of your bank account.

The downside of taking on the formidable task of building from the ground up lies in several realities. Foremost, perhaps, is the very practical matter of whether you can manage to be on site regularly to oversee construction. Other challenges, including delays, contention, and jangled nerves, are almost inescapable byproducts.

The alternative to "doing your own thing" is to purchase an existing home that comes as close as possible to meeting your expectations. Again, there are pros and cons.

One great advantage is that there is no protracted waiting time to accommodate the construction process. Assuming that prices have risen in recent years, there could be some savings to be realized in buying a home that was built at lower cost than would apply in the current new home market (even if some appreciation in value has occurred). Purchasing an existing home also often is characterized by any number of extras that were added after construction and that are now part of the sale package (for example, window treatments, built-in fixtures or adornments, carpet upgrades, landscaping, etc.).

There is also something to be said for the stability of the selling price. Once settled, it is unlikely to change. In contrast, when custom building, the original quotation may be substantially less than the final cost because of all the temptations to which the home buyer may be subjected. Sometimes it is just too much to resist modifications that add to the bottom line.

MONEY MATTERS

Flight from excessive living costs can become an imperative. People in many areas of the country have relocated out of sheer budgetary necessity. Without question, living costs are a priority consideration for most relocating retirees. Unless you enjoy unlimited financial resources, chances are you give serious attention to deciding how your income dollars will be spent. For many in retirement, it is necessary to live on a relatively fixed income, leaving little budgeting flexibility.

There are rather substantial differences from one part of the country to another in the price tag for taxes, food, housing, clothing, health care, and any number of other commodities and services found in the family budget. Unfortunately, these relative costs are in a virtually constant state of flux. Local economic conditions can change on surprisingly short notice. Given that caveat, we can proceed with examining such cost figures and still find useful indicators to help us make informed decisions.

There is no more obscure and complex issue on the cost of living agenda than taxes. Differences in the impact of the tax burden on retirees can be startling. When state, county, and local assessments are combined, the bottom line can vary from one town or city to another by several thousand dollars annually. Fortunately, for those who take their research seriously, there is no dearth of available data. One of the better, more current reference works is a 1996 soft-cover book titled *Tax Heaven or Hell—A Guide to the Tax Consequences of Retirement Relocation* (see bibliography). It analyzes state and local taxes/fees to help the reader determine the best and worst of taxing jurisdictions in America. Your public library reference shelves may have other useful sources of similar information. The most reliable and up-to-date data, of course, can be obtained directly from the state agency responsible for revenue and taxation. Contacts in that regard are given in this directory before the first profile in each state under the heading "tax facts."

It is of interest to take note here of a rather peculiar tax-related proclivity among retirees and others who contemplate relocation. It concerns the fact that so many otherwise astute people jump to a clearly faulty judgment regarding state income tax. They treat that singular issue as though it was the only critical consideration in measuring comparative tax burdens. Not so.

A state may very well impose no income tax but instead use a myriad of other revenue devices to reach into the citizen's pocketbook. Such levies may significantly offset the absence of taxes based on income. Sales tax rates can add up to substantial differences in out-of-pocket dollars given to state and local governments at the end of the year. The state tax code may provide for imposing a tax on income but with provisions of exemptions and graduated scales that can reveal important variances among different types of individual income sources. The point here is simply a word of caution. A determination of tax impact on any one family's obligations to the commonweal deserves careful examination, perhaps competent professional guidance.

Having expressed these qualifying conditions regarding income taxes, we are not inclined to omit from this account mention of those jurisdictions that tease your frugal nature and draw you toward the lure of practical savings. Some states, including Florida, Tennessee, Texas, and Washington, impose *no tax on income.*

Taxes levied on investment income, often a vital element in a retiree's resources, are collected by six states and/or by local jurisdictions within those states. Such "intangibles taxes" are collected in Florida, Georgia, Kentucky, Michigan, Pennsylvania, and West Virginia. Rates, inclusions, and exemptions vary from one location to another. An excellent recent report on this subject was published by Vacation Publications, Inc., 1502 Augusta Drive, Suite 415, Houston, TX 77057 (713-974-6903).

There will be no attempt here to examine the role of property taxes in making the retirement relocation decision. While such taxes can consume as much as 5 percent or more of the family budget, the subject is so convoluted and difficult to dissect that we will leave it to others to provide insights in that connection. Even those who specialize in developing such information differ on how to organize and present meaningful data. The problem lies in the fact that there are so many different state and local taxing authorities, infinite variations in appraisal policies and rate structures, a wide assortment of allowable exemptions and deductions, and varying degrees of inclusiveness of services covered by the tax bill, as opposed to being separately charged (e.g., street repairs, trash collection, recycling, snow removal, etc.).

For those interested in a detailed analysis of cost of living data (excluding taxes), there is pertinent information available from ACCRA, an affiliate of the American Chamber of Commerce Executives, titled *ACCRA Cost of Living Index.* Published quarterly since 1968, it sets forth useful measurements of living cost differences among urban areas around the country. The information is drawn from government survey data. The current issue can be found in the reference sections of most libraries or can be ordered directly from the publisher (ACCRA, 4232 King Street, Alexandria, VA 22302-9950).

TAKE GOOD CARE OF YOURSELF

As we near the end of the 20th century, Americans are comforted more than ever by increased life expectancy. While we read about serious shortcomings in our health care system, clearly there are more of us than ever before who are reaping the blessings of physical well-being.

This promise of longer life, of course, has given impetus to the phenomenon of "active adulthood." People who have reached an age not long ago thought to be beyond the pale of new beginnings, now take on post-retirement challenges in the work place, in the community, in leisure activities, and in their personal goal setting. Health problems for increasing numbers in the maturing population are no longer the inhibitors they once were.

Nonetheless, even those who are relatively healthy recognize the increased vulnerability that comes with advanced age. Availability of quality health care resources is always a prime concern. Certainly, if the retiree contends with one or more chronic conditions, it becomes especially important to know that there is competent medical care close at hand.

When reviewing the health care sections of the profiles in this publication, pay close attention to the locations, distances, and size of accessible hospitals. An institution with several hundred beds is likely to have more surgeons and specialists than a smaller facility. A hospital that bears accreditation from the Joint Commission on Accreditation (JCAH) indicates that it is eligible to receive federal funds and is licensed by the state to perform certain advanced procedures. It also gives the consumer reasonable evidence of acceptable standards in service delivery having been met, although it is no guarantee that deficiencies cannot be found. JCAH is a private nonprofit commission set up to certify hospital operations.

While most sizable master-planned communities do not have on-site full-service hospital facilities, often there are medical and dental offices, pharmaceutical and other related services, outpatient clinics, and health centers on or adjacent to the property. As for emergency medical response and treatment for conditions that may at some time require hospitalization, most people regardless of age, consider reasonably fast access to 24-hour comprehensive health care facilities a vital criterion in choosing a new place to live.

Health insurance is another ingredient that is worth attention as part of the evaluation process. Find out whether health care professionals at a destination area accept your policy provisions and what adjustments, if any, might be necessary.

PLACES TO GO, THINGS TO DO

For most people, opportunities for social and recreational indulgence are prominent on the menu of life style objectives. Planned retirement communities are uniquely conceived to provide a broad range of possibilities.

Wherever there is a substantial concentration of "leisure class" residents with the freedom to allocate time as they choose, there is likely to be a corresponding range of planned activities and facilities to satisfy the demand. In the larger communities there are staff specialists who arrange, promote, and implement social and recreational programs. For many, they are at the heart of the community's appeal.

These activities may include an almost endless number of clubs and interest groups, from bird-watching, bowling, and book reviews to gardening, genealogy, and gourmet cooking. Planned entertainment is apt to be a major attraction, especially when the community boasts a sizable auditorium or meeting space.

A key element of any comprehensive leisure program is effective promotion to attract participants. Regularly published newsletters are the most common medium for creating interest in planned events. Resident committees are often at the forefront of initiatives to plan and publicize special attractions. Some communities even use closed circuit television or a cable channel to get the word out.

If there is any standard feature of planned retirement communities, it is the clubhouse or activity center. Often a centerpiece of architectural dominance and appeal, it is invariably the hub of all that contributes to resident interaction. Most have meeting rooms of various sizes for crafts, games, hobbies, parties, etc. Pool and table tennis are popular draws. Indoor swimming pools, health clubs, saunas and Jacuzzi whirlpools, snack bars, and dining rooms are among typical features. If the recreation building serves as a golf/tennis clubhouse as well, the pro shop is an inevitable adjunct. Sometimes there is a gift shop, convenience store, or other retail combination to round out a more complete service center.

Perhaps most conducive to becoming better acquainted with neighbors and forming new friendships are the day trips and longer excursions that take residents from the community to various places of interest. Sometimes it is a busload to an entertainment center or an itinerary of historical sites. Sometimes it's a caravan of cars to cultural/educational attractions or to a high-appeal resort area promising new experiences or unusual amenities. Most are within a comfortable travel distance. And, of course, getting there is half the fun!

Recreation encompasses such a variety of activities that no master-planned community (not even most mid-sized cities) can begin to provide all things to all people. If there is any single, almost universal common denominator, it is the golf course. More often than not, the aesthetic quality of the graceful, manicured contours of golfing greens is the developer's enhancement of choice...the ideal landscaping around which to arrange homesites. The popularity of the game among seniors has never been greater.

A close second among recreational centerpiece features are bodies of water—ponds, lakes, rivers, canals, streams, or seashore. Like the golf course, a twofold purpose of scenic appeal and leisure options is combined in a prime outdoor asset. Fishing, boating, water skiing, and swimming are resulting byproducts that enhance livability.

Of course, there are countless other popular leisure lures that are not found right there in the neighborhood. A multiplex cinema, a family theme park, professional or collegiate sporting events, or a national forest campground are going to require more than just a short walk or drive to the community recreation center. For those whose needs in this regard are a priority, it becomes a matter of some importance to determine just how convenient it will be to reach these places, if indeed, they are available at all within a practical distance.

You may be among the 10 percent or so of the population who consider that treating yourself at least once a week to a good restaurant meal is the highest form of recreational indulgence. If so, the quality of dining at the clubhouse or yacht club on the grounds takes on added weight (no pun intended!). Access to enjoyable dining, of course, need not be inside the perimeter of your home neighborhood. Of equal interest and worth noting in your destination evaluation is the selection, value, and excellence of the eateries that are convenient to home and that best serve your family's epicurean tastes.

From a retirement perspective, one of the principal sources of social interaction lies in finding volunteer activities that one can perform well, that are needed in the community, and that result in a true sense of personal fulfillment. Many who are drawn to volunteer activity place its importance at the apex of their avocational and socialization needs.

It is a well-recognized fact that cultural assets tend to be concentrated in the larger cities. For world-renowned performers and an infinite choice of venues, one must go to the cultural citadels—New York, Los Angeles, Chicago, Boston, Washington, D.C., and San Francisco, among others.

That said, it is also true that some of the nation's outstanding symphonies and theater and dance groups can be found performing in all sorts of out-of-the-way places. Touring companies bring some of the best professional talent to the hinterlands. Colleges and universities, often located in small towns, are frequently focal points of cultural activity. Nonprofit community concert associations also thrive in spite of typically limited financial resources. Local and regional performers can keep costs to a minimum while earning the respect and appreciation of patrons from the area who make up most of their audiences. Retirement communities with comprehensive activity programs and with sizable, well-appointed auditorium facilities to match can sometimes attract national and international celebrities for dramatic, musical, and speaking appearances. And so it is that worthwhile cultural riches can be found in small-town America.

All of this is to say that while the big cities may have a lock on many cultural prizes, the artistic world seems to reach into the more remote parts of the country. To cite just a few of many examples, witness the Berkshire Music Festival in rural western Massachusetts, the Santa Fe (New Mexico) Opera, the Cumberland County Playhouse (Crossville, Tennessee), and the Hendersonville Symphony Orchestra (North Carolina), located in what is said to be one of the smallest communities in the nation to support a full symphony orchestra. Sometimes it may require the upcountry dweller to travel some extra miles to reach the attraction, but more often than not, it is no more than a comfortable distance away.

One secret weapon favoring the hinterland in competing with the big cities for cultural appeal is the role of colleges and universities. Some of the most prominent of them are located away from major metropolitan areas. It is on their campuses, more frequently than not, that the larger auditoriums and program resources are found. It is to that setting that so many of America's top touring companies are attracted.

If your retirement crystal ball shows signs of classrooms and textbooks, your attention understandably will be drawn to continuing education opportunities. A good many of our selected communities are located near fairly large cities. In those cases, there will probably be an ample variety of college-level courses that might be of interest. Some of these communities, however, may not be conveniently located near such institutions, so this factor then takes on greater importance in the destination screening process.

It is of particular interest in this connection that an increasing number of universities and community colleges around the country offer special tuition incentives and admission privileges to seniors. Often enrollment fees are greatly reduced or even entirely waived. Noncredit auditing of courses at no cost is another frequent feature of "gray campus" programs.

SAFE AND SECURE

There is no more emotional issue on today's community agenda than protecting ourselves and our families against crime. To some, more than others, it is among the most urgent considerations in making a relocation decision.

Few will agree on what constitutes the most important elements of community safety. Several factors, however, are well-recognized and generally accepted as valid:

♦ Density of population.

♦ State of the local economy.

♦ Adequacy of law enforcement resources.

♦ Neighborhood stability.

In a number of ways, the typical self-contained retirement community ranks high on the safety scale.

Master-planned communities are often gated, surrounded by a perimeter fence or wall with entrances that are access-controlled by a coded entry system or security personnel. While not completely foolproof, these features do indeed contribute to effective crime control.

Beyond physical barriers, there are other factors that have a direct bearing on the level of security:

1. *Location:* Master-planned developments, primarily because they require large tracts of land, are typically situated in suburban or rural settings, removed from urban decay, stress, and congestion. The residential population usually lives in more dispersed housing patterns than those found in a traditional neighborhood.

2. *Population characteristics:* While most retirement communities are quite diverse in terms of housing costs and income levels among residents, there are no pockets of poverty, no substandard housing. There are also few, if any, teenagers in residence, tending to eliminate the threat of vandalism or gang-related crime.

3. *Street patterns:* Typical master-planned communities are platted so as to limit avenues of entry and exit. Criminals are not apt to be drawn to neighborhoods where quick escape is hampered.

4. *Law enforcement:* Whether a community is protected by its own security personnel or by local police, there is a tendency toward a more interactive relationship between law enforcement and citizens than exists in most urban neighborhoods. Unlike a small town of comparable size, there is typically a heightened degree of cohesiveness and involvement. Citizens are likely to take more responsibility for their mutual protection and well-being.

5. *Loyal relationships:* It is also characteristic of active adult communities that there is a prevailing sense of kinship. Loyalties and interdependence arise out of shared activities and common interests. These feelings and attitudes translate readily into a kind of neighborliness that makes for a bond of mutual protection against any external threat to community peace and preservation.

6. *Neighborhood stability:* Retirees don't contend with job transfers or most other causes of involuntary relocation. More often than not, those who move to an all-adult community will spend the rest of their lives there. Consequently, there is virtually no transient population and therefore, in that respect, no negative impact on crime rates.

All this having been said, we must recognize a sociological reality of these times. It is unlikely that there can be found a truly crime-free place where people live in relatively close proximity. All we can hope for is a low incidence of criminality and a resolute community joined together with the will to do what is necessary to keep it that way.

LET'S GO SHOPPING

Proximity to the products and services you are likely to need with some regularity is a priority consideration. If your location is a significant distance from a sizable city, it becomes more important that grocers and other frequently patronized businesses are part of the local commercial makeup. A convenience store is no substitute for a full-service food market. Hardware stores, barber and beauty shops, dry cleaners, drug stores, car mechanics, and the like are too frequently on the day's errands agenda to tolerate a 30- or 40-mile pilgrimage each time there is a need.

When visiting a community that is relatively new, be cautious about impressive scale models, brochures, or architectural drawings that depict future commercial enhancements. Plans change. Sometimes good intentions fall by the wayside. Delays can seem endless. It is far better to make judgments based on what is already in place.

ALABAMA TAX FACTS

INDIVIDUAL INCOME TAX

Graduated from 2% to 5% as follows:

♦ First $500 of income @ 2%
♦ Next $2,500 @ 4%
♦ Over $3,000 @ 5%

Exemptions:

♦ Single, $1,500
♦ Married, $3,000
♦ Head of household, $3,000
♦ Dependent, $300

Twenty-nine gross income exclusions include life insurance death benefits, gifts and inheritances, interest on federal and Alabama obligations, onetime exclusion on gain on sale of personal residence if seller is at least 55 years of age, federal social security benefits, stock dividends, annuities from U.S. retirement system or disability fund, and income from trusts (stock bonus, pension, or profit-sharing plan). Rates apply to single and married persons filing separately and married filing jointly. For heads of household, income brackets are doubled.

SALES TAX

A 4 percent tax is imposed on retail sales and storage, use, consumption, and rentals of tangible personal purchases and transient accommodations (under 30 continuous days), but with special rates applicable to certain specific products and services.

PROPERTY TAX

The range of property tax rates per $1,000 of assessed value is from $4 to $40.50 for city levies and from $14.50 to $43.60 for county rates (1994). These rates are composites of locally applicable city, county, and school district rates. There may be additional levies by special districts and improvement assessments not covered in the foregoing figures.

RANKING REPORT

According to *State Government Finances*, among the 50 states, Alabama ranks 7th from the most favorable in total state taxes per capita when only state levies are considered. When comparing property taxes, however, it is clearly the lowest rate in the nation.

For more complete tax information contact the Alabama Department of Revenue, 4112 Gordon Persons Building, 50 North Ripley St., Montgomery, AL 36132, 205-242-1175.

Note: The above information is based on applicable tax law information available at the time of publication. Because such laws and tax rates are subject to change, professional assistance should be sought if tax implications are critical to a relocation decision.

STILLWATERS RESORT

DADEVILLE, ALABAMA

1816 StillWaters Dr.
Dadeville, AL 36853
205-825-7021 / 888-797-3767
Fax: 205-825-4273

Developer: The Foundation Companies

Year of initial property sales/rentals: 1971

Approximate total land area: 2,200 acres

Average elevation: 400 feet

Location: East-central Alabama; on Lake Martin; just south and west of the intersection of U.S. Highway 280 and State Highway 49; Tallapoosa County; approximately 60 miles northeast of Montgomery (state capital); 25 miles northwest of Auburn; 45 miles northwest of Columbus, Georgia;

Nearest airport with scheduled commercial service: Montgomery Dannelly Field (50 miles)

Current number of housing units with year-round occupants: 260

Projected number of housing units: 950 (2002)

Resident eligibility: There are no age restrictions for residency, but an estimated 70% of homeowners are retired or semiretired.

Community visit/tour incentive program: On-site lodging in a one-, two-, or three-bedroom apartment is made available to qualified prospective purchasers at a special rate of $50/night, subject to availability. The package includes access to all amenities (golf, other facilities, food, etc.) at the same reduced cost to which club members are entitled.

Suggested daily newspaper: *The Montgomery Advertiser*, P.O. Box 1000, Montgomery, AL 36101 (334-262-1611)

WHY STILLWATERS RESORT?

StillWaters Resort likes to consider itself central Alabama's moderately priced alternative to the resorts in Florida and the Gulf Coast. After having survived a series of lean years and financial misfortunes since its inception in the early 1970s, new ownership and an infusion of $10 million have brought the community to a promising level of revitalization. A second 18-hole golf course, with a new driving range and practice area, plus a new $3 million clubhouse complex, opened in 1996, have helped make this **Lake Martin** planned golfing community one of Alabama's top retreats for business meetings. A conference center can accommodate up to 300 attendees for programs that accentuate fun and recreation, along with more industrious pursuits. As a vacation lure, or as a permanent relocation destination for retirees, it has the necessary ingredients.

The StillWaters marina, one of 17 such docking facilities around the enormous 40,000-acre Lake Martin reservoir (which claimed title to being the world's largest artificial body of water when it was first completed in the late 1920s), recently doubled its size and installed many new improvements. The vacation ownership business (sometimes called time-sharing), is the primary focus of this family resort. Interval International (a vacation exchange network) gave a five-star rating to StillWaters in a program designed to recognize quality properties. The lake area has been heralded for military retirees as one of the 25 most affordable locations. It is said to be the only premium vacation property in the state of Alabama.

The **Church of the Living Waters** is an on-site, nondenominational, open-air A-frame place of worship with a serene view of the lake and a canopy of trees as a part of its inspirational appeal. From Memorial Day to Labor Day, vacationers join lake dwellers who come by car and by boat to hear guest clergy and lay speakers preach, musicians play sacred music, and vocalists sing favorite hymns.

WHO'S IN CHARGE?

Each property owner pays an annual maintenance fee of $247 to the **StillWaters Residential Association (SWA)**. Forty percent of the amount collected is earmarked for road maintenance, and 60 percent is used for security, common area maintenance, and amenities upkeep. Increases in the amount of the assessment is tied to the cost of living index. Payment of the fee entitles the property owner to free access and use of the clubhouse, swimming pool, tennis courts, and lakeside beach. Golfers have the option of paying for playing privileges as they go at the rates posted for members, or they may apply for membership in the golf club on an annual fee basis.

Policy development and implementation, and all operational responsibilities, rest with the developer until such time as final buildout phases are reached. At that point, proprietorship will be assumed by the residents' association. In the meantime, the SWA functions on a somewhat informal, volunteer basis, meeting regularly with the developer, initiating and coordinating social activities, and keeping lines of communication open between residents and the developer/management team.

THE WEATHER REPORT

Weather patterns in this east-central Alabama farmland country (mostly cotton, hay, and beef cattle pastures) can be said to be typical "deep south"— almost subtropical. Proximity to the **Gulf of Mexico**, situated on a broad, unobstructed savanna, the area invites summer heat and humidity and an ample rainfall (about 58 inches annually). The absence of nearby topographical barriers, however, helps assure a four-season climate, with winters that can contradict the southern latitude with below-freezing temperatures, and then a day or two later, bring sunshine and the mid-60s. If variety is the spice of life (with respect to weather, that is), this is a location that can satisfy any longing for diversity.

Average winter and summer high/low readings for nearby Montgomery (the closest weather reporting station) are reported by the U.S. National Oceanic and Atmospheric Administration as follows:

December: high 60/low 39   **January:** high 56/low 36

February: high 61/low 39   **June:** high 89/low 68

July: high 91/low 71   **August:** high 90/low 71

Annual precipitation: 58 inches (Dadeville area)
Annual snowfall: less than one-half inch (Montgomery)

HOME SWEET HOME

There is a variety of StillWaters housing options, including residential building sites ready for construction, resale homes, and vacation ownership properties (time-shares). As a full-service resort, fully furnished condominiums are featured as short-term rentals for family getaways or business conferences. There is a mix of permanent residents in homes occupied year-round, along with a substantial number of owners whose properties serve as second homes, occupied for only a portion of the year. Many of the latter group are in preretirement stages and built their second homes with the intention of eventually making them their primary residence. Most are situated on one-third to one full acre lots, many with picture-perfect views of the golfing greens and fairways of two courses.

Custom homes are created by various prominent builders from central Alabama. The selection in cost and size is virtually unlimited, beginning in the low $100,000s with 1,500 square feet, and going on up to whatever specifications and budget the owner is inclined to adopt. There are two clusters of homes designed by a single architect. One is called the Golf Colony Villas—four-plex units ranging in size from 800 to 1,500 square feet, with two or three bedrooms, and priced from the low $70,000s to less than $114,000. These units can be purchased furnished or unfurnished. Many owners choose to place these homes in the rental program managed by the developer.

A second group of preplanned dwellings, recently completed, is called Linkside Homes. These two-story, 12-unit condominiums feature patios or optional rear decks/screened porches, front porches, low maintenance exteriors, optional fireplaces, and enclosed garages. Three floor plans with three elevations, in three- or four-bedroom layouts, are offered. A new section of 50 homesites was being made ready for development as this book reached its publishing date.

MONEY MATTERS

Alabama is known to have one of the lowest tax bases in the United States (see page 29), contributing significantly to a very affordable cost of living. More than that, the cost of consumer goods and services are also among the most moderate in the country. A recent issue of the *ACCRA Cost of Living Index* (2nd quarter, 1996) showed eight of nine Alabama locations (of a total of 315 nationwide) to be below the national average. Birmingham, the one exception, was pegged at the average for all locations included in the report. The rest ranged from 2.2 percent to 11.8 percent below the average finding.

According to an Alabama guide to retirement, prepared by the Alabama Department of Economic and Community Affairs, even though the state "...develops and operates extensive community, recreational, medical, educational, social welfare, road and transportation facilities and services, (it) has the *lowest overall tax rate in the United States*...(and) has *fewer state employees* per 1,000 population than 35 other states." Added to those lofty assertions is the further distinction, according to the same source, that Alabama offers the *lowest real property taxes in the nation,* and persons over 65 years of age may have, upon request, all or a significant portion of the property tax on their homestead waived. Property taxes are based on 10 percent of the appraised value of the home and lot. That figure is multiplied by a millage rate of .030. Under this formula, a $150,000 property is taxed at $450 annually. Homestead exemptions allowed for primary residences (as opposed to vacation or second homes) can further reduce the taxable obligation by as much as $53.

Residential gas bills are said to be 9 percent less than the national average; residential electric bills as much as 47 percent less than some northern states and 35 percent less than some western states.

TAKE GOOD CARE OF YOURSELF

The nearest hospital is just 7 miles away, in **Dadeville**, StillWaters' home address town. **Lakeshore Hospital** is a 46-bed acute care, rural community hospital with a 24-hour emergency care center. Specialties include speech, physical, and occupational therapy. Surprisingly well-equipped for its size, technical capabilities include ultrasound and stress test procedures, and regularly performed surgery. A home healthcare program reaches more than 4,000 visits each month. A wellness club for seniors has been in place for more than a decade, drawing sizable audiences each month. The hospital is often characterized as a place where patients already know the staff before they are admitted, and where personal care is, in fact, a reality.

On those occasions when more comprehensive medical attention is required, the **East Alabama Medical Center** in **Opelika**, with 351 beds and complete regional diagnostic and treatment capability, is just 30 miles down the highway.

There are more than 200 beds in three specialized convalescent and nursing centers within a 10-mile radius of the community. Physical, occupational and speech therapy are primary specializations among them. At least eight physicians and dentists maintain practices in the Dadeville area.

PLACES TO GO. THINGS TO DO

Alongside the shores of Lake Martin are StillWaters' two signature golf courses, both of which have won their share of acclamation throughout the state and beyond. **The Legend**, designed by George Cobb who served as design consultant to Augusta National for many years, was built in 1972 and has served the resort well for more than two decades. In 1996, a second course, **The Tradition,** was added to put StillWaters in the forefront of southeastern resort golfing properties. Longer than its companion course, the new recreational gem was laid out with more than 200 feet of elevation change and presented a somewhat more challenging landscape than its older cousin lying adjacent. An extravagant new 20,000-square foot clubhouse with a wrap-around porch, well-groomed practice facilities, a generously stocked golf shop, locker rooms, bag and cart storage area, and a sports bar that offers three daily meals, multiple televisions, and an irresistible rendezvous for watching sporting events of the day, all combine to create an atmosphere of luxury and self-indulgence.

Golf membership plans, encompassing both courses, range in cost from $3,600 annually for a family to $2,250 annually for an individual, depending on payment arrangements. Cart plans are extra. Daily use rates are an option with green fees ranging from $10.70 to $42, depending on preference for cart rental, choice of courses, day of week, and nine or 18-hole rounds.

Two outdoor swimming pools, game and exercise rooms, six tennis courts, a spacious 2,400-acre hunting plantation, and a white, sandy lake beach round out key amenities. Great dining at the convention center and at the new clubhouse are ideal for special occasions or just well-earned relaxation after a tough day on the golf course. Two bike and walking trails add to leisure options.

The list of historic and interesting sites, outdoor attractions, and big events and festivals in **Tallapoosa County** and surrounding counties, is much too long to detail here. Among the highlights are **Wind Creek State Park** (on Lake Martin near **Alexander City**, home of the biggest campground in Alabama), **Talladega National Forest** (covering about 220,000 acres spanning four nearby counties), and **Mount Cheaha State Park** (near **Lineville** in a neighboring county where the highest elevation in the state—about 2,400 feet—affords inspirational vistas of the countryside).

The influences of **Auburn University**, about 25 miles southeast of StillWaters, perhaps have the greatest impact among off-site attractions. Its resources tend to give surrounding communities a world of culture, entertainment, and recreation that would not otherwise exist for them. Special concerts and recitals are regularly performed at the **AU Theatre**. Touring groups, including symphony orchestras and Broadway road shows, opera and ballet companies, make frequent appearances. Collegiate sports rotate around some of the most exciting athletic conferences in the country. An outstanding library boasts more than 1.8 million volumes, two million microforms and 1.8 million government documents. For area residents, such functions, resources, and activities contribute substantially to the quality of life they enjoy within the sphere of influence of a major university.

SAFE AND SECURE

StillWaters is a secured community with a 24-hour gated entrance and random patrols operating seven days a week to help assure controlled access. Local crime statistics, according to community sources, confirm the complete absence of any violent crime for the past three years. Only one burglary (breaking and entering) was reported during that period. Truly an enviable record in this day and time.

The **Tallapoosa County Sheriff's Department** and the **City of Dadeville Police Department** share law enforcement responsibilities. StillWaters has its own volunteer fire and rescue department with assistance, as needed, from another nearby volunteer department.

LET'S GO SHOPPING

People like to talk about "a safari around the lake" in search of antiques and "junque." There are those who insist there are treasures to be found in the least expected places. Wherever you go around Lake Martin, they say, there is a shop with a dealer who has a specialty and a love of the past. Imported and locally crafted furniture and accessories, books, glassware, and linens share the antiques and collectibles spotlight. Artisan-owned shops offer a dazzling variety of handmade crafts, creating displays that are a treat to behold.

The nearest mainline grocery shopping is 7 miles away, in Dadeville. Two supermarkets there cater to a sizable rural market. Major enclosed malls, with prominent anchor department stores, food courts, and the usual collection of specialty shops, are 25 to 30 miles down the highway in Auburn.

ARIZONA TAX FACTS

INDIVIDUAL INCOME TAX

Graduated from 3% to 5.6% (for married couples filing jointly, $7,000 standard deduction), $4,200 exemption, as follows:

- First $20,000 of income @ 3%
- Next $30,000 @ 3.5%
- Next $200,000 @ 5.2%
- Next $50,000 @ 4.2%
- Over $300,000 @ 5.6%

Other information:

- $2,100 over 65 exemption/person; Social Security income exempt; no deduction for federal income tax paid.
- Up to $2,500 exemption for local, state, and federal government pensions.

SALES TAX

Retailers collect a 5 percent sales tax. Other sellers collect sales/use taxes in a range from 3.75 percent to 5.5 percent. Additional sales tax is authorized to be imposed by local jurisdictions (cities, counties, towns, special districts, etc.).

PROPERTY TAX

The range of property tax rates (1994) per $1,000 of assessed value was from $11.094 to $16.77. These rates are composites of many locally applicable city, county, and school district levies. There may be additional special district and/or improvement assessment rates that are not covered in this general range. State tax for education allows a maximum limit of 47 cents per $100 of assessed value.

RANKING REPORT

According to *State Government Finances*, among the 50 states, Arizona ranks 32nd from the most favorable in total state taxes per capita when only state levies are considered. In property taxes, *The Rating Guide to Life in America's Fifty States* ranks it 29th.

For more complete tax information contact the Arizona Revenue Department, Taxpayer Assistance, 1600 West Monroe, Phoenix, AZ 85007, 602-542-2076; (fax) 602-542-3073.

Note: The above information is based on applicable tax law information available at the time of publication. Because such laws and tax rates are subject to change, professional guidance should be sought if tax implications are critical to a relocation decision.

DEL WEBB'S SUN CITY GRAND

SURPRISE, ARIZONA

Del Webb Communities, Inc., 13950 Meeker Blvd.
Sun City West, AZ 85375
602-546-5108 / 800-528-2604
Fax: 602-546-5104

Developer: Del Webb Corporation

Year of initial property sales/rentals: 1996

Total land area: 4,000 acres

Average elevation: 1,000 feet

Location: South-central Arizona; Maricopa County; off U.S. Highway 60/93; less than 15 miles west of Interstate 17; 18 miles northwest of Phoenix.

Nearest airport with scheduled commercial service: Sky Harbor International/Phoenix (23 miles)

Current number of housing units with year-round occupants: 175

Projected number of housing units: 9,500

Resident eligibility: At least one member of the household must be at least 55 years of age; no one in permanent residence under age 19.

Community visit/tour incentive program: "Vacation Getaway" packages offer four- and seven-night stays in more than 100 fully-furnished, on-site vacation courtyard villas and include a complimentary 18-hole round of golf, an orientation breakfast, and a wine and cheese party. All-inclusive rates for one- and two-bedroom units range from $335 ($180 off-season) for the shorter stay in a smaller unit, to $840 ($525 off-season) for the full week in a two-bedroom home.

Suggested newspaper: *Daily News Sun,* P.O. Box 1779, Sun City, AZ 85351 (602-876-2513)

WHY SUN CITY GRAND?

Innovation in the development of master-planned communities for active adults is not easily achieved. Recreation programs and other leisure activities tend to follow familiar patterns. It is fair to say that at **Sun City Grand (SCG)** a new concept has emerged that is likely to have significant impact in the planning of many other retirement-oriented projects in the years ahead. It is a fresh approach to personal fitness. It is a recognition of the fact that growing numbers of retirees assign high priority to their ability to maintain good health. It was in that connection that decision-makers at SCG departed from earlier program strategy in terms of how their residents would take to reduced emphasis on shuffleboard and lawn games (not that they would be entirely discarded) in favor of a stronger focus on combining cutting-edge technology with fitness and health education. The result has been the first known program of its kind in a master-planned retirement community. (See "Places to Go, Things to Do.")

Sun City Grand is the newest of four **Del Webb Corporation** active adult communities in Arizona, (three in the **Phoenix** area), and now one of 10 such developments there and in four other states—Nevada, California, Texas, and South Carolina. With a post office address in **Sun City West,** SCG is actually located in the town of **Surprise**, a northwest suburb of Phoenix, between **Sun City** and Sun City West. According to industry analysts, the pace of home sales here has led the area's planned community market since its opening in late 1996. Trademark Del Webb amenities including multi-million dollar clubhouses and recreation centers, generous home features and options, championship golf courses and other quality recreational features, are unmistakably in evidence. New home architectural designs make for a more distinctive desert-oasis ambiance and add character to the resort-like environment. Natural desert vegetation, great panoramic views of the **White Tank Mountains**, and lots of soothing water features enhance the appeal.

WHO'S IN CHARGE?

Management responsibility and administrative control of community affairs during the present startup phase of progression rest with a three-member board of directors of the **Sun City Grand Community Association**, all of whom represent the developer. Two additional member seats representing the community residents will be created when the development reaches an appropriate stage. Established as an incorporated nonprofit entity, the board's primary responsibilities include the establishment of operating policies, promulgation and implementation of budgetary guidelines, and the promotion of effective communication between and among homeowner constituents. An unofficial management liaison team of residents is in place to help maintain an open flow of information, to coordinate with the governing body, and to launch mutual interest activities for which support has been demonstrated. Once a sufficient number of homes are built and occupied, a formalized homeowners association will take shape with appropriate rules and regulations to guide its operation, and ultimately, to take on full management and proprietorship responsibilities.

An annual fee of $425 per household entitles residents access to all amenities other than golf (which is a separate, optional assessment, the cost of which depends on several alternative plans within a range of $1,400 to $2,600 annually). This fee also covers administrative and maintenance costs for staffing and common grounds/facilities upkeep.

THE WEATHER REPORT

Phoenix, and other parts of Arizona's **Valley of the Sun**, are known far and wide as a sanctuary for winter escape from frosty northern climes. It is a mountain/desert alternative to tropical, maritime Florida for such a retreat. The joys of those mild winters, of course, are counterbalanced by the temperature extremes of summer. For those who make their home year-round in the desert southwest, a stout disregard for the discomfort of 100-plus degree heat is a helpful constitutional asset. That's where the mercury is likely to stand for most of June through much of September. Nighttime readings at that time of year typically do not drop below the mid-80s. Even the low humidity cannot be said to offer much relief when temperatures reach those excessive levels. One saving grace—summer thunderstorms do tend to cool things off a bit for a temporary respite. Many would say, of course, that those who inhabit this land in that season seldom find themselves at the involuntary mercy of the sun, content to spend most of their waking hours in air conditioned comfort, whether at home, traveling, shopping, or being entertained. Those who worship the more oppressive of outdoor solar influences will be found on the golf course or cavorting around the pool.

The valley in which the community is located is part of the **Sonora Desert**. Humidity, from late spring to early summer, can be as low as 10 percent. The few meager inches of rain that fall (mostly in winter and early spring, and then again in mid-summer) are what sustain the desert environment.

Normal high and low temperatures for the Phoenix area are reported by the U.S. National Oceanic and Atmospheric Administration as follows:

December: high 62/low 43   **January:** high 66/low 43

February: high 70/low 49   **June:** high 106/low 79

July: high 106/low 80   **August:** high 104/low 80

Average annual precipitation: 7 inches
Average annual snowfall: trace
Average annual humidity at maximum temperature: 10-20%

HOME SWEET HOME

Twenty floor plans and 18 on-site models give home shoppers an exceptional opportunity to inspect and consider a multitude of home design options. Floor plans range from 1,100 to 2,900 square feet, priced from the $90s to the $200s. Interiors are characterized by open living spaces and great room concepts. All homes are single-family, detached. There are no condominiums or attached town houses on the property. A compound for RV storage is available for a monthly fee that is determined by the size of the vehicle.

MONEY MATTERS

According to the *ACCRA Cost of Living Index*, (2nd quarter, 1996), living costs among 315 selected U.S. metropolitan and nonmetropolitan areas shows Phoenix to be a moderate 3 percent above the composite average for six weighted spending categories in the study. Analysis of the six groupings shows the following above or below average findings: groceries, 4.3 percent above; housing, .7 percent below; utilities, 9.8 percent above; transportation, 1.3 percent above; health care, 15.2 percent above; and miscellaneous, 1.2 percent below (this is the category with the single heaviest weighting—more than one-third of the total value, thereby accounting for what would otherwise be a considerably higher composite percentage).

Local property taxes are described as being 1.3 percent of the total purchase price of a home.

TAKE GOOD CARE OF YOURSELF

Sun City Grand residents share with their neighbors in **Sun City** and **Sun City West** (the two original bellwether Del Webb all-adult communities) access to the **Del E. Webb Memorial Hospital** (203 beds), practically adjacent to the property, and **Walter O. Boswell Memorial Hospital** (305 beds), about 6 miles away. The two institutions have combined medical staffs of more than 400 physicians, representing more than 40 medical specialties. Both have been cited for outstanding patient care with reaccreditation "with commendation," an honor accorded to only 3 percent of hospitals seeking accreditation from the **Joint Commission for the Accreditation of Healthcare Organizations (JCAHO)**. Both have also received national recognition for cost management and effectiveness systems.

Webb Memorial is a modern acute-care facility with many unique service capabilities, including a state-of-the-art cardiac catheterization lab, a special procedure for use of laminar flow air-purification technology for selected surgeries, and a center for adult behavioral health. Boswell Memorial is the largest healthcare facility serving the northwest valley and is one of Arizona's leading providers of care for most of the common diagnoses for older adults, including cardiac care (one of the most experienced providers of coronary bypass surgery and other sophisticated cardiac procedures), joint replacement and follow-up rehabilitation (as well as other orthopedic programs), oncology, and emergency care.

There are 20 principal medical centers in Phoenix and more than a dozen related special service agencies, most of them within a half-hour of Sun City Grand. There is virtually no health care specialty that cannot be found among them.

PLACES TO GO, THINGS TO DO

The Village Center is a complex of five buildings, the axis around which a myriad of social, cultural, and recreational activities revolve. Its focal point is the $7.7 million, high-tech, 29,000-square-foot **Adobe Spa & Fitness Center** with an imaginative program utilizing the latest in exercise equipment, an indoor walking track, indoor and outdoor swimming pools, and a system of highly individualized tracking and training for prescriptive health and fitness benefits. Participants are given the opportunity to take personal control of their state of wellness—to allay fears, to motivate, to promote consistency, and to avoid boredom.

Beyond this extraordinary fitness facility, the Village Center also has four tennis courts, courts for bocce ball, an outdoor amphitheater for staging festivals and special events, a billiards room, and classrooms for computer instruction and a wide variety of other subjects to be provided as interest is demonstrated.

The 18-hole **Desert Springs Golf Course,** open to the public, was designed by **Billy Casper**, one of America's top professional golfers, and **Greg Nash**, a highly regarded golf course designer. Opened in late 1996, it is the first of four championship courses with three now under construction or planned for future play as the community grows. Playability for seniors is featured in a setting of 17 lakes and panoramic views.

Lake Pleasant Regional Park, a short 20-mile ride away, features a 10,000-acre lake for boating, fishing, and marina relaxation, along with shoreline picnic areas. **White Tank Mountain Regional Park** near **Peoria**, and about 30 miles from SCG, was once inhabited by the **Hohakam Indians**. Its 26,000-plus acres is laden with hiking, equestrian, and mountain bike trails. Periodic nature hikes are scheduled. Camping sites are plentiful.

Phoenix, Arizona's capital city, is one of only 14 U.S. cities with its own resident symphony, theater company, ballet, and opera company. It is the home of a long string of museums, performing arts venues, and world-class resorts. The nationally acclaimed **Heard Museum**, nestled within one of central Phoenix's restored historical districts, is best known for its exhibits of Native American arts and crafts, culture, and lifestyles. The **Phoenix Art Museum**, recently undergoing a major expansion and renovation, houses one of the nation's outstanding collections of 19th and 20th century Western art and apparel. Contemporary technology is the focus of the **Arizona Science Center.** Other principal museums spotlight ancient Indian heritage, turn-of-the-century western folklore, aerospace technology, and vintage aircraft, among many preservation specialties. **Taliesin West,** outside **Scottsdale**, showcases the architectural genius of **Frank Lloyd Wright.** The **Gammage Center for the Performing Arts** (another Wright creation), on the **Arizona State University** campus in **Tempe**, regularly books top Broadway road shows and other touring companies.

The **Phoenix Zoo**, 125 acres of mammals, reptiles, and birds, is the largest privately owned, self-supporting zoo in the country. Adjacent, in **Papago Park,** is the **Desert Botanical Garden**, a remarkable display of the delicate plant life of the arid earth.

The **PGA Phoenix Open** golf tournament, held annually in Scottsdale, is said to be the pro golf event that draws more people than any other in the world (an estimated 600,000 spectators). The Valley also hosts the annual **Fiesta Bowl** parade and football classic in late December and early January, drawing national attention to days of revelry and special events. "Cactus League" spring training for major league baseball teams has become a major seasonal attraction. The 10,000-seat **City of Peroria Sports Complex**, located practically next door to Sun City West, is the spring training home of the **Seattle Mariners** and the **San Diego Padres**.

SAFE AND SECURE

The city of Surprise provides law enforcement protection to SCG through its municipal police agency, including round-the-clock patrol coverage. Fire-fighting and prevention services come from Sun City, Sun City West, and Surprise resources. A volunteer posse, similar to those established in other Del Webb communities, is in the planning stage and will be organized as soon as the population is large enough to support such a program.

LET'S GO SHOPPING

Across and a bit down the highway in Sun City West, there are more than 70 businesses of various descriptions. A few blocks further on, in Surprise and along the main thoroughfare, there are additional major retail shopping clusters. All of this, within a mile or so of SCG, puts a major grocery store, restaurants, shops, and a hotel practically within walking distance. A major discount mall, opened in 1994, is the **Wigwam Outlet Stores**, a 34-unit complex with a full food court, about 12 miles from the Grand.

Within easy reach too (about 10 miles away), is the 1.3 million square foot **Arrowhead Towne Center**, opened in 1993 and one of the largest super-regional shopping malls in the state—five major department stores, more than 130 specialty shops, three full-service restaurants, and a modern food court. Also uniquely featured in this massive commercial development is a community hospital **Satellite Resource Center** and a **Customer Service Center** where, among other things, shoppers can request an escort or golf cart transportation to their cars in the parking lot.

FAIRFIELD HOMES GREEN VALLEY

GREEN VALLEY, ARIZONA

P.O. Box 587
Green Valley, AZ 85622
800-528-4930 / 520-625-4441
Fax: 520-648-2145

Developer: Fairfield Homes, Inc.

Year of initial property sales/rentals: 1972

Total land area: 18,000 acres

Average elevation: 2,900 feet

Location: Southeastern Arizona; Pima County; in the Santa Cruz River Valley; on Interstate Highway 19; 25 miles south of Tucson; 45 miles north of the Mexican border city of Nogales (Arizona).

Nearest airport with scheduled commercial service: Tucson International (23 miles); 12 regional and national carriers

Current number of housing units with year-round occupants: 10,900

Projected number of housing units: 17,900 (2010)

Resident eligibility: Operates under the Fair Housing Amendments Act of 1988, requiring that at least one person in a household must be age 55 or older, although in a limited number of homes, the oldest occupant may be younger than age 55. Those under 18 years of age are not allowed in permanent residence, but there are no restrictions on children visiting for limited periods.

Community visit/tour incentive program: Guest room and suite accommodations are available at reasonable rates. Some restrictions apply.

Suggested newspaper: *Arizona Daily Star/Tucson Citizen*, 4850 So. Park Avenue, Tucson, AZ 85714, (520-573-4400)

WHY GREEN VALLEY?

The town of **Green Valley** is unique in its composition and structure. Established in 1964, it is described as an unincorporated adult community primarily devoted to families in retirement. It is approximately 8 miles long and 2 miles wide. It has 45 homeowner associations within its borders, each representing an independent retirement community. All of the communities are organized under an umbrella organization known as the **Green Valley Community Coordinating Council (GVCCC)**. An estimated 90 percent of the residents in the town are older than 55 years of age. Adjacent communities are open to young families, many with small children.

A 1996 issue of *New Choices* magazine named Green Valley among the 20 best of 2,000 American retirement communities surveyed. In praising Green Valley virtues, the article suggested that, "Anyone who loves a desert setting would be entertained by the **Santa Rita Mountains**, stately saguaro cacti, yucca plants, and pecan orchards..." The article went on to describe the community as "the highest value for your retirement dollar."

WHO'S IN CHARGE?

Fairfield Homes Green Valley is a major institutional member of the GVCCC. Its properties are divided into three components or neighborhoods within Green Valley: Las Campanas, Ridgetop, and Vacation Villas. GVCCC, established in 1973, functions as a nonprofit, cooperative, volunteer local government. A board of representatives is elected from constituent organizations. It exercises final authority on all matters within its jurisdiction. Members elect officers every two years who are responsible for maintaining 15 standing committees to serve the broad needs of the community at large. The next higher level of governmental authority is vested in the **Pima County Board of Supervisors**, whose jurisdiction relates to those public services and responsibilities that extend to the entire county (public library system, justice courts and public safety, health care and educational services, etc.).

Homeowners pay fees to their associations to cover costs of common area maintenance and various other services that may be included in the dues package (recreational programs and facilities, trash collection, special events, etc.). Membership is mandatory. The amount of such fees generally ranges from $228 to $336 annually.

For more than 25 years, GVCCC has compiled and distributed the *Green Valley Area Community Directory* to local residents free of charge, listing all residents by their home towns. The directory is sustained by advertising revenue and donated time from dedicated volunteers drawn from the various member associations.

THE WEATHER REPORT

Green Valley enjoys more moderate summer temperatures and lower humidity than **Phoenix**, its metropolitan neighbor to the north (some 140 miles), a consequence of its 2,900-foot elevation. Winters, of course, are the time of year when desert climes lure "snowbirds" from the northern states.

Typical of the area's summers is the rapid cooling that nightfall brings. Even when the thermometer soars at midday, nights are generally quite comfortable. The community boasts more than 300 days a year of sunshine, making it a magnet for outdoor sports enthusiasts.

A 12-year weather summary from the Green Valley reporting station reveals the following average high and low temperature readings:

December: high 65/low 37	**January:** high 65/low 37
February: high 69/low 41	**June:** high 100/low 66
July: high 98/low 71	**August:** high 95/low 71

Average total annual precipitation: 16 inches
Average annual snowfall: none
Average relative humidity at 5 p.m: 25%

HOME SWEET HOME

Fairfield Homes, Inc., the principal builder in Green Valley since 1972, offers an unusually wide selection of site-built, single-family residences. There are 18 different models and six different exterior architectural styles from which to choose (contemporary, southwestern contemporary, traditional, Santa Fe traditional, ranch adobe, and territorial). Plans vary in size from 1,269 to 2,550 square feet. Prices range from $108,000 to $300,000. There are also two townhouse models with 985 to 1,246 square feet selling in two different styles and ranging in price from $89,000 to $100,000. Prices include a standard homesite. Premium sites are available at additional cost.

There is a sizable inventory of new homes on the market at any given time, allowing for immediate purchase and occupancy. Custom homes, constructed to the owner's specifications, are a popular alternative. The two neighborhoods in Green Valley in which Fairfield construction is centered are at opposite ends of town. Ridgetop is especially notable for homesites that are situated high on elevations that offer spectacular views of the Santa Rita Mountains and the lush fairways of the **San Ignacio Golf Club**.

Two full-service apartment rental complexes offer long-term leases on unfurnished units beginning at $300 a month. Furnished apartments are available during the winter season starting at $900 a month.

MONEY MATTERS

The fact that most community amenities are shared by so many groups of homeowners makes the cost per household quite modest. Depending upon the association(s) to which a property owner belongs, membership dues (covering the maintenance of all common areas and facilities, program activities, and management supervision costs) will vary, but any combination of such costs is considered an excellent value.

Residential property is appraised at market value. Assessments are based on 10 percent of value for an owner-occupied domicile. Local taxes generally amount to approximately 1.1 percent of the property's assessed value.

A late 1996 survey of living costs among popular retirement cities and towns ("Chart of Living Costs: How 99 Cities Compare in *Where to Retire* magazine; based on cost of living indexes from ACCRA) showed **Tucson** (nearest to Green Valley of those compared—only 25 miles distant) to have a lower cost of living index than 29 of the 39 major cities cited. Its score was precisely the same as Baltimore and Atlanta, each considered to be in the lower to moderate range among comparable metropolitan areas. In *Where to Retire*, an older survey of real estate, utility, and health costs, Tucson ranked 48th from the least expensive among 78 retirement-oriented cities and towns. In that survey, real estate and utility costs were 17 percent below the summary average, while health care was 16 percent above average.

TAKE GOOD CARE OF YOURSELF

Within Green Valley there are four medical clinics affiliated with nearby major hospitals. There are six dental offices, an ambulance service with trained emergency medical technicians, a highly rated nursing home, and two assisted living facilities. Numerous specialists with practices in Tucson regularly schedule visits to Green Valley. There are no fewer than 10 major hospitals in and around Tucson, most less than a 30-minute drive from the community. They include the **University Medical Center**, the only physician training institution in the state, operating under the **University of Arizona College of Medicine**.

PLACES TO GO, THINGS TO DO

Recreational activity and community social life revolve around a $10 million collection of facilities administered by **Green Valley Recreation (GVR)**, a nonprofit membership organization that functions much as a municipal parks and recreation department. It provides community-wide sports, recreation, and leisure activities through five social center complexes and six neighborhood recreation centers. About 60 staff members are required to operate an impressive program calendar.

Benefits and specific activities are too extensive to fully recite here. Heated pools and Jacuzzis, water aerobics, state-of-the-art fitness equipment, 13 tennis courts (eight lighted for night play), dance and language classes, day trips and tours, entertainment packages, plays and concerts, arts and crafts, and hobbies of every description are all part of the GVR agenda. More than 160 social, game/hobby/activity, place of origin, religious, fraternal, military, political, service, and cultural clubs and organizations dot the leisure landscape. More than 100 classes are offered in everything from painting, ceramics, and sculpture to square dancing, swimnastics, and conversational Spanish or German. Volunteer opportunities are plentiful, many involving work with GVR staff at recreation facilities, hobby shops, and special events.

The **Greater Green Valley Arts Council** is a collection of approximately 40 different organizations. Member interests and activities center on visual arts (including painting, needlework, pottery, and woodwork), dance groups, historical preservation, literary pursuits, music (including opera, band concert, jazz, and choral) and theater. Access to the GVR is available to Green Valley residents for the modest annual dues of $292.

As you might expect, golf carts are parked in lots of garages and driveways. The San Ignacio Golf Club, designed by **Arthur Hills**, has a full slate of professional and dining services and is one of seven courses in the community. Twenty-five more are minutes away in Tucson and in smaller nearby towns. PGA and LPGA tournaments are commonplace.

For those who want to explore the surrounding countryside, there is no end to the choices of interesting places to visit. There are venerable Spanish missions, canyons populated by rare vegetation and wildlife, prized recreational lakes, movie location studios, national parks and monuments, majestic mountain peaks and ski resorts, caves, historic towns, wineries, planetariums and observatories, sports stadiums, rodeos, and race tracks. Most such enticements are within an hour's drive. Just 40 miles to the border, the charms of colorful Mexico are almost on your doorstep.

Educational opportunities are abundant, too. The **University of Arizona**, one of the top 20 research universities in the nation (with more than 35,000 students on a 347-acre campus in Tucson), offers 131 undergraduate programs, 137 master's, and 95 doctoral programs. The **UA Extended University** operates an off-campus facility in Green Valley with many course offerings. Other academic programs are under the auspices of the **Pima Community College**.

SAFE AND SECURE

Green Valley is an open community without entry gates or perimeter walls. Law enforcement is centered at a substation of the Pima County Sheriff's Department. Twenty deputies and more than 50 sheriff's auxiliary volunteers provide around-the-clock policing services. The GV Fire District contracts with a private company for both property protection and paramedic services.

LET'S GO SHOPPING

The community has all the retail and professional services of a city with a much larger population. There are more than 350 business establishments and service locations. Included are a major supermarket, two full-service drug stores, discount department stores, apparel shops, restaurants, and numerous specialty stores. Five banks maintain six local offices, along with three savings and loans and seven brokerage firms. There are seven different shopping centers.

PEBBLECREEK RESORT COMMUNITY

GOODYEAR, ARIZONA

3639 Clubhouse Dr.
Goodyear, AZ 85338
602-935-6700 / 800-795-4663
Fax: 602-935-6767

Developer: Robson Communities

Year of initial property sales/ rental: 1993

Total land area: 760 acres (Phase I)

Average elevation: 1,235 feet

Location: South-central Arizona; Maricopa County; 2 miles north off Interstate 10; 17 miles west of the intersection with Interstate Highway 17 and downtown Phoenix.

Nearest airport with scheduled commercial service: Sky Harbor International (22 miles)

Current number of housing units with year-round occupants: 735

Projected number of housing units: unknown

Resident eligibility: At least one person in most households must be 55 years of age or older, and no permanent residents under age 19. A limited number of homes may be occupied with one family member at least 40 years of age.

Community visit/tour incentive program: "Preferred Guest Program" offers four-days/three-nights' stay in an on-site luxury home, including $150 worth of meals and recreation, a round of golf (subject to availability); weekday arrivals required. Discounted guest rates for the package range from $109 to $299, depending on season of visit.

Suggested daily newspaper: *Arizona Republic*, 120 E. Van Buren St., Phoenix, AZ 85004 (602-257-8300)

WHY PEBBLECREEK?

PebbleCreek is one of three **Robson Communities** in the **Phoenix** metropolitan area. A fourth sister community is in the Tucson vicinity. The developer is the largest privately owned retirement community builder in the state of Arizona. Its list of awards and honors is impressive—among them is inclusion in *New Choices* magazine's "Top 20 Retirement Communities in America" for three successive years through 1996. In 1994, the **National Association of Home Builders** and the **National Council on Seniors** awarded Robson Communities the Silver Seal Award for exceptional service in meeting the housing needs of older Americans. **The President's Council**

on **Physical Fitness and Sports** bestowed on the organization the prestigious Silver Eagle Award for **MaxLife**, an exemplary health and fitness program benefiting older adults. A score of other awards received during the 1990s covered such categories as interior home design, construction quality, sales and merchandising, and model home presentation.

Phoenix, the seventh largest city in the United States, and 22 other communities comprise the **Valley of the Sun.** The area lies along the northern edge of the **Great Sonoran Desert**, a wondrous landscape that displays more cacti and other plant and animal species than any other desert in North America. Within a 3- to 5-mile radius of PebbleCreek are four championship golf courses, a new medical center, factory outlet stores, a popular five-star resort, a community college, supermarket, banks, service stations, a wide variety of retail and professional services, and an air force base. The location is truly the ultimate in convenience.

WHO'S IN CHARGE?

The **PebbleCreek Homeowners' Association (PCHOA)** is a nonprofit organization of residents whose representatives are elected to a board of directors. It is their responsibility to set policy and to maintain coordination with the developer's representatives in managing the affairs of the community. Such responsibilities include enforcement of rules and regulations to preserve quality-of-life conditions, preserve the integrity of recreational amenities, etc. Meetings are held monthly. A typical meeting of the board might include a report from the general manager on property improvements, new tee time schedules for golfers, appointment of committee members, revision of homeowner rules and regulations, standing and/or *ad hoc* committee reports, and determining appropriate action to take on recommendations presented.

An annual homeowner's fee of $726 is charged for each home site based on two members per household. The income is used for maintenance and program support of all club facilities (except for golf and the MaxLife fitness center, which are supported by user fees), upkeep of common grounds, and evening neighborhood patrols. Membership in the fitness center is $275 annually. Golf course green fees range from a low of $11 to a high of $32, depending on season and on whether it's a nine-hole or 18-hole course. An annual golf fee as low as $1,100 per person eliminates separate user charges.

The *PebbleCreek Eagle* is a newspaper published monthly for PC residents. It is supported by a very active advertising program and has the appearance of a commercial tabloid-size publication, with content covering a broad range of editorial commentary, news, and photos. Emphasis is given to features on individuals and families in the community, club activities, meeting reports, and future scheduled events, along with locally inspired poetry, announcements, and recipes.

THE WEATHER REPORT

Any discussion of climate in the desert southwest is likely to acknowledge the daytime summer temperatures soaring well over the 100-degree mark. It is an equally well-known fact that "it's low humidity heat," and therefore not nearly as oppressive as it might sound. Valley of the Sun residents enjoy at least 300 days of sunshine during the year, an attraction for those who wish to escape the overcast marine climate that prevails in many more moderate climes in the Pacific northwest, along the southern Atlantic seaboard, or in parts of the Gulf coast.

That it gets very hot in summer cannot be denied. The flip side, of course, is that winters in the Phoenix area are heavenly retreats for those seeking to flee the harsh winters of the nation's northern tier. "Snowbirds" on seasonal migrations south are a great boost for the local economy.

Official normal daily high and low temperatures for Phoenix are summarized by the U.S. National Oceanic and Atmospheric Administration as follows:

December: high 66/low 42   **January:** high 66/low 41

February: high 71/low 45   **June:** high 103/low 73

July: high 106/low 81   **August:** high 104/low 80

Average annual precipitation: 8 inches
Average annual snowfall: trace
Average summer humidity at maximum temperature: 10-20%

HOME SWEET HOME

All housing is built by the developer. All are single-family detached dwellings with model selections of more than 30 floor plans and more than 100 elevations. Custom refinements create almost unlimited variations. Concrete block, steel reinforced construction is used throughout. It is said to be superior to wood frame structures with regard to insulation against the elements, fire resistance, security, maintenance, sound retardation, and termite resistance. PebbleCreek homes are marketed with a strong emphasis on "energy advantage" certification for meeting exacting government specifications. High-efficiency appliances and energy-saving construction techniques (such as insulated windows, extra weather stripping, and natural gas heating systems, ranges, water heaters, and dryers) are credited with significantly holding down energy costs. An architectural control committee is responsible for maintaining a desirable appearance. Additions, exterior painting, landscaping or decorative alterations, repairs, excavations, roof replacement, or any other alteration of lot or building appearance must be approved before work is begun.

Homes range in size from 1,110 square feet, with prices starting from the low $100s, to the units that are as much as 3,400 square feet, selling up to the high $200s, depending on exterior design and options incorporated. An estimated 95 percent of housing sales are new construction, with the remainder on the resale market. Lots are not sold separately—they're only sold in home/lot packages. A normal construction time frame is four to five months. An RV parking/storage area is available. The community is served by central municipal systems for both water supply and sanitary sewer lines.

MONEY MATTERS

The most reliable data available, the *ACCRA Cost of Living Index* (2nd quarter, 1996) comparing living costs among 315 selected American metropolitan and nonmetropolitan areas, shows Phoenix to be just 3 percent above the average composite index. The study draws a cost analysis for six different categories of typical family expenses and, using weighted values for each grouping, produces a composite index as a combined cost comparison. The six categories showing above or below average results for Phoenix are as follows: groceries 4.3 percent above, housing .7 percent below, utilities 9.8 percent above, transportation 1.3 percent above, health care 15.2 percent above, and miscellaneous goods and services (representing one-third of the total value) 1.2 percent below.

Property taxes are set by individual governmental jurisdictions. The valuation of real and most personal property is assessed by county authorities. Residential property is assessed at 10 percent of current value and personal property at 25 percent. The property tax on a typical home valued at $136,000 is approximately $1,896 annually.

TAKE GOOD CARE OF YOURSELF

There are three hospitals within a 15-mile radius of the community. The nearest among them is the 213-bed **Maryvale Samaritan Regional Medical Center**, only 10 miles away, at the western outskirts of Phoenix. Samaritan operates a satellite health center in the PebbleCreek home city of **Goodyear**, located just a few minutes away across the interstate. One of the most exciting medical care developments in recent years has been the establishment and expansion (in **Scottsdale**, eastside neighbor of Phoenix) of a major branch of the renowned **Mayo Clinic** of Rochester, Minnesota, including a large medical research center. The **Maricopa Health System** operates 12 valley-wide family health centers, one of which is minutes away in neighboring **Glendale.** Two other major hospitals with comprehensive services and specialties are within a 15-mile radius—**Phoenix Memorial** and **Walter O. Boswell Memorial** in Sun City, the latter with 360 beds. **Palm Valley Medical Plaza,** opened in 1997 and just blocks away, is a cluster of medically oriented offices for physicians, dentists, and other health care professionals.

Perhaps the best of facilities for promoting and preserving good health is the MaxLife active adult total fitness program on the PebbleCreek site, a national model in its field. It provides professionally supervised activity that is designed to improve cardiorespiratory efficiency, body strength, muscular endurance, joint flexibility, reduced body fat, and all-around fitness. More than simply an exercise regimen, it is a well-conceived educational program as well. Testimonials to its successful results are found in abundance.

PLACES TO GO, THINGS TO DO

A magnificent, sprawling **Eagle's Nest Clubhouse** has almost 40,000 square feet of floor space. In a setting of mountain vistas, fountains, lakes, palm trees, and golfing greens, the facility is a nucleus of recreational and social interaction among residents. Its regal architecture and furnishings complement an array of amenities that leave little to be desired—a massive ballroom/auditorium and stage, a formal dining/banquet and lounge area, meeting rooms, pro shop, men's and women's lockers and showers, fitness center, library, indoor pool/spa, and a sumptuous lobby and reception area. A spacious covered veranda, complete with a snack bar, extends almost the full length of a long side of the building, overlooking an idyllic landscape. Outside is an oversized heated swimming pool, and just beyond that is a championship-quality tennis center with seven lighted courts and its own clubhouse and covered patio for viewing matches.

A new arts and crafts center is a stand-alone, thoughtfully planned building housing an array of avocational pursuits and hobbies. Built around a center courtyard, there are separate rooms and studios for painting and drawing, ceramics and sculpture (with kilns), crafts, sewing and quilting, photographic development (dark room), multipurpose activities, a resource center, billiards, and even an arts and crafts store. Other leisure activities include woodcarving, silversmithing, stained glass, and lapidary. There are groups formed around cards and other table games, dance, music and theater, exercise, golf and tennis, softball, and a score of clubs that involve everything from computers and travel to investments and dining out. Religious and service organizations further expand the community's options.

When it comes to off-site attractions, there are virtually endless temptations. Within a five- to 10-mile radius of PebbleCreek is a wildlife zoo, a five-star golf resort, a community college campus, and the **Phoenix International Raceway** (motor car racing). Just a few miles further into the Phoenix center city are the **America West Arena** (home of the **Phoenix Suns,** powerhouse of professional basketball, and of the **Phoenix Coyotes,** newcomers to the **National Hockey League**) and the **Arizona Center** (a mammoth downtown complex of entertainment and restaurants). The

Phoenix Zoo is the largest nonprofit zoo in the country, featuring more than 1,300 animals in surroundings that imitate their natural environments. **Desert Botanical Garden** displays some 20,000 desert plants in an incredible variety of native vegetation.

Patrons of the arts are treated to a cornucopia of outstanding museums and performing arts companies. The **Phoenix Art Museum** boasts a permanent collection of more than 13,000 master works, with strong collections of western, Chinese, and contemporary work. The **Scottsdale Center for the Arts** houses not only an impressive exhibit of modern art, but offers outdoor craft festivals and classic film screenings as well. **The Heard Museum**, famous for its widely acclaimed primitive and modern Native American art, is a top priority for visiting fine arts aficionados. Even **Sky Harbor International Airport,** near downtown Phoenix, is adorned with public art collections throughout its terminals. The **Phoenix Symphony** has risen in stature to one of the nation's leading orchestras. The **Arizona Opera** and two prominent theater companies enjoy enthusiastic community support. **Arizona State University** contributes much to the classical world, as well as to an intercollegiate sports calendar that has few equals. The list of cultural, entertainment, and educational highlights goes on and on.

SAFE AND SECURE

The gated community provides its own paid safety patrol, on duty seven days a week. This includes neighborhood patrols, vacation watch and home inspections, parking restriction enforcement, vehicle and residential lockout response, and other services normally identified with such programs. The city of Goodyear provides fire and police protection services, as well as emergency response units.

LET'S GO SHOPPING

Two miles south of PebbleCreek lies the freeway with quick access to just about any kind of shopping need. **Westridge Mall**, a major retail emporium in **Glendale** (next door to Goodyear), is but 10 miles away and one of three malls in the area. The **Wigwam Outlet Mall** in Goodyear, a big drawing card for those who appreciate discount values, is little more than a long walk from the PebbleCreek front gate. Within a 25- to 30-mile distance, there are more regional malls, specialty shops, countless restaurants of every taste and price range, and professional/household services of every description.

SADDLEBROOKE RESORT COMMUNITY

TUCSON, ARIZONA

64518 E. SaddleBrooke Dr.
Tucson, AZ 85739
520-825-3030 / 800-733-4050
Fax: 520-825-2301

Developer: Robson Communities

Year of initial property sales/rental: 1986

Total land area: 1,790 acres (phases I and II)

Average elevation: 3,200 feet

Location: Southeastern Arizona; Pinal County; 14 miles north of Tucson; some 100 miles south of Phoenix; about 75 miles north of the Mexican border town of Nogales, Ariz.; off State Highway 77, just below its intersection with the terminus of State Highway 79.

Nearest airport with scheduled commercial service: Tucson International (35 miles)

Current number of housing units with year-round occupants: 1,650

Projected number of housing units: 4,000

Resident eligibility: At least one person in most households must be 55 or more years of age and no permanent residents under age 19. A limited number of homes may be occupied with one family member at least 40 years of age.

Community visit/tour incentive program: A "Preferred Guest" program entitles prospective home buyers to a welcome package at generously discounted rates that offers a visit of up to three nights and four days to experience the community. Included are luxurious accommodations, swimming, tennis, and a complimentary round of golf, and an opportunity to personally visit with current homeowners. The total package cost ranges from $129 to $299, depending on the season.

Suggested daily newspaper: *Arizona Daily Star*, P.O. Box 26807, Tucson, AZ 85726 (520-573-4511)

WHY SADDLEBROOKE?

SaddleBrooke is billed with good reason as "the mountain view collection." While Arizona does indeed have more than its share of **Rocky Mountain** rapture, few of the state's comparable adult communities rest so comfortably close to the majesty of post-card vistas and seemingly endless grandeur. Lying before the rise of the **Santa Catalina Mountains** (locale for numerous Hollywood productions), punctuated by glistening man-made lakes, it is a scene reminiscent of an exclusive world-class five-star resort. Given the lavish amenities set in the captivating American desert heartland, and just minutes from a major metropolitan center, it is a combination of environmental characteristics seldom encountered in a single location.

Surprisingly enough, in a world of escalating real estate costs, this package of residential/recreational quality comes at prices that are affordable to many who never thought they could retire to quite so appealing a lifestyle. The fact that so many SaddleBrooke families have come to this nesting place from all across the nation and beyond attests to the value of the product.

In 1997, **Robson Communities** celebrated its 25th year of developing active adult, master-planned villages. SaddleBrooke, the second of four such Arizona enterprises, shares with two of its sister communities, both in the **Phoenix** area, the honor of having been named by *New Choices* magazine (a *Reader's Digest* publication) among the "Top 20 Retirement Communities in America."

WHO'S IN CHARGE?

The **SaddleBrooke Home Owners Association (SBHOA)** has title to the community's recreational properties and common areas and is responsible for maintaining facilities and programs. In fulfilling that obligation, it collects a fee from resident member households in the amount of $64.75 per month ($777 annually). Those owners who live in Villa Homes (duplex units) pay an additional $115 per month, which covers all exterior building maintenance and a variety of services applicable to that neighborhood. Some recreational activities, including use of the golf course and certain special classes, require separate user fees. The Robson Communities management team continues to be responsible for operations of facilities and programs until such time as full administrative control is turned over to the SBHOA, anticipated to occur in January 1999.

The SBHOA Board of Directors is elected by resident members. Much of its work is carried out by standing committees of member volunteers, such as those concerned with architecture and landscaping, finance, golf and tennis programs, property maintenance, community rules and regulations, social and recreational activities, and street maintenance. The *SaddleBrooke Progress* is a tabloid-size newspaper that carries substantial advertising and is published monthly with news, comments, and various features of interest to local residents.

THE WEATHER REPORT

While **Tucson** experiences characteristics of the desert valley climate, average summer temperatures are not as high as those found in Phoenix, more than 100 miles to the northwest. Overnight lows are typically as much as 10 degrees below Phoenix readings, and daytime highs about three to five degrees lower. The SaddleBrooke area, being closer to the mountains and at an elevation of more than 3,000 feet, enjoys yet a further moderation of weather extremes. Average summer highs, however, are close to the three digit mark, with nighttime readings falling to the low 70s (quite comfortable with the very low humidity level).

There is no weather data available for the specific SaddleBrooke location. The following temperature summary from the U.S. National Oceanic and Atmospheric Administration is for nearby Tucson and, as stated, is likely to be somewhat warmer at any time of the year:

December: high 65/low 39   **January:** high 64/low 38

February: high 67/low 40   **June:** high 98/low 67

July: high 98/low 74   **August:** high 96/low 72

Average annual precipitation: 11 inches
Average annual snowfall: ½ inch
Average humidity at maximum temperature: 25%

HOME SWEET HOME

Robson bywords, in marketing homes, are *flexibility* and *affordability*. Much emphasis is directed toward giving the home buyer ample opportunity to personalize floor plans, alter or add features, or create new concepts and still keep costs in check. Home sales in 1996 increased by more than 60 percent over the prior year, surpassing previous sales records.

A model home village displays a representative cross section of state-of-the-art innovations for interior design, as well as for the infinite variety of exterior elevations. One of the largest and most luxurious of new home models was recently introduced (The Lexia), ranging in size from 3,200 to 3,497 square feet. It showcases dramatic interior treatments from a sweeping circular stairway to a well-equipped gourmet kitchen (built-in desk, oversized pantry, work space island, and a cozy breakfast area overlooking the back patio), an elegant dining room, lots of storage space, and a variety of options to satisfy different needs. The unit is priced from the $230s.

Single-family, detached homes are offered in sizes ranging from 1,270 to 3,497 square feet, at prices from the low $120s to the mid-$250s (or higher depending on site selection). Attached town house units are available with floor plans of 1,466 to 1,724 square feet, priced in the $120s to the high $130s. Some 95 percent of home purchases are new construction, the remainder from a limited resale market. Long-term rentals are available in a wide assortment of sizes at lease rates from $1,000 to $2,500 a month. Central water and sanitary sewer systems are provided by agencies of nearby local government.

MONEY MATTERS

Living costs can reasonably be expected to mirror those found in the metropolitan Tucson area, because SaddleBrooke is almost close enough to be called a suburb. In a comparison analysis among 99 popular retirement cities ("Chart of Living Costs: How 99 Cities Compare" in *Where to Retire* magazine) Tucson was found to reflect precisely the same overall cost level as Atlanta and Baltimore and fell within three percentage points higher or lower than such places as Dallas, Harrisburg, Kansas City (Missouri), Minneapolis, Orlando, St. Louis, and Tampa. It was at least 20 percent less expensive than Anchorage (21 percent below), Boston (29 percent below), Hartford (20 percent below), Honolulu (44 percent below), Philadelphia (22 percent below), New York City (55 percent below), San Francisco (42 percent below), and Washington, D.C. (20 percent below). These findings were based on seven categories of expenditures (originally published by ACCRA) covering housing, food, clothing, transportation, health care, utilities, and miscellaneous goods and services.

In *Where to Retire*, a separate report on relative living costs released several years earlier and based on a broader range of factors, including average wages and property taxes, as well as real estate, utilities, health care, and food costs, Tucson was ranked number 48 on a list of the least to the most expensive of 78 popular retirement cities. The authors pointed out that the rankings were for just the 78 towns and cities listed and were not based on any national average, and that the rankings should be used only as a rough guide to indicate relative costs of living.

Local property taxes on real estate are based on actual value. The owner of a home valued at $136,000 would pay approximately $1,632 annually.

TAKE GOOD CARE OF YOURSELF

There are 14 hospitals with more than 2,370 beds in the Greater Tucson area. Professional medical services include more than 2,000 physicians, dentists, health care specialists, and health maintenance organizations. **Columbia Northwest Medical Center,** with 162 beds is approximately 12 miles from SaddleBrooke and is the nearest in-patient facility. A nearby medical plaza houses a broad selection of physicians and other health care professionals in private practice. Other such offices are located in **Oro Valley** (including an audiology clinic), just north of Tucson.

A second major medical facility on the north side of the city, about 17 miles distant, is **Tucson General Hospital** with 106 patient beds. It offers a full range of diagnostic and therapeutic services with a medical staff of more than 250 physicians, including 39 specialties.

PLACES TO GO, THINGS TO DO

Whatever sport, hobby, or special interest is on one's priority list of activities, it is likely to be found at SaddleBrooke. If not, chances are it could be created with just a little initiative and a modicum of effort. All the expected amenities are in place—a grand 25,000-square-foot two-story clubhouse, a 27-hole championship golf course, eight lighted tennis courts, heated indoor/outdoor swimming pools and whirlpools, an arts and crafts center, a state-of-the-art 5,000-square-foot-plus health club, and fine dining and lounging.

Holiday parties, concerts, variety shows, theme dances, social hours, and special events fill the evening calendar. About nine miles from **Catalina State Park**, and spread before a mountain backdrop fit for an artist's canvas, it is a lifestyle that seems somehow beyond the pale of reality—too good to be true.

The 1997 residents' activity guide lists more than 50 clubs and organized activities, each briefly described and showing the name and phone number of the contact person. All the usual card games, sports and fitness activities, arts and crafts, and service/religious groups are there, plus a good many not-so-usual—like motorcycle touring, UFO education, creative writing, landscape weaving, jewelry making, and a table game called hoss-pfeffer (whatever that might be!).

Tucson, Arizona's second largest city (population almost a half million) has within its limits of nearly 500 square miles, all the cultural, entertainment, and educational assets one could expect to find in a major metropolitan center. It is a modern city with a curious mixture of high-tech industry and a desert frontier heritage. A multibillion dollar tourist industry is a major part of its economic base. As such, it has spawned a reputation for appealing to visitors yearning for escape to historical origins and for a different kind of recreational environment.

One example of the uniqueness of area attractions is found just 10 miles south of the city. **Mission San Xavier del Bac,** also known as the "Sistine Chapel of North America," is said to be an art restoration classic and the finest example of mission architecture in the United States. **Tombstone**, the "town too tough to die," features the famous **OK Corral, Boothill Cemetery, Bird Cage Theatre,** and **Crystal Palace Saloon**, all indelible landmarks of America's wild west ancestry. It is little more than an hour's drive away. About 45 miles south is the town of **Tubac,** Arizona's oldest European settlement and an internationally known artists colony where ruins from the 17th century are preserved. American Indian life and history are preserved on nearby reservations and in museums that honor Apache warriors and other "first Americans." The Mexican border town of **Nogales** is 64 miles down the highway from Tucson, a convenient gateway to a neighboring country and culture where "Americanos" have long been lured by shopping bargains and enchanted with the charms of Hispanic civilization.

If you're interested in science or technology, about 40 miles south you can catch the **Titan Missile Museum,** housing the underground silo of its famous weapon namesake. Not far beyond is the **Kitt Peak National Observatory**, home of the world's largest collection of astronomical telescopes (including the largest solar telescope), anchored atop a 7,000-feet-high mountain loft. One of Tucson's most fascinating points of international notoriety is the scientific project known as Biosphere II, located just north of SaddleBrooke.

Beyond all these special area attractions, there are, in Tucson, 18 museums and art galleries, 17 libraries, 96 parks, four lakes, 28 golf courses, and 11 bowling alleys. **University of Arizona** athletic programs and a full calendar of educational and cultural events add further recreational choices.

SAFE AND SECURE

SaddleBrooke retains its own neighborhood patrol, supplemented by the county sheriff's department for law enforcement functions. The SB contingent provides services typical for such units, including neighborhood patrol, vacation watch, enforcement of community parking and traffic regulations, and emergency response to residents' needs.

LET'S GO SHOPPING

A new on-site commercial center for SaddleBrooke opened in mid-1997. Tenants include a "super convenience store" and gas station, hair salon, bank, coffeehouse, post office, financial services offices, and a golf cart sales and service shop. The towns of **Catalina** (population about 5,000), almost within walking distance of SaddleBrooke, and Oro Valley, a bit larger and just a few more minutes further down the road, offer convenient supplementary shopping for most day-to-day personal and household needs. There is also a large full-service food market and a major departmental drug store.

For more serious shopping, there are two major malls on the side of Tucson nearest to SaddleBrooke, each within a 20- to 25-mile radius. **The Tucson Mall**, most popular in the area, features several department stores (including a Sears and a JCPenney) and a busy food court.

SUN LAKES RESORT COMMUNITY

SUN LAKES, ARIZONA

25025 South E.J. Robson Blvd.
Sun Lakes, AZ 85248
602-895-9600 / 800-321-8643
Fax: 602-895-0675

Developer: Robson Communities

Year of initial property sales/rentals: 1972

Total land area: 3,500 acres

Average elevation: 900 feet

Location: South-central Arizona; Maricopa County; in the east valley of metropolitan Phoenix; 7 miles south of Chandler; about 23 miles southeast of downtown Phoenix; 3 miles east of Interstate 10.

Nearest airport with scheduled commercial service: Sky Harbor International/Phoenix (21 miles)

Current number of housing units with year-round occupants: 7,200

Projected number of housing units: 10,000-plus

Resident eligibility: At least one person in most households must be 55 or more years of age, and no permanent residents under age 19. A limited number of homes may be occupied by one family member at least 40 years old.

Community visit/tour incentive program: Prospective home buyers can arrange for a four-day, three-night stay at very attractive guest rates. Included in the "Preferred Guest Package" are luxurious on-site accommodations and approximately $150 in meals and recreational activity. Weekday arrivals are required. Discounted rates for the full package range from $129 to $299, according to season.

Suggested newspaper: *Arizona Republic*, 120 E. Van Buren St., Phoenix, AZ 85004 (602-257-8300)

WHY SUN LAKES?

Among four **Robson** communities in Arizona, **Sun Lakes** is the company's flagship development and the largest in acreage and population. Part of its uniqueness lies in its five separate country club neighborhoods, each with its own clubhouse and golf course. An investment in excess of $70 million has produced upscale amenities that rival any exclusive resort destination in the country. The community has grown steadily since its inception in 1972, adding new features and amenities with each passing year. Its most recently developed third-phase subdivisions have introduced new levels of elegance in clubhouse decor and functional satisfaction in the design of activity facilities. Sun Lakes has been listed among the "Top 20 Retirement Communities in

America" by *New Choices* magazine for four consecutive years (1993-1996). Two of its sister communities have earned that distinction for the last three of those years.

It might be assumed that a community with five 18-hole golf courses devotes most of its leisure interest to the greens and fairways. Not necessarily so. The new private **Oakwood Health & Tennis Club** showcases the award-winning **MaxLife Fitness Program** and no less than 14 lighted courts, including two sunken, stadium configurations and four clay courts. This top-rated complex is now the site of the **Seniors Doubles Pro Scramble**, an annual event featuring many of the world's most celebrated professional senior players. Some Sun Lakers who swing a serious racket are on community teams that travel to distant tournaments.

Few all-adult communities can lay claim to a nationwide reputation for road show performances by talented residents who give new meaning to the word "retiree." **The Dancin' Grannies,** all from Sun Lakes, have been taking their high-stepping aerobic stage production all over the country for years. They appear at senior health fairs and other special events with a mission to change attitudes and stereotypes about grandmothers in particular and about people in general who have passed the first half century of their lives.

If Robson Communities has had a watchword since its inception, that word has been *value.* In a highly competitive market, their objective has been clear—quality housing and exceptional amenities at an affordable cost. Anyone familiar with today's costs of most active adult resort communities will acknowledge that they have done well in meeting that goal.

WHO'S IN CHARGE?

The Sun Lakes complex is divided into three phases. In each of the first two phases, almost all lots have been sold and new home construction completed. Each of those communities is under the management control and ownership of its own homeowners association. Those entities are responsible for maintenance of facilities and operation of programs. HOA #1, with a golf course, clubhouse, and two swimming pools, collects a $400 annual fee from resident members for upkeep of facilities and common grounds. HOA #2, with two golf courses and clubhouses, four swimming pools, additional tennis facilities, and about twice the acreage, has an $800 yearly assessment. Both have their own general manager and staff. Phase III, still in active development, is currently administered by Robson Communities. Meantime, however, this last component has its own residents' association playing an active coordinating role with the developer in planning and executing programs and in formulating policy. Annual dues in Phase III come to $726.

In order to keep mandatory HOA assessments to a minimum and to provide an equitable program of recreational options, separate user fees are charged for golf and for a privately operated health and tennis club. A tabloid-size newspaper is published monthly for distribution to Sun Lakes residents, generating extensive advertising revenues and moderate subscription fees to maintain complete self-sufficiency.

THE WEATHER REPORT

The **Phoenix** area claims more sunshine days per year than any other city in the United States. In-season weather (October through March) brings hordes of winter "snowbirds" from frosty north country climes. Those who reside in the desert valley all year round are folks who can tolerate summer temperatures that are into the 100-plus range much of June through early September. It is not unusual for the mercury to reach 110 degrees in the afternoon and remain above 80 through the night. The low humidity, for which the region is so well-known, makes the moderately high temperatures much more bearable, but offers little relief when the thermometer reaches the upper 90s and on up into three-digit territory.

The flat, oval-shaped **Salt River Valley**, with an average elevation of more than 1,000 feet, is home to metropolitan Phoenix. The topographical features that characterize this **Sonora Desert** land include surrounding mountains, the highest of which is **Superstition Mountain**, about 30 miles to the east and rising to as much as 5,000 feet above sea level.

Normal high and low temperatures for Phoenix are reported by the U.S. National Oceanic and Atmospheric Administration as follows:

December: high 66/low 42   **January:** high 66/low 41

February: high 71/low 45   **June:** high 103/low 73

July: high 106/low 81   **August:** high 104/low 80

Average annual precipitation: 8 inches
Average annual snowfall: trace
Average summer humidity at maximum temperature: 10-20%

HOME SWEET HOME

Robson Communities is both developer and builder. A full-service design center assists home buyers in planning and executing a construction contract that may incorporate any of a wide variety of interior and exterior features. The "Premiere Series" offers floor plans from 1,544 to 2,022 square feet with prices from the low $130s to the mid-$160s. The "Luxury Series" begins at 1,330 square feet and goes up to 3,497 square feet with prices from the low $140s to the mid-$250s. A third home series called "The Villas" offers sizes from 1,466 to 1,724 square feet, with prices from the low $120s to the low $130s. Prices include a standard homesite. Many variations can substantially affect the final selling price.

An extensive list of included features for each of the three series of homes covers special luxury appointments, bathroom/kitchen/flooring/garage specifications, and a long list of miscellaneous features that make for extra comfort and eye appeal. Concrete block construction, natural gas appliances, and dual-pane windows maximize energy efficiency. An award-winning model home village showcases 14 different plans and price points.

Long-term rental units are often available in a wide selection of sizes, depending on the time of the year and prevailing market conditions. Storage and recreational vehicle parking are available on the property. Homesites are not sold without construction contracts. Some electric/telephone lines are under ground, some above.

MONEY MATTERS

A cost-of-living comparison of 27 cities compiled by Robson Communities showed Phoenix to have a slightly higher cost than Tucson, but lower than 22 of the places reviewed. Cities shown to have the same or within 3 percent of the same cost ratio as Phoenix were Billings (Montana), Cleveland, Denver, Harrisburg, Lansing (Michigan), Milwaukee, Minneapolis, Montpelier (Vermont), Richmond (Virginia), and Syracuse (New York). New York City costs were 54 percent higher; San Francisco, 39 percent; Boston, 24 percent; Philadelphia, 19 percent; and Anchorage, 18 percent. Only three of the listed cities were significantly lower than Phoenix: Omaha at 12 percent, Kansas City (Missouri) at 8 percent, and Dallas at 5 percent. The Robson analysis was based on cost of living data drawn from indices prepared by ACCRA, a research group.

Sun Lakes homeowners' dues vary from $400 to $800 annually, depending upon the phase in which the home is located (see "Who's In Charge?" section). Golf fees are determined by how many courses are to be accessed and the frequency of play. Those costs range from $500 to $1,491 a year. The MaxLife Fitness Program annual membership costs $275 per person.

Local real estate property taxes are based on 1.4 percent of the purchase price of the home. The annual tax bill on a $136,000 home would amount to approximately $1,904.

TAKE GOOD CARE OF YOURSELF

An on-site **Sun Lakes Health and Education Center** opened in the spring of 1997. The facility offers SL residents a comprehensive menu of health care services, including primary and specialty physician offices, urgent care, x-ray and diagnostic imaging, physical therapy, dentistry, and social services. It places a variety of out-patient medical resources at everyone's doorstep. There are also two pharmacies in the community. For those who require in-patient care, **Chandler Regional Hospital,** a 142-bed facility with all but the most nontraditional diagnosis and treatment programs, is but 6 miles down the road. It sponsors a strong program of community education, featuring support groups for a wide variety of medical conditions, along with lectures and workshops on related topics of broad public interest.

Desert Samaritan Hospital in **Mesa,** just 11 miles from Sun Lakes, is a larger and more comprehensive institution providing 495 beds, including a short-term nursing unit. More than 100 physicians and other health care providers maintain practices within a 15-mile radius of the community.

PLACES TO GO, THINGS TO DO

Sun Lakes residents need not go far to satisfy recreational appetites. Five golf courses (and three driving ranges), separate well-appointed clubhouses, arts and crafts centers, lighted tennis courts, heated swimming pools, appealing dining rooms, spacious auditoriums, whirlpools, and impressive libraries top the list of amenities.

While golf and tennis may define the essence of Sun Lakes living, there are alternatives on a grand scale for those who don't swing a club or racket. There are activities for more than 100 social clubs, organizations, and leagues—two dozen kinds of arts and crafts alone. More than 15 different table games draw players together. Eleven different types of exercise groups match choices with physical capabilities. Musical interests, both voice and instrumental, beckon those with performing talent and those who just appreciate. No fewer than 10 dance groups span the entire spectrum of form—including ballroom, ballet, jazz, country, line, square, and round. Other creative pursuits include community theater, writing, and book discussions. Twenty-three hobby groups and clubs leave few possibilities overlooked. Added to all of this are service and religious organizations and a diverse collection of health and support groups. The greatest challenge for many newcomers (and old-timers, too!) is to decide which activities are most likely to produce the greatest personal satisfaction.

For those who yearn for a change of scenery or something in the way of in-town attractions, metropolitan Phoenix is bountiful. Within a 20- to 30-mile radius, there are outstanding museums, performing arts stages, and symphony venues. Professional and collegiate sports teams play in some of the nation's prime stadiums and arenas (such as **Arizona State University's Sun Devil Stadium**, site of **Super Bowl XXX** and the annual New Year's **Fiesta Bowl** classic). Eight major league baseball teams descend on the Phoenix area in a perennial spring training ritual. Nearby **Scottsdale** is host every January to the **PGA Phoenix Open** golf tournament. Thoroughbred horses, greyhounds, and sports cars race past grandstands and around perfectly groomed ovals that are among the best in their respective circuits. **The Original Coors Rodeo Showdown** comes around every October, one of the most prestigious of U.S. rodeo championships, pulling in upwards of

35,000 fans from far and wide. A new 24-screen cinema complex is just 7 miles away. An outstanding zoo, wildlife park, botanical gardens, nature centers, and casinos all provide plenty of leisure opportunity.

If communing with nature is your thing, the world-famous **Apache Trail,** just east of Phoenix, cuts through Superstition Mountain and features volcanic debris, canyons, sparkling lakes, monumental saguaro cacti plants, and wildflowers without end. A two-hour drive up Interstate 17 leads to **Sedona** and the magnificent red sandstone cliffs at **Oak Creek Canyon**, an international mecca for art lovers and for those who especially appreciate authentic Native American crafts. Only a four-hour drive from Phoenix is the granddaddy of all America's natural wonders—the mighty **Grand Canyon.** It's like no other place on earth, which may explain why people from all over the planet beat an unremitting path to its breathtaking perimeter.

SAFE AND SECURE

For those who prefer the added peace of mind derived from living in a gated community, two of the four Sun Lakes subdivisions have entry access control stations, some staffed by round-the-clock personnel. The entire community, however, is served by its own safety patrol and sheriff's posse. In addition to policing functions, homeowners are provided with such services as vacation watch, motorist assistance and accident reports, and vehicle/ residential lockout. Emergency response and assistance is provided by the Sun Lakes fire department, which maintains two facilities on-site with trained paramedics.

LET'S GO SHOPPING

Sun Lakes has its own shopping center near the model homes village. It is a sizable strip shopping mall anchored by a major food market and joined by about 20 retailers and service outlets, including vendors of golf carts, hardware, and videos, a florist, and large drug store. Service establishments include mortgage and title companies, a bank, library, cable television provider, beauty salon, investment broker, real estate office, and a gas and auto service station. Regional mall shopping is easily accessible in Mesa, about 11 miles away, and still more extensive in Phoenix, **Tempe**, and **Chandler**, all within a 15- to 25-mile radius.

ARKANSAS TAX FACTS

INDIVIDUAL INCOME TAX

Graduated from 1% to 7 % as follows:

- ♦ First $2,999 of income @ 1%
- ♦ Next $3,000 @ 2.5%
- ♦ Next $3,000 @ 3.5%
- ♦ Next $6,000 @ 4.5%
- ♦ Next $10,000 @ 6%
- ♦ Over $25,000 @ 7%

Other information:

- ♦ No deduction for payment of federal income tax.
- ♦ Exemption on first $6,000 of public or private pensions.
- ♦ Social security benefits exempt.
- ♦ Various standard deductions, credits, and rebates.

SALES TAX

Retailers collect 4.5 percent; local jurisdictions are permitted to levy additional tax, generally in the 1.5 percent to 2 percent range.

PROPERTY TAX

Political subdivisions (counties, cities, and school districts), rather than the state, impose taxes on real and personal property based on valuations. There are variations in tax rates and policies for each such jurisdiction. Information should be obtained from the county assessor and local tax collector at the location of interest.

RANKING REPORT

Among the 50 states, Arkansas ranks 9th from the most favorable in total state taxes per capita when only state levies are considered, but 3rd from the most favorable when local data (property taxes) are included, according to the *1995 State Policy Reference Book*. The average annual dollar amount for the combined state and local tax tab is $1,514, compared to the national average of $2,178.

For more complete tax information contact the Arkansas Department of Finance & Administration, Taxpayer Assistance Office, P.O. Box 1272, Room 216, Little Rock, AR 72203, 501-682-7751, (fax) 501-682-7900.

Note: The above information is based on applicable tax law information available at the time of publication. Because such laws and tax rates are subject to change, professional assistance should be sought if tax implications are critical to a relocation decision.

BELLA VISTA VILLAGE

BELLA VISTA, ARKANSAS

210 Town Center
Bella Vista, AR 72714
501-855-3776 / 800-228-7328
Fax: 501-855-6634

Developer: Cooper Communities, Inc.

Year of initial property sales/rentals: 1965

Total land area: More than 36,000 acres covering more than 50 square miles

Average elevation: 1,100 feet

Location: Far northwestern corner of Arkansas; Benton County; in the Ozark Mountain Range; on US Hwy 71; just south of the Missouri border; 110 miles east of Tulsa; 90 miles southwest of Springfield (Missouri).

Nearest airport with scheduled commercial service: Fayetteville Municipal (30 miles)

Current number of housing units with year-round occupants: 7,600; number of property owners—more than 38,000; number of year-round residents—approximately 14,000.

Projected number of housing units: 17,000 (2009)

Resident eligibility: No age restrictions, but an estimated 80% of population is retired or semiretired; estimated fewer than 10% of households with children under 18 years of age.

Community visit/tour incentive program: Mini-vacation plans available to qualified guests to occupy fully furnished single-family private homes and townhouses; incentive program for present property owners to refer new prospects for relocation.

Suggested newspaper: *Benton County Daily Record,* c/o Community Publishers, Inc., 104 SW "A" St., Bentonville, AR 72712 (501-271-3700)

WHY BELLA VISTA VILLAGE?

Bella Vista Village is the flagship community of its developer, **Cooper Communities, Inc.** It is one of five such planned residential communities under the Cooper banner located in four different states. It is the oldest among them (established in 1965), making the project one of the truly pioneering ventures of its kind.

The Cooper organization, founded in 1954, is one of the country's earliest builders of master-planned subdivisions. The company has been awarded numerous honors for outstanding and innovative developmental practices.

It has been repeatedly recognized for an unwavering commitment to the preservation of large portions of the natural environment in its planned communities.

The Village is unique in many respects. In terms of size alone (more than 36,000 acres), it is among the largest privately built and owned sites in real estate subdivision development. For its residents, the magnitude of space and population translates into many quality amenities, valued at some $35 million and available to residents at very low per capita cost. An impressive array of leisure amenities and programs revolve around no fewer than seven golf courses, eight private lakes, three country clubs, a yacht club and marina, 10 parks (six developed, four in the natural state), four recreation centers, five swimming pools, and three tennis complexes.

Topographical features of the area include hilly terrain, mountain streams, and unspoiled forests. Twenty-five percent of the total area of the community is, and will always remain, in its natural state. These 9,000 preserved acres provide a green belt that borders every recreational facility and joins each piece of residential property. It includes lakefront and golf course settings, park and picnic areas, and endless stretches of dense woodlands populated by towering pines and mature oaks, maples, elms, and sweetgums.

The Village is situated less than 10 miles north of **Bentonville**, home of corporate giant Wal-Mart, the world's largest retailer and pioneer in discount merchandising. The two communities share a single chamber of commerce and are bound closely together in common interests centering on economic and infrastructure development, tourist promotion, volunteer activity, and citizen interaction.

WHO'S IN CHARGE?

The **Bella Vista Property Owners Association (POA)** is a nonprofit corporation under the direction of a nine-member board of directors elected from and by BVV resident members. The Association has complete responsibility for administering the affairs of the Village, including financial control, the purchase, use, and storage of all supplies, materials, and equipment, maintenance of roads and facilities, water sources and waste disposal, fire protection, emergency medical services, public safety, etc. A general manager is hired as the chief executive officer who directs a departmental staff.

Membership in the POA is granted to all owners of lots or living units. Residents currently pay an incredibly low $14 a month assessment, which sustains all community operations and entitles property owners access to the full range of facilities, programs, and services outlined elsewhere in this profile. While there are some user fees (e.g., golfing green charges), most recreational amenities impose no additional costs.

THE WEATHER REPORT

Northwestern Arkansas is generally described as having a four-season mild climate. Situated at a moderate elevation in the **Ozark Mountains**, snowfall, icy conditions, and frigid temperatures are relatively infrequent. Spring invites dogwood and flowering redbud trees. Summer is a lush green, and fall follows with the vibrant colors that attract tourists from far and wide, particularly from neighboring states to the south that are not so blessed with the bursting colors of the season.

A 12-month weather summary recorded in 1995 by the BVV resident weather observer showed the following *average high and low* temperature readings:

December: high 43/low 28   **January:** high 45/low 25

February: high 51/low 28   **June:** high 80/low 60

July: high 85/low 65   **August:** high 90/low 67

Average annual precipitation: 45 inches
Average annual snowfall: 8 to 9 inches

HOME SWEET HOME

In a wide range of architectural styles and landscape options, housing choices center on detached single-family homes and clustered townouses. Home sites vary in cost in accordance with size and enhancements, such as proximity to a lake or golf course, location, etc. An estimated 20 percent of residential properties are available for new construction by Cooper or other builders of choice. The remaining 80 percent of homes for sale is on the resale market.

Most homes are built off the main roads, many on short, winding circles or culs-de-sac. Virtually all are on lots that border a natural feature of the property. Currently there are approximately 6,650 single-family homes, more than 950 townhouses and more than 100 apartments (assisted care units) occupied by permanent residents. An RV park and storage area is provided.

Vacant lots generally range in size from ¼ to a full acre. Prices range from $1,000 to $125,000. An average homesite costs approximately $13,500. Those on or within view of a lake or golf course start at about $18,500. Single-family homes are priced from $79,000 to $250,000, with floor space from 1,200 to 3,500 square feet. Townhouse prices start at $145,000 and go up to as much as $350,000, with plans that vary from 1,200 to 3,500 square feet. Long-term leasing units can be found at rates from $500 to $1,500 a month, in sizes ranging from 900 to 2,000 square feet.

Electric and telephone line placements are mixed above and below ground. The sanitary system encompasses both central sewage disposal and septic tanks (in some neighborhoods). Bella Vista Village operates its own municipal water supply under the supervision of the BVV Property Owners Association.

MONEY MATTERS

Northwestern Arkansas has an enviable reputation for its extremely low living costs. An *ACCRA Cost of Living Index* survey conducted for the first quarter of 1996 shows the Bella Vista/Bentonville area to be a haven for those who enjoy seeing their dollar stretch to the limits of value. Prices were analyzed for grocery items, housing, utilities, transportation, health care, and miscellaneous goods and services. The northwest corner of Arkansas was rated at 5.4 percent below the national average, among the lower rankings for U.S. metropolitan areas.

In a state that is among the nation's lowest in taxation, local jurisdictions also offer very gentle assessments. **Benton County** adds a moderate 1.5 percent to the state sales tax (4.5 percent). Prescriptions are among the exemptions. Bella Vista Village imposes no additional supplement at the city level. The only local property tax is for either of two school districts. The Bentonville School District is $42.60 per $1,000, with property assessed at 20 percent of the true market value. The **Gravette** School District is pegged at $33.80 per $1,000, with the same rate of assessment.

TAKE GOOD CARE OF YOURSELF

Bella Vista Medical Center is in the community, minutes from every resident's doorstep. Owned and operated by **St. Mary's Hospital** in nearby **Rogers**, the facility maintains three full-time physicians (all accept Medicare) and offers a full complement of visiting primary and specialty medical services, including urology, cardiology, surgery, mammography, x-ray, dietary counseling, and laboratory services. A self-contained continuing care/ assisted living facility with a fully staffed intermediate care nursing center is also within the Village.

The closest full service hospital is 70-bed **Bates Medical Center** in Bentonville, with a staff of more than 100 physicians, about 8 miles from Bella Vista. Specialized departments include intensive and coronary care, cardiac rehabilitation, physical and respiratory therapy, diagnostic imaging, and a 24-hour emergency service. A particularly innovative Bates program is its Center for Health, Wellness, and Disease Prevention. St. Mary's Hospital in Rogers, 16 miles away, has more than 100 beds and state-of-the-art technology. Ten miles further south in **Springdale** is the **Northwest Medical Center,** a still-larger acute care facility with 150-plus beds and a wide array of medical specialties.

PLACES TO GO, THINGS TO DO

With seven golf courses and five pro shops, one can assume the popularity of golf carts in the Village. Newcomers to BVV who never before swung a club are among those taking lessons from the pros. User fees are minimal. There's even miniature golf. For tennis buffs there are 12 hard-surface lighted courts. Fishing on the community's eight well-stocked lakes and any number of other nearby recreational lakes, rivers, and streams, offer the angler a harvest of bass, crappie, catfish, bream, and perch, among other varieties. The **Loch Lomond Marina,** adjacent to the **Bella Vista Yacht Club** is fishing head-quarters and source of boat and slip rentals, guide service, and a complete stock of artificial lures, live bait, and tackle. The **Bella Vista Trout Farm** is the place to catch your own, virtually guaranteed.

Boating and water sports satisfy the outdoor spirit. Some Bella Vista lakes (ranging in size from 22 to 477 acres) allow water skiing with no horse-power limits. Some have launching ramps. Some feature swimming areas. Sixteen miles to the southeast is 36,000-acre **Beaver Lake** that annually attracts thousands of campers and water sports enthusiasts.

Seven swimming pools (one indoor), shuffleboard, basketball, and racquet ball courts contribute to recreational choices. Well-appointed picnic areas offer restrooms, electricity, and covered grills. Bella Vista boasts more than 150 clubs and civic groups! Interests and activities center on golf and tennis, arts and crafts, bowling, camping, games, dance, health, music, and theater. Clubs meet regularly around just about every conceivable activity, from bike riding, bird watching, and book reviews to volunteer services, singles, and shriners. A full-time activities director coordinates all programs. The 120-seat nondenominational **Mildred B. Cooper Memorial Chapel** is an architectural masterpiece in the village open to the public for meditation or quiet relaxation, as well as for weddings, concerts, christenings, memorial services, and such.

BVV residents have their own library. A wide-screen cinema is located on site. More than 40 churches representing 14 denominations are inside the Village or within a 10-mile radius (including two nondenominational congregations).

Just 26 miles away, exotic animals from around the world roam free at the **Wild Wilderness Safari,** where families can drive through for close-up communion with other species. Canoeing on the **Elk River** is just 5 miles from home. **Eureka Springs,** the "little Switzerland of the Ozarks" less than an hour's drive away, is a unique tourist destination that draws hundreds of thousands of visitors each year.

Thirty miles to the south is **Fayetteville,** home of the **University of Arkansas** main campus and scene of every imaginable collegiate sport, entertainment, and cultural genre. Top-ranked football and basketball programs are a long-nurtured tradition. Theater and dance companies feature both local and touring performers. Countless exhibits of fine art, historical collections, native crafts, and such are ongoing public attractions.

The **North Arkansas Symphony**, also in Fayetteville, is a worthy reflection of its big-city cousins. The five-city core of northwest Arkansas—Bella Vista, Bentonville, Rogers, Springdale, and Fayetteville—offers a breathtaking year-round calendar of events that includes festivals of every sort, a slew of arts and crafts shows, little theater, concerts in the park, rodeos, golf tournaments, holiday celebrations, antique and toy shows, quilt fairs, fishing tournaments, and "Opera in the Ozarks" at neighboring **Inspiration Point** in **Eureka Springs**. From mid-October through November is the "Flaming Fall Revue," the season of glorious autumn color in the "Natural State."

There are several historical landmarks in the area. Of special interest are two civil war memorial parks, both a short drive from Bella Vista. **Pea Ridge National Military Park**, just south of the **Missouri** border, is the site of a battle that ended a campaign to keep the State of Missouri under Federal control. **Prairie Grove Battlefield State Park** marks the ground upon which 20,000 Confederate and Union soldiers clashed, creating more than 2,500 casualties in a struggle to control Northwest Arkansas.

The **1875 Peel Mansion and Historic Gardens,** located in neighboring Bentonville, is a magnificent villa tower Italianate mansion that was a working farmstead surrounded by 180 acres of apple trees. The site is also an outdoor museum of historic 19th-century roses, perennials, and native plants.

SAFE AND SECURE

The POA funds a Bella Vista Division of the Benton County Sheriff's Office to provide for public safety. They maintain a 15-man substation in the Village. A security patrol is on duty around the clock, seven days a week. A BVV fire station is fully equipped and manned on a 24-hour schedule.

LET'S GO SHOPPING

The developers of Bella Vista have long conducted an energetic program of commercial promotion to bring more retail and service establishments to the community. Residents enjoy the convenience of a full-service grocery market that anchors its main shopping center. There are few types of retail outlets and service establishments that are absent from the selection of businesses in the Village and within a 10-mile radius. Regional mall shopping is available in and around Fayetteville, only 30 miles away.

FAIRFIELD BAY

FAIRFIELD BAY, ARKANSAS

P.O. Box 1400
Fairfield Bay, AR 72088
501-884-3324 / 888-244-4386
Fax: 501-884-6062

Developer: Fairfield Communities, Inc.

Year of initial property sales/rentals: 1968

Total land area: 10,155 acres

Elevation range: 490 to 1,250 feet

Location: North-central Arkansas; Van Buren County; on Greers Ferry Lake; on State Highway 16; 17 miles east off U.S. Highway 65 at Clinton; approximately 80 miles north of Little Rock; 130 miles north of Hot Springs.

Nearest airport with scheduled commercial service: Little Rock National Airport (80 miles)

Current number of housing units with year-round occupants: 1,000

Projected number of housing units: 1,400 (2015)

Resident eligibility: There is no age restriction for living in the community, but an estimated 80% of the population is either retired or semiretired. Not more than 20% of households is estimated to have family members in full-time residence under the age of 18.

Community visit/tour incentive program: None

Suggested newspaper: *The Fairfield Bay News* (weekly), P.O. Box 1370, Fairfield Bay, AR 72088 (501-884-6012)

WHY FAIRFIELD BAY?

Fairfield Bay is a resort/retirement community nestled in the foothills of the **Ozark Mountains,** along the north shore of 40,000-acre **Greers Ferry Lake.** Earliest development began in 1968 as a privately owned and operated residential subdivision. In 1993 the community was incorporated as a municipality with most amenities and the common areas remaining under the control of the local property-owners association, the **Fairfield Bay Community Club.**

Greers Ferry Lake is a multipurpose project, completed in 1962, for the control of floods and generation of hydroelectric power, along with the creation of a mammoth recreational playground (about 50 miles long with 343 miles of shoreline). The lake and its nearby leisure facilities were recognized in 1994 as the state's top tourist attraction.

In 1995, "The Bay" was recognized by the state for a second time as a "Volunteer Community of the Year," an annual competition among Arkansas towns and cities for encouraging and facilitating citizen community service.

WHO'S IN CHARGE?

The Fairfield Bay Community Club (FFBCC) was established when the community was first organized in 1967. Throughout the years, it has exercised the authority to collect dues and maintain common properties that were deeded to them under the original covenants. Membership dues are mandatory for property owners and are currently pegged at $18 a month. That fee includes membership in the country club and access to all amenities, including swimming pools, golf courses, tennis courts, etc. *The Fairfield Bay News,* a newsletter in full-size newspaper format, is published weekly by the FFBCC.

The board of directors is composed entirely of property owners. In 1993, the community was incorporated as a city, electing its own municipal officers. The new status left the FFBCC with its established budget and operational responsibilities, leaving to the newly formed city council responsibility for matters of state-local contracts and relationships, building, zoning and health standards, etc. There is no assessment of city taxes.

THE WEATHER REPORT

Located in the transition area between the Arkansas delta flat lowlands and the Ozark Plateau uplands, the area's climate is described as four-season modified continental. Temperature extremes are uncommon. The weather recording station at **Greers Ferry Power House** reports the following normal daily temperatures for the summer and winter months:

June: high 89/low 68	**July:** high 93/low 71
August: high 92/low 70	**December:** high 53/low 34
January: high 51/low 32	**February:** high 55/low 36

Average annual precipitation: 50 inches
Average annual snowfall: 3 inches

HOME SWEET HOME

A range of housing options includes condominiums, single-family detached, and mobile homes. It is estimated that some 10 percent of the housing stock is available for sale at any given time. A generous inventory of home construction sites are on the market, some with lake or golf course views. Building costs for a standard construction home is said to be about $60 per square foot and $70 per square foot for premium features.

Single-family detached homes range in cost from $45,000 to $350,000 for floor plans of 800 to 6,000 square feet. About 90 percent of dwellings are in that category. The remainder, condominiums, duplexes, and mobile homes, sell for between $25,000 and $50,000 in sizes between 700 and 1,200 square feet. A good selection of long-term rentals among the latter units can be leased for $200 to $500 a month. Standard vacant lots generally cost between $2,000 and $4,000. Golf course and lake frontage sites are higher.

Extra storage facilities are available on site as is separate mobile home parking. Water supply is from a private source. The waste treatment facility is operated by the community club.

An age-restricted (62 years of age or older), $5.5 million residential apartment complex with 50 units was opened in 1990. Residents have an on-site dining room and several multipurpose rooms for meetings, parties, arts and crafts, etc. Exercise and laundry rooms, a woodworking shop, library, greenhouse, beauty and barber shops, garden plots, a park, and an in-house post office are among the amenities provided.

MONEY MATTERS

Virtually any list of the most affordable places to live will find Arkansas locations well-represented. The *ACCRA Cost of Living Index* (2nd quarter, 1996) provides data for four key Arkansas locations. The nearest among them to Fairfield Bay is the **Little Rock** metropolitan area, some 80 miles to the south. Among 315 metropolitan and nonmetropolitan areas profiled in the survey, Little Rock was shown to have the lowest cost of living with a composite index 16.8 percent below the national average. Housing costs were found to be the biggest bargain of all (comparing five more expense categories, in addition to housing, including groceries, health care, utilities, transportation, and miscellaneous goods and services), with an incredible index of 28.9 percent below average. A glance at housing costs reflected in the preceding section of this profile tends to support the survey conclusion.

Local real estate and personal property millage tax rates are .0369 and .0374, respectively. According to figures published in 1996 by the City of Fairfield Bay for homes in the 1,425 to 3,200 square foot range, the property tax would amount to between $600 and $1,330 annually. Personal property within those parameters would run from $76 to $270. Taking an average for the two comes to $95 a month for total property taxes. When combined with the exceptionally favorable state tax structure (shown at the beginning of the Arkansas profiles), it is readily apparent that the tax picture is among the most attractive to be found anywhere.

TAKE GOOD CARE OF YOURSELF

The nearest in-patient hospital, **Van Buren County Memorial**, is a 70-bed facility in **Clinton**, 11 miles from the Bay. A larger regional hospital with more diversified technology and specialization is located in **Conway**, 58 miles south. In Little Rock, another 30 miles further south, are the ultimate health care facilities of a major metropolitan area. There are two health care clinics within the community—**Baptist Health Center** and **Fairfield Medical Clinic**. A full-time resident physician serves the community and specialists are scheduled in on a weekly basis.

There are chiropractic clinics in Clinton, **Edgemont**, and **Greers Ferry**, all just minutes away. Four dental practices are also located in the Fairfield Bay-Clinton vicinity. A volunteer rescue service operates in the community with registered nurses, trained emergency medical technicians, and two fully equipped ambulances.

PLACES TO GO, THINGS TO DO

The north-central Ozark plateau and foothills region has more than its share of attractions that appeal to all sorts of leisure tastes. With a 40,000-acre lake at their doorstep, Fairfield Bay residents devote much of their recreational time to water-related activities—boating, rafting, fishing, swimming, water skiing, and other aquasports. But beyond the water, there is a plethora of options for landlubbers. Campers can find no more enticing sites to pitch a tent, barbecue some ribs, or commune with nature. Trails for hiking, bird-watching, and exploring scenic woodland, are seldom equaled for sheer environmental delight.

Two outstanding golf courses within the community, one for the private use of Fairfield Bay residents, the other a semiprivate course, have won praise from the pros and from *Golf Digest*, one of the sport's primary periodicals. Together they host the Arkansas PGA and ASGA tournaments. The tennis program at the Bay, headed by a highly regarded professional director, has been home to the world's largest mixed doubles tourney since 1974. Ten lighted courts are featured.

The community center offers a variety of activities, including pool tables, pinball machines, video games, semiweekly coffee klatches, and regularly scheduled bridge games. Also available are exercise, aerobics, dancing, and live entertainment at the racquet club. The marina is a busy place for fishing contests, sightseeing shuttles, and sunset cruises. A popular conference center can accommodate gatherings of up to 500 persons. There are musical reviews in the park, hayrides, and cookouts. An under-21 club caters to the community's sparse teenage set. There's shuffleboard, horseshoes, and junior/adult volleyball. A full-time activities director coordinates programs. The **Fairfield Bay Riding Stables** at **Lazy M Ranch** offer guided equestrian trail exploration, mountain bike rentals, and horse-drawn carriage and coach rides.

Festivals, jamborees, and exhibitions crowd the annual events calendar. Just about every holiday is celebrated with a dance, a fair, or some form of merriment. **Sugar Loaf** is a mountain island in the middle of Greers Ferry Lake with a summit more than 1,000 feet high. Its nature trail draws some 35,000 hikers annually to a matchless bounty of vegetation and wildlife. **Indian Rock House,** tucked away on one of the Bay golf courses, is a massive sandstone cave with archaeological evidence of having been home to a primitive people dating back to around 1000 BC.

Movie theaters are located in nearby Clinton and **Heber Springs**. The roster of Fairfield Bay clubs and activity groups number more than 30 different centers of interest. The arts and crafts cluster alone has separate groups for painting, quilting, basketweaving, woodcarving, stained glass, and ceramics. There are pockets of local interest in performing and visual fine arts, but understandably, the main attractions in that regard call for a trip to Little Rock, some 80 miles down the road. Major collegiate sports are also centered there.

SAFE AND SECURE

A city department of public safety employs a chief of police, seven patrol officers, and five dispatchers. Two patrol cars travel the community continually. The fire department operates with a cadre of 24 volunteers, all certified by appropriate authorities. A 911 emergency phone system is in place.

LET'S GO SHOPPING

A 100,000-square-foot, five-building shopping mall within the community houses 28 convenient shops and services. Included are a food market, deli, three banks (in the immediate vicinity), investment brokerage, travel agency, Realtor, pharmacy, insurance agency, law firm, video store, barber and beauty shop, eye and hearing clinic, florist, various apparel shops, and other retail outlets. Seven other grocers are located in the nearby towns of Clinton, **Shirley**, and Greers Ferry.

Some interesting shopping options are found in Clinton, including discount store operations and a collection of antique and arts and crafts hideaways. Serious shopping for major or specialized purchases would likely require a trip to Conway (58 miles) or further on to Little Rock (about 80 miles) for the most complete selections.

HOLIDAY ISLAND

HOLIDAY ISLAND, ARKANSAS

2 Holiday Island Dr.
Holiday Island, AR 72631
501-253-7810 / 800-643-2988
Fax: 501-253-6969

Developer: Holiday Island Development Company

Year of initial property sales/rentals: 1970

Total land area: 4,500 acres

Average elevation: 1,500 feet

Location: Far northwest corner of Arkansas; Carroll County; on the Missouri border; along the shores of Table Rock Lake; about 5 miles north of the junction of U.S. Highway 62 and State Highway 23 at Eureka Springs; 180 miles northwest of Little Rock; 50 miles northeast of Fayetteville; 40 miles southwest of Branson (Missouri).

Nearest airport with scheduled commercial service: Fayetteville Municipal/commuter service (46 miles); Springfield Regional (90 miles)

Current number of housing units with year-round occupants: 980

Projected number of housing units: 5,000

Resident eligibility: There are no restrictions regarding the age of residents, but an estimated 65% of the population is retired or semiretired. An estimated 30% of resident families have children under 18 years of age living in the home.

Community visit/tour incentive program: Such programs are available but vary in cost and format depending on seasonal and other conditions at time of visit.

Suggested newspaper: *Arkansas Democrat-Gazette* (Northwest Edition), P.O. Box 2221, Little Rock, AR 72203 (800-482-1121)

WHY HOLIDAY ISLAND?

Holiday Island is more than a planned community. It is unto itself a municipality, with a population of approximately 2,000, carved out of the Ozark wilderness. Its berth is on an Arkansas finger of sprawling 53,000-acre **Table Rock Lake**, a U.S. Corps of Engineers creation, most of which lies on the Missouri side of the state border. A unique topographical feature of the development is a 500-acre triangular island appendage that extends into Table Rock Lake, connected to the mainland by a bridge over a narrow inlet.

Ozark Mountain vistas behind fresh water landscapes provide idyllic settings framed in heavily forested hillsides and valleys. The booming northwest Arkansas business expansion corridor along U.S. 71 to the west, from Bentonville to Fayetteville, is less than an hour's drive away. Neighboring **Eureka Springs,** a little more than 5 miles to the south, is aptly dubbed the "Little Switzerland of the Ozarks." It is a noteworthy mid-America tourist attraction with all sorts of festivals, exhibitions, and celebrations highlighting the calendar of events throughout the year.

Established in 1970, Holiday Island has experienced steady growth, especially during the past decade. Much of the impetus for population increase is credited to the Arkansas reputation for low living costs, its natural scenic endowment, and its removal from urban sprawl. Because Holiday Island is a combination of a vacation resort as well as a permanent residential community, natural recreational amenities tend to be more expansive than they might be otherwise.

WHO'S IN CHARGE?

All contributing assets in the form of utilities and recreational facilities are under the control and ownership of community property owners. Each adult resident has one vote in electing five commissioners to serve on the **Holiday Island Suburban Improvement District (HISID),** each for a three-year term. A general manager is employed to supervise staff in administering public services and internal management. A remarkably modest annual assessment of $335 for each property owner provides for the upkeep of recreational facilities, utilities, and road maintenance. Residents pay no user fees for recreation facilities and no green fees for golf play. More than $30 million in assets are said to be virtually debt-free, with substantial reserves on hand.

The community owns and operates its own water system. State approved water is taken from deep wells. A central sewer system serves every home. There is not a septic tank in the entire development. Along with a sizable clubhouse, two golf courses, a marina and other recreational facilities, and 80 miles of private roadways within the community, electric and other utilities were donated by the developer with the transfer of control and ownership to the independent governing body.

THE WEATHER REPORT

Located in the heart of the Ozark Mountains, but at a relatively moderate elevation, this area of the state enjoys a four-season climate but avoids the extreme midsummer and winter temperatures normally associated with the open prairies of the nation's midsection.

Weather information collected by local observers record the following *average high and low* temperature readings for the Holiday Island area:

December: high 51/low 30   **January:** high 48/low 28

February: high 52/low 31   **June:** high 86/low 64

July: high 91/low 67   **August:** high 91/low 66

Average annual precipitation: 45 inches
Average annual snowfall: under 9 inches

HOME SWEET HOME

Housing includes everything from estate homes and custom single-family dwellings, to multifamily units, townhouses, and time-share condominiums. Some are clustered together on smaller, low-maintenance lots while others are situated on oversized parcels in more secluded sections. Street patterns feature culs-de-sac throughout the development, providing optimal residential privacy and limiting through-street traffic to the principal arteries connecting neighborhoods, community facilities, and entry/exit points.

New construction is handled by a number of independent builders, all of whom must clear the **Holiday Island Planning Commission** before construction can begin. Unlike a community in which the developer is the exclusive builder, or one among several, in this situation there is no consistent pattern of floor plans or price parameters. Each newcomer who chooses to build a new home contracts with a builder of choice. Construction costs generally fall in the range of $70 to $90 per square foot, depending on specifications and optional features selected. Floor plans run from 1,200 square feet all the way to 4,000 square feet and larger.

Lots available for residential construction generally range in size from a half acre to two acres at prices beginning as low as $2,500 and progressing up to $100,000. Of the 5,000 lots on the property, about 400 remain to be sold. Many others are held by owners for future development. Long-term rental units can be leased from $500 to $750 a month with 1,000 to 2,000 square feet living space.

MONEY MATTERS

Any comparison of living cost factors between and among states will find Arkansas at or near the top of the list in affordability. National surveys typically disclose from 10 to 20 percent of the top 25 low-cost U.S. towns and cities to be in Arkansas. Newly accelerated economic activity can readily impact on such conditions, of course. There have been signs of upward pricing movement, for example, in towns along the developing commercial strip between **Fayetteville** and **Bentonville** in the state's far northwest corner. But living in the Ozarks is still very much a bargain.

It can be further stated as axiomatic that rural areas tend to have lower living expenses across the board when compared to urbanized centers, especially when separated by more than an hour's driving time. In this instance, Holiday Island is far enough from the nearest major cities, but close enough to smaller but well-developed communities, to access products and services normally found only in more densely populated places.

The *ACCRA Cost of Living Index* covering the first quarter of 1996 shows a nearby section of northwestern Arkansas (the "metroplex" cluster of Arkansas towns that includes Fayetteville, **Springdale**, and **Rogers**) with a composite index (among six consumer cost categories) of 5.4 percent under the national average. Grocery items were 4.1 percent below average, housing 13.8 percent below, transportation 7.7 percent below, and health care 11.6 percent below. Two categories were just slightly above average: utilities just 0.1 percent, and miscellaneous goods and services at 1.6 percent.

TAKE GOOD CARE OF YOURSELF

There are two out-patient clinics in the community, both opened in 1996. One is affiliated with **Washington Regional Hospital** in **Fayetteville** (a 300-bed, full-service facility, the largest within a 50-mile radius of Holiday Island). Two family practice physicians are on staff, along with a dentist, optometrist and several other health care specialists. A second clinic is jointly affiliated with the **Carroll Regional Medical Center** in **Berryville** (60 beds, 15 miles to the east), and the **Springdale Memorial Hospital**, just north of Fayetteville. This local clinic offers a multifaceted rehabilitation program, a psychological services department, and a fitness center to which HI residents may belong for a modest monthly fee. A heliport serves as an evacuation station for emergency cases requiring quick transport to major hospitals in the larger cities.

Eureka Springs Hospital, a member of the **Washington Regional Medical System**, is the closest in-patient facility to Holiday Island (four miles away). It is an acute-care hospital with 24-hour emergency services, out-patient surgery, lab services, x-ray and ultrasound, mammography and echocardiograms, cardiac stress testing, various therapy specialties, and home health services, among other departmental functions.

PLACES TO GO, THINGS TO DO

Holiday Island combines the recreational advantages of a private residential community with the amenities expected to be found at a vacation resort. The development is bordered by two national forests. Two golf courses—18-holes for a full-day outing or a nine-hole executive course for shorter rounds—provide opportunities for satisfying play at any level of game proficiency. There's tennis, shuffleboard, volleyball, outdoor racquetball, basketball, table tennis, horseshoes, miniature golf, and softball for those who thrive on outdoor games. Homeowners do not pay recreation user fees nor any green fees on the golf courses. The clubhouse accommodates up to 286 conferees or partygoers and can be rented to property owners at a reasonable cost for private affairs. A separate recreation complex, in addition to swimming pools and aforementioned games, also offers meeting rooms at no charge to residents. Some 20 community clubs and interest groups maintain busy calendars, coordinated by a full-time activities director.

Table Rock Lake invites water-skiing, scuba diving, sailing, power boating, and swimming. The lake is also great for fishing for largemouth and spotted bass, and walleye, as well as crappie, bluegill, white bass, and catfish. Even rainbow trout have been introduced into the lake. A full-service marina offers boat rentals, bait and tackle, rental slips, and dry storage. A private yacht club adds to the festive environment for enjoying lake-centered activity. **Beaver Lake**, another 28,000 acres of recreational waters just a few miles to the southwest, is especially known as striped bass country where stories of 20- and 30-pound catches are told and retold around area campsites, clubhouses, and party boats.

One of the truly great prizes HI residents enjoy is their proximity to Eureka Springs, one of the most popular vacation spots in all of Ozark country. Literally at their back door, just a few minutes away, is a galaxy of attractions that draw visitors from all over the country and beyond. The **Great Passion Play**, with a cast of some 250 performers is billed as America's top attended outdoor drama. More than a quarter of a million guests are in the audience every season to witness the inspirational bible story production. "The Springs" is home to a steam locomotive nostalgia adventure where the elegant flavor of the 1920s aboard the Eurekan dining car takes passengers to an unforgettable revival of a bygone era. Seven miles south of Eureka Springs is **Turpentine Creek Wildlife Refuge**, a 450-acre ranch where lions, tigers, cougars, leopards, bears, and monkeys roam. **Eureka Springs Gardens** is Arkansas' 33-acre premier botanical display. From early spring through late fall, there is a brilliant collage of color and floral glory. There's an antique doll and toy museum, live theater, concerts, dance performances, and more than 75 restaurants to assure that every culinary taste is gratified.

And then there's **Branson, Missouri,** only 35 miles to the northeast, mid-America's upstart answer for family enjoyment—star-studded entertainment (mostly country music celebrities) but without any gambling and licentious shows. For those who crave the excitement of collegiate sports, the **University of Arkansas** main campus in Fayetteville is less than an hour's drive. Beyond athletic team competition, there is the predictable swirl of cultural and entertainment attractions that surrrounds any major university center, drawing upon not only students and faculty, but upon residents of towns and cities from all around the region.

SAFE AND SECURE

The last significant crime spree in Eureka Springs ended in a shoot out with bank robbers in 1922! Law enforcement is in the hands of the **Carroll County Sheriff's Department**. Neighborhood watch organizations provide volunteers to supplement crime prevention measures. Coordination of security patrols (1,600 hours during 1996) is credited for preserving a community reputation for a crime-free environment.

Holiday Island has its own fire department. The HI fire rating is the lowest of any town in the county. Fully staffed 24-hour paramedic emergency response units are provided by an agency of county government.

LET'S GO SHOPPING

A new on-site commercial center, called **The Park**, was in operation by early 1997. Tenants include a 27,000-square-foot food market, a large variety store, two medical clinics, already described (see "Take Good Care of Yourself"), and two banks, a pharmacy, restaurant, dry cleaner, florist, travel agency, framing shop, dental and chiropractic offices, law firm, investment brokerage, insurance agency, and a newspaper office, among other retail and service establishments. Also opened in 1997 were a U.S. Post Office and a lawn and garden center. Approximately 75 new businesses are projected upon completion of construction.

Shopping in Eureka Springs is a convenient supplement to HI outlets, especially for the great selection of eating establishments. For regional malls, discount chains, and major department stores, Fayetteville compares favorably with cities twice its size.

HOT SPRINGS VILLAGE

HOT SPRINGS VILLAGE, ARKANSAS

P.O. Box 970
Hot Springs Village, AR 71902
501-922-0250 / 800-451-4311
Fax: 501-922-1076

Developer: Cooper Communities, Inc.

Year of initial property sales/rentals: 1970

Total land area: 26,000 acres

Average elevation: 700 feet

Location: West-central Arkansas; Garland and Saline Counties; on State Highway 7; 22 miles northwest of Hot Springs; 52 miles southwest of downtown Little Rock.

Nearest airport with scheduled commercial service: Little Rock Regional Airport (60 miles)

Current number of housing units with year-round occupants: 6,000

Projected number of housing units: 9,000 (2007)

Resident eligibility: There are no age restrictions for living in the community, but more than 83% are retired.

Community visit/tour incentive program: Subject to conditions of visit, discounted lodging at $45 per night, furnished home or townhouse, for up to three nights' stay.

Suggested newspapers: *La Villa News* (semiweekly), 121 DeSoto Center Dr., Hot Springs Village, AR 71909 (800-833-4050); *Hot Springs Sentinel-Record*, 300 Spring St., Hot Springs, AR 71901 (501-623-7711)

WHY HOT SPRINGS VILLAGE?

Hot Springs Village, with amenities and natural features that have attracted residents from all 50 states and several foreign countries, is unique in its infrastructure and in the scope of its facilities. Its sheer size (more than 26,000 acres stretching 12 miles in one direction and 6 miles in the other) and population (about 13,000) give it the human and economic resources necessary to sustain a vibrant community program and commercial support system. Nestled in the foothills of the **Ouachita Mountains**, at the perimeter of **Hot Springs National Park**, this community is in harmony with its natural environment. Fully 25 percent of the total acreage is dedicated to common areas—unspoiled landscape reflecting the appeal of virgin hardwood forests and abundant plant and wildlife.

Entering the Village at the main entrance leads immediately to the principal thoroughfare, DeSoto Boulevard. It is the spinal cord of the development.

Traveling along its 12-plus mile course from one end of the property to the other, is in itself a unique experience. Only rarely can a home or commercial building be seen from the main road. Residences are hidden from view, tucked away along culs-de-sac and little-traveled neighborhood connecting streets. DeSoto Boulevard itself, thickly wooded to either side, appears to be out in the country, away from any population encroachment.

Each residential property is connected to a greenbelt common area (dense woodland or a golf course fairway) or lake front. No neighbor's backyard adjoins another. A large back deck is a feature that demands inclusion in any floor plan if the pristine surroundings are to be fully enjoyed. Many homesites offer views of nearby foothills, rocky hillsides, and heavily timbered landscape.

The city of **Hot Springs**, with a population of more than 40,000, is less than a half-hour drive from the HSV main entrance and has been consistently included among the nation's most popular retirement destinations. It is also the most popular tourist attraction in Arkansas, drawing as many as two million visitors every year.

Mature Outlook magazine described the Village as an "invitingly priced community with diversions for vacationers and retirees alike" in an article touting the best in retirement havens. *Where to Retire* magazine, in its winter 1996 issue, named Hot Springs/Hot Springs Village among the top 10 retirement destinations. The finance editor of *New Choices* magazine, rated the area "among the best retirement locations in America." Recognition in the two latter articles was based on factors such as proximity to a major airport, low cost of living, rich cultural amenities, outdoor recreational opportunities, low crime rate, medical care, and broad choices in housing.

WHO'S IN CHARGE?

The **Hot Springs Village Property Owners Association (HSVPOA)** is a nonprofit corporation organized for the purpose of preserving values and to promote the health, safety, and welfare of the residents and business establishments of the Village. All recreational amenities are community-owned. Operations are under the direction of a general manager who is hired by the board of directors, which is in turn elected by the property owners. The POA is responsible for maintaining more than 450 miles of streets within the village, the water supply and sewage treatment plants, a fully staffed security department, and fire and ambulance stations. The monthly assessment to each property owner to fund the POA is a very modest $26, which includes access to recreational programs and facilities. This fee can be increased only with a majority vote of the owners. Support of the recreational facilities (lakes, golf course, parks, pools, fitness center, tennis courts, marina, etc.) is supplemented by user fees, also exceptionally moderate.

THE WEATHER REPORT

Hot Springs Village is located at the eastern rise of the Ouachita Mountains, just west of the **Mississippi River Valley**. Airflow from the ridges and hills tends to keep warm air relatively stable. A modified continental climate includes exposure to all of the different North American air masses. Proximity to the **Gulf of Mexico** tends to mark summers with prolonged periods of warm and humid weather. Winters are generally mild, but Arctic outbreaks are not uncommon.

Average high/low temperatures for 1996, provided by the Southern Regional Climate Center, Office of Climatology, showed the following readings for the three winter months and three summer months:

December: high 55/low 38   **January:** high 52/low 29

February: high 60/low 33   **June:** high 89/low 67

July: high 92/low 70   **August:** high 89/low 67

Average annual rainfall: 52 inches

Average annual snowfall: Not recorded in this source report, but winter conditions in this area of the state are generally described as producing infrequent freezing precipitation, with snowfall typically measuring less than 4 inches.

HOME SWEET HOME

Among almost 6,000 homes built to date, approximately 85 percent are individual, free-standing dwellings. The remaining 15 percent are townhouses. Recreational vehicle storage is available.

All home construction is subject to approval by the architectural control committee of the HSVPOA. Mobile or modular homes are not allowed. Interior homesites range in price from as low as $5,000 to upwards of $15,000. Golf view and golf front sites are in the range of $10,000 to $72,000. Lake-enhanced lots cost from $20,000 to $265,000. The HSV real estate market includes townhouses, custom homes, model homes, and resale homes. An average newly constructed home is approximately 2,100 square feet with a price tag of $140,000. Square footage costs of construction vary widely (depending on a wide array of design features, appliance selection, custom options, etc.), ranging from $45 to $110. An active resale market includes townhouses in a price range from the $50s to the $150s, and single-family detached homes from the $80s to more than $400,000.

MONEY MATTERS

When state and local taxes are totaled, including property taxes, Arkansas residents are among the least burdened in the country. According to the *State Policy Reference Book*, Arkansas ranks 49th in per capita state and local taxes, paying an average of only $1,191 annually, compared with a national average of $1,888. Property taxes in Hot Springs Village are either .0319 or .0366 per $100 of assessed value, depending upon in which of two school districts the property is located. Assessments are based on 20 percent of a home's market value. That translates to $600 a year on a home valued at $100,000. Purchases made within the city of Hot Springs are subject to a 1 percent sales tax on top of the state levy of 4½ percent (still below the percentages applied in most states).

Confirming this condition of bargain living costs, the *ACCRA Cost of Living Index* (2nd quarter, 1996) shows the **Little Rock** metropolitan statistical area (less than 50 miles from HSV) to have the very lowest composite index among any of the 315 cities and nonurban places included in the survey! That composite is a combination analysis that includes weighted costs of groceries, housing, utilities, transportation, health care, and miscellaneous goods and services. The 83.2 composite index for Little Rock means that all six categories of cost factors taken together are 16.8 percent below the average for all places in the survey.

TAKE GOOD CARE OF YOURSELF

The Village has its own impressive health care resources right on site. In 1993, **St. Joseph's Regional Health Center**, a major hospital in Hot Springs, opened a 13,000-square-foot medical clinic in Hot Springs Village. The facility provides primary care physicians, diagnostic laboratory and radiology services, a cardiac fitness center, ophthalmology and physical medicine specialties, a home health agency, and various offices and examination rooms.

AMI National Park Medical Center, a second principal Hot Springs hospital, operates an urgent care clinic across from the HSV main gate. Services focus on full-family health care, including lab and x-ray facilities and a walk-in emergency department. Physicians' offices are located in each of four on-site commercial centers. **Good Samaritan Cedar Lodge**, with 82 independent living apartments and a 40-bed intermediate care unit, is often an ideal place for HSV residents to recuperate following surgery or a serious illness.

Both St. Joseph's and NPMC hospitals, with satellite outreach at HSV, have their principal facilities in Hot Springs, each with a full range of comprehensive services, programs, and equipment to meet specialized patient needs that extend beyond those available at the on-site clinics. Another medical institution in the area is the **Hot Springs Rehabilitation Center Hospital**, specializing in physical, occupational, and speech therapies, spinal cord, orthopedic, and brain injuries, and stroke treatment.

PLACES TO GO. THINGS TO DO

The list of recreational amenities is awesome. There are seven 18-hole golf courses (several of which have garnered national acclaim) and pro shops; three country clubs; four restaurants; 16 lighted tennis courts in two complexes with a pro shop; three swimming pools (one indoor, open all year); two recreation centers; six recreational lakes with a total of more than 1,800 acres; two marinas with five boat ramps; a swimming beach; more than 14 miles of hard- and soft-surface bike and walking/jogging paths and nature trails; miniature golf; lawn bowling; basketball, volleyball, and shuffleboard courts; a softball diamond; a lake pavilion; and two parks!

Diamante, completed in 1995, is a private facility for those who own property in the Diamante neighborhood. Managed by **Club Corporation of America**, it features a championship 18-hole course with a 9,000-square-foot clubhouse and pro shop, executive locker rooms, a swimming pool, four tennis courts, and fine dining. **Magellan**, the Village's newest golf course (completed in 1996) features a 3,000-square-foot pro shop, a driving range, and practice putting green. The **Coronado Recreational Complex**, an 18,000-square-foot building on a 24-acre lake shore site, includes 13 lighted tennis courts, a tennis pro shop, along with the village library, a dance floor, kitchen, conference rooms, and offices. More than 100 social, civic, and recreational clubs and organizations meet there regularly. The **Coronado Natatorium and Fitness Center** offers full Nautilus equipment and free weights, stairmasters, treadmills, a 25-meter indoor pool, sauna, whirlpool, and massage therapy programs.

High on the Village pride scale is the **Ponce De Leon Performing Arts Center**. Completed in 1992, this $2.5 million state-of-the-art 654-seat auditorium stages theatrical productions, musicals, art exhibits, and choral performances, among other attractions.

As if the Village didn't have sufficient leisure pursuits, one need not venture beyond Hot Springs (less than 20 minutes away) or Little Rock (about an hour's drive) to find the ultimate in diversion. The city of Hot Springs, boyhood home of **President Bill Clinton**, offers an array of lake sports and pleasures, the comforting thermal waters of historic bathhouse row, and the excitement of **Oaklawn Park**, where thoroughbred horse racing draws the third largest track attendance in the country. (More than 30 Oaklawn entries have qualified for the Kentucky Derby, a record unbeaten by any other U.S. racetrack). **The Grand Promenade**, a brick walkway high above and overlooking bathhouse row, is a favorite place for vacationers and residents to stroll or to sprawl on a parkside bench and watch the passersby.

Mid America Museum, the state's largest, is a hands-on world of science. Among the many local tours in and around Hot Springs is one that takes visitors on a ride aboard a 31-foot-long amphibious vehicle built to amble along the streets of the city and then slip into **Lake Hamilton** for a leisurely boat ride. **Music Mountain Jamboree** is an original music and comedy show with everything from impersonations to live country and western, gospel, pop, and patriotic musical productions. A 400-passenger riverboat, the **Belle of Hot Springs**, sails Lake Hamilton with live narration on points of interest and sightseeing. It also offers lunch and sunset dinner/dance cruises, featuring award-winning cuisine.

Little Rock, the state's capital and largest city (with a metropolitan population of more than a half million), has all the assets of a major city. It is a city rich in cultural and recreational appeal. Beautiful riverside parks, many museums, professional and collegiate sports, a ballet, a symphony, live theater (including Broadway productions), an outstanding zoo, and scores of fine restaurants all contribute to a galaxy of enticements to which Village residents are drawn.

SAFE AND SECURE

HSV has its own security force of 19 trained county deputy sheriffs. Four entry control gates, both manned and with card access, provide effective visitor screening. The community's fire department operates out of three fire stations and includes ambulance service staffed by paramedics with life support equipment and an emergency 911 system.

LET'S GO SHOPPING

Within the orbit of Hot Springs Village there are five separate shopping centers. The **Cordoba Center** is just outside the main entrance on State Highway 7. Tenants include a full-service food market, a bank, a well-stocked hardware store, medical offices, beauty shop, dental clinic, and pharmacy. Three other centers, scattered strategically around the property, house retail establishments such as a bakery-deli, service station, gift shop, watch repair, bookstore, pharmacy, video store, cosmetics shop, and convenience store. Service outlets include a stock brokerage, laundry, restaurants, travel agency, dental and eye clinics, and a credit union. Opening in 1997 was the fifth commercial enclave, **La Plaza,** located at the far eastern end of the Village on State Highway 5. Three main buildings provide a covered connecting pedestrian walkway. A 10,000 square foot HSV sales and information pavilion is the centerpiece of the development, plans for which include a food market and movie theater.

CALIFORNIA TAX FACTS

INDIVIDUAL INCOME TAX

Graduated from 1% to 11% (for married couples filing jointly) as follows:

- First $9,816 of income @ 1%
- Next $13,448 @ 2%
- Next $13,450 @ 4%
- Next $14,254 @ 6%
- Next $13,446 @ 8%
- Over $64,414 @ 9.3%

Other information:

- Rates shown are for tax year 1996 and apply to joint filers and surviving spouses with dependents.
- Singles and marrieds filing separately use same rates but on half of income brackets for joint return filers.
- Exemptions of $67 apply to singles, heads of households, and age 65 or older; for marrieds, $134.

SALES TAX

The combined state and uniform local sales tax rate is 7.25 percent. Actual rates vary by locality, generally by adding from .25 percent to 1.25 percent. Differences are due to transactions and use taxes imposed by transit districts where applicable.

PROPERTY TAX

According to *The Rating Guide to Life in America's Fifty States*, California's $602-per-capita property tax revenue ranks near the average (27th from the most favorable). That compares with Alabama, with the nation's lowest burden in this category at $163, and Alaska, with the highest levy at $1,246.

RANKING REPORT

Among the 50 states, California ranks 27th from the highest in state tax revenue with a revenue figure of $73.04 per $1,000 of personal income, as compared with a 50-state average of $69.03. That contrasts with Alaska (ranked most expensive) at $170.36 and New Hampshire (ranked least expensive) with $41.00.

For more complete tax information contact the Controller—Taxation, P.O. Box 942850, Sacramento, CA 94250, 916-445-2692, (fax) 916-322-4404.

Note: The above information is based on applicable tax law information available at the time of publication. Because such laws and tax rates are subject to change, professional guidance should be sought if tax implications are critical to a relocation decision.

DEL WEBB'S SUN CITY ROSEVILLE

ROSEVILLE, CALIFORNIA

6000 Sun City Blvd.
Roseville, CA 95747
916-774-3500 / 800-633-5932
Fax: 916-774-3553

Developer: Del Webb Corporation

Year of initial property sales/rentals: 1994

Total land area: 1,200 acres

Average elevation: 200 feet

Location: North-central California; Placer County; 25 miles northeast of Sacramento; less than 5 miles northwest from the intersection of Interstate 80 and State Highway 65.

Nearest airport with scheduled commercial service: Sacramento International (20 miles)

Current number of housing units with year-round occupants: 1,400

Projected number of housing units: 3,100 (2000)

Resident eligibility: At least one member of the household must be 55 years of age or older, although a small percentage of homes may be occupied by residents who do not meet that requirement. Additional restrictions apply, including occupancy by children under age 18.

Community visit/tour incentive program: A "vacation getaway program" provides qualified visitors access to a spacious, fully-equipped villa, a wine and cheese reception, a narrated bus tour, a round of golf and/or other activity goodies, for about $50 a night for two people for two, three, or four nights.

Suggested newspaper: *Sacramento Bee*, 21st and Q Streets, Sacramento, CA 95814 (916-321-1111)

WHY SUN CITY ROSEVILLE?

Each year since its opening in 1994, **Sun City Roseville** (SCR) has been leading new home sales for communities of any description in all of northern California. The development was among the top 20 retirement havens in America, so distinguished in 1996 by *New Choices* magazine. The **Superior California Building Industry Association** that same year honored SCR as "Community of the Year." The project was the first active-adult venture in northern California by the **Del Webb Corporation**, acknowledged to be the earliest of the nation's few pioneering developers of master-planned retirement enclaves.

The community is positioned about equidistant from two of California's prime vacation haunts—**San Francisco** and **Lake Tahoe** (both within approximately a 100-mile radius). Just 25 miles from downtown **Sacramento**, the state capital, and inside the perimeter of the city of **Roseville** (population about 60,000), this Sun City archetype can claim its location as a key asset. Its residents have a unique blend of stimulating resources conveniently at hand.

There is much to commend the elegance of community amenities. The most striking of SCR's handsome qualities, perhaps, is the **Timber Creek Recreation Lodge**. Its huge expanse of 52,000 square feet (more than an acre of indoor space), with all its attendant internal appointments and external enhancements, is a fitting image for any picture post card. It is the community's center of activity and source of its pride and energy. It is symbolic of the quality of activity programming and lifestyle opportunities awaiting those who cross its threshold.

WHO'S IN CHARGE?

The **Sun City Roseville Community Association (SCRCA)** is the administrative mechanism through which residents exercise their influence over the decision-making process in community governance. Currently, the seven-member board of directors has representation from both the Del Webb Corporation and elected representatives from the neighborhoods. Three resident directors hold monthly open forums at which any homeowner can bring to the floor and discuss any matters of association business. Beyond that, the executive director of the SCRCA conducts a monthly "listening post" meeting where any item of general interest can be raised and appropriate action considered. Other special forums are presented by the community relations committee of the board when issues of significant broad concern are on the table.

SCRCA fees are less than $85 per month per household and are reviewed annually. These fees cover use of the recreational facilities, maintenance of the commonly-owned recreation lodge, golf course, green belts and related staffing. *The Village Courier* is a community association newsletter that provides overviews on important issues, along with extensive reporting on club activities and special events. Communication is further facilitated through use of a closed-circuit television channel devoted to community news and announcements.

THE WEATHER REPORT

The Sacramento area has abundant sunshine most of the year. Summers are generally dry with most of the rainfall coming from late fall to early spring. Mountains to the north, east, and west protect against the effects of winter storms. Summer temperatures are occasionally moderated with the flow of cool ocean air through the lower Sacramento Valley and river delta. Hot spells during summer are generally accompanied by very low humidities, sometimes as low as 20 percent, making the heat much more tolerable than would otherwise be the case. Light to moderate morning fog may occasionally descend on the area during the colder wet season, particularly in the midst of winter.

High and low average temperatures during three winter and three summer months reported by the U.S. National Oceanic and Atmospheric Administration are as follows:

December: high 53/low 38   **January:** high 53/low 38

February: high 59/low 41   **June:** high 87/low 55

July: high 93/low 58   **August:** high 92/low 58

Average annual precipitation: 21 inches
Average annual snowfall: rare

HOME SWEET HOME

Sun City Roseville offers 18 different models in four distinctive series of homes. All are single-family, one-story detached units ranging in size from 968 square feet to 2,619 square feet and priced from the mid-$120s to $280,000. Easy maintenance is a high priority in use of construction materials. A well-organized design center gives the home buyer practical assistance in deciding on countless choices among standard and optional features, fixtures, and appliances. Landscape consultants are also available to help with yard and patio alternatives to meet personal preferences and budget parameters. **Fairmount Mortgage Company,** a subsidiary of Del Webb Corporation, offers a number of financing programs to meet individual family needs.

The standard lot size varies by series floor plans. Each home plan offers a choice of three exterior designs with stone, brick, wood siding and/or stucco. Water and sanitary sewer systems are provided by the city of Roseville. Telephone and electric utility lines are below ground.

MONEY MATTERS

It is widely acknowledged that most of California endures higher living costs than those of other states. San Francisco shares with New York City the dubious distinction of being the most expensive cities in the continental United States in which to live. And while not every part of California has excessive living costs, most metropolitan areas are well above average.

There are no known data available showing such comparative costs for Sacramento or its neighboring **Placer County** towns. The closest parallel might be drawn to **Santa Rosa** which is about 60 miles north of San Francisco (Roseville is a little more than 100 miles northeast) and for which cost of living analysis has been published in the *ACCRA Cost of Living Index* (2nd quarter, 1996). The referenced study shows Santa Rosa to be at a hefty 130.2 percent of the average for the 315 locations included in the survey. That is a composite figure combining six categories of living expenses. Housing, the second most heavily weighted of the six headings, was shown to be by far the single most elevated component with a 73 percent above average rating. Health care costs came in at second from the highest level at 31 percent above average. It should be pointed out that the Sacramento/Roseville area, like most of the state's inland population centers, is likely to be notably less expensive than Santa Rosa, but these findings provide useful indicators as the nearest location with available data.

It is well to point out, in light of this information, that housing costs at Sun City Roseville are certainly not higher to the degree indicated than comparable communities in other parts of the country. Many factors contribute, no doubt, to the Del Webb pricing formula that seems to have succeeded in keeping home construction costs within reasonable limits.

Annual real estate taxes are estimated to be 1¼ percent of the total purchase price of a home. Local school bond indebtedness is currently estimated at $36 to $48 per $100,000 of assess valuation and is included in the foregoing annual percentage estimate.

TAKE GOOD CARE OF YOURSELF

Roseville has become part of an increasingly important medical community in the greater Sacramento area. The new **Sutter Roseville Medical Center**, with 168 beds and 330,000 square feet of floor space, is the closest in-patient hospital to Sun City, just 7 miles away. It operates a senior services program at a Roseville community center at which lectures and discussions revolve around a variety of related topics bearing on exercise and fitness, nutrition, resource utilization, caring for aging family members, etc.

Kaiser Permanente Medical Clinic, also less than 10 minutes away in Roseville, is an out-patient complex of professional offices and out-patient services. The Kaiser organization also operates a full-service, 326-bed hospital in Sacramento, about 20 miles from Sun City Roseville.

PLACES TO GO, THINGS TO DO

Within the walls of the commodious recreation lodge, creative juices flow in all directions. It may be in the ceramics or arts studio or in the sewing center. It may be in the computer room or the rather well-stocked library, or in the truly unique "Wall Street room," where people gather to monitor investments and maybe share an inside tip with a neighbor. There's a ballroom in this grand building, complete with a stage and site of banquets, stage productions and social events. The **Lifestyle Fitness Center** has a variety of exercise equipment and trained personnel to conduct classes, counsel with members, and supervise activity. A dance and aerobics center, with a cushioned wood floor, is a place where residents come together to trim down, firm up, or to generally improve their physical well-being.

A sparkling 25-meter indoor swimming pool supports aquatic exercise classes, water volleyball games, and lap swimming. An outdoor resort-style pool is ideal for sun and water relaxation. Six lighted tennis courts, two paddle tennis courts, a basketball half-court, and special spaces for bocce ball and horseshoe pits all contribute to activity choices. The 27-hole **Billy Casper** signature golf course winds around a meandering creek. To accommodate the expert and the novice, the course features several tee boxes at each hole. Complementing the course is a practice driving range and putting greens and a full-service pro shop staffed by PGA professionals. A network of walking and jogging trails wind through the community. Roseville's **Mahany Park** is adjacent to Sun City, a pleasant off-site escape to meditate or people watch.

Volunteer activity among Sun City residents has been shown to be about 45 percent, in contrast to a national Gallop survey indicating that about 38 percent of seniors across the country contribute their time and talents to worthy causes. SCR volunteers concentrate most of their energies to local schools, hospitals, law enforcement agencies, the library, museums and, to a significant extent, to their own SCR Community Association.

For off-site diversion, Roseville has more than its share of leisure attractions. The **Placer County Fair** is a midsummer gala that brings five days of family fun, exhibits, and entertainment. A Downtown Street Faire every fall features three blocks of antiques, hand-crafted items, exhibits, food, and excitement. The parks and recreation department regularly schedules sports leagues, special interest classes, and community events. Annual business/ community/industrial tours bring diverse segments of the population together to encourage broad perspectives and economic education. **Music in the Park** takes center stage for spring, summer, and fall concerts. Virtually every holiday is cause for a public celebration. The **Roseville Public Library** operates an information and referral service designed to help local residents connect with governmental and private resources that can help with a long list of possible needs. Special attention is given to senior citizen assistance. The **Maidu Community Center** publishes a monthly senior newsletter with a complete program of activities for older adults, along with its own information and referral system

Roseville's **Aquatics Complex** houses an Olympic-size swimming pool with a generous wading area and a huge, twisting waterslide that would be worthy of a full-scale recreation park. **Royer Park** is a great place for people to mingle with ducks and geese amid majestic trees that provide a cool summer canopy. The park is a favorite place for summer concerts and all sorts of cultural events organized by **Performing Arts of Roseville**.

If Roseville has a unique reputation that sets it apart from many of its neighbors, it is the attention and resources it devotes to bicycling. One of its distinguishing program components in this regard is an elaborate system of off-street bike paths through surrounding areas of creeks, meadows, and woodlands. The city publishes a detailed map showing all the existing and planned bikeway routes, lanes, and paths.

Less than a half-hour away are the cultural, educational, and entertainment resources of California's capital city of Sacramento, with a county-wide population of more than one million inhabitants. There, of course, one can find all the fulfillment and indulgence that the pocketbook will allow.

SAFE AND SECURE

Crime rates drawn from the *Sourcebook of Criminal Justice Statistics* for cities in the 50,000 to 90,000 population range show the California incidence of violent crime against persons to be 1,120 per 100,000 compared to a national average of 746 per 100,000. Contrary to the state ranking however, Roseville's rate of 621 was substantially below the national average.

Police and firefighting services are provided by the City of Roseville. A safety patrol/neighborhood watch program is run by resident volunteers with assistance from the **Roseville Police Department.** Special attention is paid to the needs of families who leave their homes for several days or longer, during which time precautions can be taken to safeguard the unoccupied property. Local police are active in promoting various educational and crime prevention programs. The **Roseville Fire Department**, in addition to fire prevention and control, provides many types of rescues, safety training, first aid instruction, and advanced life support.

LET'S GO SHOPPING

Within about 4 miles of the SCR entrance, in Roseville, are banks, restaurants, cleaners, and a full-service grocery store. A bit further on into town there are numerous shopping areas, including **Centerpoint Marketplace**, a 50-acre retail center. **The Brickyard** and **Albertson's Plaza** are other commercial clusters within a 10-mile radius. Just six miles beyond Roseville, in **Citrus Heights** (a city of more than 100,000 population), is **Sunrise Mall**, with more than 100 shops and department stores, including Sears, JCPenney, and Macy's. Ten miles east of Roseville, in **Folsom**, is **Natoma Station**, a factory outlet mall. Just minutes further down Interstate 80, in the city center of Sacramento, begins the virtually endless assortment of retail and service establishments, including several more major malls.

LEISURE WORLD LAGUNA HILLS

LAGUNA HILLS, CALIFORNIA

23522 Paseo de Valencia
Laguna Hills, CA 92653
714-597-4360 / 800-711-9273
Fax: 714-472-1397

Developer: Golden Rain Foundation

Year of initial property sales/rentals: 1964

Total land area: 2,100 acres

Average elevation: 383 feet

Location: Southwestern California; southern Orange County; in Saddleback Valley; off Interstate Highway 5 at County Highway S18 at the southern extremity of metropolitan Los Angeles; less than 10 miles inland from the Pacific Ocean; about 10 miles south of Newport Beach; 75 miles north of San Diego.

Nearest airport with scheduled commercial service: John Wayne Airport (8 miles)

Current number of housing units with year-round occupants: 12,736

Projected number of housing units: 12,736

Resident eligibility: At least one occupant of a household must be 55 years of age or older.

Community visit/tour incentive program: Personal tours available in conjunction with a reduced-rate vacation "getaway" package offered through a local hotel (includes a free round of golf and access to other recreational facilities).

Suggested newspaper: *Orange County Register*, 625 No. Grand Ave, Santa Ana, CA 92701 (714-835-1234)

WHY LEISURE WORLD LAGUNA HILLS?

Leisure World Laguna Hills (one of seven Leisure Worlds around the country from which it is completely independent) is the largest community of its kind on the U.S. West Coast. It is a mini-city with a population of 18,000, offering residents a mix of housing, recreational, and demographic distinctions that have a unique life-style appeal. Because of the age restrictions (primarily requiring at least one person in a dwelling be older than 55 years of age), residents tend to share parallel interests. Virtually all come to the community from other places, so there is a catalytic effect on socialization. There is a heavy emphasis on providing escape from responsibilities normally associated with home ownership.

LWLH has been the recipient of numerous awards over the years. In 1991, it was recognized by the **Community Associations Institute** for excellence in all aspects of operations and management. Other commendations have come from California for waste reduction, from the **International Society of Aboriculture** for outstanding landscape beautification, from the **South Orange County Chamber of Commerce** for new environmental solutions, and from the **Professional Grounds Management Society** for best maintained planned community. All of these recognitions suggest the abundant, impeccably maintained landscaping that meets the eye upon entering the property.

Surrounded by chaparral-filled hills, Leisure World's eastern vista looks upon the looming **Saddleback Mountains**, providing a dramatic natural skyline. Proximity to the boundless attractions and resources of metropolitan **Los Angeles** equates with unlimited choices in entertainment, recreation, shopping, etc. But even without leaving the community gates, there is a staggering array of discretionary activities, attractions, and conveniences to satisfy just about every want and need. All of this in a Southern California setting amid the scenic glory for which that land is famous.

WHO'S IN CHARGE?

Community affairs have been managed by a professional management company since 1973, under contract with the **Golden Rain Foundation**, a nonprofit corporation that owns or holds in trust all tangible facilities including six clubhouses, an administration building, golf course, stables, trailer parking area, and certain streets and common areas. Under a somewhat complex structure of relationships, each resident is a member of one of three "mutual" corporations that operate under different organizational plans, depending upon the nature of the housing ownership arrangement. (One is a cooperative in which the corporation maintains ownership in the dwelling units occupied by its members; the other two are variations of a condominium form in which members own their respective homes and hold an undivided interest in common areas.) Each of these entities collects fees from resident members based on costs involved in each instance, and each is governed by an elected board of directors chosen from among such members.

Monthly costs for these memberships vary depending on the housing services delivered to the homeowner. They range from $286 to $500, the higher amounts covering a broader menu of benefits. In the case of cooperatives, for example, such amounts include both property taxes and mortgage payments. All assessments include exterior home maintenance, landscaping, and recreational activities. Most recreational activities/facilities/services are also included in this monthly assessment, with the exception of the golf course, equestrian center, garden center plots, movies, recreational vehicle storage, and certain special events, each of which charges a very nominal user fee to members. A fare-free 15-bus transportation system is included in the services provided under the community operating plan.

A community newspaper, *The Leisure World News,* is distributed to residents by subscription.

THE WEATHER REPORT

There is no part of the United States with more enviable weather conditions than southern California. Described as a near-perfect Mediterranean climate, well-suited to an active outdoor life style, the sun is said to shine about 80 percent of the year. Rarely during July and August does the thermometer top 90 degrees. Freezing temperatures are unknown.

The **Pacific Ocean** is the overriding influence on such moderate barometric behavior. During winter months, high temperatures are typically in the upper 60s, and lows in the mid-40s. Summer highs seldom rise above the low 80s, with lows in the high 50s. Significant is the fact that low relative humidities make infrequent heat waves quite tolerable for most people. Thunderstorms are relatively infrequent.

Average high and low temperatures for the three summer months and three winter months in this part of the California coast are reported by the U.S. National Oceanic and Atmospheric Administration as follows:

December: high 67/low 45	**January:** high 67/low 45
February: high 68/low 47	**June:** high 77/low 60
July: high 83/low 63	**August:** high 84/low 65

Average annual precipitation: 12 inches
Average annual snowfall: trace

HOME SWEET HOME

All exterior maintenance and landscaping is done by a full-time staff of carpenters, plumbers, painters, and gardeners. Housing style options include single-family dwellings and single or multi-story condominiums and cooperatives with up to three bedrooms and a selection of more than 90 floor plans. **Rossmoor Towers**, twin high-rises overlooking the golf course, feature luxury condominiums for those who choose to have maid service and daily dinner meals as a part of their housing package.

Of more than 12,700 living units, approximately 4 percent are available for resale at any given time. Leisure World homes, also called manors, fall into two ownership categories—condominiums or cooperatives (see "Who's In Charge"). Both are governed by homeowner associations called mutuals, operated by elected boards of directors. A condominium resident owns the actual structure in which the dwelling unit is located, along with an undivided interest in the common areas. These owners pay monthly assessments as determined by the mutual's board of directors for maintenance and management of the common areas. Condominium owners are responsible for the mortgage payments and taxes for their individual units.

In a cooperative, residents are members of a corporation which owns all real property, including the living units, carports, and laundry facilities. As a corporate member, each resident enters into an occupancy agreement to pay a share of the corporation's mortgage payments, property taxes, maintenance, and other operations expenses.

The cost of Leisure World homes ranges from $49,000 to $500,000. Floor plans vary in size from 900 to 2,600 square feet. Long-term condominium rentals are available at rates from $1,000 to $2,000 a month in sizes ranging from 900 to 2,600 square feet. There are no homesites available for new construction. Use of two recreational vehicle storage lots is available for a fee.

MONEY MATTERS

It is no secret that California, and **Orange County** in particular, imposes high living costs. A 1995 *Money* magazine report showed this upscale enclave to be almost 24 percent above the index average among 299 cities and other political subdivisions around the country. The median cost of a three-bedroom home is some 59 percent above the national average, although housing values have declined by more than 6 percent since 1995 while the national average climbed more than 4 percent. These community-at-large figures do not necessarily apply to home prices and values at Leisure World, where the economics of housing are unique.

Real property is taxed in Orange County at 1.25 percent of the purchase price. The largest share of such revenues goes to support local school districts. Only 6 percent of the typical property tax dollar supports the county general fund, the lowest county share in the entire state. The sales tax, with local and state options applied, comes to 7.75 percent.

TAKE GOOD CARE OF YOURSELF

There is an unparalleled world of medical, dental, and specialized caregivers just beyond the community gates. More than 100 health care offices/clinics are located adjacent to or within 20 miles distance of Leisure World. Five fully accredited hospitals are within a 10-mile radius. **Saddleback Community Medical Center** in **Laguna Hills**, with 220 beds, is adjacent to the community. It offers 24-hour emergency services and any number of specialized departments, including a heart institute and wellness center, pediatrics, radiology, a rehabilitation wing, home and transitional care, a women's hospital and breast center, and community education. The 250-bed, full-service **Irvine Medical Center** is just 4 miles from LW. Its programs include strong emphasis on consultation with seniors, and other related services. **Mission Regional Medical Center** in **Mission Viejo**, adjacent to Laguna Hills (about 6 miles away), operates an innovative service called "Health Whys," a health information phone line staffed by a registered nurse. They offer answers to questions troubling individuals who want some preliminary input short of making a trip to a doctor or hospital.

Within walking distance of the LW entry gate is a 1,500-resident assisted living, skilled nursing, and transitional care facility. In the same general area are services for treatment of a full range of health issues, including cardiovascular and heart disease, Parkinson's, and physical therapy.

PLACES TO GO, THINGS TO DO

Six well-maintained clubhouses feature such amenities as hobby and game rooms, meeting and billiards rooms, five large swimming pools, hot pools, lawn bowling greens, shuffleboard courts, and well-equipped fitness centers. One of these centers of activity boasts a 834-seat theater. There are two golf courses, one a championship 27-hole links, the other a three-par, nine hole executive course. A driving range, practice putting greens and chipping area, along with a well-stocked pro shop, two full-time golf pros, and electric golf cart rentals, round out a complete golfing complex. Resident golf fees are only $3.25 for nine holes and $5.50 for a round of 18.

An eight-court tennis complex includes a clubhouse and two lighted courts for night play. An upscale equestrian center boards and rents horses for a nominal fee and provides riding lessons and guided trail rides, along with a grandstand and show ring. An arts and crafts center offers professional equipment and instruction for classes in jewelry-making, sewing, woodworking, photography, painting, and ceramics. Two garden centers provide individual plots of land where residents can give full rein to their green thumbs.

More than 200 community-based service clubs and organizations serve virtually every leisure interest and activity. There are choral groups, ballroom dancing events, music concerts, theater performances, spectator and participatory sports, literary functions, bridge and other game tournaments, and a seemingly endless calendar of stimulating directions one can follow. A staff of 140 full- and part-time employees are involved in the extensive recreational programs, aided by about 450 volunteers who teach classes, staff the library, and help host hospitality areas, among other things. Clubhouse conference/meeting rooms, dining rooms, lounges, galleries, outdoor patios, etc., can be rented by residents for remarkably modest fees.

For those who desire to add educational dimension to their lives, instructional courses in a wide range of subjects are available through the **Emeritus Institute**, a fully accredited division of nearby **Saddleback College**. Active seniors attend classes on such varied topics as art appreciation, computer technology, U.S. political issues, and conversational Spanish—more than 100 courses in all. Enrollment in the institute numbers nearly 8,500. The goal of these mature students is not to earn academic credits or an academic degree, but rather to experience the sheer joy of learning and for the simple reward of expanding personal knowledge.

All of this and more, within the community itself. To step outside Leisure World leads within a relatively short distance to some of the nation's greatest pleasure-time attractions. Whether seeking the best in visual and performing arts, world-class museums, spectacular natural wonders (like the **San Bernardino Mountains, Balboa** and **Catalina Islands**, and Pacific Ocean beaches), top collegiate and professional sports, internationally renowned tourist centers (**Disneyland, Universal Studios, Hollywood, Knotts Berry Farm,** and **Crystal Cathedral,** to name just a few), or fascinating historical sites, a 60-mile radius will turn up the ultimate experience. When it comes to educational resources, there are within that same distance around LW no fewer than 20 colleges and universities, eight of them in Orange County. Among them are some of the top academic institutions in the country.

SAFE AND SECURE

Leisure World is surrounded by a decorative block wall, with guarded gatehouses and 24-hour mobile patrols throughout the community. Entry can be made into the property only through one of the several manned gate stations. Compared to the crime rate in surrounding areas and in southern California in general, Leisure World has an extremely low crime rate. There has been virtually no violent crime against people or property. Records reveal an average of two stolen cars per year, plus minor theft and vandalism incidents.

Employed directly by LW, the community's security force emphasizes crime prevention and promotes educational programs toward that end. Security personnel work closely with the county sheriff and fire departments to ensure prompt and effective response to emergencies.

LET'S GO SHOPPING

Residents have easy access to the whole gamut of recreational services within the LW development using the community's private bus service. This same bus system transports residents fare-free to any of the many retail outlets and service establishments heavily clustered nearby—banks, restaurants, houses of worship, and shopping centers, etc. (There are no commercial establishments within Leisure World.) **Laguna Hills Mall**, with more than 90 specialty shops and four major department stores, is on the well-traveled LW route. Those driving their own vehicles can easily find practically any type of outlet or service within a 2- to 10-mile trip from home.

OAKMONT VILLAGE

SANTA ROSA, CALIFORNIA

310 White Oak Dr.
Santa Rosa, CA 95409
707-539-1611 / 888-625-6668
Fax: 707-539-6537

Developer: H.N. Berger Developers & Planners

Year of initial property sales/rentals: 1964

Total land area: 1,745 acres

Average elevation: Varies from 150 to 500 feet

Location: Northwestern California; Sonoma County; near the intersection of U.S. Highway 101 and State Highway 12; about 55 miles north of San Francisco, less than 25 miles inland from the Pacific coast; 7 miles southeast of the city of Santa Rosa.

Nearest airport with scheduled commercial service: Sonoma Airport/Santa Rosa (15 miles); San Francisco International (60 miles)

Current number of housing units with year-round occupants: 2,800

Projected number of housing units: 2,950 (1999)

Resident eligibility: One resident in the household must be at least 55 years of age.

Community visit/tour incentive program: None

Suggested newspaper: *The Press Democrat*, 427 Mendocino Ave., Santa Rosa, CA 95401 (707-546-2020)

WHY OAKMONT VILLAGE?

Oakmont Village has twice been chosen by *New Choices* magazine as one of the top 20 retirement communities in the United States. Its **Sonoma County** location in the historic **Valley of the Moon**, heart of the state's vaunted wine country, is considered by many to be one of the most scenic regions in all of northern California. It was adventure author **Jack London**, whose home was in the nearby vineyard country, who is credited with giving the ancient Indian "Valley of the Moon" name to the **Sonoma Valley**.

Situated 7 miles east of the center of **Santa Rosa**, a city with a population of about 135,000, Oakmont is distant enough from the downtown bustle to enjoy a country atmosphere of quiet contentment, but close enough to benefit from municipal services. The community is sheltered by **Annadel State Park**, 5,000 forested acres with miles of hiking trails. Two other state parks are nearby. Many Oakmont homes are perched on hillsides with splendid views of the **Mayacamas Mountains** whose peaks rise to more than 2,000 feet. Less than 30 minutes to the west are inviting coastal beaches and scenic drives. Along the way is **Armstrong Woods**, where magnificent redwood forests tower over the landscape. Added to all this is the great convenience of being no more than an hour's drive from **San Francisco,** one of America's most irresistible cities.

WHO'S IN CHARGE?

The **Oakmont Village Association (OVA)** is a mutual benefit nonprofit corporation organized under the laws of the state of California. Its mission is to take title to, maintain, and operate Oakmont community property on behalf of its members. Association dues for 1997 were set at $12.50 per person per month, paid annually. Membership in the association is mandatory for all persons who own property in the community. Oversight functions are under the policy supervision of the resident-elected board of directors. The assessment covers the recreation centers, including tennis courts, swimming pools, lawn bowling greens, bocce ball courts, and fitness facilities.

The **Oakmont Golf Club** is a separate entity, independent of OVA, and run by its own nine-member board of directors, made up entirely of Oakmont residents. The golf club, course, and related facilities are separately funded and supported by those who make use of them. Residents who play no golf pay no fees. The *Oakmont News* is a semimonthly 24-page community newspaper owned and published by OVA, written by resident volunteers, but produced by a professional printer. The publication is sustained by lots of display advertising and reflects a quality of content and layout fit for a commercial newspaper. Each Oakmont home receives a mailed copy at no charge.

THE WEATHER REPORT

Sonoma County is a climatic patchwork. A summer day can be in the upper 50s on the coast and in the upper 90s no more than 20 miles inland. Towns located just five or 10 miles south of Santa Rosa have typical daytime summer temperatures in the high 60s and low 70s, while a few miles north and east, it will be in the upper 80s and lower 90s. It is these broad swings in temperatures in different parts of the county on the same day that are called "microclimates." Those locations with lower summer daytime readings are cooled by fog that slips through the Petaluma gap, running along the river of the same name, and emptying into **San Pablo Bay.** The fog may be a heavy blanket or a light wisp, but when combined with the moderating influences of the **Pacific Ocean** and the patterns of coastal hills and valleys, the results can be dramatic. Average annual rainfall too, can reveal startling variables—from a low of about 24 inches to a high of almost 74 inches—all within the same county! Snowfall, if any, is generally limited to a light dusting at nearby Mayacamas Mountain peak elevations.

Average high and low temperatures for Santa Rosa during the three summer months and three winter months, drawn from the U.S. National Oceanic and Atmospheric Administration data by local weather observers are as follows:

December: high 58/low 38   **January:** high 58/low 37

February: high 63/low 41   **June:** high 81/low 50

July: high 84/low 51   **August:** high 84/low 52

Average annual rainfall: 30 inches
Average annual snowfall: rare

HOME SWEET HOME

Hundreds of customized individual homes overlook the fairways, with tree-covered mountains that rim the valley as a background. There's a wide range in home sizes and elevations, floor plans, locations, and price tags. Choices in housing include detached single-family and townhouses. Prices on free-standing homes range from $185,000 to more than $500,000, with living space generally running from 1,200 to 3,500 square feet. Townhouses are priced from $150,000 to $250,000 in sizes from 1,200 to 1,800 square feet or more. Currently, about one-third of home sales are for new construction, the remainder for resales. A few long-term lease units are available. No vacant lots for future construction are for sale.

Also within Oakmont is **Oakmont Gardens**, an assisted living complex primarily for residents who no longer wish to maintain their own homes. Such residents lease apartments and are entitled to participate in all that Oakmont Village offers.

A site is available for recreational vehicle, boat, or small household storage. Water and sewer systems are provided by Santa Rosa municipal utility agencies.

MONEY MATTERS

The Santa Rosa metropolitan area is no exception to the relatively high cost burdens found in most parts of California. The most reliable and comprehensive living cost data available, the *ACCRA Cost of Living Index* (2nd quarter, 1996), shows this location to be well below that of nearby San Francisco (the second most expensive city in the United States, behind New York City) but still substantially above average. The survey shows a composite index for six measured categories of living costs in Santa Rosa to be 30.2 percent above the average for 315 metropolitan and nonmetropolitan areas analyzed. Measurements for the six individual components, all above the weighted averages, were as follows: groceries, 10.4 percent; housing, 73 percent; utilities, 3.6 percent; transportation, 24.9 percent; health care, 31.3

percent; miscellaneous goods and services, 11.1 percent. It should be noted with regard to housing costs, that private, planned communities sometimes are able to offer home construction values that are more appealing than those reflected in the norms found in surrounding incorporated areas. Such differences in costs may be a result of economies of site development, concentration of construction activity, or other factors common to such projects.

Sonoma County property—whether residential, commercial, or industrial—is appraised at market value as it existed on March 1, 1975, with increases limited to 2 percent annually. Properties created or sold since that date bear full cash value as of the time created or sold, plus the 2 percent annual increase. Local property taxes throughout the state of California are limited by law (Proposition 13) to 1 percent of the value of residential property ($1.00 per $100 appraisal of fair market value) plus any taxes levied to cover bonded voter-approved indebtedness for county, city, schools or other taxing agencies.

The sales tax in Santa Rosa is 6 percent (state portion), plus 1 percent levied by the city, 0.25 percent by the county, and 0.25 percent by the district, for a total of 7.5 percent.

It should be noted that Oakmont's association fees of $12.50 a month per person are very moderate when measured against other comparable communities.

TAKE GOOD CARE OF YOURSELF

A recently opened on-site health center, operated by **Santa Rosa Memorial Hospital**, provides convenient state-of-the-art outpatient medical and related services.

Santa Rosa has four general hospitals, all within a 6- to 12-mile radius of Oakmont, with a total bed capacity of 569. There is also a physical rehabilitation hospital with 141 beds, eight convalescent facilities, seven community clinics, two chronic dialysis clinics, three psychology centers, two surgical clinics, seven health and hospice facilities, five centers serving people with developmental disabilities, and numerous home health agencies. There are more than 600 physicians and surgeons serving Sonoma County. In Santa Rosa alone, there are almost 100 dentists, 20 optometrists, more than 100 chiropractors, and 30 physical therapists.

PLACES TO GO, THINGS TO DO

The centerpieces of Oakmont are two challenging 18-hole golf courses. Facilities include two pro shops, a driving range, practice putting greens, a lounge and restaurant (with a spacious deck overlooking the fairway), a snack shop, and a clubhouse for member functions. It takes a staff of almost 40 administrative and maintenance personnel to keep golf operations on track.

There are approximately 65 clubs and activities at Oakmont. A two-page calendar of meetings and events (appearing monthly in the community newspaper) sets forth listings six days a week for anywhere from five to 18 different scheduled activities each and every day! On most days there are a dozen or more resident groups in collective pursuits ranging from an anglers' club, a yoga demonstration or an investment forum, to a ceramics or French class, fitness club, or choir rehearsal. Sunday mornings offer a choice between a community nondenominational church service held in the community center (there are numerous off-site denominational congregations of choice, just minutes away) or a symposium in the recreation center—a weekly forum for lectures and discussion of topics of broad general interest.

Few table games known to humankind are missing from the organized leisure agenda. There's bridge, of course, in all its variations. There's canasta, cribbage, dominos, bingo, and pinochle. For those who lean toward more physical activity, there's shuffleboard, table tennis, lawn bowling, bocce, dancing, tennis (six hard-surface courts on the property), and a wide assortment of exercise classes. A classical music club and an arts association regularly present outstanding performances and lectures. Three large recreational centers serve as focal points for social activities. Each has a swimming pool, spa, multipurpose room, large meeting hall, and a kitchen. Residents who are single have a very active club that caters to their particular needs and interests. A full-time office staff helps plan, promote, and implement programs.

Through special arrangements with local travel agencies and the OVA, a significant segment of the population is on the go at any given time with a bewildering selection of group tours and vacation trips to almost every imaginable destination. One recent series of announcements included a one-day excursion to hear the **San Francisco Symphony**, to a 13-day escorted trip to the Canadian Maritime Provinces, a 12-day cruise steamboating the Mississippi River, or a six-day adventure to Mexico to explore the Mayan ruins and experience other south-of-the-border treasures.

Cultural and recreational resources in Sonoma County include 96 churches; two performing arts centers; four libraries; 45 neighborhood, community, and state parks (most of which have playgrounds), a lake (a favorite spot for fly casting); 16 theaters; an ice arena; two roller skating rinks; and several bowling centers. The Sonoma County and **Napa Valley** wine country are just minutes away, a scene visited by hundreds of thousands of visitors throughout the year. There is a heavy concentration of art and artists in the area. Festivals, special musical productions, live theater, and scores of extravagant charity fund-raising events create a steady diet of pleasurable attractions.

Santa Rosa Junior College is highly acclaimed for the quality of its academic programs and services to the community. **Sonoma State University**, about 12 miles from the Oakmont entrance, offers a full four-year educational curriculum along with a generous agenda of campus activities, many of which are open to local residents. For those who choose to venture further from home, but only an hour or so away, there is, of course, the unlimited universe called San Francisco. Virtually no need or want is likely to go unsatisfied in that citadel of civilized enlightenment, be it world class entertainment, cultural stimulation, spectator sport, or any of countless mainline attractions that draw visitors from all corners of the earth.

SAFE AND SECURE

Police protection and firefighting services are provided by the city of Santa Rosa. A fire station is maintained within the community. A private security company patrols the common areas nightly. An emergency response team is less than a mile away. A county-wide "Vial for Life" program, implemented by volunteers, involves placing a small container inserted with vital information (about medications, health conditions, etc., of family members) placed in the refrigerator of each participating household. The procedure gives emergency crews prompt access to sometimes crucial life-saving information.

The **Oakmont Property Owners Association**, working with the city of Santa Rosa, takes on educational program responsibilities with seminars featuring local officials discussing various aspects of community crime prevention, fire safety, and health maintenance. The incidence of law violations over the past several years at Oakmont is described as "inconsequential" and limited to property crimes, with but one exception.

LET'S GO SHOPPING

Commercial development inside Oakmont consists of several small service and retail businesses, including real estate offices, three banks, a restaurant, a post office, a service station, and a newly constructed medical/dental clinic. An OVA shoppers' bus carries residents (at a nominal fee) to variously scheduled destinations, sometimes considerable distances south of San Francisco to reach special shopping needs.

A chain-operated mega food market is about 2 miles from the Oakmont entrance. A major retail shopping mall is 8 miles off in Santa Rosa. Other commercial concentrations are closer, within about 4 miles. As might be expected in a city the size of Santa Rosa, there are three large malls and a full spectrum of retail and service outlets throughout the city, including major department and discount stores.

PRESLEY'S SUN LAKES COUNTRY CLUB

BANNING, CALIFORNIA

5062 Rolling Hills Ave.
Banning, CA 92220
909-845-2123 / 800-368-8887
Fax: 909-845-7321

Developer: Presley Homes

Year of initial property sales/rentals: 1987

Total land area: 963 acres

Average elevation: 2,350 feet

Location: Southern inland California; Riverside County; south off Interstate 10 between Beaumont and Banning, just east of State Highway 79; about 90 miles east of Los Angeles; 27 miles east of Riverside and 28 miles west of Palm Springs.

Nearest airport with scheduled commercial service: Palm Springs Regional (28 miles); Ontario International (40 miles)

Current number of housing units with year-round occupants: 2,150

Projected number of housing units: 3,600 (2004)

Resident eligibility: Residences must be occupied by at least one person at least 55 years of age (the qualified resident). All others must be 45 years of age or older (with several specific and limited exceptions). Visiting guests of any age may stay for cumulative periods not to exceed 60 days/year.

Community visit/tour incentive program: A "Try Before You Buy" program invites relocation prospects to visit the community and experience the amenities and life style. Options are available for two-night weekend or mid-week stays in a fully furnished on-site home at rates of $129 for one couple and $179 for two. Includes a free round of golf and a complimentary meal at the clubhouse restaurant.

Suggested newspaper: *Riverside Press Enterprise*, 3166 W. Ramsey St., Banning, CA 92220 (909-849-4531)

WHY SUN LAKES?

Shimmering lakes, tile-roofed homes, and stately palms give the **Sun Lakes Country Club (SLCC)** community an aura of Mediterranean flavor. It is situated along the summit of the **San Gorgonio Pass Area**, a mountain barrier formed by **Mt. San Gorgonio** and **Mt. San Jacinto**. Their snow-capped peaks glistening in the distance adds a majestic ambiance. *New Choices* magazine, a national publication focusing on active-adult retirement communities, ranked SLCC among the top 20 such developments in the country for the first two consecutive years of its annual selections, beginning in 1992. Only two other southern California retirement communities were named in that illustrious company. Evaluations made by the magazine's editors were based on discussions with industry experts and representative residents, and on such criteria as design, climate, amenities, security, environment, and property values. Magazine commentary at the time underscored the fact that all communities selected "...provided the highest dollar value...and each had a distinctive 'personality' that is readily apparent to residents."

The **Presley Companies**, developers of Sun Lakes, was founded in 1956. A telling part of their reputation for quality and value is said to center on the fact that almost one-third of all residential sales are made as a result of a referral by someone who already owns a Presley home.

The geographic location of SLCC also presents a noteworthy life style advantage. There are, within a 30-mile radius, three principal population centers, each offering significant convenience to a plethora of leisure attractions and daily living resources. **Riverside**, with a population of more than 225,000, **San Bernardino,** with almost 165,000, and their two combined counties with more than 2.5 million inhabitants, provide Sun Lakes residents easy access to a vast cultural, educational, entertainment and recreational domain. The third, **Palm Springs**, (population about 40,000) is an international winter playground and one of America' premier resorts, icing on the cake of recreational diversion for Sun Lakes fun-seekers.

WHO'S IN CHARGE?

The **Sun Lakes Country Club Homeowners Association** is established as a nonprofit corporation under the laws of California. It is empowered to enforce established rules and regulations intended to preserve living standards and protect property values. The association operates and regulates the use of community facilities under its ownership. It functions through an elected board of directors, committees appointed to help implement major portions of its programs, and the developer, acting as managing agent. Under this master association, there are three subassociations, each with its own directorate and committees, and each representing a particular neighborhood or sector of the total community.

The master association holds a proprietary interest in all recreational facilities except the two golf courses. Residents can individually join the country club for golfing privileges, but all residents pay a monthly fee to help defray a portion of the cost of maintaining the golf course, in recognition of the fact that it is an aesthetic community attribute to golfers and nongolfers alike. Each purchaser also pays a one-time, nontransferable initiation fee of $950 per lot for membership in the country club. The monthly assessment to each resident is $113.05 which pays for maintenance of all private streets and common areas within the community, round-the-clock security, club-houses and recreational facilities. An optional cable television package may be added for $19.95 a month.

A seven-member communications advisory committee to the board of directors assembles a community newsletter called *Sun Lakes Lifestyles*. Published monthly, residents are encouraged to contribute articles about any of the great variety of club and interest group activities constantly taking place around the community. The *Sun Lakes Life*, in addition, is a commercial newspaper, published monthly by the *Record Gazette* (an area publication), exclusively for the Sun Lakes community.

THE WEATHER REPORT

At an elevation of more than 2,000 feet, effects of the desert southwest weather characteristics are somewhat moderated. Situated in a pass between two dominating mountain ranges, the **Banning** area is typically quite a bit cooler than the desert floor below—sometimes by as much as 15 to 20 degrees in nighttime lows. It is not uncommon in winter to see shirt-sleeved golfers on the fairways with generous snow covering the mountains in the background. It is of particular interest to point out that while summer temperatures can be persistently in the high 90s and past the 100 degree mark, evenings are dramatically cool with typical lows in the high-50s and low to mid-60s.

The only weather information available for the Sun Lakes area was for the year 1996 (as opposed to data collected over an extended period of time, as has been presented in the other profiles). Assuming that 1996 was a relatively normal temperature year, however, we can draw reliable inferences from this limited summary of average high/low readings for three winter and three summer months:

December: high 63/low 41	**January:** high 65/low 41
February: high 66/low 43	**June:** high 91/low 54
July: high 99/low 62	**August:** high 100/low 62

Average annual precipitation: 18 inches
Average annual snowfall: none

HOME SWEET HOME

There were four series of homes being offered during the 1997-98 season, all detached, single-family. The "Executive Series" is being built around the new executive golf course which opened for play in the spring of 1996. Square footage for these floor plans run from 1,266 to 1,803 at prices from the low $100s to the high $150s. Three other series celebrated a grand opening in the summer of 1996, offering a string of nine models for inspection. Plans range from 1,288 to 2,250 square feet, priced from the low $120s to the low $220s, with considerable variation in accordance with lot location and exterior elevation style. A full-year Presley warranty program covers virtually all fixtures and systems in every home. It is said to be the most comprehensive builder-backed new home warranty in the industry, surpassing many 10-year warranties that often cover only major structural defects.

Attached townhouse units are no longer being built, but there is a notable resale market for units ranging from 900 to 1,500 square feet. An RV storage area for 250 units is available. Central water and sewer services are provided by the city of Banning. Electric and telephone utility lines are below ground.

MONEY MATTERS

In a state well-known for high living costs, the Riverside area (the nearest available data site, just 27 miles from Banning), enjoys something of an absolution from that dubious reputation. The *ACCRA Cost of Living Index* (2nd quarter, 1996) compared 315 selected metropolitan and rural areas of the country. The composite indices for eleven California locations showed that all were above the national average (measuring six different categories of spending), ranging from a modest 4.2 percent above average (Bakersfield) to a whopping 64.3 percent (San Francisco). Riverside, on that same scale, weighs in at 9.7 percent above average, clearly among the less costly places in California to live.

Comparing the six measured components (groceries, housing, utilities, transportation, health care, and miscellaneous goods and services), healthcare was the only category shown to be more than 12 percent above the national average, with a factor of 27.8 percent.

The property tax rate for **Riverside County** is approximately 1.25 percent of the residence purchase price. A separate assessment bond to pay for a railroad overpass that serves the community comes to between $258 and $343 annually, depending on the size and type of home.

TAKE GOOD CARE OF YOURSELF

Just a mile or so from the Sun Lakes front gate is the 68-bed **San Gorgonio Memorial Hospital**. Small, but with full technical support facilities (x-ray, lab, monitoring equipment, etc.), special attention is given to short-term urgent care for illnesses or injuries that are not life threatening. It is a lower cost, fast-track program that minimizes waiting time and is backed by a full staff of board-certified specialists and a 24-hour emergency room prepared for more serious conditions. The hospital maintains a helicopter service for quick transport to the 800-bed **Loma Linda University Medical Center** (21 highway miles away), the largest and most comprehensive health care facility in the region, and to the 280-bed **Eisenhower Medical Center** in **Rancho Mirage** (south of Palm Springs, about 40 miles from Sun Lakes), where complete diagnosis and treatment resources are also available. The **Riverside General Hospital & University Medical Center** in Riverside (about a half-hour drive) also offers complete in-patient and out-patient services, including 60 specialty clinics.

The **Banning Health Center**, a facility of the county department of health, offers health education, physical examinations, nutrition programs, routine testing, and public health nurse visiting, among other services, short of emergency or after-hours care. Physician and surgeon individual and group medical practice offices, along with dentists and other health care professionals, are infinite in number throughout the many county cities and towns.

PLACES TO GO, THINGS TO DO

A sprawling, well-appointed, 18,000-plus square foot main clubhouse, always bustling with activities, features a library, a spacious ballroom, billiards room, arts and crafts studio, travel desk, restaurant, staff offices, and the **Bob Mathias Health and Fitness Center**. It is the center of community-wide social events, including holiday parties and special performances. A proposed expansion will add another 5,000 square feet. Outdoor amenities include an 18-hole championship golf course (which is regularly the site of celebrity and professional tournaments, along with amateur play), two tennis courts, a swimming pool with adjacent locker rooms and a Jacuzzi, and pathways for walking, jogging, and cycling. A smaller, but equally inviting north clubhouse covers 8,500 square feet, sporting a nine-hole executive golf course (later to be expanded to 18 holes) and pro shop, a staged auditorium, another outdoor pool and Jacuzzi, meeting and game rooms, etc. Yet a third such facility is proposed, adding six more tennis courts, bocce and paddle tennis courts, and more exercise space.

A glance at the monthly activities calendar reveals a bewildering daily schedule of events—everything from a variety of exercise programs, dance groups, and card games, to club activities centering on quilting, bible study, computer education, investments, drama and tennis mixers. A recent roster of clubs and activity groups listed 44 different entries. A homeowners travel group has an ongoing schedule of group excursions ranging from day and overnight trips to nearby attractions, to grand cruises to foreign lands, African safaris, and 'round the world tours. There are seminars and workshops on everything from dealing with sore feet to home and community security, astronomy or mapping the family genealogy tree. Each month the schedule includes one or more special events such as talent shows, holiday dinner dances, concerts on the green, and theater parties. There are free swimming lessons, health and personal issues support groups, special activities for singles, and neighborhood barbecues.

One need not wander far from home to find a whole slew of other activities. More than a dozen major parks and lakes within a 30- to 50-mile radius offer campsites, fishing, lake swimming, pedal boats, rockclimbing, hiking, boating, picnicking, cycling, pony rides, or solitude. Museums in the area display Indian artifacts, historical memorabilia, antique furniture, and natural science exhibits, as well as a generous selection of sculpture and other art media. Area cherry orchard harvests give rise to an early summer festival that has been celebrated in these parts for almost 80 years. If gaming is your thing, the casino on the **Morongo Indian Reservation** is just east of Banning, a tempting alternative to Las Vegas.

SAFE AND SECURE

The community has enjoyed a virtual immunity from any noteworthy crime, according to local spokespersons. Entry to the property is controlled by a manned security gate that operates day and night, seven days a week. An internal security patrol is on duty throughout the night. Law enforcement and fire protection is provided by the city of Banning.

A Safety Advisory Committee has developed an emergency preparedness action plan that provides guidelines for implementation in the event of a community-wide emergency or natural disaster. The plan is detailed and each resident plays an important role in its function.

LET'S GO SHOPPING

Sun Lakes Village is a shopping center located at the entrance to the community, giving maximum convenience to residents for day-to-day needs. Principal tenants include a major food market, a popular-priced department store, a chain drug store, and a cluster of specialty shops and service establishments. **Moreno Valley Mall**, about 20 freeway miles toward Riverside, is a modern, enclosed emporium with nationally known, main-line department stores and the usual galaxy of specialty shops that normally accompanies such shopping configurations.

Eight miles in the opposite direction is the **Desert Hills Premium Outlets** collection of more than 100 shops featuring some of the world's leading designers and brand names in top fashion apparel, sportswear, sporting goods, shoes, home furnishings and housewares, luggage and leather goods, toys and children's wear, and gifts and specialty items. Antique marts and galleries can be found with ease. For those looking for the highest-end premium merchandise, **Palm Desert Towne Center** is less than 30 minutes away.

SONORA HILLS

SONORA, CALIFORNIA

19601 Greenley Rd.
Sonora, CA 95370
209-532-3600 / 800-223-2346
Fax: 209-532-3077

Developer: California Gold

Year of initial property sales/rentals: 1988

Total land area: 44 acres

Average elevation: 1,825 feet

Location: Central California; Tuolumne County; near the intersection of State Highways 108 and 49; 51 miles northeast of Modesto; 133 miles and 70 miles straight east from San Francisco and Stockton, respectively; 105 miles southeast of Sacramento; 51 miles west of entrance to Yosemite National Park.

Nearest airport with scheduled commercial service: Stockton Metro (65 miles); Sacramento Metropolitan (110 miles)

Current number of housing units with year-round occupants: 190

Projected number of housing units: 235 (1999)

Resident eligibility: Occupancy is restricted to at least one person/spouse 55 years of age or older.

Community visit/tour incentive program: None

Suggested newspaper: *The Union Democrat,* 84 South Washington St., Sonora, CA 95370 (209-532-7151)

WHY SONORA HILLS?

Sonora Hills is a community of high-end manufactured homes featuring innovative dwellings produced by one of the foremost companies in the U.S. prefabricated housing industry. The site is nestled in the central **Sierra Nevada** foothills on the edge of the **Stanislaus National Forest.** The community's elevation and topography place it below the winter snow line but above the seasonal inversions that keep valley country to the west in shrouds of fog for extended periods of time during winter months. **Sonora,** the county seat with a population of nearly 5,000, is situated less than an hour from one of America's premiere national treasures—**Yosemite National Park.** Easily accessible from Sonora, is a spellbinding attraction underlined on every tourist's agenda. **Tuolumne County** is said to attract literally millions of visitors each year who are drawn to the internationally popular California mountain wilderness and the abundant recreational activity within and around it.

The area has proven irresistible to Hollywood and television producers. For more than 70 years, the film and broadcast industries have found this part of the world to be an ideal setting for many story lines brought to the big screen and into the nation's living rooms.

WHO'S IN CHARGE?

There are two organizations to which residents have the option of belonging. The **Sonora Hills Residents Association** has an elected board chosen from among homeowners. They collect no dues and have no budget. Their purpose is to serve as a communication link between homeowners and the developers who maintain fiscal and administrative management responsibilities. The association convenes monthly meetings with its resident constituents and separate meetings with the development owners and management staff in order to address problems and consider proposals.

The **Sonora Hills Social Club**, as the name implies, initiates and coordinates all sorts of leisure activities for participation by those residents who choose to become members for an annual fee of $5. This group too, elects a board of officers and directors, along with nine standing committees. An independent group of volunteers produces a monthly magazine-format newsletter covering activity calendars, resident biographies, favorite recipes, featured columns, and commentary and guest articles.

THE WEATHER REPORT

The **Tuolumne County Chamber of Commerce** claims the area has 328 days of sunshine annually. Considering that natives are inclined to describe the climate as "Bay Area without the fog," one has to be careful about separating objectivity from home-town pride. It is quite true that significant snowfall is somewhat out of the ordinary during a typical winter. An occasional "dusting," they say, generally disappears in a matter of hours. But summer temperatures, unlike **San Francisco**, are quite capable of climbing to as high as 100 or more degrees. The saving grace is that when the sun goes down on such a day, it will generally cool to the mid- to upper-50s. No hot, sticky, sleepless nights here. A humidity of less than 30 percent for much of the time makes the peaks of summer heat quite tolerable.

The following is a partial summary of a 50-year monthly average temperature record compiled by *The Union Democrat*, published in Sonora:

December: high 56/low 33   **January:** high 55/low 33

February: high 58/low 35   **June:** high 86/low 56

July: high 95/low 59   **August:** high 94/low 57

Average annual precipitation: 32 inches
Average annual snowfall: very light; measurement data unavailable

HOME SWEET HOME

The ultimate number of homes to be built in Sonora Hills is 236, now about 80 percent completed. Approximately 90 percent of home sales are for newly built units, the rest for resale. The price range for these homes is on the high end of those associated with such housing, featuring a long list of appointments not found in less expensive construction. Ten different floor plans vary from 1,289 to 1,830 square feet at selling prices between $105,000 and $134,000. Elevations resemble traditional site-built homes rather than the mobile home box construction so often used. Standard features, too numerous to fully recite here, include dual-glazed windows, designer hardware, prewiring for cable television, walk-in closets, and fully landscaped front yards with automatic irrigation. Any number of optional touches of luxury can be incorporated at additional cost.

Typical of developments offering manufactured housing, building sites are offered on a lifetime land lease, binding for as long as the home ownership is maintained. Home resales by the owner are handled in much the same way as any other real estate transaction. The lease is assignable to the new buyer at no additional cost to them and converts to a renewable 20-year term. The arrangement contributes significantly to keeping home ownership investment costs to a minimum. The monthly land lease cost pays for the ongoing maintenance of all common areas, upkeep of private roads, sidewalks, lights, and maintenance of the clubhouse, pool, and spa. Such payments also include front yard landscape maintenance and property taxes on the lot. Exterior maintenance and property taxes on the dwelling itself are the responsibility of the homeowner. The lease fee for 1997 was set at $449 a month. There are no additional homeowner or association fees.

Residents have access to a storage area for recreational vehicles for a moderate monthly charge. Water and sewer systems are serviced by the county utility district. Sources of water supply originate in the snowy Sierra Nevada Mountains, leading to an extensive system of man-made storage and distribution facilities. Captured so close to the source, contaminants are avoided, resulting in a very high quality of water for both domestic and industrial use. Electric and telephone service lines are under ground.

MONEY MATTERS

County property taxes are based on a formula that assesses the value of a home at 70 percent of the purchase price, with 1 percent of the assessed value as the basis for the amount of taxes owed, less the homeowner's exemption of $70 per year. According to that standard, a $100,000 home would have a property tax assessment of approximately $630 per year. A combined utilities budget (trash collection, water, sewer, gas, electricity, and cable television) can be expected to come to $150 to $200 a month. Average home insurance is estimated to come to between $30 and $35 a month.

There are no known data available to compare living costs for consumer products and services at retail (food, health care, durable goods, etc.). Median housing prices in Tuolumne County, however, are more than 40 percent lower than the state-wide average, according to local real estate figures released through the California Department of Finance. Rentals too, are substantially below state averages (by 31 percent) with the median rent paid by residents at only $392 per month.

TAKE GOOD CARE OF YOURSELF

There is a total of 191 hospital beds, in two separate facilities, within a mile of Sonora Hills. **Tuolumne General** dates back to the mid-1800s and today features a variety of specialized services. Among them are a 24-hour emergency department, cardiac rehabilitation, wellness programs, comprehensive diagnostic facilities, home health care, both inpatient and one-day surgery, and a psychiatric unit. **Sonora Community Hospital**, a not-for-profit institution, is the largest private employer in the county. It operates satellite clinics and medical centers at locations scattered throughout the area, making primary family care immediately available in many of the smaller outlying county towns.

Both hospitals accept most insurance coverage. Some physicians maintain offices within walking distance of the Sonora Hills entrance. A recent roster of health care professionals in the county showed 93 physicians and surgeons, 38 dentists, 18 chiropractors, 10 optometrists, and 14 physical therapists, among others. There are three convalescent hospitals and nine residential care homes.

PLACES TO GO, THINGS TO DO

An 8,000 square foot clubhouse is equipped with a large kitchen, great room, library, billiards parlor, and an activities room that is available for arts and crafts as well as exercise. Residents have access to the clubhouse for meetings, parties, and special occasions. A year-round heated pool and spa are also part of the facility. A horseshoe pitch and a barbecue/picnic area complement the facility. Asphalt-paved walking trails wind throughout the community, accented by a waterfall, pond, and gazebo. An active travel club arranges for residents to journey together to all sorts of enticing destinations.

There are five public golf courses within a 10- to 20-minute drive from the community. The published annual Tuolumne County calendar of events is loaded with every imaginable attraction—from music, film, and food festivals to Indian tribal celebrations, craft fairs, rodeos, and art exhibitions. There are 78 lakes in the county of all shapes and sizes, offering opportunities for boating, water skiing, and fishing (especially trout). The **Tuolumne River** is one of the premiere whitewater rafting and kayaking magnets in the west. More than 2,000 developed campsites in dozens of campgrounds entice hikers to return year after year to conquer 480 miles of developed trails. Downhill and cross-country skiers from across the U.S. and abroad find excellent resort amenities in the county's eastern high-country reaches and in neighboring **Calaveras County.**

A healthy arts community is punctuated by three highly respected professional theater groups and a host of local musical organizations that present programs—mostly outdoor presentations in any of three different parks—ranging from big-band to jazz. A summer-long interpretive program includes wildflower and wildlife walks, star-gazing shows, and local history journeys into some of the fascinating gold-rush towns that still maintain much of their dramatic heritage. The **Central Sierra Arts Council Gallery** in downtown Sonora, offers many shows featuring works from the large colony of local artists in the area.

Columbia College in Sonora provides a two-year post-high school program offering technical and vocational, remedial, and community education, noncredit courses for adults, and special instruction for businesses and other organizations with appropriate needs and objectives.

SAFE AND SECURE

Entry and departure from the community are controlled by access gates. A private security company is employed to patrol neighborhood streets from 9 p.m. until 5 a.m., making rounds three times each evening. Management services are available 24 hours a day. The Sonora police and fire departments are responsible for public safety programs. An FBI uniform crime statistics report in 1993 showed Tuolumne County to have one of the lowest crime rates in northern California.

LET'S GO SHOPPING

Shopping outlets lie directly across the street from the Sonora Hills entrance. Also featured are cinemas, a library, senior center, pharmacy, banks, restaurants, gas station, and a hardware store. Professional offices include physicians, therapists, dentists, optometrists, a podiatrist, a veterinarian, and a hearing center. Main-line shopping is available in **Stockton** (with a population of more than 200,000), a little more than an hour's drive from Sonora.

COLORADO TAX FACTS

INDIVIDUAL INCOME TAX

Residents are taxed on all income, regardless of where it is earned. Income is taxed at 5 percent of the federally adjusted gross income with modifications, less deductions and exemptions. For the tax year 1996, a federal tax exemption of $2,550 was allowed.

SALES TAX

There is a tax of 3 percent on retail sales or use, storage or consumption within the state. Tax applies to lodging rentals under 30 days.

PROPERTY TAX

Residential realty is assessed by 21 percent of actual value. The range of property taxes per $1,000 of assessed value is from $3.03 to $11.317. These rates are composites of locally applicable city, county, and school district rates. There may be additional levies by special districts and improvement assessments not covered in the foregoing figures.

RANKING REPORT

Data published in *The Rating Guide to Life in America's Fifty States* in 1994, showed Colorado ranking 33rd from the most favorable with regard to property taxes.

For more complete tax information contact the Colorado Revenue Department/Taxpayer Services Division, 1375 Sherman St., Denver, CO 80261, 303-866-5565, (fax) 303-866-2400.

Note: The above information is based on applicable tax law data current at the time of publication. Because such laws and rates are subject to change, professional assistance should be sought if tax implications are critical to a relocation decision.

HEATHER GARDENS

AURORA, COLORADO

2888 South Heather Gardens Way
Aurora, CO 80014
303-755-0652
Fax: 303-745-5253

Developer: Environmental Developers, Inc.

Year of initial property sales/rentals: 1973

Total land area: 198 acres

Average elevation: 5,300 feet

Location: North-central Colorado; Arapahoe County; at the southwestern edge of the Denver suburb of Aurora; about 5 miles southeast of the center of downtown Denver; on Interstate Highway 225; connecting to Interstate Highways 25 to the southwest and 70 to the north.

Nearest airport with scheduled commercial service: Denver International (20 miles)

Current number of housing units with year-round occupants: 2,426

Projected number of housing units: 2,426 (completed)

Resident eligibility: Each unit must be occupied by at least one individual who is 39 years of age or older. No residents under age 16 are permitted as permanent occupants. An estimated 90% of the resident population is retired or semiretired.

Community visit/tour incentive program: None

Suggested newspapers: *Aurora Sentinel*, 1730 So. Abilene, Aurora, CO 80012 (303-750-7555); *Denver Post*, 1560 Broadway, Denver, CO 80009 (303-820-1010)

WHY HEATHER GARDENS?

Few active adult communities are located inside a major metropolitan area. **Heather Gardens** lies in the shadow of modern business towers and among a multitude of hotels and other commercial establishments, just beyond the southeastern outskirts of the **Denver** city limits. With a population of about 3,800 people, a 1997 operating and capital reserve budget of just under $6.5 million, and more than 50 employees on the payroll, the community has been called a city within a city. It also has been suggested as a model for the housing needs of active older adults that will be sustained well into the new century.

The entire development of 35 multistory buildings (three, four, or six floors) and 316 townhouses and patio homes is under a condominium ownership plan. Those who purchase residential units, as in any instance of condominium participation, actually own the space occupied, rather than the physical property itself, along with an undivided fractional interest in the ground under the property and the common areas and buildings. All real estate (land and structures) belongs to the association—that is, to all the owners together. It is a form of ownership that has had more than its share of interest from retirees, in part as a result of the fact that exterior maintenance becomes the responsibility of the collective owners, leaving the individual occupant free of such cares.

Title to the entire property was vested in the original developer for the first 10 years of operations and subsequently, in early 1983, transferred to the resident-owners through their elected representatives in the governing association.

WHO'S IN CHARGE?

As a result of a series of historical developments since the community was first established, there are now four different resident organizations, each serving a separate purpose. The **Heather Gardens Association (HGA)**, a private nonprofit corporation, is composed of all the homeowners. Its sole function is management of the owners' common elements and to provide activity programs. The association operates under the authority and control of an elected board of directors that oversees a staff employed to implement programs and manage facilities. HGA owns no real property.

A second association, also with its own board of directors made up of elected homeowners, is the **Heather Gardens Metropolitan District (HGMD)**. It is a public government entity created to incur bonded indebtedness in order to purchase all the recreational properties (community center, golf course, etc.) and maintenance facilities from the original owner-developers after their 10-year limited tenure had terminated and they were required by law to relinquish proprietary interests. As a government agency, HGMD (and therefore the homeowners) benefits from numerous advantages in connection with property, income, and sales tax exemptions, as well as state lottery and license fee income derived as a Colorado political subdivision.

A third community entity is the **Area Representatives Organization (ARO)**. It provides a link among residents, management staff, and the HGA and HGMD boards of directors. This group is composed of elected representatives from each multistory building and from each cluster of townhouses and other single-family groupings.

The fourth organization, the **Seville Recreational Association**, represents only those resident-owners of units in six of the multistory buildings, each of which has its own inner park area, tennis court, and swimming pool, and therefore whose agenda may have special application only to their particular set of needs and interests.

Mandatory homeowners' fees are based on the size of the living unit. The monthly assessment ranges from $145 to $415. A monthly newsmagazine, *Heather 'n Yon,* is published by HGA, providing information and news about residents and the community.

THE WEATHER REPORT

The "mile-high city," ensconced along the eastern slope of the central **Rocky Mountains**, enjoys a more moderate climate than one might expect, given its high country image. The altitude is high enough to provide a bracing fresh air from early fall until late spring, yet not so high as to invite the unforgiving harshness found at higher elevations. In summer, the area is largely immune from extended warm weather spells found at some of Colorado's lower level climes. Autumn is the most pleasant time of year here. Severe cold fronts and thunderstorms are few and far between. Even in the dead of winter, more often than not, frigid Canadian air masses are typically drawn off to the east where the lower plains offer an unobstructed wide track to the east and south. The Chinook winds, a product of the topographical mountain patterns, can bring midwinter temperatures into the 60s with little fanfare.

All of this is not to say that the Denver area has an idyllic climate. Colliding polar air with warm, moist air from the Gulf of Mexico can and does bring on rather abrupt and severe weather changes. Denver, indeed, produces one of the highest snowfall readings in the state among cities at the moderate to lower elevations. Overnight lows in midwinter are likely to drop into the teens.

Average high and low temperatures in the Denver area for the three summer months and three winter months are reported by the U.S. National Oceanic and Atmospheric Administration as follows:

December: high 44/low 17   **January:** high 43/low 16

February: high 47/low 20   **June:** high 81/low 52

July: high 88/low 59   **August:** high 86/low 57

Average annual precipitation: 15 inches
Average annual snowfall: 60 inches

HOME SWEET HOME

The total of 2,426 dwelling units at Heather Gardens consists of 2,110 apartments housed in 35 multistory condominium buildings, 252 duplex homes, and 64 townhouses. The apartments range in size from 850 to 2,200 square feet, priced between $65,000 and $180,000. The duplexes and townhouses offer between 1,200 and 2,412 square feet of space, with prices ranging from $120,000 to $210,000. All together, there are 46 different floor plans. An architectural control committee exercises active control over all exterior and interior structural changes to assure conformity and harmony with the overall development and to maintain the structural integrity of all HGA properties.

Because all construction of new housing was completed some years ago, only resales are available on the market. Such sales are said to be characteristically of short turnover, an indication that property values in the development have held up well. While most units are occupied by owners, there is a limited number of leased condominiums normally available at monthly rates ranging from $650 to $1,100. Water and sewer services are provided by the city of Aurora. Utility lines are below ground.

MONEY MATTERS

The overall comparative cost of living in the Denver metropolitan area is moderately above average. Data published in the *ACCRA Cost of Living Index* (2nd quarter, 1996) compares relative price levels for consumer goods and services in 315 participating metropolitan and nonmetropolitan areas. The composite index (combined cost for all measured components) for Denver was 3.1 percent above average. Three of six weighted cost categories showing higher than average costs were: housing at 17.7 percent, transportation at 6.2 percent, and health care at 21.8 percent. The three cost categories with pricing below average were: groceries at 1.6 percent, utilities at 27.1 percent, and miscellaneous goods and services (with a weighted value of slightly less than one-third of the total values assigned) at 4 percent.

The total millage rate levy for the jurisdiction in which Heather Gardens is located comes to $106.88, based on 10.25 percent of purchase cost. That translates to a total property tax burden of $1,620 on an HG home costing $146,300.

TAKE GOOD CARE OF YOURSELF

There are 24 hospitals in Denver and the surrounding suburbs. At least eight of them are within a 10-mile radius of Heather Gardens. The nearest full-service facility is **Columbia Medical Center of Aurora,** which actually consists of two separate hospitals in Aurora, some 2½ miles apart. The south campus of the institution is almost within walking distance of the HG entrance. Together, the two hospitals provide 346 patient beds, a staff of approximately 400 physicians, and a continuum of primary and specialized services. Adjacent to the north campus is the **Columbia Spalding Rehabilitation Hospital.** The complex also serves as a dispatch center for a helicopter and fixed wing emergency transportation system.

All sorts of health care providers maintain offices throughout the immediate area and surrounding neighborhoods. Relief is just minutes away for virtually any type of health problem.

PLACES TO GO, THINGS TO DO

A sprawling community center of just less than 27,000 square feet is open 16 hours a day, seven days a week all year-round except for Thanksgiving, Christmas, and New Years Day. A staff of two full-time and approximately 50 part-time employees (and almost 100 volunteers) keep the wheels of leisure activity spinning. A typical annual roster of more than 65 instruction classes crowd the calendar—everything from ballroom dancing to woodworking, ceramics and quilting to bridge and billiards, to seminars and lectures on local topics and current affairs. Every year there are more than 85 special travel excursions and group tours, many of them day trips to nearby places of interest, some extended vacation stays at popular tourist destinations. Recent low-cost one-day escorted outings have been to such diverse places as an ostrich farm, a gambling casino, a U.S. Air Force Band concert, and lunch at the Colorado Institute of Culinary Arts.

A billiards room at the center accommodates six regulation-size pool tables. A library with books donated by residents and others, offers an impressive collection of reference materials as well as fiction and nonfiction. There's a multipurpose auditorium, a restaurant, golf shop, indoor swimming pool and locker rooms, exercise rooms, saunas and a whirlpool, classrooms, an art studio, and two card rooms. Outside facilities include a nine-hole executive golf course (rated in 1993 as the premiere course of its size in the country), two tennis courts, an outdoor swimming pool, and a picnic pavilion. The center hosts plays and concerts performed by area talent, an arts and crafts fair, a flea market, a health fair, and a spring talent show put on by local residents.

Thirty or so clubs and organizations appeal to most every taste for leisure and socialization. Some focus on games, others on hobbies, politics, religion, or working with charities or other volunteer pursuits. Several devote their programs only to widowed persons who may have special needs or inclinations.

Outside the Heather Gardens perimeter lies Denver, with endless attractions. Minutes away are museums of every description—art, science, aviation, railroad, etc. There are historic parks and gardens, nature centers, galleries, and a zoo. There are recreational parks galore, performing arts centers for music, opera, theater and dance, and spectator sports that cover every conceivable professional and collegiate team competition. All of this is within a 15- to 20-mile radius of the HG community.

SAFE AND SECURE

A resident can reach HGA security 24 hours a day, 365 days a year. Services include emergency coordination in connection with plumbing, electrical and heating problems, checking residences while families are on vacation, car and home lock-out incidents, etc. Security personnel conduct neighborhood watch meetings, regularly patrol neighborhoods, test fire alarms, and assist with medical emergencies. The staff of five police professionals qualify annually for use of weapons and for cardiopulmonary resuscitation (CPR) life-saving procedures. All Heather Gardens employees are CPR-qualified.

A year-end 1996 security report showed 1,716 activity responses, the great major of which were rendering some type of personal assistance to residents, including gaining entry to a home lock-out, lost and found property search, pet complaints, rescue assistance to trained medical and fire rescue personnel, and various types of vehicular and other accidents. There were only 32 cases of petty theft and minor vandalism (to vehicles) noted for the year and no burglaries or other more serious crimes. There has not been a violent crime committed in the community in more than 12 years.

Aurora municipal police and fire departments cover Heather Gardens as they would any other part of the city. HG security maintains radio communications with both agencies in coordinating response activity.

LET'S GO SHOPPING

Full service grocery shopping is but a half mile from the HG entrance. **Aurora Mall**, a major enclosed retail center, is 4 miles away. Two other shopping centers, **Cherry Creek** and **Park Meadows**, are 10 and 15 miles distant, respectively.

FLORIDA TAX FACTS

INDIVIDUAL INCOME TAX

Florida's constitution prohibits a state personal income tax. It is among the six states that levy no such tax.

INTANGIBLES TAX

The state has an *ad valorem* levy that applies to stocks, mutual funds, notes, bonds, and certain receivables. The rate is two mills annually. Exemptions range from $20,000 to $100,000 per person and double that amount for a husband and wife filing a joint return.

SALES TAX

The retail sales tax is 6 percent for most tangible personal property sold to the ultimate consumer. Some counties levy a discretionary sales surtax up to an additional 1 percent. Groceries, prescription medicines, household fuels, and most services are exempt.

PROPERTY TAX

There is no state-level property tax. Such levies are imposed by counties, cities, and special districts. The state has a constitutional homestead exemption on the first $25,000 of assessed valuation of an owner-occupied residence.

RANKING REPORT

According to *State Government Finances,* among the 50 states, Florida ranks 12th from the most favorable (tied with Oregon) in total state taxes per capita ($1,037) when only state levies are considered. According to *The Rating Guide to Life in America's Fifty States,* it is 28th in property taxes per capita ($612).

For more complete tax information contact the Florida Department of Revenue, Office of Taxpayer Assistance, 5050 West Tennessee St., Tallahassee, FL 32399-0100, 904-488-6800.

Note: The above information is based on applicable tax law data available at the time of publication. Because such laws and tax rates are subject to change, professional assistance should be sought if tax implications are critical to a relocation decision.

THE COUNTRY CLUB OF MOUNT DORA

MOUNT DORA, FLORIDA

1400 Country Club Blvd.
Mount Dora, FL 32757
352-735-0115 / 800-213-6132
Fax: 352-735-1706

Developer: Morrison Homes

Year of initial property sales/rentals: 1991

Total land area: 440 acres

Average elevation: 180 feet

Location: North-central Florida; Lake County; on U.S. Highway 441, just north of its intersection with State Highway 46; 30 miles northwest of downtown Orlando; 10 miles east of Leesburg.

Nearest airport with scheduled commercial service: Orlando International (48 miles)

Current number of housing units with year-round occupants: 325

Projected number of housing units: 745 (1999)

Resident eligibility: There are no age restrictions for residency. It is estimated, however, that more than 65% of homeowners are retired or semiretired with only about 5% of the households having children under the age of 18 as permanent occupants.

Community visit/tour incentive program: None

Suggested newspaper: *Orlando Sentinel,* 633 N. Orange Ave., Orlando, FL 32801 (800-359-5353)

WHY THE COUNTRY CLUB OF MOUNT DORA?

Atlanta-based **Morrison Homes**, a subsidiary of the largest and oldest homebuilder in Great Britain (George Wimpey, PLC), is a company that has vigorously competed with new U.S. housing markets in recent years. California, Georgia, Florida, Texas, and Arizona have been principal target states to date, with additional expansion likely in the near future.

The word "quaint" must have found its way into the English language after someone touring Florida found **Mount Dora**, a town with a population of less than 8,000. Few small towns in America have enjoyed more generous media attention. The *New York Post*, never known to be a promoter of southern migration, proclaimed Mount Dora to be "as rare as a snowflake in the Sunshine State." *Sunshine,* the magazine of South Florida, called it "nirvana," the place for a blissful life. *Money* magazine's retirement panel, after analyzing climate, housing and living costs, cultural and educational amenities, available health care, and the incidence of crime, went so far as to rank Mount Dora first in Florida and third in the nation as the best of all places to retire. The magazine of the largest travel club in the country—the *American Automobile Association*—painted an elegant and detailed picture postcard description of a town whose streets take you back to a bygone era, reminiscent of a classic movie about idyllic life in small-town New England.

The countryside of **Lake County** is not typical Florida. In a state characterized by flatlands and endless stretches of sand, this part of the tropical peninsula is embellished with approximately 1,400 named, freshwater lakes, undulating hills and more oaks than palm trees. Mount Dora is on the chain of lakes that connects with the inland waterway and the **Atlantic Ocean**. With elevations of more than 180 feet above sea level, Mount Dora qualifies as a mountain retreat by Florida standards. Proximity to one of the most popular entertainment/educational attractions on earth—**Disney World** and all its satellite leisure inducements—puts the **Country Club of Mount Dora (CCMD)** less than an hour from a place that people travel thousands of miles to experience. If ever there was an incentive for grandchildren and other loved ones to visit, what could be more motivating? All in all, this is a town with a leg up on most of the competition in the retirement sweepstakes.

WHO'S IN CHARGE?

The Country Club of Mount Dora (CCMD) is a deed-restricted community with a homeowners association serving 12 separate neighborhoods. Infrastructure construction is performed by a community development district (CDD) created for that purpose. Water and sewer systems are owned and serviced by the city of Mount Dora. Roads and drainage are maintained by the CDD, the HOA, and the city. Morrison Homes will relinquish control of the property when all or a substantial number of remaining units are sold. The nonprofit **Homeowners' Association of the Country Club of Mount Dora (HOA)** will at that point become the owners and administrators of the development. Until then, a master HOA board of directors, consisting of three representatives of the developer and two elected by residents, is responsible for administrative oversight and policy development. A $41 per month fee paid by residents is used to sustain property management staffing, and to maintain common grounds, street lights, and dusk-to-dawn security arrangements. Mandatory complete lawn care (including fertilization, weed and insect control, mulching, tree and shrub trimming, as well as mowing, edging, and clean up) is required in seven of the 12 community entities for a fee of $70 to $80 per month.

A property management firm is retained by the developer to carry out administrative and maintenance responsibilities. The services of such a company will likely continue after transfer of ownership and operational responsibilities pass to the HOA at a future date. An architectural review board deals with the development and enforcement of property modification standards. A bimonthly newsletter is published under the sponsorship of the community activities committee of the HOA. All writing, editing, and layout functions are done by volunteer residents. In addition to serving as a medium to disseminate community information about developments and operations, it also serves up a lively potion of personal anecdotes collected and submitted by neighborhood reporters.

THE WEATHER REPORT

The winter season, for as long as there have been paved roads, train rails and airports, has signaled the massive tourist and vacation pilgrimage from north to south. From New England and the Ohio Valley, to deep within the Canadian interior, it sometimes seems that all but a few have deserted home and hearth for the comfort of America's prime winter escape hatch. For those who choose Florida as a year-round residence, however, that migratory direction does have a reverse gear. Summers in the "Sunshine State" can be less than perfect. High humidities and temperatures well into the 90s are not for everyone. It is also true, however, that this region of Florida does not spawn quite the same heat extremes as those found further south. Fortunately, the rainy season does favor summertime, tending to moderate high seasonal temperatures with afternoon thundershowers. Florida's reputation for hosting hurricanes does not really apply to this inland part of the state. This hinterland location offers substantial protection from the wrath of the severe storms that can ravage coastal areas.

Using **Orlando** weather data (the nearest reporting station to Mount Dora), average daily high and low temperatures for three winter months and for three summer months are as follows:

December: high 73/low 51   **January:** high 71/low 49

February: high 73/low 50   **June:** high 90/low 72

July: high 91/low 73   **August:** high 91/low 73

Average annual rainfall: 54 inches
Average annual snowfall: trace

HOME SWEET HOME

Approximately 95 percent of housing is single-family, detached construction. The rest are attached cottages. Detached units vary widely in price from the low $130s to upwards of $500,000, with floor space ranging from 1,580 to as much as 6,000 square feet. Custom homes in the upper brackets of this category are contracted with a highly regarded local independent builder. Attached golf villas with about 1,322 square feet are priced near $120,000.

A collection of nine model homes gives prospective buyers an opportunity to inspect every detail of construction and options for interior features. The community has won several awards from the **Lake County Parade of Homes** for both exterior and interior innovations. Standard features include concrete block construction; complete landscaping with sprinkler system; covered lanai; ceramic tile flooring at entry, baths, and kitchen/breakfast nook; double vanities and Roman tubs in master bath; underground utilities; and a Morrison blanket warranty program.

MONEY MATTERS

The nearest location to Mount Dora for which cost-of-living research data can be found is Orlando. While it is true that there may be cost impact factors affecting one or the other of the two areas, this is the only practical parallel that can be drawn. Greater Orlando is found to have a surprisingly moderate level of living cost. Survey findings on selected categories of consumer spending show a composite index of 1.6 percent below the average of 315 metropolitan and nonmetropolitan areas of the country that are included in the survey. Among six weighted groups of products and services analyzed, utilities showed the highest comparative cost at 16.3 percent above the average, and health costs at 8.7 percent above average. The remaining four categories showed below average results, each with more heavily weighted factors: groceries, 3.3 percent; housing, 6.5 percent; transportation, 1.5 percent; miscellaneous goods and services (the most heavily weighted of all categories), 2.8 percent.

Property taxes, after a $25,000 exemption for qualified households, are based on a millage rate of 22.8740 per $1,000 of assessed value (includes county, schools, and special districts). Membership in the country club requires an initiation fee in varying amounts from $750 (single/social) to $3,500 (full golf/family option), with monthly dues ranging from $35 to $165 within those same membership parameters. Proportionate fee reductions are given for seasonal golf applicants (six months of the year). Membership in the club is prerequisite to residents having access to amenities located there (golf, tennis, swimming, etc.).

TAKE GOOD CARE OF YOURSELF

A 182-bed in-patient health care institution with 125 affiliated physicians, **Florida Hospital/Waterman**, is in nearby **Eustis**, just 7 miles from the CCMD entrance. A new out-patient extension facility was opened in late 1997 with physician offices and a diagnosis/evaluation/surgery center. Five other hospitals serve Lake County. A recent count of practicing health care professionals showed 224 physicians and 68 dentists. **Florida Hospital/ Orlando**, about 35 minutes away, is the largest cardiac treatment center in the state with the most experience in bypass surgery, ranking third in the nation in that specialty.

Eleven extended care/assisted living/nursing home facilities, with a total of more than 1,300 beds, are located in the county. Two of them are within a 5-mile radius of CCMD.

PLACES TO GO, THINGS TO DO

It should come as no surprise that golf holds center stage on the recreational calendar. The 18-hole, par-72 championship course, designed by **Lloyd Clifton**, has more than its share of distinctive qualities. The layout provides ample variation and playability. Each hole seems to have its own unique character. Fairways are decorated with generous stands of oaks and pines. Water features grace all but four of the 18 holes.

The elegant clubhouse caters to golfers in style, with a full-service pro-shop and complete locker rooms. Golf lessons and seminars are regularly scheduled. More than a golfer's sanctuary, it is the social center for all residents. Residents have access to four lighted tennis courts, a heated pool with Jacuzzi and cabana baths, a game room, a dining room, outdoor patio dining, and a bar and grill.

Clubs and interest groups center on bridge, men's/women's/couples golf and tennis, water aerobics, a monthly "coffee connection" featuring outside speakers, and travel and investment clubs. Free first-run movies are shown weekly. Group travel covers everything from day trips to extended international cruises. Art lessons are offered for beginners and intermediates.

Off-site leisure activities expand to almost unlimited choices and preferences. In Mount Dora and neighboring **Tavares,** there are 10-pin bowling alleys with year-round league play. Mount Dora is the home of one of the nation's largest lawn bowling clubs, carrying on an ancient tradition brought to America by early British and Scottish immigrants. The **Mount Dora School of Fine Arts** offers instruction and lectures in watercolor, oil, and acrylic painting; hand lettering; and rug hooking. The local YMCA operates a "wellness center" with complete fitness programs.

Long dubbed "the festival city," Mount Dora hosts special events and celebrations in numbers disproportionate to its size and resources, sometimes attracting upwards of 200,000 visitors. Art festivals, antique auto and boat shows, sailing regattas, invitational golf tournaments, bicycle assemblies, pet parades and contests, craft and garden fairs, Christmas lighting ceremonies and holiday parades, flea market festivals and fashion shows all vie for public attention. There's live indoor theater and Shakespeare in the Park. All these attractions are at hand for CCMD residents to pick and choose if off-site adventure beckons.

The ultimate exposure to great entertainment and educational enlightenment is a little more than 40 miles from CCMD. **Disney's Magic Kingdom** and **EPCOT Center, Universal** and **MGM Studios**, and **Florida Sea World**, are at the center of an area filled with attractions. It is the theme park hub for approximately 65 other similar attractions, ranging from giant expositions to small, nature-oriented, one-of-a-kind showcases. A bit further out is another top attraction, **Cypress Gardens**, in **Winter Haven**, about 45 miles southwest of Orlando (about 55 miles from Mount Dora). Claiming title to being "Florida's first theme park" (established in 1936), it features a star-studded ice show, variety acts, and a widely acclaimed reptile "discovery" program. All said and done, central Florida is a destination that draws millions of visitors from throughout the world, and it's practically on the CCMD doorstep.

SAFE AND SECURE

A dusk-to-dawn private security officer patrols the property seven days a week. Police and fire protection are provided by the city of Mount Dora, including an emergency response system. A combination police/fire station is located about 2½ miles from the community entrance. A volunteer crime watch program was initiated in 1997—a communications network linking residents, block captains, CCMD security, and the local police department.

LET'S GO SHOPPING

A full-service grocery store is a mere half mile from the CCMD entrance. Mount Dora is a great place for antiques (more than a dozen shops), crafts, gifts, fashions, books, jewelry, flowers, and such. A vintage English tea room, ice cream parlors, candle and doll makers, and a clock shop together add an element of charm not found in many places. All are within a few blocks.

Florida Twin Markets, also known as **Renninger's**, open on weekends, is advertised as the state's largest indoor antiques and collectibles market with a medley of shops representing more than 200 dealers. For more serious shopping in the realm of household needs and professional services, where variety of selection and price levels is a priority, there is **Leesburg** (about 10 miles off), and ultimately Orlando (little more than 30 minutes away). It's just a few minutes' drive to **Lake Square Mall**, located between Leesburg and Tavares, where 85 retail outlets, including local and national chains, leave few shopping needs unmet.

CRESCENT OAKS

TARPON SPRINGS, FLORIDA

1017 Kings Way Lane
Tarpon Springs, FL 34689
813-937-7661
Fax: 813-934-4280

Developer: U.S. Home Corporation

Year of initial property sales/rental: 1989

Total land area: 850 acres

Average elevation: less than 15 feet

Location: On the Gulf coast of mid-Florida; Pinellas County; far northern suburb of the Clearwater-St. Petersburg peninsula; off Alternate U.S. Highway 19; about 35 miles northwest of downtown Tampa.

Nearest airport with scheduled commercial service: Tampa International (15 miles)

Current number of housing units with year-round occupants: 310

Projected number of housing units: 434 (1999)

Resident eligibility: There is no age restriction, but it is estimated that more than half the permanent residents are retired or semiretired. Only about 10% of households are said to have children under 18 years of age living at home.

Community visit/tour incentive program: Three preview models available; no lodging incentive package

Suggested newspaper: *St. Petersburg Times,* P.O. Box 1121, St. Petersburg, FL 33731 (813-893-8111)

WHY CRESCENT OAKS?

Crescent Oaks was developed by **U.S. Home Corporation (USHC),** one of the nation's 10 largest single-family homebuilders. **Rutenberg Homes,** since 1953, has been the luxury home division of USHC. The recipient of numerous honors, it is the nation's only three-time winner of the "National Builder of the Year" award by the National Association of Home Builders, most recently in 1994. That same year, USHC was singled out of more than 12,000 of its industry peers by **Home Buyers Warranty Corporation** as a "Blue Diamond Builder" for its commitment to excellence in construction and customer satisfaction.

The Crescent Oaks property layout map shows that most homesites are bordered by a golfing green, a wooded conservation area, a pond, or a combination of these features, while the architecture lends a Mediterranean ambiance.

Its geographical location in the **Tampa-St. Petersburg-Clearwater** retirement enclave places the community in the midst of a metropolitan area of abundant activity and appeal for mature adults.

Tarpon Springs, home of Crescent Oaks, is truly a unique place. It was a fashionable winter resort before the turn of the 20th century. Its strong heritage of Greek origins has had a substantial influence on its contemporary character. It was from that country's sponge-producing industry, transplanted on the west coast of Florida, that the town became a world-famous sponge diving center. Tarpon Springs is also the site of one of the best known Greek Orthodox churches in America, home of the largest and most elaborate Epiphany rituals in the country. Nowhere is the Greek flavor more evident than in the many ethnic restaurants serving Moussaka, Felo, Keftedes, and roast leg of lamb (with a generous Greek salad on the side).

WHO'S IN CHARGE?

The community is under the administrative control and direction of a professional management company. It is supported by membership fees generated by the nonprofit homeowners association. The management company is accountable for all typical oversight and maintenance responsibilities (security arrangements, common area upkeep, enforcement of deed restrictions, facility maintenance, etc.). It operates in tandem with the homeowners group in setting fees and making policy decisions.

THE WEATHER REPORT

The **Tampa Bay** area, perched on the **Gulf of Mexico**, enjoys land and sea breezes that tend to moderate the subtropical climate. The west coast of the Florida Peninsula has been aptly described as the "suncoast." Late spring days typically offer the most consistent sunshine. On a year-round basis, one can expect clear skies for as much as 70 percent of the daylight hours. Mild winters, of course, have been the big attraction for generations of "snowbirds" running from the harsh winters of the northern states and Canada. Normal winter lows in the 50s and highs in the lower 70s are hard to resist as an alternative to icy streets and frost-bitten toes.

As with virtually all climate choices, for most people it is not perfection. The subtropical temperatures of summer can be troublesome to those who do not tolerate heat very well, especially when combined with high humidity (often in the 80s early in the day but dropping into the mid-60 range later on). But humidity levels are not as oppressive as one might expect and late afternoon and early evening summer temperatures can drop rather quickly from the low 90s to the low 70s whenever a thunderstorm blows in. Average daily high and low temperature readings for three winter months and three summer months are reported by the U.S. National Oceanic and Atmospheric Administration as follows:

December: high 72/low 52   **January:** high 70/low 50

February: high 71/low 52   **June:** high 89/low 73

July: high 90/low 74   **August:** high 90/low 74

Average annual precipitation: 44 inches
Average annual snowfall: extremely rare

HOME SWEET HOME

U.S. Home built and sold more homes during 1995 than any other Tampa Bay area builder, according to an industry report published that year. The company places great emphasis on value and affordability while offering purchasers a wide variety of floor plans, elevations, and interior options. A strong warranty program is also in place.

The Coventry neighborhood at Crescent Oaks offers one- and two-story villas ranging in size from 1,575 to 2,694 square feet. Pricing begins at $156,950 and tops out at $207,950 (as of November 1996). Other sections feature homes that range from 2,200 to 4,995 square feet, priced from $210,450 to more than $300,000. There are no condominiums, townhouses or apartments in the development. All are custom-built single-family dwellings. The size of homesites ready for residential construction are generally 14,000 to 16,000 square feet, priced from $70,000 to $149,000.

The overall development has been projected for no more than 434 homes. With a total property size of 850 acres, there is a generous ratio at buildout of almost two acres per household. All utility lines are below ground. Water supply and a waste disposal system are provided by municipal and county utility services.

MONEY MATTERS

A ranking of 78 U.S. towns and cities in *Where to Retire* (1991) showed the Tampa/St. Petersburg metropolitan area to be 45th from the least expensive among those compared. While real estate and utility costs were 22 percent and 19 percent, respectively, below the average of the entire sample, health costs were 15 percent higher. In another statistical review, Tampa was shown to have a lower cost of living in all but five of 39 selected cities with which it was compared. Only one of the five with lower costs, Omaha, revealed a relatively significant difference. Tampa scored precisely even with Kansas City and St. Louis, Missouri, and Orlando, Florida. The indices used in the tabulation were drawn from data in the *ACCRA Cost of Living Index* (2nd quarter, 1996), covering housing, food, transportation, health care, utilities, and miscellaneous goods and services.

Membership fees at Crescent Oaks depend in part upon the neighborhood in which you live. Coventry, the area in which the more moderately sized and priced villas are located, require homeowner participation in both the

Coventry and the **Crescent Oaks Master Association**. The former affiliation ($80 a month) provides for yard sodding and lawn maintenance, pest control, exterior painting, sidewalks, and sprinkler system upkeep. **The Master Association**, to which all residents belong ($70 a month) without benefit of the aforementioned services, covers security gate operations, lake maintenance, and upkeep on entrances, streets, and lighting.

There are various options for membership in the country club. The most expensive, for a full privilege package that includes golf, tennis, swimming, fitness, and clubhouse access, requires $5,700 in transferable and nontransferable initiation fees plus $226 a month dues for a family ($191 for single). A "grand slam" membership provides for full privileges for everything but golf, which is limited. Initiation fees drop under this category to $2,250 with an $88 a month dues payment for a family. A social membership (without tennis or golf) calls for a $500 initiation fee and $45 a month dues.

TAKE GOOD CARE OF YOURSELF

The Tampa Bay-St. Petersburg metropolitan area has been one of the nation's preeminent retirement centers for many decades. As a result, there is an abundance of health care facilities and services throughout the region. Every conceivable specialization, especially for older people, is readily at hand. Medicare-approved hospitals with round-the-clock emergency service, all within a 5- to 15-mile distance from Crescent Oaks, include **Columbia New Port Richey** with 414 beds and a number of specialized care units. Other notable full service hospitals include **Morton Plant Hospital** in Clearwater, **Mease Dunedin** (in nearby downtown **Dunedin**), and **Mease Countryside** in **Safety Harbor**, just east of Clearwater. The **University Psychiatry Center** on the campus of the **University of South Florida** (Tampa) is a fully accredited and licensed facility dealing with a broad range of emotional and chemical dependency problems.

PLACES TO GO, THINGS TO DO

The preeminent recreational focal point is the Crescent Oaks championship 18-hole par-72 golf course. The greens stretch 6,575 yards, encircling the entire community. A driving range, locker room facilities, and a complete pro shop complement the facility. A seasoned PGA professional arranges tournaments, provides expert instruction, and assists members with whatever needs they might have. Men's and ladies' golf associations dominate the residents' leisure activity calendar.

The clubhouse makes a grand impression. It is a sprawling structure topped with an exquisite Spanish tile roof. A porticoed main entrance, an elegant dining room, a well-appointed meeting room and other appealing features make for a popular community social center. Bridge, mah jong, and canasta clubs meet regularly. An adjacent Olympic-size swimming pool and four plexipave tennis courts accent the complex.

Entertainment and cultural attractions are located within minutes of the community in the nearby metropolitan area. Performing arts, museums, libraries, sports stadiums, historical landmarks, and yacht clubs abound. A 10-screen cinema is just 6 miles from the Crescent Oaks entrance. **John Chestnut Park**, an enchanting haven, is 10 minutes away. Every imaginable water activity and performance spectacle is found nearby. The **Konger Coral Sea Aquarium** in Tarpon Springs is a magical display of sea life indigenous to the Gulf of Mexico and the Caribbean waters. Professional sports teams, most notably the **Tampa Bay Buccaneers**, in recent years have brought an energetic fan devotion to the area. A new major league baseball team is scheduled to come to bat in 1998.

The world-renowned **Busch Gardens** in Tampa draws throngs of visitors to behold more than 3,000 exotic animals in an untamed wilderness, to view dolphin and "Hollywood on Ice" shows, and to experience some of the great thrill rides for which the park is famous. Theme parks, botanical gardens, race tracks, and the outstanding **Florida Aquarium and Marine Science Center** (along the revamped downtown Tampa waterfront) are here, too. The **University of South Florida** and the **University of Tampa** are prized educational institutions that provide collegiate enrichment in sports and entertainment, as well as learning opportunities.

The coastal accents of Clearwater and St. Petersburg long have been popular attractions for visitors and residents alike. Spotless beaches, unspoiled islands, and gentle surf along with affordable prices attract a steady stream of sun worshippers. St. Petersburg boasts a thriving arts community that includes the **Salvador Dali Museum** and a host of local art galleries.

SAFE AND SECURE

Access to the development is controlled at manned entrance gates. The **Pinellas County Sheriff's Department** provides law enforcement. An emergency 911 phone system is in place.

LET'S GO SHOPPING

While there are no business establishments within the community, there is within a 1- to 3-mile radius of the entry gate a virtually endless variety of retail and service outlets. Among them are major food markets, branch banks, specialty shops, outlet stores, and a full range of professional services. Major malls and stand-alone department stores are all within a 10- to 20-minute drive. **Boatyard Village** in Clearwater, nestled in a cove on Tampa Bay, is a recreated 1890s fishing village, featuring an appealing variety of restaurants, boutiques, and galleries. It is one of many such shopping and dining showcases in the area.

FOUR LAKES GOLF CLUB

WINTER HAVEN, FLORIDA

990 LaQuinta Blvd.
Winter Haven, FL 33881
941-299-4777 / 800-826-7076
Fax: 941-299-7826

Developer: CRF Communities

Year of initial property sales/rental: 1995

Total land area: 500 acres

Average elevation: Under 150 feet

Location: Mid-state interior; Polk County; on State Highway 544, off U.S. Hwy. 27; 3 miles northeast of Winter Haven; 35 miles southwest of Orlando; 45 miles east of Tampa; 15 miles east of Lakeland.

Nearest airport with scheduled commercial service: Orlando International (40 miles)

Current number of housing units with year-round occupants: 150

Projected number of housing units: 850 (2003)

Resident eligibility: 80% of the households must have at least one person 55 years of age or older. Other occupants must be at least 40 years of age.

Community visit/tour incentive program: A two-night, three-day stay is offered to "qualified" prospective buyers.

Suggested newspaper: *The Ledger*, 401 So. Missouri Ave., Lakeland, FL 33801 (941-687-7000)

WHY FOUR LAKES GOLF CLUB?

A community of prefabricated homes, **Four Lakes Golf Club** is one of 433 such developments in this one Florida county! The FLGC developer, **CRF Communities**, is the largest provider of its kind in the state, with 11 developments. There are 26 CRF communities across central Florida, 23 of which are completely sold out. FLGC, the newest of CRF's properties to come on the market, is one of the three communities that are still available. The manufactured home industry, here in the most dynamic of the nation's leading retirement states, has made a huge impact on home-buying patterns among retirees. Value and affordability have been the watchwords for tens of thousands of relocated families who have chosen the prefabricated home option.

CRF Communities has been recognized on four separate occasions by *Sunshine State Senior Citizen Magazine* as "Manufactured Home Community Developer/Operator of the Year," a testimonial to the firm's resident relations standards. Unlike most traditional site-built retirement communities, the developer in this instance maintains ownership and property management responsibilities for the life span of the community, rather than turning the property over to a homeowner's association after all site sales have been completed.

Located at the geographical center of the Florida peninsula, **Winter Haven** (population about 25,000) is at the Four Lakes doorstep (only three miles from the entry gate) and serves as the off-site commercial, entertainment, and activity center for residents. Less than an hour's drive to the northeast or to the west are two of Florida's major cities, **Orlando** and **Tampa,** each with major metropolitan leisure and educational attractions, regional health care resources, and international air travel terminals.

WHO'S IN CHARGE?

Ownership of homesites and all amenities, and responsibility for all community facilities, common area upkeep, security, and program planning/implementation rests with the developer under a permanent commitment. Funding for support of the clubhouse and all of the foregoing services is derived from an annual lifetime land lease for the site upon which each home is built (see housing section).

Free of financial and operational obligations, resident volunteers take an active part in promoting and arranging social activities, including publication of a monthly newsletter.

THE WEATHER REPORT

The central Florida terrain is characterized by inland lakes, which tend to keep relative humidity high year-round. Summer nighttime levels often reach 90 percent, with afternoon readings in the comfortable 40- to 50-percent range, and with further moderation during winter months. Scattered afternoon thunderstorms are common during the rainy season (June through September) and tend to keep temperatures more bearable, rarely rising to above 95 degrees. Summer breezes generally contribute further to comfort levels.

During the winter season when Florida bulges at the seams with tourists and resort visitors, rainfall in this part of the state is light. Temperatures after sundown can turn chilly, rising rapidly during the day with typically bright sunshine and pleasant afternoons. The inland location around Winter Haven is relatively safe from hurricanes, because such severe storms lose much of their gusto as they travel over extended stretches of land.

Average daily high and low temperatures for three winter months and three summer months are approximately the same as for the Orlando area, summarized by the U.S. National Oceanic and Atmospheric Administration as follows:

December: high 73/low 51   **January:** high 71/low 49

February: high 73/low 50   **June:** high 90/low 72

July: high 91/low 73   **August:** high 91/low 73

Average annual precipitation: 48 inches
Average annual snowfall: trace

HOME SWEET HOME

As in most manufactured home communities, residents at Four Lakes buy their homes and lease the lots upon which the home stands, thereby avoiding a significant part of the purchase outlay. Such lot leases range from $220 to $450 a month, in accordance with location and size.

All homes are detached, single-family dwellings. Prices range from $55,000 to $120,000. Floor plans are virtually limitless, with custom options readily incorporated into basic layouts. Sizes range from 900 to more than 2,400 square feet. Seventeen models are open for inspection. Standard features include solid brick foundations, fully equipped kitchens, aluminum carports, central heat and air conditioning, fully landscaped lots with underground sprinkler systems, screen rooms, drapery and carpeting, window treatments, and a variety of other practical and cosmetic components. Home exteriors are virtually maintenance free.

An early purchase program enables a buyer to close on a new home and then place it in either a leaseback or rental program. Under the former, the developer uses the home as either a model or guest house, leaving the owner with a variety of tax benefits and deductions until he or she is ready to occupy. The rental program allows the owner to simply rent the property prior to occupancy or turn it over to the developer, wherein the home is marketed to seasonal guests for short-term use, providing significant income potential in addition to tax write-offs. A delayed closing program allows the buyer to select and hold a lot of choice and freeze the current price for a specified period of time.

MONEY MATTERS

Orlando is the nearest location for which there is reliable cost of living data available. Only 35 miles from Four Lakes and sharing central inland characteristics, it can be assumed to be reasonably close in these measurements (perhaps slightly higher for being a metropolitan area, as compared to the less-urbanized Winter Haven). The composite index among selected urban areas for the categories analyzed showed Orlando to be 1.6 percent under the average for all cities in the survey. Four of the six measurements (groceries, housing, transportation, and miscellaneous goods and services) were shown to be below the national average. Two, utilities and health care, were well above average (utilities by a substantial 16.3 percent).

The lot lease payment, mentioned in the "Home Sweet Home" section, includes the cost of the lot, professional management staffing to sustain community programs, maintenance of common property, and the security system. Of particular significance is the fact that there are no property taxes on the assessed value of the lot and home other than a very modest "decal" fee of $150 (on an average-size manufactured unit). The lease amount on the lot includes taxes due the state. Sales tax on retail purchases is limited to the basic state levy of 6 percent. **Polk County** jurisdictions patronized by Four Lakes residents do not exercise any add-on option permitted under law.

TAKE GOOD CARE OF YOURSELF

Winter Haven Hospital is a 579-bed community-operated, not-for-profit, accredited facility with 24-hour emergency room service. Just 5 miles from Four Lakes, it is staffed by physicians and surgeons representing virtually all fields of medical practice. Also in Winter Haven is **Regency Medical Center,** a 50-bed hospital specializing in obstetrics and gynecology and also offering an eating disorders treatment program. There are five more hospitals in Polk County, including **Lakeland Regional Medical Center**, and ten clinics with outpatient services. Approximately 200 physicians and dentists maintain offices within the county. The **Tampa Bay** and Orlando metropolitan areas, less than an hour away, boast the ultimate in high technology medicine and treatment.

PLACES TO GO, THINGS TO DO

The 16,000 square foot Four Lakes clubhouse is the social and recreational centerpiece of the community, housing its own restaurant/lounge, pool/game room, a fully equipped exercise room and sauna, an arts and crafts room (with a kiln), and a library. The adjoining 6,300-yard-long, 18-hole championship golf course is accented by rolling fairways and manicured greens. Concrete cart paths wind about the entire course. An Olympic-size heated swimming pool, lighted tennis and shuffleboard courts, and hard surface hiking and walking trails add to the generous mix of recreational choices. A unique activities program hosted by the developer provides for ongoing intercommunity social events that bring residents from many of the neighboring CRF communities together.

The Four Lakes community affairs committee promotes and supports a long list of activities. Among them are golf, bowling, and shuffleboard tournaments, community dances, pot-luck dinners, arts and crafts classes, day tours to nearby attractions, fishing trips, holiday and special event parties, bingo, extended group travel trips, swimming aerobics, and game clubs.

The Winter Haven/Polk County area might well be dubbed the Minnesota of the south. More than one-third of the city's surface consists of small lakes.

The county encompasses more than 2,000 square miles, within which there are more than 500 lakes!

Cypress Gardens, one of Florida's most popular tourist attractions, is just outside Winter Haven's city limits. Drawing more than one million visitors annually, this 223-acre botanical Eden features a world-famous water-ski revue and a butterfly conservatory. The state's premiere visitor magnets—**Busch Gardens**, the **Walt Disney World Resort Complex**, **Disney-MGM Studios, Sea World, Universal Studios,** and the **Kennedy Space Center**, among others, are all within an easy drive. Less than 75 miles east or west are the famous beaches of the Atlantic Ocean and the Gulf of Mexico.

Theatre Winter Haven, highly acclaimed as one of the finest community theaters in the southeast, stages five productions each season in the city's 350-seat auditorium in the **Chain O'Lakes Convention Center.** **Polk Community College** boasts a 500-seat theater that draws regional and national talent for music, drama, and dance. Music lovers flock to the annual two-day **Bach Festival,** which celebrated its 20th anniversary in 1995. Fifteen movie theaters and a senior center add to the mix of entertainment options.

Eighteen of Winter Haven's lakes are interconnected, forming the area's "Chain of Lakes" character. Public boat ramps are scattered along lake shores, some with beaches, piers, or picnic grounds. Winter Haven is recognized as one of the water-skiing capitals of the world. Fishing, of course, is popular, with countless anglers on the banks or adrift in boats.

Winter Haven is also a baseball fan's spring training delight. It is here that the major league **Cleveland Indians** tune up their team before each season's play. Golf, tennis, bowling, shuffleboard, and roller skating dominate the participatory sports scene.

The local public library, founded in 1910, houses more than 50,000 volumes, as well as records, video and audio cassettes, compact discs, cameras, art prints, and sculpture. Other features include book reviews, children's reading programs, and a computerized index and research system.

SAFE AND SECURE

An attractive entry gatehouse signals a comprehensive security arrangement. Access to the property is under manned supervision seven days a week, 10 hours a day. Gates remain locked to outsiders the rest of the day. Twenty-four-hour patrol personnel assure optimal protection from intruders. The **Polk County Sheriff's Office**, along with CRF civilian security personnel, provide a program that involves neighborhood watch and educational programs to help homeowners maximize anticrime measures. Street patrols in Sheriff's Department vehicles, as well as in marked community guard cars, cover the development around the clock.

LET'S GO SHOPPING

Such close proximity to Winter Haven makes the town a primary marketplace for most household purchases and service needs. Department stores, specialty shops, and mini-malls offer a full selection of retail merchandise, professional services, and trade outlets. During harvest seasons, citrus juices and related products are selling at every turn, typically at very attractive prices. Full-service food markets are conveniently located within a 3- to 5-mile distance from Four Lakes. A regional shopping mall is about 10 miles away.

KINGS POINT IN TAMARAC

TAMARAC, FLORIDA

7600 Nob Hill Rd.
Tamarac, FL 33321
954-722-0121 / 800-233-6569
Fax: 954-721-5833

Developer: Lennar Homes, Inc.

Year of initial property sales/rentals: 1983

Total land area: 350 acres

Average elevation: 12 feet

Location: East coast of south Florida; Broward County; off the Florida Turnpike, just north of the Everglades Parkway (U.S. 75); about 15 miles northwest of Fort Lauderdale; 35 miles north of Miami.

Nearest airport with scheduled commercial service: Fort Lauderdale/Hollywood International (20 miles)

Current number of housing units with year-round occupants: 2,650

Projected number of housing units: 5,471

Resident eligibility: At least one person in the household must be at least 55 years of age.

Community visit/tour incentive program: None

Suggested newspaper: *The Sun Sentinel*, 5555 Nob Hill Rd., Sunrise, FL 33313 (305-572-2000)

WHY KINGS POINT?

By any measurement of Florida retirement community expectations, **Kings Point** is among the largest and most well-appointed. A multimillion-dollar, 60,000-square-foot clubhouse reflects the comprehensiveness of its programs and activities. **Lennar Homes, Inc.**, the developer, is Florida's largest homebuilder and prominent among the nation's most experienced promoters of active adult communities. The company began its home construction operations in this state in 1954 and maintains a separate active adult home-building division. More recent new markets have been opened in Texas, Arizona, and California.

Kings Point is billed as the "gateway to **Coral Springs**," strategically located between **Fort Lauderdale** and **Boca Raton**, two of Florida's higher-profile cities. It is in the midst of a highway network that makes freeway travel readily accessible. The concentration of towns and cities in the area makes virtually any kind of activity or service available within minutes of

147

home. **Tamarac**, the community's address location, has an estimated population of over 50,000, with more than 2,400 business establishments.

WHO'S IN CHARGE?

Lennar Management Corp., a property administration arm of the developer-owner, is responsible for maintenance and control of the recreation satellite community. Monthly maintenance fees range from $208 to $224, depending upon the neighborhood in which the home is located, standard or premium lot selection, and size of the dwelling. These assessments pay for a rather extensive list of services and benefits, including water and sewer, trash collection, landscaping, external pest control, neighborhood recreation area maintenance, main clubhouse maintenance, private bus transportation system, cable TV, guard house and roving security, emergency alert system, and reserves for roof replacement, painting, and pavement resurfacing. In addition to such maintenance fees, each homeowner purchases a proprietary share in community recreation facilities. Such investments can be paid in advance ($5,988) or set up on a 30-year fixed-rate mortgage at $52 a month.

Each of the subdivisions has its own homeowners association, responsible for upkeep of amenities located within its neighborhood. A master association of homeowners is responsible for those common grounds, facilities, and programs that benefit the residents of the entire development, without regard to neighborhood. Once the community nears completion of property sales (now at almost 50 percent of projected buildout), ownership and operation of the entire project will be turned over to the residents' association.

A monthly newsletter is published by the clubhouse staff with contributions from management, residents, and outside interests. Primary attention is given to scheduling activities, classes, and neighborhood news.

THE WEATHER REPORT

Florida owns the sun. Or so one would think, noting the endless stream of tourist promotional brochures and glossy advertisements that saturate the media. "The Sunshine State" is no coincidental sobriquet. The planet's unimpeachable source of solar energy is packaged as one of its most important resources, luring winter vacationers for more than a century. From a more pragmatic perspective, the lower east coast of Florida is essentially a subtropical marine climate. Long and warm summers, with plentiful rainfall, are followed by pleasant, relatively dry winters. Prevailing easterly winds typically make higher seasonal temperatures more tolerable than they would be at an inland location. Real temperatures, regardless of wind conditions, also tend to be considerably lower on or near the coast than at interior locations. Freezing temperatures rarely reach coastal communities.

The hurricane season (normally during September and October) is often a concern but seldom a reality for the north-of-**Miami** portion of the coastline.

Construction codes here, and throughout most of the peninsula's eastern shores, maximize protection against wind damage.

Using Miami data (the nearest official reporting station), average daily high and low temperatures for three winter months and for three summer months are reported by the U.S. National Oceanic and Atmospheric Administration as follows:

December: high 77/low 61   **January:** high 75/low 59

February: high 76/low 60   **June:** high 88/low 75

July: high 89/low 76   **August:** high 89/low 77

Average annual rainfall: 56 inches
Average annual snowfall: none

HOME SWEET HOME

There are currently nine separate and distinct subdivisions or neighborhoods at Kings Point, with further future expansion on the drawing boards. Each has its own recreation center, consisting largely of a swimming pool, tennis and/or shuffleboard courts, and a cabana or pavilion. Some have additional athletic facilities. Most of the more than 3,300 living units are condominiums, each part of a modern four-story building and each accommodating between 44 and 64 apartments. The remainder are one-story villas, joined together in clusters of six to eight adjoining units.

Condominiums range in size from 839 to 2,658 square feet. Prices start at $60,000 and go up to $180,000. Villas are generally 1,830 to 2,272 square feet, with prices ranging from about the $120s to the mid-$150s. Homesites are typically adorned with sparkling waterways or landscaped gardens. Purchase packages include gourmet kitchens, well-appointed master suites, and screened terraces.

Water and sanitary sewer systems are provided by the city of Tamarac. Electric and telephone utility lines are underground.

MONEY MATTERS

A published survey of 78 U.S. towns and cities in *Where to Retire* (1991) placed the Miami area at 57th in the ranking from the least to the most expensive. The data showed real estate prices to be 10 percent under the average for the entire sample, 20 percent under for utility costs, and 15 percent over for health care costs. More recent living cost data in the *ACCRA Cost of Living Index* (2nd quarter, 1996) shows a composite index for six categories of products and services for Miami/**Dade County** (adjacent to Kings Point's **Broward County**) to be 8.4 percent above the average for all 315 locations in the survey. A breakdown of the six categories showed Miami to be above the norm in all groupings, as follows: groceries, 1.8 percent; housing, 9.2 percent;

utilities, 21.2 percent; transportation, 1.4 percent; health care, 13.5 percent; miscellaneous goods and services, 8.7 percent.

Monthly taxes for condominium units are based on the purchase price and applicable millage rate, currently 2.8 percent. Estimated monthly taxes on a home costing $95,000 would come to about $136; on a residence with a selling price of $140,000, taxes would be about $234 (figured with homestead exemption).

TAKE GOOD CARE OF YOURSELF

There is no dearth of health care providers and wellness specialists along the Coral Springs/Margate/Tamarac/Sunrise corridor. Within that 15-mile stretch of side-by-side communities, there are countless walk-in centers, medical officess, specialized therapeutic and rehabilitation services, assisted living and nursing home facilities, as well as full-service hospitals and clinics.

The closest inpatient care is **University Hospital,** a 269-bed acute condition facility located in Tamarac. In addition to emergency care and diagnostic surgical and rehabilitative services, a key program recently inaugurated is the **Arthritis Awareness Center** where customized treatment for each patient is a primary feature. A highlight of this modern resort-like setting is an indoor temperature-controlled therapeutic pool equipped with a hydraulic lift and other types of hydra-massage and exercise jets. **Florida Home Health,** for both Medicare and private patients, has been part of this hospital's program for more than two decades. Services include skilled nursing; physical, occupational, respiratory, enterostomal, and intravenous therapies; speech pathology; psychiatric nursing; medical social work; nutritional counseling; and home health aide services.

Other nearby hospitals include the 200-bed **Coral Springs Medical Center**, with a strong family and pediatrics program, and **Northwest Medical Center** in Margate (just minutes from Tamarac), which is an affiliate of **Columbia Healthcare Corporation**. Diabetic care and wound care centers are among their specialized programs.

PLACES TO GO, THINGS TO DO

The main clubhouse at Kings Point is one of the community's two crown jewels. It is a sprawling complex that offers considerably more leisure options for residents than might be expected. It has both indoor and outdoor oversized heated swimming pools. There are indoor and outdoor whirlpools to match. Embellishing the outdoor pools is the **Cabana Royale**, a shaded oasis accented by graceful palm trees and equipped with a generous spread of lounge chairs and tables.

Lighted tennis courts are just a few steps from the building. There is a weight room, a fully equipped aerobics center, and a cardiovascular unit. Three separate rooms are set aside for cards and other table games. Ping pong and billiards have their own enclosed space. Designated rooms for arts and crafts and for ceramics (with an enclosed kiln room) are popular corners of activity.

The 700-seat **Cabaret Royale,** off the main lobby, has been the glamorous showcase for an endless parade of show business celebrities, who appear on its stage season after season. And as if this wasn't enough of an entertainment lure, construction was completed in 1997 on **The Palace Theater for the Performing Arts,** the community's other crown jewel. This most impressive 1,000-seat auditorium, with its state-of-the-art production equipment and art-deco-style design, provides community social directors with a matchless venue to attract the top road-show and regional-theater talent available, including Broadway musicals and plays, symphonies, and yesteryear's big bands.

The roster of clubs, classes, and interest groups is said to number more than 200! Activities are designed for singles as well as couples, all under the supervision of a full-time activities director. The variety of choices has no parameters—bingo, bowling, ballroom dancing, drama, painting, photography, softball, group trips, line dancing, pottery, golf and tennis clubs for men and for women, table tennis, billiards, and on and on. Exercise and nutrition programs at the health club are designed for active adults who can take part in "aquacise" in the pool, group workouts, health-walking, and informative lectures on fitness and healthful menus.

Within a 35- to 40-mile stretch of highway from **West Palm Beach** to the north, and to Miami and **Coral Gables** to the south, there are unlimited leisure attractions. Professional and collegiate football, baseball, basketball, and hockey are practically around every corner. Just a few minutes from the Kings Point doorstep is the famed city of Fort Lauderdale, still a great drawing card for visitors looking for lots of vacation options—from shipwreck and reef diving to historical attractions, scattered waterfront resorts, discovery cruises, swamp safaris, recreation parks, and a string of first-rate museums. Among Fort Lauderdale's unique features are the brick pedestrian promenades lined with sidewalk cafes along its inviting sandy beaches.

There are golf courses without end throughout the area. The **Coral Springs City Centre Theatre** brings to town top stars of stage and screen, including Broadway productions and live performances especially for kids. The seashore is about 20 minutes away. There's pari-mutuel thoroughbred racing at world-famous **Hialeah,** harness racing at nearby **Pompano Park,** jai alai in Miami, and greyhound tracks just about everywhere, including neighboring **Hollywood.** The **Miami Metrozoo** is a 290-acre cageless showcase of more than 100 species of rare and exotic animals. The **Miami Seaquarium** is an internationally known marine life park. A few miles west of Tamarac into the **Everglades** is **Sawgrass Recreation Park,** where tours and exhibits offer insights into one of the nation's most interesting natural preserves.

There are numerous continuing education opportunities. Privately operated **Lynn University** in Boca Raton, less than 20 miles up the coast, offers a full complement of professional and continuing studies programs. Courses include nursing, interior design, human resources management, business information systems, and international business. **Florida Atlantic University,** at its two Fort Lauderdale campuses, offers classes in business, communication, criminal justice, and education, among others. **Broward Community College** serves 54,000 post-secondary students, many enrolled in its continuing education department. Electronics, engineering, journalism, and child care development are among its offerings at the north campus in **Coconut Creek,** no more than 10 minutes from Kings Point.

SAFE AND SECURE

An attended gatehouse or an automatic entry gate tied to a closed circuit television system stands at the entrance to each Kings Point neighborhood, enabling residents to screen all guests. Each home has an emergency medical alert and home intrusion system. At the touch of a button on a wall monitor or personal remote unit, an emergency signal is sent to a central control station from which police or medical assistance can be dispatched to the caller.

Police services are provided by the **Broward County Sheriff's Office.** The **City of Tamarac Fire Department** includes KP within its jurisdiction. Roving patrols of the KP internal security force make three rounds each night through the entire development.

LET'S GO SHOPPING

A full-service food market is within a mile of the community entrance. A major shopping mall in the adjacent town of Sunrise is about three miles distant. **Coral Square,** not much further in the opposite direction, is a 100-acre, meticulously landscaped regional mall with five major department stores, a food courtyard, and more than 140 specialty shops. **The Festival Flea Market** is the largest indoor enterprise of its kind in the area. More extensive commercial development is found in and around Fort Lauderdale. Widely known as a bargain-hunter's delight, **Sawgrass Mills,** the nation's largest outlet mall, is a collection of 270 name-brand discount shops, a major tourist attraction in itself. The elegant **Galleria,** one of several first-rate shopping malls, is chock-full of designer and luxury merchandise.

Casual beachside cafes, sidewalk trattorias, and elegant dockside restaurants dish up just about every cuisine known to the American appetite.

The Kings Point royal coach transportation system regularly schedules trips to area supermarkets, banks, medical facilities, and malls.

ROYAL HIGHLANDS

LEESBURG, FLORIDA

6001 Monarch Blvd.
Leesburg, FL 34748
352-365-2303 / 800-325-4471
Fax: 352-365-6221

Developer: Pringle Development

Year of initial property sales/rentals: 1996

Total land area: 779 acres

Average elevation: 105 feet

Location: In north-central Florida; Lake County; about equidistant from the Atlantic Ocean and the Gulf of Mexico; on U.S. Highway 27, off the northernmost stretch of the Florida's Turnpike; 11 miles south of Leesburg; 45 miles northwest of Orlando.

Nearest airport with scheduled commercial service: Orlando International (50 miles)

Current number of housing units with year-round occupants: 170

Projected number of housing units: 1,500 (2002)

Resident eligibility: 80% of residents must be at least 55 years of age. More than 90% are estimated to be in retirement or semiretirement status.

Community visit/tour incentive program: Guest home accommodations available for evaluation visit; call for details.

Suggested newspaper: *Daily Commercial,* P.O. Box 490007, Leesburg, FL 34749 (352-365-8246)

WHY ROYAL HIGHLANDS?

For those with a pioneering spirit who relish moving into a community that is in its earliest stages of development—getting in on the ground floor, so to speak—**Royal Highlands** offers the opportunity to influence patterns of activity and governance, and to help shape future directions. The sense of communion among residents, all of whom are newcomers, tends to accelerate socialization and the process of building new friendships. All are sharing the same experience of transition and, for many, a new and uncertain lifestyle. It is a condition that makes for reaching out and bonding with others.

Pringle Development has spent more than eight decades nurturing its reputation as one of central Florida's most creative residential developers. The company has been awarded by the **Lake County Home Builders Association**'s annual "Parade of Homes," recognizing best overall community attractiveness, layout and amenities, and superior home design and construction.

153

Lake County, home of Royal Highlands, contains within its borders more than 1,400 named spring-fed lakes, covering 202 square miles. **Leesburg**, the RH post office address, is the largest town in the county with a population of about 15,000. Unlike most parts of Florida, these central highlands are graced by rolling countryside and roads that wind through protected conservation lands. Many roads are shaded by stately oak trees draped in Spanish moss. One third of Royal Highlands' total acreage is forever preserved as natural wetlands and lake surface. The community's upper midstate location is convenient to two of America's favorite playgrounds—**Orlando** (about 45 miles southeast) and **Tampa/St. Petersburg** (approximately 80 miles southwest). It's no trick at all to entice visits from children and grandchildren with such easy access to some of the greatest visitor attractions on earth, including **Disney World** and the **Kennedy Space Center**.

WHO'S IN CHARGE?

A nonprofit homeowners association was established in early 1997, soon after the first homes were built and occupied. Management and policy control will be retained by Pringle Development until the community reaches its final stages of buildout. At that time, the entire property will become resident-owned. Until then, the association functions primarily as a communication linkage mechanism between Pringle Development and property owners so that mutual concerns and objectives can be addressed and volunteer board leadership developed.

A monthly fee of $77 is assessed for all households to cover clubhouse and other common property and amenities upkeep, as well as cable TV service.

A monthly newsletter is published by the developer. It features columns and articles by various Pringle managers and staff specialists, covering community news and activities. Residents contribute to its pages, too, with human interest and personal stories to share with neighbors.

THE WEATHER REPORT

The central section of the Florida peninsula, as has already been noted, is a land teeming with lakes. As such, even though some distance from the east and west coastlines, humidities are relatively high throughout the year, particularly after sundown. Readings do tend to moderate considerably during sunny afternoons, especially during the winter months. The rainy season begins in early summer and typically extends into October. Afternoon thunderstorms and lively winds are frequent at that time of year and help bring temperatures down to more bearable comfort levels than would otherwise be the case. Hurricanes seldom cause alarm in these parts. The inland location is protection enough since such storms are generally rendered relatively anemic after passing over a substantial stretch of terrain.

Using Orlando weather data (the nearest official reporting station), comparable average daily high and low temperatures for three winter months and for three summer months are as follows:

December: high 73/low 51   **January:** high 71/low 49

February: high 73/low 50   **June:** high 90/low 72

July: high 91/low 73   **August:** high 91/low 73

Average annual rainfall: 48 inches
Average annual snowfall: trace

HOME SWEET HOME

There are two types of residential construction offered in the standard selection—single-family and garden homes. Buyers can select from a wide range of lot sizes, many with waterfront or golf course views. Garden homes are fully detached dwellings, but are on narrow lots. Pringle Development prides itself on offering customers the option of making minor design changes to their basic model plans, or to completely customize to the owner's layout and feature preferences. Pringle management officials like to say that no two homes are alike. They produce and distribute a "blue book" on how to buy a home in Florida—30 pages of helpful information about special construction considerations, communities and life styles, cost of living factors, financing and reselling, and a host of other topics of interest to anyone planning to relocate to the land of sunshine and citrus.

Among the homes built to date, minimum basic floor plan sizes are 1,151 square feet and go up to 1,925 square feet. Prices range from under $100,000 to the mid-$160s, including the lot.

The development is tied to municipal water and sewer systems. Utility lines are below ground.

MONEY MATTERS

Surprisingly, greater Orlando (the outskirts of which Leesburg is not far beyond) shows a relatively moderate level of living costs. Available data on selected categories of consumer spending show a composite index of 1.6 percent below the average of 315 metropolitan and nonmetropolitan areas of the country that are included in the survey. Among the six weighted segments of products and services measured, utilities showed the highest comparative cost at 16.3 percent above the average and health costs at 8.7 percent above average. The remaining four groupings showed below average measurements, each constituting more heavily weighted factors: groceries, 3.3 percent; housing, 6.5 percent; transportation, 1.5 percent; and miscellaneous goods and services (weighted at one-third of the total value of all categories), 2.8 percent. Clearly, the sustained healthy tourist economy and growing population of the central Florida market has not brought with it undue upward pressure on prices.

Costs related to living at Royal Highlands have certain notable advantages over some other retirement communities. A good illustration is the fact that those who are not golfers pay nothing toward the maintenance of the course. Such expenses are met through separate golf membership and use fees.

Property taxes, after homestead exemption, are based on a millage rate of $16.16 per thousand dollars of assessed value. Under that formulation, taxes for a $100,000 home (with exemption) would come to approximately $1,200. Combining all city utilities (water, sewer, gas) and trash pickup, telephone and electricity, the average estimated total comes to $172 a month. Adding the $77 a month homeowners dues (previously referenced), the monthly single-family home expense, exclusive of taxes and insurance, comes to $249.

TAKE GOOD CARE OF YOURSELF

In part because Lake County has a substantial population of adults over the age of 55 (almost a third are reported to be over 65), there has been a strong county planning program to cater to the needs of older residents. State-of-the-art medical resources have taken root, creating a highly responsive health maintenance and recovery system. Ample numbers of physicians, medical specialists, and dentists are nearby.

Leesburg Regional Medical Center has provided Lake County with a full range of medical and surgical services since 1963. Just 6 miles from the Royal Highlands entrance, this 294-bed facility was recently named one of the 100 top performing hospitals in the nation out of 3,575 general care institutions graded on quality, efficiency, and financial stability. Leesburg Regional offers a long list of specialties including cardiopulmonary rehabilitation, diagnostic imaging, a 24-hour emergency department, lithotripsy, obstetrics and gynecology, occupational, physical, speech, and respiratory therapy, a sleep disorder center, and several wellness centers. Two other modern hospitals within the county, **South Lake Memorial** in **Clermont** and **Florida Hospital Waterman** in **Eustis**, each within 20 to 30 minutes, offer additional diagnosis and treatment programs.

PLACES TO GO, THINGS TO DO

A recreational calendar of activities within the community is emerging as more newcomers arrive. **The Monarch** is a 6,050-yard, par-72 golf course with the look and feel of the early Scottish links. It is the centerpiece of on-site leisure attractions. In addition to the home course, there are more than 30 other golfing centers within driving distance. Together with the golf clubhouse, a recreational complex offers tennis, swimming, Jacuzzi, shuffleboard, billiards, horseshoe pits and bocce, along with a variety of clubs and interest groups—from quilting and macrame to fishing, model airplanes, gardening, and antique cars. Royal Highlands' private lakes are made to order for fishing and canoeing.

Just north of RH is **Lake Griffin,** the largest of nine lakes that make up the **Harris Chain,** home of sailing regattas and fishing tournaments. Boaters can actually cruise all the way to **Jacksonville** in northernmost Florida, more than 100 miles through connected lakes and man-made canals. No lakeside cove is far from pure wilderness where egrets, herons and the American Bald Eagle congregate. Central Florida's world-famous tourist destinations clustered around Orlando are less than an hour away—the **Magic Kingdom, EPCOT Center, Disney-MGM Studios**, and a host of exciting attractions that comprise **Walt Disney World. University Studios Florida** and **Sea World** share the Orlando spotlight with comparable appeal. The **Cypress Gardens** in **Winter Haven,** about 60 miles south of Royal Highlands, is known as "the water ski capital of the world" and features water and stage shows, a magnificent botanical garden, and a butterfly conservatory. A little closer, in **Kissimmee,** is **Green Meadows Farm,** where a "hands-on" two-hour guided tour of more than 300 farm animals gives visitors an opportunity to milk a cow, ride a pony, or take off on a hayride.

Some of the more adventurous outdoor activities in these parts are found at places such as the gliderport at **Clermont** featuring motorless sailplane rides and flying lessons. Three championship-level water ski schools stand ready to hone the athletic talents of those with daredevil propensities. No challenge has been more enthusiastically embraced by more retirees than the Florida bicycle craze. Neon and spandex-clad cyclists, for more than two decades, have descended upon central Florida for the **Annual Mount Dora Bicycle Festival.** Roadway bike lanes, an inordinate number of bicycle retailers and repair shops, and a state coordinator for such activity, are hallmarks of the attention being given to this popular and growing form of fitness fun.

SAFE AND SECURE

A gated entrance is staffed by security personnel seven days a week, 24 hours a day. Patrol vehicles roam the development on a regular schedule. Municipal police and firefighting services are provided by the city of Leesburg. A 911 emergency phone system is in place.

LET'S GO SHOPPING

Lake Harris Square in Leesburg is a 60,000-square-foot shopping center, about 6 miles from the RH gate. It is anchored by a 48,000-square-foot major food market chain that includes a pharmacy, deli/restaurant, full service photo center, and a dry cleaner. Other retailers include a beauty shop, a video shop, and a family sports pub. Also in Leesburg, a bit further away, is **Lake Square Mall,** featuring four popular department stores and approximately 75 smaller shops. For special needs, Orlando is less than an hour away and offers the full array of consumer products and services one would expect to find in a major metropolitan center.

Lake County is known as an antique and collectibles paradise. Most of the county towns have lots of small boutiques and specialty stores. **Mount Dora**, not more than 20 minutes east of Leesburg, has an eight-block downtown area that is an especially appealing collection of quaint shops and congenial restaurants.

STONEYBROOK GOLF & COUNTRY CLUB

SARASOTA, FLORIDA

8801 Stoneybrook Blvd.
Sarasota, FL 34238
941-966-1611
Fax: 941-966-0165

Developer: U.S. Home Corporation

Year of initial property sales/rentals: 1994

Total land area: 475

Average elevation: 25 feet

Location: Central Florida's west coast; Sarasota County; in a southern suburb of the city of Sarasota; off U.S. Highway 41, about 3 miles west of Interstate 75 at Central Sarasota Parkway; about 60 miles south of Tampa; 15 miles south of Bradenton.

Nearest airport with scheduled commercial service: Sarasota/Bradenton International (17 miles)

Current number of housing units with year-round occupants: 350

Projected number of housing units: 940 (1998)

Resident eligibility: There are no restrictions regarding age requirements of residents. It is estimated, however, that approximately 80% of homeowners are retired or semiretired, and fewer than 3% of families have children living permanently in the home.

Community visit/tour incentive program: A "Fly & Buy" program provides for the developer to pay up to $500 in reimbursement for travel expenses at the time of closing.

Suggested newspaper: *Sarasota Herald Tribune*, 801 So. Tamiami Trail, Sarasota, FL 34236 (941-953-7755)

WHY STONEYBROOK?

U.S. Home Corporation, developer of **Stoneybrook Golf & Country Club**, is one of the nation's oldest and largest publicly held homebuilders. Established in 1954, it has operations in 31 metropolitan areas in 12 states. A substantial portion of its properties is devoted to the retirement and active adult/second home market, concentrated in Florida, Maryland, Nevada, New Jersey, and Texas. **Rutenberg Homes** is the home construction subsidiary of USHC, the only builder ever to have been honored three times as the "National Builder of the Year" by the **National Association of Home Builders**. The proud and extensive corporate display of awards and trophies is testament to more than four decades of home-building experience and customer satisfaction.

The purchase of a home at Stoneybrook includes an automatic membership in the country club and an ownership stake in the golf course and club facilities. Even for those purchasers who are not golfers, this arrangement is an appealing bonus, providing access to social and recreational programs without any additional equity investment.

The community location on the southern outskirts of **Sarasota** gives access within minutes to miles of gulf beaches that locals claim have the world's whitest and softest sand. The city of Sarasota (population about 51,000), according to a recent edition of *Southern Living Magazine,* is "the nation's per capita arts capital." Nearly four times as many performing artists are said to live and work in the area as in any other part of the state. **Sarasota County** reportedly has the third-highest per capita income in Florida, yet cost-of-living indicators do not reflect correspondingly high pricing patterns. In another category of "the biggest and best," the county has some 17,000 pleasure boats registered which, by most any standard, is a reflection of nautical supremacy.

WHO'S IN CHARGE?

There are three associations involved in the overall community operating structure. The **Stoneybrook Golf & Country Club (SGCC)**, owned by the residents, is the central activities focus. Its annual membership fee of $1,072 covers full club membership privileges and sustaining funds to maintain the clubhouse, golf course, and recreational facilities. What might be considered an initiation or equity fee is included in the purchase price of a home (as indicated in the previous section). Within that organization, and included in the SGCC membership fee, is a separate entity, the **Stoneybrook Boulevard Commons Association.** Its functions include entry and main boulevard maintenance, common area liability insurance, and management/state fees. The third entity is the **Palmer Ranch Master Association**, to which residents make a $78 semiannual payment for upkeep of common areas (including public parks, main roadway, signage, etc.) within the 10,000-acre-plus property within which Stoneybrook and other communities are located.

Condominium owners belong to any one of 18 separate associations to which a fee of $144 per month is paid to cover the services they receive, including ground and recreational facilities maintenance for their area, property and liability insurance, water/sewer services, pest control, and general reserves. Some of these condo units are in multistory buildings, while others are attached villas.

Each of the multiple community segments within Stoneybrook (separate single-family, villa, and multifamily) is under the direction of a private management company. When property sales reach 90 percent of buildout, control is turned over to an elected board of residents. In most instances, that entity continues to employ the firm originally enlisted by the developer.

THE WEATHER REPORT

Everything about weather is relative. What is hot? What is humid? So much depends on our own tolerance for extreme temperatures and climatic conditions and what each of us has been conditioned to perceive as reasonably comfortable. That the Florida coasts experience summer heat and humidity requires no validation. That some relief is afforded by ocean-borne breezes and afternoon showers is also a matter of established fact. The high 80s to the low 90s may seem downright cool to someone accustomed to the kind of heat typically experienced in the desert southwest and parts of the south-central plains. It is, of course, the other eight or nine months of the year that has made the "Sunshine State" the seasonal migratory destination of hordes of northerners determined to swap winter snow shovels for sunglasses and tanning cream. They come for the winter respite.

The nearest official reporting weather station is **Tampa**, 60 miles to the north, which shares the same coastline. While there may be some topographical influences that affect the two locations in different ways, it can be assumed that the Tampa temperature profile is a satisfactory parallel. Average daily high and low readings for the three winter months and the three summer months are as follows:

December: high 72/low 52   **January:** high 70/low 50

February: high 71/low 52   **June:** high 89/low 73

July: high 90/low 74   **August:** high 90/low 74

Average annual precipitation: 60 inches (Sarasota County)
Average annual snowfall: none

HOME SWEET HOME

U.S. Home has been recognized as a premier homebuilder in the **Tampa Bay** area for almost two decades. Providing the buyer with a wide range of choices in floor plans, price points, design options, and premium fixture/ appliance brand names has been a cornerstone of USHC practice. Company marketing emphasis is given to affordability, in part arising out of superior national buying power, and guarantees of defect-free construction backed by a strong warranty program.

Single-family detached homes account for about one-third of inventory at Stoneybrook, ranging in price from the mid-$200,000s to more than $300,000 with 1,900 to 3,000-plus square feet. Luxury "Veranda" and "Clubside" condominiums, the largest single category of dwelling options, come with prices beginning at just under $100,000 and go up to the mid-$160,000s with 1,150 to 1,650 square feet of space. A small number of larger townhouses have been built, selling for between $169,900 and the low $200,000s. Buyers have ample opportunity to customize floor plans. A complete in-house mortgage financing program is readily available.

Long-term rentals are generally available in a $1,500 to $1,700 per-month lease rate for condos with 1,300 to 1,600 square feet. Lots are not sold without construction contracts. Utility lines are below ground. The county provides central sanitary sewer and water services.

MONEY MATTERS

With few exceptions (primarily **Miami/Dade County** and the **West Palm Beach** metropolitan area), most Florida population centers reflect living costs close to the national average. The Sarasota area is just a fraction of one percent above average, according to data originated by ACCRA, covering housing, food, transportation, health care, utilities, and miscellaneous goods and services. Among the six expense categories, two were significantly above average (utilities, 12 percent and health care, 10.2 percent), but both had the lowest level of impact on household budgets. A third above-average finding was only moderately elevated, but for the second highest category of importance (housing, 3.9 percent). The remaining three groupings were below average (groceries, 2.6 percent; transportation, 11.6 percent; and miscellaneous good and services, the heaviest weighted item, 2.6 percent). The composite index for all these factors came to .3 percent above the national average.

The absence of a state personal income tax in Florida is given further impact by the fact that permanent residents pay no property taxes on the first $25,000 of a home's appraised value. The Sarasota County property tax millage rate is said to be among the lowest in the state, amounting to approximately 1 percent per year of the purchase price.

TAKE GOOD CARE OF YOURSELF

Sarasota is ranked fourth in the state for the number of physicians in practice—almost 800. There are more than 200 dentists and six hospitals with a combined total of more than 1,600 beds. **Sarasota Memorial** and **Doctors Hospital** are both within a 10-mile radius of Stoneybrook. There are three assisted or long-term care facilities with a total of almost 200 beds, all within 2 miles of the community.

PLACES TO GO, THINGS TO DO

The regulation, par-72 golf course at Stoneybrook was designed by one of the world's most prominent architects of such properties—**Arthur Hills**. It was Hills, in 1992, who became the first in the 10-year history of the *Golf Digest* Awards to win top honors in both the "best new private course" and the "best new public course" categories. The course was planned in a manner that offers challenge to novice and pro-class alike.

The 20,000-square-foot country club has a gourmet dining room, full-service lounge, a pro shop, private locker rooms, card room, a heated swimming pool, four lighted tennis courts, a fitness program area, a driving range and putting green, and administrative offices. Condominium neighborhoods have their own swimming pools and tennis courts. Nearby are paved and dirt walking trails. There are no formalized activities programs, but a number of clubs and interest groups have been organized around bridge and other table games, golf and tennis, water aerobics, walking, and investments. Some of these clubs sponsor their own dinners and dances. A 40-acre park is within walking distance of the Stoneybrook front gate, featuring a lake, nature trails, playground, and a basketball court.

Sarasota Bay, less than 20 minutes from Stoneybrook, provides more than 35 miles of gulf beaches. Four barrier islands across the bay contribute especially prized sandy shores to this world-famous coastal enclave. An abundance of inlets, canals, and freshwater lakes dot the nearby landscape. Trout, redfish, pompano, and flounder are found in the inland waters. Kingfish, mackerel, grouper, and gamefish give anglers a run for their money offshore. There are lots of boat ramps, marinas, and boat charter agencies. No fewer than 65 public, private, and semiprivate golf courses satisfy every skill level on the fairways. Fourteen tennis court locations around the city make it relatively easy to gain access to the nets.

Point of Rocks on **Siesta Key**, just south of the city, features sponges, exotic shells, and colorful tropical fish found in less than 10 feet of water. Reef and wreck diving in the **Gulf of Mexico** can be experienced 8 to 10 miles offshore. There are state park recreation areas, a notable marine aquarium, a planetarium, botanical and jungle gardens, a bird sanctuary, historical landmarks—even a stallion ranch. Sarasota is in the midst of major league baseball spring training camps, where fans come out in droves to watch their favorite teams.

Cultural and historical attractions are much in evidence. The **Gamble Plantation** unveils the workings of an antebellum sugar plantation. The one-of-a-kind **John and Mable Ringling Museum** takes visitors back to the early days of the "big tent," the development of the world's greatest circus, and the story of the man who breathed life into this Florida town in the early 1900s. There, old masterpieces and fine contemporary art serve as a counterpoint for circus-related memorabilia. The county's high per capita income supports a wide variety of arts organizations, including live theater, ballet, opera, and international film festivals. Other festivals celebrate children's art, jazz and other musical themes, sailing, sand sculpture, and antique cars. Educational institutions in Sarasota County include the **University of South Florida at Sarasota** and **Sarasota University**, both of which offer fully accredited undergraduate and graduate level courses of special interest to active adults.

For those who wish to seek out yet more sophisticated stimulation, it is little more than an hour's drive to the Tampa/St. **Petersburg/Clearwater** metropolitan area. There, world-class attractions include **Busch Gardens** and one of the nation's outstanding science centers. More than 15 art galleries and museums include the world's largest collections of works by surrealist artist **Salvador Dali.** The list of special events, sports attractions (both collegiate and professional), historic districts, and native wildlife habitats is endless.

SAFE AND SECURE

Stoneybrook is a controlled access community with entry gates staffed by security personnel around the clock, seven days a week. Police and fire protection and paramedic services are provided by Sarasota County government. A neighborhood crime watch program supplements preventive initiatives to help assure a safe environment.

LET'S GO SHOPPING

There is a prime shopping strip within a mile of the front gate. A dozen or so businesses include a full-service grocery store. About a half-mile further on is **Sarasota Square Mall,** an enclosed regional center with several anchor department stores and a substantial number of boutiques and specialty shops.

STRAWBERRY RIDGE

VALRICO, FLORIDA

4419 State Road 60
Valrico, FL 33594
813-689-9423 / 800-344-8995
Fax: 813-684-1642

Developer: Blair Group

Year of initial property sales/rentals: 1971

Total land area: 120 acres

Average elevation: 75 feet

Location: Mid-Florida's west coast; Hillsborough County; suburb of Tampa, about 10 miles east of the central city; on State Road 60, approximately 7 miles east of intersection with Interstate 75.

Nearest airport with scheduled commercial service: Tampa International (21 miles)

Current number of housing units with year-round occupants: 525

Projected number of housing units: 865

Resident eligibility: At least 80% of households must have a family member 55 years of age or older. No children under age 18 are permitted as permanent residents.

Community visit/tour incentive program: A guest visitation program is made available to prospective purchasers who are within 12 months of relocating. A fully decorated home is provided for two nights and three days at a special rate of $89, and includes enjoyment of on-site recreation facilities, as well as golf at a nearby course.

Suggested daily newspaper: *Tampa Tribune*, 202 So. Parker, Tampa, FL 33606 (813-685-4581)

WHY STRAWBERRY RIDGE?

Florida's coastal areas are generally flat with little topographical variation. **StrawBerry Ridge**, consisting of manufactured homes, has the distinction of being perched atop the highest ridge of land in **Hillsborough County**, at elevations of more than 100 feet above sea level. The downtown skyline of **Tampa** can be seen on the western horizon. To the east are groves of orange trees and fields of strawberries. The community runs counter to similar all-adult developments, because most are located some distance from a major metropolitan area (partly because of lower land costs). In this instance, the Tampa/**St. Petersburg/Clearwater** Metropolitan Statistical Area, of which StrawBerry Ridge/**Valrico** is a suburb, is among the nation's 25 largest

MSAs, with a population of more than two million people. That means StrawBerry Ridge has access to a superabundance of leisure opportunities.

The **Tampa Bay** area was given a mark of distinction when *Money* magazine, in its July 1996 issue, placed it among the top 15 "Best Places to Live in America," and third best among cities with a population of more than one million. High marks were garnered for a healthy economy, desirable climate, and a plethora of world-class entertainment and recreational attractions. The planned community of StrawBerry Ridge itself has been the recipient of the "Circle of Excellence Award" for the last five years. The recognition comes from the two home manufacturers whose product is sold here, and is based on independent surveys of home buyers with regard to the level of satisfaction with their new homes and with the communities in which they have chosen to locate. The scores SR earned were well above the award's requirement.

The manufactured home has evolved over the past decade or so into a formidable housing alternative to site-built construction, with emphasis on affordability and durability. Contemporary designs, workmanship, and production techniques have transformed old stereotypes of such housing so that today's product bears little resemblance to its predecessors.

WHO'S IN CHARGE?

The **StrawBerry Ridge Homeowners Association** sponsors, plans, and implements the various social and recreational activities and special events. Its representatives meet quarterly with the developer to discuss matters of mutual interest and to share information on issues and developments. The HOA does not share proprietary rights or management responsibilities with the developer/owner, but is given an ongoing opportunity to express opinions, suggestions, and concerns. Residents pay an optional $12 annual fee to their all-volunteer association. Minimal expenses are covered by the developer out of land lease revenues.

Purchasers of property in this community, typical of other manufactured home developments, lease the land upon which their home is situated and to which they hold title. Monthly lease payments range from $205 to $295 (depending on lot size and location). In addition to payment on the homesite itself, the lease also covers professional management services, gated entry and 24-hour security, upkeep on two clubhouses and all the recreational amenities and programs connected with them, and a full-time activities director to keep it all together.

StrawBerry Toppings is a monthly community newsletter carrying limited advertising. It delivers commentary from staff and residents, a crammed-full activities calendar, and reports from various clubs and interest groups regarding current and planned programs.

THE WEATHER REPORT

The Florida climate has been a magnet for winter "snowbirds" from the north for as long as seasonal migration became practical with the advent of modern transportation. And for those who can afford to make Florida their permanent home, the tropical peninsula is more than a temporary escape from the miseries of numbing cold, icy streets, and skyrocketing heating bills. No matter what time of the year, sunworshippers will find plenty of pleasant weather to enjoy.

Weather patterns in the Tampa Bay area are especially noteworthy for the summer thunderstorm season. From June through September, afternoon downpours can suddenly drop temperatures from the low 90s to a pleasant 70 degrees. Thanks to the sea breezes and frequent showers, seldom does the thermometer rise above the low nineties, a condition that inland locations in the southern states can only wish for. Freezing temperatures in winter are rare. Measurable snowfall has occurred only a few times in the last century. Average daily high and low temperature readings for three winter months and three summer months are as follows:

December: high 72/low 52   **January:** high 70/low 50

February: high 71/low 52   **June:** high 89/low 73

July: high 90/low 74   **August:** high 90/low 74

Average annual precipitation: 44 inches
Average annual snowfall: extremely rare

HOME SWEET HOME

Manufactured housing at StrawBerry Ridge features amenities that not long ago were unknown among such products. Fireplaces, skylights, gourmet kitchens, walk-in closets, luxurious master bathrooms, deluxe closet shelving, cathedral ceilings, and complete landscaping packages are among the standard and optional components available in most models. All homes include a carport (garage optional in some models), utility room, screened porch or patio, central air and heat, choice of carpeting, cabinets, wall coverings and draperies, and electric range and refrigerator. There are usually already-constructed homes available for purchase. A model center is open seven days a week for prospective buyers to inspect all elements of residential design and fixture and appliance specifications.

A manufacturer's five-year warranty provides protection against any defects in construction or workmanship. A full one-year "white glove" warranty is offered by the developer, which includes a home inspection after the structure arrives from the factory, plus quality control checks throughout the construction phase.

Floor plans range from 764 to 2,200 square feet at prices ranging from the mid-$40s to more than $110,000. There are no rental units available, nor vacant lots for sale. Water and sewer systems are supplied by the county. All utility lines are underground.

MONEY MATTERS

A ranking of 78 of the nation's towns and cities several years ago showed the Tampa/St. Petersburg metropolitan area to be 45th from the least expensive among those compared in the analysis. While real estate and utility costs were 22 percent and 19 percent, respectively, below the average of the entire sample, health costs were 15 percent higher. In another statistical review, Tampa was shown to have a lower cost of living than all but five of 39 selected cities with which it was compared. Only one of the five with lower costs (Omaha) revealed a relatively significant difference. Tampa scored precisely even with Kansas City and St. Louis, Missouri, and with Orlando, Florida. The indices used in the tabulation were drawn from data originated by ACCRA, covering housing, food, clothing, transportation, health care, utilities, and miscellaneous goods and services.

StrawBerry Ridge management has estimated the annual cost of living for the fixed expenses that might be anticipated (rates will vary in accordance with property size and value and usage patterns):

Homesite lease	$2,994
	(average for $205-$295 monthly range)
Electric	$1,056
Water & sewer	$360
Trash collection	$168
Homeowner insurance	$742
Registration decal and tax	$150
Total	$5,470 ($455.80 a month)

Homeowners pay no property tax, because the land upon which the house stands is leased, rather than owned. The only related cost is that of a "tag" fee to the state of between $125 and $175 per year (depending on the size of the home), insignificant when compared to the usual property taxes on site-built dwellings.

TAKE GOOD CARE OF YOURSELF

Columbia Brandon Regional Medical Center is within 5 miles of the SR entrance. The 255-bed facility, opened in 1977, has 425 affiliated physicians. Among its key departments are a 24-hour emergency/trauma center, a day surgery unit, a home health care program, an adult counseling center, a regional wound care unit, and a senior friends association. **Tampa General Healthcare** is a considerably larger hospital with more than 40 departments and specialties that range from a blood bank, brain injury treatment, and a burn center, to treatment for sleep disorders, strokes, and speech pathology. The institution operates six outpatient family care centers, five occupational health service locations, and a variety of specialty clinics and services, such as physical therapy, sports medicine, and weight management. The Tampa General main campus is situated on **Davis Islands** on the southern fringe of downtown Tampa, less than 12 miles from StrawBerry Ridge.

PLACES TO GO, THINGS TO DO

With all the things to do in Tampa Bay so close by, it might be expected that folks at StrawBerry Ridge would depend almost entirely on that world for its diversion. Not so. The community has what can be described as a rich activities program under the direction of a full-time coordinator. There are bingo and bridge games. There are clubs for golfers, bowlers, gardeners, and those interested in boating and fishing. Groups gather regularly to visit museums, attend the theater, or go on shopping excursions. There are clubs for dancing, photography, cooking, literary and religious pursuits, and veterans' interests. A "solo" club is especially active for those who are widowed or otherwise single.

Two clubhouses offer more than 20,000 square feet of social and recreational opportunities, including a tropical indoor heated swimming pool, outdoor pool, therapy spa, billiards room, library, ceramic and woodworking shops, and game courts for tennis, shuffleboard, horseshoes, and bocce ball. Regularly scheduled social mixers come in the form of potluck suppers, card parties, pancake breakfasts, exercise classes, and choral group practice and performance. Any activity that smacks of competition is likely to have a league attached to it and a tournament in which to participate.

Golfers have a choice of nearby courses—six within a 15-minute ride. Other off-site leisure attractions include some that draw visitors from all over the country and beyond. World-famous **Busch Gardens** in Tampa features spectacular midway rides, extravagant live shows, and thousands of exotic animals in their natural habitat. Right next door is **Adventure Island**, with water rides, white-sand volleyball courts, and thrilling speed slides. Tampa Bay's stunning **Florida Aquarium** is home to more than 4,300 aquatic animals and plants native to Florida. There, a wetlands gallery holds everything from alligator-filled swamps and rivers of playful otters to fleeting stingrays and delicate seahorses.

The incomparable gulf beaches of Clearwater and St. Petersburg are about 30 minutes away. Party boats take revelers out into the **Gulf of Mexico** for dining, dancing, live entertainment, and Las Vegas-style casino gaming. The **Museum of Science & Industry** boasts Florida's largest IMAX dome theater—a 10,500-square-foot screen that puts the audience in the midst of the action. The **Tampa Bay Performing Arts Center**, a state-of-the-art complex with four theaters and performance halls, is the largest facility of its kind south of the Kennedy Center in New York. There's also NFL football, high-speed jai alai, greyhound and thoroughbred horse racing, polo, and hockey.

SAFE AND SECURE

An electronically controlled access entrance and bright street lights are two of the community's security measures. Police protection is provided by the **Hillsborough County Sheriff's Office**. Residents of the community serve on volunteer patrol duty and neighborhood watch assignments. A county fire station is located less than 2 miles from StrawBerry Ridge. An emergency phone system is in place.

LET'S GO SHOPPING

Brandon, little more than walking distance from the StrawBerry Ridge entrance, has developed into a popular retail center, drawing customers from well beyond its borders. A full-service food market is less than 2 miles from the SR entry gate, along with a pharmacy, hardware store, and other specialty shops. Auto repair, banks, and restaurants are also in the same general area. Just a block away is a convenience store, a beauty salon, and a walk-in health care clinic. A regional mall in Brandon is 4 miles away, and another is in Tampa, only 11 miles away. Again, proximity to the Tampa Bay tri-cities makes virtually any kind of shopping need easy to satisfy. **MacDill Air Force Base**, located on a peninsula stretching to the south from downtown Tampa, operates a major commissary, available to families of qualified discharged or retired military personnel.

TIMBER PINES

SPRING HILL, FLORIDA

2368 Fairskies Dr.
Spring Hill, FL 34606
352-683-8435 / 800-541-3111
Fax: 352-666-6203

Developer: U.S. Home Corporation

Year of initial property sales/rentals: 1982

Total land area: 1,420 acres

Average elevation: 40 feet

Location: Upper west coast of Florida; southwest corner of Hernando County; on U.S. Highway 19, near the intersection of State Highway 578; approximately 35 to 50 miles north of the Tampa/Clearwater metropolitan area; 1½ miles off the Gulf of Mexico shoreline.

Nearest airport with scheduled commercial service: Tampa International (50 miles)

Current number of housing units with year-round occupants: 2,500

Projected number of housing units: 3,460 (1998)

Resident eligibility: At least one person in the household must be 55 years of age or older. Children under age 16 may not remain for visits of more than eight weeks. Children under 16 years of age are not permitted in permanent residence.

Community visit/tour incentive program: A "Hospitality House" program offers a three-day, two-night stay in the community for a reduced cost of $98.

Suggested newspaper: *St. Petersburg Times*, P.O. Box 1121, St. Petersburg, FL 33731 (813-893-8111)

WHY TIMBER PINES?

Timber Pines was singled out in 1994 by an impartial panel of judges for the **National Association of Home Builders** as "America's Best Designed Active Senior Housing Community." *New Choices* magazine, for three years in a row through 1996, named the development one of the "Top 20 Retirement Communities in America." With more than 40 years experience, the developers of Timber Pines, **U.S. Home Corporation**, is one of the largest and most successful homebuilders of retirement and active adult communities in the nation.

With the purchase of a new single-family home or villa, families moving into the community receive access to $15 million in amenities with no up-front costs or initiation fees. All amenities are owned by the residents and administered through the homeowner's association, of which all property owners are automatically members.

Having been a natural preserve in the form of a tree farm before the development was created, the terrain reflects much of its original character. Its proximity to the tri-city **Tampa Bay** area (**Tampa, Clearwater,** and **St. Petersburg**) provides convenient access (less than a 45-minute drive) to innumerable cultural, entertainment, and educational attractions.

WHO'S IN CHARGE?

The **Timber Pines Community Association** is a nonprofit organization established in 1982, soon after the first residents moved in. A basic community service fee of $89 a month for single-family homeowners includes the cost of providing 24-hour security, maintenance of private roads, parks, and clubhouse, access to all recreational amenities, and *free greens fees* on either of two 18-hole executive golf courses. Villa homeowners pay $168 a month, which includes the basic association fee in addition to lawn maintenance and exterior house painting.

THE WEATHER REPORT

Located only about 50 miles north of metropolitan Tampa and on the **Gulf of Mexico, Spring Hill** can be looked upon as having virtually the same climatic characteristics as its larger neighbors to the south. Prevailing winds off the Gulf tend to modify the otherwise typical subtropical weather patterns. Summer temperatures above the low 90s are infrequent and winter highs seldom fail to reach the 60s (although it can fall to below freezing on rare occasions). Summer thunderstorms in the late afternoon often bring quick relief from heat extremes. Afternoon humidity is typically in the 60-percent range during summer and somewhat lower for the rest of the year.

Average daily high and low temperatures for three winter months and three summer months are as follows:

December: high 72/low 52   **January:** high 70/low 50

February: high 71/low 52   **June:** high 89/low 73

July: high 90/low 74   **August:** high 90/low 74

Average annual precipitation: 44 inches
Average annual snowfall: trace

HOME SWEET HOME

There are two basic housing configurations—single-family detached and villas. The former make up about two-thirds of the total inventory. Villa owners pay an additional $79 a month in homeowner association dues over the

$85 base amount. The extra assessment provides for the individual owner's lawn care, underground sprinkler system, and exterior house painting, as needed.

Model homes are open for inspection to help visualize space and feature variations and options. Prices for single-family detached homes begin at $112,950 with square footage of 1,277. At the top of the range is a unit with 2,321 square feet, selling in the low $170s. One- and two-unit (duplex) villa homes are offered at a low end of $82,950 and graduated upward through seven models, the most expensive of which is under $120,000. These dwellings range in size from 1,111 to 1,605 square feet. All prices include the lot and free equity membership in the golf and country club. Vacant lots ready for construction sell for $30,000 to $75,000 with square footage from 7,150 to 8,250.

There are storage facilities available for boats and recreational vehicles. All utility lines are below ground level. Water and sanitary sewer services are provided by the county.

MONEY MATTERS

An estimate of average monthly homeowner's fixed expenses prepared by community sources showed the following cost summary:

	Single-family	Villas
Community service fee (includes 36 holes of golf, without green fees; heated pools; security; capital improvements; common grounds maintenance; all activities; and pay for salaried club employees)	$89	$168
Taxes (school, property; approximately 1 3/4% of cost of home, including $25,000 homestead deduction)	$165	$145
All-electric home cooling and heating	$90	$75
Water/sewer, with automatic sprinkler system	$55	$25
Private line telephone	$25	$25
Cable television/basic package (32-plus channels)	$25	$25

Homeowner's insurance	$40	$30
Trash pickup	$5.50	$5.50
Totals:	$494.50	$498.50

Considering the very moderate level of homeowner association fees (see the "Who's In Charge?" section), living costs at Timber Pines appear to be well below expectations for similar locations elsewhere in Florida.

TAKE GOOD CARE OF YOURSELF

There are four fully accredited regional hospitals within a 20-minute radius of Spring Hill. **Columbia Oak Hill Regional Medical Center**, the largest among them, is a full-service facility with 370 beds, located in Spring Hill, about 8 miles from Timber Pines. Also in Spring Hill, about the same distance away, is the **Spring Hill Regional Hospital** with 91 beds. This institution operates a local enrichment center offering comprehensive programs in health education, support groups, exercise, and several related activities.

A senior service directory compiled by the **Hernando County Medical Society Alliance** shows a list of more than 80 support and health-related organizations and 10 nursing homes and continuing care communities. All manner of specialized therapeutic services are available within a 3- to 15-mile radius.

PLACES TO GO, THINGS TO DO

Country club living with no initiation fee and no annual membership fee gives Timber Pines a value seldom matched by other comparable communities. Two 18-hole executive golf courses impose no green fees for member residents. The third and newest course is the **Grand Pines Championship Course**, with longer yardage than the executive layouts and demanding a higher level of play. Residents pay a very modest user fee to tee off there. A noted golf pro is available for lessons.

The 10,000-square-foot country club offers both casual and formal dining, as well as a well-appointed fitness center under the direction of an on-site instructor. A separate 18,000-square-foot clubhouse/lodge, located on more than 7 acres of lush wooded hillside, is devoted to continuing rounds of activity under the supervision of a full-time staff social director. It boasts two lighted tennis courts (among a total of eight on the property), as well as six shaded shuffleboard and bocce courts, a large sun deck, and open porches. Rooms are set aside for arts and crafts (with kilns and easels), woodworking, table games, billiards, and social gatherings. There are classes in art, ballroom and country dancing, bridge, ceramics, chorus, and defensive driving, among others. Forty different activities cater to almost every imaginable interest, many of them organized under the banner of any of a dozen different clubs.

There's a library and a travel desk that arranges for individual and group excursions. A large auditorium accommodates dances, shows, parties, and such. Further supplementing indoor facilities is an 800-seat performing arts center. Two Olympic-size heated pools and spas, along with a cabana and friendship gazebo, driving range, and 7 miles of paved walking trails round out a notable collection of amenities.

For those seeking other diversions outside Timber Pines, there is a new eight-screen cinema only 4 miles away. Bowling lanes are no more than 2 miles down the road. A variety of professional and collegiate sports teams (including baseball spring training) are within an hour's drive. Beaches, salt water fishing places, picnic areas, and playgrounds abound. **Weeki Wachee Springs**, just minutes away, is the home of the world's only underwater mermaid show. Thirty miles south is **Tarpon Springs** where old world Greek traditions and culture provide a special charm to the contemporary scene. **Stage West** in Spring Hill is a new theater for live performances. In less than an hour, TP residents can be in the Tampa Bay metropolitan area, where entertainment and cultural attractions are generous and diverse.

SAFE AND SECURE

The Pines is a three-gated community manned by a private, professional security force around the clock, seven days a week. These officers also provide vehicle patrols at scheduled intervals. Their service is supplemented with official law enforcement from the county sheriff's department. Fire protection and emergency ambulance services are provided by the city of Spring Hill in conjunction with a 911 response system. Crime statistics are not available, but are said to be insignificant, in part as a result of security measures in place.

LET'S GO SHOPPING

An abundance of retail and service establishments are clustered around the Timber Pines main gate. National chains such as Wal-Mart, Kmart, Walgreens, and Kash 'n Karry are within walking distance, along with a string of independent merchants who cater to personal needs, pets, hobbies, and dining out. **Gulfview Square Mall,** a regional center in **New Port Richey** with a galaxy of prime shopping outlets, is only 16 miles south off the highway to Tampa/Clearwater, where 35 miles further along, are the endless shopping alternatives of a major urban area.

THE VILLAGES OF CITRUS HILLS

HERNANDO, FLORIDA

2450 No. Citrus Hills Blvd.
Hernando, FL 34442
352-746-0527 / 800-323-7703
Fax: 352-746-0527

Developer: Citrus Hills Investment Properties

Year of initial property sales/rentals: 1983

Total land area: 12,000 acres

Average elevation: 150 feet

Location: About two-thirds of the distance north of the southernmost reach of the peninsula's Gulf coast; Citrus County; main sections of the development lie within a triangle formed by US Highway 41, State Highway 44, and County Road 491; 5 miles southeast of Inverness, 24 miles southwest of Ocala; less than 10 miles inland from the Gulf of Mexico.

Nearest airport with scheduled commercial service: Orlando International or Tampa International (both approximately 90 miles)

Current number of housing units with year-round occupants: 3,000

Projected number of housing units: 10,000 (2030)

Resident eligibility: There are no age restrictions for residency, but an estimated 60% of the population is retired or semiretired; approximately 10% of households have children under 18 years of age in permanent residence.

Community visit/tour incentive program: A "life-style preview" inspection trip for a couple for three days and two nights, including air fare, is available at a total cost of $299, subject to prior qualifying conditions.

Suggested newspaper: *Citrus County Chronicle*, 1624 No. Meadowcrest Blvd., Crystal River, FL 34429 (352-563-6363)

WHY CITRUS HILLS?

By Florida standards, and to some extent by the standards in any state, **The Villages of Citrus Hills** is a development of considerable size. On 12,000 acres, with an ultimate housing inventory of as many as 10,000 dwellings (currently at about 3,000), it has the potential of matching the population of a sizable city. As such, because of the extent of its resources, its amenities tend to be numerous and diverse. It is a community of 15 villages, each with its own distinctive features. Two have their own clubhouse and adjacent golf course. One has a swim and fitness club. Another features an equestrian center with white-fenced horse trails. Some have tennis courts and/or swimming pools. Some simply bask pleasantly among the rolling hills and mature trees.

A jewel in the community's crown is the **Ted Williams Museum** and **Hitters Hall of Fame.** The major league baseball idol to whom this shrine is dedicated is a resident of the community and, although retired long ago from public life, he has maintained a hand in the ongoing programs and activities sponsored by the museum and its supporters. An anniversary celebration in 1996 was hosted by stars of the sports and entertainment worlds and, like previous events, admitted three more retired baseball batting greats to the "hitters hall of fame" roster in the presence of nationally prominent political, athletic, and show business luminaries. Ted Williams's appearances around the country are reported regularly in Citrus Hills publications.

Citrus Hills Construction Company was recognized in 1996 for the second year in a row as the recipient of **Citrus County's** "Builder of the Year" award. Nominations for the honor come from the county builders association, made up of builders and building trade professionals, with final voting by the association's 20-member board of directors. In 1996, Citrus Hills was voted the best real estate development and the best banquet facility in the county, and was voted honorable mention in six other categories, including best golf course, best retirement community, and best country club.

WHO'S IN CHARGE?

Each of the 15 villages has its own relatively informal property owners' association. Most community management responsibilities are in the hands of the developer, but each residents' organization maintains an architectural control board to assure compliance with neighborhood appearance standards and also directs security patrol activities. A modest fee of about $80 a year is paid by homeowners to sustain these functions. Street maintenance is carried out by the county.

A semiannual *Highlights* publication, in a slick magazine format, updates and summarizes key village developments and activities and focuses on Citrus Hills newcomers and personality profiles. Yet another publication is distributed by the **Citrus Hills Golf and Country Club**—a monthly activities guide that also includes community and club "insider" news.

THE WEATHER REPORT

Citrus County weather survey data was provided by the community, based on records obtained from the National Weather Service at **Brooksville,** 25 miles from the CH Villages. The report reveals an incredible 345 days a year of sunshine, although other local authorities claim a more conservative average of 294 cloudless days annually. Most rainfall occurs during the months of June, July, and August, each of which normally registers between 7 and 8 inches. The information further reveals that, on average, 219 days of the year (60 percent of the time) fall into a "comfort zone," during which period neither heating nor cooling is required. Average high and low maximum and minimum readings for the three winter months and three summer months were as follows:

December: high 70/low 51   **January:** high 73/low 53

February: high 71/low 51   **June:** high 89/low 71

July: high 90/low 72   **August:** high 90/low 72

Average annual precipitation: 51 inches
Average annual snowfall: none
Average annual humidity: 72%

HOME SWEET HOME

Green belts, wide curving interior streets, culs-de-sac, and lot sizes ranging from ¼ to more than a full acre characterize neighborhood layouts. Warranties include a 10-year structural guarantee, a two-year protection against failure of mechanical systems, and a one-year "bumper to bumper" warranty that provides for periodic home inspections designed to automatically assure attention to any problems experienced after move-in. Concrete block and framing construction is said to exceed Florida's very demanding building codes.

Single-family detached homes range in price from the mid-$80s to $200,000 or more, in sizes from 1,600 to 3,000 square feet. About 100 villas are priced from the low $80s to the mid-$130s, with floor plans of between 1,500 and 2,500 square feet.

MONEY MATTERS

Citrus County has one of the lowest cost of living indices in the state. Auto insurance is cited as an example of substantial savings over rates applied in most of the nation's other metropolitan centers. The cost of electric power (base rate of 5.8 cents per kilowatt hour) is compared with the Long Island suburbs of New York City, where the base charge is said to be nearly 19.6 cents per kilowatt hour. Property taxes, helped by Florida's generous $25,000 homestead exemption, are generally much lower than levies collected elsewhere. A typical annual Citrus County real estate tax assessment ran between $900 and $1,500, based on the cost of the home. County commissioners for the 1995-96 fiscal year cut taxes by 3 percent, bringing assessments down to the 1988 level. It was the fifth consecutive year they had brought about a millage rate reduction, said to be the result of streamlining and consolidating administrative costs.

An estimate of approximate average monthly homeowner's fixed expenses prepared by community sources showed the following cost summary:

Property taxes	$118.08
Electricity	$110.00
Homeowners insurance	$51.38
Auto insurance	$45.00
Lawn care	$35.00
Utilities (other than electric)	$22.36
Cable television	$19.73
Trash collection	$15.00
Telephone	$14.00
Association dues	$7.50
Total monthly expenses	$438.05

Optional membership in the CH Golf and Country Club comes in three different plans—golf, tennis, and social. All offer unlimited use of clubhouse facilities and programs but varying degrees of access to the two principal amenities (golf course and tennis courts). Each type requires a one-time refundable deposit: $7,000 for golf, $700 for tennis, and $200 for social. Annual dues for single and family memberships in 1997 were $1,260/$1,780 for golf, $264/$396 for tennis, and $125/$150 for social.

TAKE GOOD CARE OF YOURSELF

The closest full-service hospital is **Citrus Memorial** in **Inverness**, 8 miles from the CH entrance, with 171 beds, a 24-hour emergency room, and around-the-clock lab services. It also has extensive specialized services, including a cardiac catheterization lab, diagnostic imaging, physical, occupational, and respiratory therapy, laparoscopic surgery, and social services. A bit further toward the coast at a distance of about 14 miles, **Seven Rivers Community Hospital** in **Crystal River** is a smaller facility (128 beds), but is well-equipped and offers a women's and family center, a psychiatric unit, an orthopedic center, an intensive and coronary care unit, and radiology and mammography services.

Two highly regarded assisted living/continuing care facilities are within a 3-mile radius, one of which has a unit devoted to Alzheimer's patients. There are five other nursing and rehabilitation centers in the county. The Citrus County health and medical directory also lists three outpatient clinics, more than two dozen dental offices, five health clubs, nine home health care services, eight pharmacies, more than a dozen chiropractors, and an extensive roster of health care professionals dealing with everything from acupuncture and alcohol addiction to optical services and prosthetic devices.

PLACES TO GO, THINGS TO DO

Inside, or immediately adjacent to the Citrus Hills compound, there are 72 holes of golf, miles of rivers, lakes, and streams for fishing and exploration, lighted tennis courts, swimming pools, exercise facilities, horseback riding, social clubs, travel clubs, and a world-famous sports museum. A newly designed **Citrus Hills Entertainment Complex** features a 14,000-square-foot activities center with a theater, pool tables, game rooms, a fitness center, lap pool, and meeting rooms. Country club activities stagger the imagination—group tours and cruises, oil painting classes, holiday celebrations, casino nights and other special events, comedy dinner shows, horse farm excursions, pot luck socials, day trips, junkets to athletic events, flower-arranging lessons, golf and tennis tournaments—the list goes on and on.

Less than 15 miles away, in places such as Inverness and Crystal River, there are pontoon boat rides, canoe rentals, scuba lessons, parks, and even flying lessons. A 47-mile paved bike trail within the county provides a great way to enjoy the natural surroundings. Hikers can enjoy a wide range of walks through sandhill, scrub, hardwood, hummock, hydric swamp, prairie, and marsh landtypes. At **Tillis Hill,** in the Citrus tract of the **Withlacoochee State Forest**, there is a stable that accommodates 20 riding horses, as well as a 37-site camping area. Anglers come from all over the country to Citrus County to find and catch trophy tarpon. Freshwater choices include sunshine bass, speckled perch, catfish, and the Florida Largemouth Bass. For those with a liking for saltwater species, grouper, snapper, sea trout, Spanish mackerel, cobia, sheepshead, redfish, and whiting are among the more frequent guests on the end of a baited line.

Diving and snorkeling enthusiasts can find no better playground. Crystal clear, spring-fed waters and an underwater cavern make for perfection. And then there's the manatee—that big, lovable water creature that is found in the greatest concentrations inhabiting the Crystal River, a waterway considered among the county's treasures.

Scarcely a week goes by without a festival, fair, arts and crafts show, or other special event. There are antique and classic car and boat shows, statewide fiddling championships, river raft races, art in the park exhibitions, fishing, golf, and tennis tournaments, country music jamborees, and wildlife celebrations—just about anything to please a crowd and have a good time.

Cultural attractions are not neglected either. The **Central Florida Symphony**, with 50 to 60 musicians and a full-time conductor, tours the mid-state area on a regular schedule of classical and pops engagements. One of its performance sites is in **Lecanto**, no more than 15 minutes from Citrus Hills. A new library opened in early 1996, a short distance from one of the CH clubhouses, featuring the latest information retrieval technology.

SAFE AND SECURE

According to the *Florida Atlas,* published by the **Institute of Science and Public Affairs** at **Florida State University**, Citrus County is one of Florida's lowest crime areas for both violent and nonviolent offenses.

The **Citrus County Sheriff's Department** provides police services to the community, supplementing a private, uniformed internal security force. An innovative program under the county agency's auspices has been the establishment of a sheriff's posse, which allows a group of unarmed, trained equestrians to aid sworn officers in various low-risk activities. These volunteers are called upon to conduct evidence searches for crime investigations, work traffic and security at special events (festivals, parades, etc.), and participate in search and rescue missions for lost or missing persons. It is the responsibility of the contracted security service personnel to maintain surveillance in the community, including ongoing neighborhood vehicular patrolling.

LET'S GO SHOPPING

The **Shoppes of Citrus Hills** is anchored by a new giant food market located on the development's perimeter. It is a strip mall shared by about a dozen retailers. **The Citrus Center Shopping and Theater Complex,** located 2 miles outside the far southeastern corner of the Villages property, features a Wal-Mart and another recently expanded and remodeled food market. It is now one of the largest (more than 46,000 square feet) and most elegant outlets of its kind, with a one-hour photo lab, a dry cleaning service, a pharmacy, a bakery and deli, and a 40-seat cafe, among the 35 or so businesses located there. Its eight-screen cinema is expected to expand to more than double that number by 1998.

The Crystal River Mall, about 12 miles from the Villages, has all the attributes of a full-scale regional mall, with four department stores, a 12-screen cinema, a food court, an enticing selection of restaurants, and an appealing collection of boutiques and specialty shops. The mall has attracted widespread attention because of its unique tent-like construction.

THE VILLAGES OF HIGHLANDS RIDGE

SEBRING, FLORIDA

P.O. Box 768
Sebring, FL 33871-0768
941-471-1171 / 800-922-8099
Fax: 941-471-1743

Developer: Highlands Ridge Associates

Year of initial property sales/rentals: 1991

Total land area: 453 acres

Average elevation: 110 feet

Location: Near the geographic north-south and east-west midpoint of the Florida peninsula; Highlands County; between the towns of Sebring and Avon Park; on Lake Bonnet; about 10 miles north of the intersection of U.S. Highway 27 and State Road 17; about equidistant from Tampa (approximately 85 miles east) and Orlando (approximately 85 miles south).

Nearest airport with scheduled commercial service: Orlando International (86 miles)

Current number of housing units with year-round occupants: 265

Projected number of housing units: 750 (2005)

Resident eligibility: At least one person in the household must be 55 years of age or older. No children under 19 years of age are permitted as permanent residents.

Community visit/tour incentive program: A "Preview to Purchase Program" offers visitation packages for one or two nights at $85 and $159, respectively (lower from May through Sept.), for accommodations in a fully furnished private home (absentee owner), with or without 18 holes of golf, optional participation in scheduled resident events and use of a golf cart for property transportation (if available).

Suggested newspaper: *Highlands Today/Tampa Tribune*, 231 U.S. Hwy. 27 North, Sebring, FL 33870 (941-382-1163)

WHY THE VILLAGES OF HIGHLANDS RIDGE?

For those retirees who truly want to distance themselves from noise and congestion, polluted air, and all those other troubling ills of urban life, this is about as far as you can go inland in Florida without setting up permanent camp in **The Everglades** or the **Big Cypress National Preserve**. The six villages at **Highlands Ridge** are nested in an environment that has more than its share of nature's bounty. When this community made the 1996 prestigious list of "20 Best Retirement Communities in America" (the fifth annual such survey by *New Choices* magazine), it was not only the first time it appeared in that select company, it was one of only two winners from Florida. It repeated the honor in 1997. The property lies at the edge of more than a mile of **Lake Bonnet** shoreline. Almost a quarter of its acreage is preserved for native wildlife and habitat. There are many rare species of plant life and native foliage unique to the area. Highlands Ridge was recently awarded top recognition by the **Florida Native Plant Society** for its commitment to preservation of natural resources.

While most of the Florida landscape is typically pictured adorned with palm trees, VHR is more accurately characterized with the presence of old oak trees and natural "scrub vegetation." Hilly terrain is an uncommon description for most of the state's countryside, but here is found the exception. Unlike the flat coastal lowlands, this inland retreat more closely resembles the undulating land of an upland piedmont region featuring picturesque ravines, running brooks, and small ponds. **Sebring** (population about 11,000), the anchor town for Highlands Ridge, is surrounded by citrus groves and grazing pasture lands. It is a town off the beaten track that found its way to notoriety in the world of international sports car racing in the early 1950s.

WHO'S IN CHARGE?

Highlands Ridge Associates, the project's developer, continues to maintain ownership and management/fiscal control of the property. A monthly fee of $127 paid by each homeowner provides for upkeep of all common grounds and recreational facilities, street maintenance, access to amenities, and unlimited participation in all social activities. The fee also includes lawn service to each home, but excludes golf course charges that are paid for separately with membership initiation (unless waived) and greens fees.

It is the developer's stated intention to retain ownership and management responsibility for the community after the project reaches completion, estimated to occur by the year 2005. Raises in the amount of fees charged to residents are limited to increases in the consumer price index.

THE WEATHER REPORT

There was no climatological data readily available for this specific Florida location. It is reasonable to assume, however, that information applicable to another central inland area, about 100 miles north, would have a comparable weather profile. Both regions are about the same distance from gulf and ocean shores and both are heavily endowed with lakes, indicating higher humidity levels than would otherwise be expected.

Significant rains begin in early summer and typically extend past the end of September. It's a time when thunderstorms and lively winds tend to moderate high midsummer afternoon temperatures. Florida's reputation for hurricanes has little application here. Protection from potentially destructive offshore storms is provided by the considerable land surface over which such turbulence would have to travel.

Weather data collected at the **Archbold Biological Station** in **Highlands County** shows the following mean daily high and low temperatures for three winter months and three summer months (recorded over a period of more than 50 years):

December: high 75/low 49	**January:** high 75/low 47
February: high 75/low 48	**June:** high 92/low 69
July: high 94/low 69	**August:** high 93/low 70

Mean annual precipitation (reported locally): 54 inches
Average annual snowfall: rare

HOME SWEET HOME

Somewhat unusual is the fact that Highlands Ridge housing is more than half double-wide manufactured homes (built on a permanent concrete foundation homesite with a "guaranteed lifetime base rent"), but with the remainder of the inventory being single-family, site-built construction that includes land ownership. Among the former, site-built double garages and verandah rooms are part of the standard package. Each type of housing is located in its own separate neighborhood.

Site-built homes range in price from the high $70s to the mid-$170s with floor plans from 1,625 to 3,400 square feet. All are constructed to meet or exceed Florida's strict building codes. Particular attention is given to maximum energy efficiency and minimum maintenance requirements. The price range for prefabricated homes begins in the mid-$50s and goes up to $100,000 for between 1,000 and 2,300 square feet. Rentals are available at between $650 and $1,975 per month in sizes to more than 2,400 square feet. Vacant lots are not sold without a home purchase.

Highlands Ridge has its own government-regulated water and sewer plant. On-site storage facilities and mobile home parking are available.

MONEY MATTERS

There is no known location-specific information on living costs for the Sebring/**Avon Park** area. It may be said, however, that most places in Florida reflect cost of living levels that hover at or near the national average. Exceptions to that general observation are greater Miami, the coastal cities of West Palm Beach and Boca Raton (and some neighboring towns), and to a lesser extent, the Sarasota/Bradenton area south of Tampa. These areas contain more highly exclusive upscale communities where buying habits are more extravagant. As in the instance of most relatively remote rural areas anywhere in the country, the costs for many necessities, especially housing, tend to be lower than in the urban centers where expensive land and more costly government services can dramatically affect consumer prices. To the extent that these observations are valid, one could expect overall living costs in the Sebring area to be at or a bit below the national average for housing, health care, groceries, and basic consumer goods and services.

TAKE GOOD CARE OF YOURSELF

Small-town, neighborly health care, but with impressive advanced technology, might best characterize the type of healing arts found in "the heartland" area. Two hospitals in Sebring serve a Highlands County population of almost 80,000 people. Both are less than 10 minutes from the VHR gate, together providing innumerable diagnostic services and treatment options. **Florida Hospital Heartland Medical Center**, opened in late 1997, is a three-story edifice with almost a quarter of a million square feet of floor space. All 101 beds are in private rooms. Facilities and services include a 12-bed intensive care unit, birthing and pediatric suites, three surgical suites with microsurgery and laser capabilities, a CT scanner, MRI, radiation therapy, and chemotherapy facilities, endoscopy and cystoscopy rooms, a state-of-the-art emergency department, and a community education center and library, offering free and low-cost community classes, screenings, and resource information.

A second full-service hospital in Sebring is the 126-bed **Highlands Regional Medical Center**, offering emergency care (including "quick care" emergency admitting), in- and outpatient services, and a new outpatient surgical center. Also just a few minutes away is **The Surgical Center of Central Florida**, a nonemergency, multispecialty facility featuring total patient care, convenience, and cost-effective treatment alternatives. The center has 20 surgeons on staff.

Yet another institution devoted to promoting a healthy populace, is the **Heartland Wellness Center**, with a focus on comprehensive illness prevention and postrehabilitation fitness. Technical equipment and staffing skills are especially attentive to health problems such as asthma, diabetes, cardiac stress, arthritis, strokes, and skeletal ailments.

There are three assisted living facilities within a 15-mile radius of VHR, with a combined total of more than 600 beds.

PLACES TO GO, THINGS TO DO

A spacious lakeside clubhouse, with a full-time activities director in charge, is the social nucleus of the community. Tennis, shuffleboard, billiards, and a large swimming pool/sun deck are some of the special features. A busy calendar of activities includes golf, tennis, and bowling teams scheduled for lively competition. Bingo and poker games beckon those with gaming inclinations. For those with alternative tastes, there are horseshoes and table tennis. Classes in ceramics, walking and aerobics groups, line dancers, and pot luck suppers can also be found on the schedule for the month. A morning coffee every Monday and an occasional pool party, pancake breakfast, or ice cream social enliven neighborly interaction and invite new friendships. There are ladies luncheons, casino nights, day trips, and even a Hawaiian Luau now and then.

When it's time to venture out of the community for more eclectic stimulation, Sebring has some surprisingly sophisticated attractions for a town of its size. **Highlands Little Theatre** is a noteworthy enterprise run entirely by volunteers and sponsored by a host of local businesses. A typical five-play season is likely to run from late October through August with a month off here and there. Productions may include musical comedy, serious drama, riveting mystery, or almost any Broadway favorite. There's a local bowling alley that hosts tournaments and league play. The downtown **Children's Museum** offers a wide variety of hands-on activities. Two cinema complexes offer a total of 14 screens. The annual **Sebring International Motor Races** are the main events of any year, drawing visitors from all around the country.

Sebring High School and **South Florida Community College** have teams competing in many sporting events, all open to the public. The college presents a cultural series of professional-level programs, including live theater, dance groups, and instrumental and vocal soloists and ensembles. The college library is also available to area residents, free of charge.

Highlands County is home to more than 30 fishing and boating lakes, with more than 35 public boat ramps. **Lake Istopoga** is the largest by far with 28,000 acres of water. Four others are more than 3,000 acres and seven more are in the range of 250 to 800 acres. **Lake Jackson** is considered the jewel of the greater Sebring area with 3,400 acres and a circumference of 11 miles, hosting every variety of water and beach sport. The **Allen Altvater Cultural Center** on Lake Jackson, near downtown, is home to the public library (with Internet access), the **Lakeside Playhouse**, the **Highlands Museum of the Arts**, the civic center, and the city pier. **Highlands Hammock State Park**, just minutes away, functions as a campsite, wildlife sanctuary, and recreation area. A tram ride gives visitors a safe and comfortable view of park wildlife, including alligators, deer, raccoons, otter, armadillos, and more than 200 species of birds. You might even spot an occasional bald eagle or Florida panther.

SAFE AND SECURE

Access to the community is controlled by automated security gates. The **Highlands County Sheriff's Department** provides police protection. A volunteer fire department in Sebring deals with control and prevention activity. There is an active volunteer neighborhood watch program. The county is said to be among those with the lowest incidence of crime in the state.

LET'S GO SHOPPING

The up-to-date **Lakeshore Mall** in Sebring, with more than 600,000 square feet of enclosed shopping, became the first major retail center for Highlands County and beyond in 1992. Situated on more than 100 acres, it can accommodate almost 3,000 cars and features four anchor department stores, along with a string of specialty shops and boutiques. Only 5 miles from the VHR gate, there is little residents cannot find to satisfy needs. A full-service grocery market is equally convenient, along with other product and service businesses and professional offices.

THE VILLAGES OF LADY LAKE

LADY LAKE, FLORIDA

1100 Main St.
Lady Lake, FL 32159
352-753-2270 / 800-346-4556
Fax: 352-753-6224

Developer: Harold S. Schwartz/H. Gary Morse

Year of initial property sales/rental: 1983

Total land area: 7,360 acres

Approximate elevation: 100 feet

Location: North-central Florida; Lake, Sumter, and Marion Counties; on combined Interstate Highways 27 and 441; about 50 miles northwest of Orlando; 23 miles southeast of Ocala; 8 miles north of Leesburg.

Nearest airport with scheduled commercial service: Orlando International (58 miles)

Current number of housing units with year-round occupants: 8,000

Projected number of housing units: 23,549 (2021)

Resident eligibility: No permanent residents under age 19. An estimated 80% of the population is retired or semiretired.

Community visit/tour incentive program: A "retirement preview plan" provides for complimentary on-site hotel or private villa accommodations, continental breakfasts, and access to golf courses and other recreational amenities.

Suggested newspaper: *Daily Sun* (Village Ed.), 1153 Main St., Lady Lake, FL 32159 (352-753-1119)

WHY THE VILLAGES OF LADY LAKE?

Although the **Villages of Lady Lake** community has more than 7,000 acres spanning parts of three counties (**Lake, Sumter,** and **Marion**), the development has maintained a quaint, small-town flavor. In many ways, it seems more like a municipality than a family-owned-and-operated master-planned community, because it offers so much of the convenience normally found only in a public jurisdiction. The entire enterprise, in fact, is 13 separate and distinct villages, all under one management. According to *Florida Trend* magazine, it is the fourth largest master-planned community of any type in the entire state of Florida.

The **Village of Spanish Springs,** part of the **Town Square District,** is essentially the "downtown" core. It is distinguished by its appealing

Spanish-style, turn-of-the-century architecture and the extensive variety of retail outlets, professional offices, and service establishments. Golf carts are seen not only cruising the fairways, but rambling about between the food market and the hardware store, serving as an alternative to the family car for community errands. A well-appointed 48-room hotel with a hacienda design, along with two modern 32-lane bowling centers, share the marketplace spotlight.

WHO'S IN CHARGE?

The ownership and administrative arrangements at The Villages is something quite different from the typical retirement community. Issues of legal possession and control of property are complex matters that cannot readily be described in this limited space. Suffice to say that there is a gradual transition in the decision-making process, wherein after the developer completes planning, construction, and marketing phases, and as more homeowners settle in, a reorganization takes place. Under Florida law, when an appropriate point is reached in the evolution of the project, a **Community Development District (CDD)**, a quasi-governmental entity, becomes the mechanism through which revenues are collected to sustain the infrastructure, recreational amenities, security operations, etc., and to protect the financial integrity of the community as it matures. At the time of this writing, the assessment (in lieu of taxes) paid by homeowners in that connection is in the range of $22 to $54 a month, part of a total $99 monthly fee that pays for the entire amenities and programs package.

The **Community Improvement Council (CIC)** is composed of residents who assist the developer and the CDD in identifying opportunities for community improvement. This activity is accomplished, in part, through a system of suggestion stations located throughout the property, inviting ideas, concerns, or problems to which any resident may wish to draw attention and seek response. A representative group of the CIC meets regularly with the developer and the CDD. **The Villages Homeowners Association** is a not-for-profit corporation established to promote and foster goodwill and effective communication among the various constituencies. The organization publishes a monthly newsletter and holds monthly meetings. Token membership dues of $6 a year per household satisfy budgetary needs. Affiliation by residents is optional.

THE WEATHER REPORT

Inland Florida in the north-central region is endowed with many lakes. The presence of so much surface water tends to raise humidity levels higher than otherwise would be the case. The rainy season begins in early summer and normally goes into October. Thunderstorms are not uncommon in the afternoons at that time of year, and when they occur, they are mostly short-lived and help bring temperatures down to more comfortable levels. The Villages is located far enough away from the coasts to be relatively free from the threat of hurricanes. Local climate statistics compiled and distributed by community sources show the following average daily high and low temperatures for three winter months and three summer months:

December: high 72/low 44   **January:** high 72/low 41

February: high 76/low 43   **June:** high 89/low 67

July: high 94/low 69   **August:** high 95/low 68

Average annual precipitation: 52 inches
Average annual snowfall: rare

HOME SWEET HOME

Standard homesites are 60 feet by 90 feet, completely developed with wide, paved, and curbed streets and gutters, sod and landscaping, central sewer and water systems, street lights and signage, storm sewers, and underground utilities. A collection of fully furnished model homes and villas is open to visitors seven days a week to inspect features first-hand. Villages homes were recognized for quality and value with the "Best in American Living Award" from *Better Homes & Gardens* magazine.

Currently, there are 22 models of single-family detached homes in three different series, ranging from 905 to 2,310 square feet and at prices from under $60,000 to more than $180,000. Custom dwellings have been built at costs exceeding $300,000. A series of five "Courtyard Villas" offer one- and two-bedroom units from 960 to 1,179 square feet in a price range from the low $70s to the high $80s. Five "Patio Villas," also one- and two-bedroom plans, are the most economical, with floor space ranging from 834 square feet to a maximum of 1,190 square feet. The price spread on these units is from the low $50s to the high $60s. The two Villa series are intended to emphasize privacy and low maintenance, notwithstanding proximity to neighboring homes. They also feature unique "car and cart" garages.

MONEY MATTERS

The greater **Orlando** area is the closest location for which there is any living cost data available. In the *ACCRA Cost of Living Index* (2nd quarter, 1996), six selected categories of consumer spending show a composite cost index of 1.6 percent below the average of 315 metropolitan and nonmetropolitan areas of the country. Among the six weighted segments of products and services measured, utilities showed the highest comparative cost at 16.3 percent above average, and health costs at 8.7 percent above average. The remaining four groupings showed below average values, although each constituted more heavily weighted factors: groceries, 3.3 percent; housing, 6.5

percent; transportation, 1.5 percent; and miscellaneous goods and services, 2.8 percent.

An estimated minimum monthly cost of living projection was prepared by Villages resources for an average home in the community. Recognizing that such costs will vary considerably depending on the size and lot location of a home and the usage habits of occupants, the following summary nevertheless was suggested as a guideline:

Amenities fee (covers access to all recreational facilities and social programs)	$99
Water and sewer	$38
Electricity (including heating and cooling)	$100
Trash collection	$15
Telephone	$14
Cable television	$27
Insurance	$42
Taxes	$125
Development District Assessment	$37
Total monthly expenses	**$497**

TAKE GOOD CARE OF YOURSELF

The community's own medical center is **The Villages Hometown Health Care**. It provides "one-stop" outpatient medical service, including x-ray and laboratory facilities and on-site physicians. **The Village of Homewood**, an on-site 40-unit assisted living facility, opened its doors in January 1998. For full-range hospital services, **Leesburg Regional Medical Center**, about 8 miles south of Lady Lake, is a facility with comprehensive specialties that include cardiac catheterization, nutritional counseling, home rehabilitation, pain management, and treatment of sleep disorders. In **Ocala**, a little more than 20 miles to the north, is **Columbia Ocala Regional Medical Center**. Major service components include dedicated treatment centers for diabetes, cancer, and cardiovascular conditions. The hospital also offers a large home health care agency, a satellite physical rehabilitation center, and a wound care unit.

PLACES TO GO, THINGS TO DO

There are 99 holes of golf in The Villages. Three are country-club, 18-hole, par 72, championship courses of more than 6,000 yards, the longest at 6,835.

Residents are automatically members of all three clubs, whether they are golfers or not, and are entitled to a broad spectrum of social and recreational amenities. Five executive nine-hole courses complete the variety of choices, satisfying any skill level, from novice to advanced. All five executive courses offer unlimited free play for residents (it's included in the basic amenities fee). Green fees on the larger country-club courses come to less than a dollar a hole, and even less for more frequent golfers who opt for an available extended-play discount program. An aqua driving range is available for practice swinging.

For those whose leisure time is not mostly absorbed by golf, there are literally hundreds of organized activities going on virtually every week of the year. A recreation department of more than 30 staffers keeps an incredible number of programs going, along with operating and maintaining the golf courses, five recreation centers, swimming pools, and such. A regularly distributed brochure more than 20 pages long details information on hobby and interest groups, music, dance, drama, crafts, and sports activities, and a seemingly endless number of clubs devoted to everything from cards, chess, mah jong, cribbage, and scrabble to travel, exercise, astrology, photography, and computers.

Add to all of this leisure, 10 heated swimming pools (one an oversized tropical hour-glass-shaped creation with a cascading waterfall), 14 courts for tennis, 22 for bocce ball, 18 for shuffleboard, 18 for pickleball, and one each for sand volleyball and outdoor basketball. Then there's a softball diamond, a table tennis room, six miles of pedestrian and bicycle paths, 12 horseshoe pits, 50 acres of private community lakes stocked for fishing, three lakeside parks, 11 wildlife preserves, a library, a six-table billiards room, and the 32-lane state-of-the-art bowling centers, complete with pro shops and lounges. There's even a polo field under construction. If bingo is your thing, there are no less than six different times and places during the week where you can challenge the odds. Oh yes, did we mention a couple of paddle boats for lake exploration?

Off-site recreational and educational standouts of a different sort are on tap in nearby communities and, of course, at the internationally renowned **Walt Disney World, Universal Studios**, and **Sea World** in the Orlando area, all within an hour's drive from The Villages. **Silver Springs**, just outside of Ocala and less than a half-hour away, is a 350-acre multi-theme nature park with great features, such as the "lost river voyage," "jeep safari," glass-bottom boats, a petting zoo, and animal shows.

Beyond recreation, there is much to be enjoyed in cultural and educational enrichment and in the wonders of nature. There are museums in Orlando, Ocala (population 65,000), and all around that celebrate not only the fine arts and sciences, but also railroads, drag racing, aviation, American heritage, ancient life forms, and pre-Columbian artifacts. Gorgeous gardens and nature preserves abound.

North-central Florida is the heart of equestrian country, where thorough-breds are raised, trained, and boarded on more than 400 horse farms. **Ocala National Forest**, on the **Lady Lake** doorstep, is a sprawling retreat for camping, fishing, hiking, lake swimming, and water sports. Live entertainment of every description, tours and cruises, and colossal theme parks combine to make decisions about where to go first almost too much to contemplate.

Uncharacteristic of most master-planned communities, there are three houses of worship inside The Villages parameters, two of them nondenominational. All major denominations are represented at off-site locations nearby.

SAFE AND SECURE

All entrances to The Villages are controlled by automated card-access gates or manned guard stations. In addition to police protection provided by municipal and county law enforcement agencies, **The Villages Neighborhood Watch** monitors the community with mobile patrols around the clock, seven days a week. Special attention is given to homes that have been vacated by residents for extended periods of time. A three-county 911 emergency telephone system is in place, coordinated between the community's on-site fire station and emergency medical services and local police agencies. A senior citizens helpline is provided by volunteers through the **Lake County Sheriff's Department**.

LET'S GO SHOPPING

Shopping in The Villages belies a community of its size. The variety and number of retail and service establishments and professional offices is un-characteristic of most master-planned communities. The Town Square District and the Village of Spanish Springs are the focal points of more than 600,000 square feet of commercial space. Two principal business sections feature two major chain food markets, a national departmental drug store, and vendors of apparel, hardware, golf carts and accessories, health foods, liquor, cards and gifts, baked goods, flowers, jewelry, and home furnishings. There's a convenience store/gas station, three banks, a post office, insurance and travel agencies, medical clinics, dental offices, an optometrist, dry cleaners and Laundromat, and styling salon, along with attorney and financial services offices.

MARYLAND TAX FACTS

INDIVIDUAL INCOME TAX

Graduated from 2% to 5% as follows (for joint filers, surviving spouses, or heads of households):

- First $1,000 of income @ 2%
- Next $1,000 @ 3%
- Next $1,000 @ 4%
- Over $3,000 @ 5%

Exemptions:

- Age 65 or over, $1,000
- Personal or elderly dependent, $1,200
- Not under 20 percent and not more than 60 percent of state income tax is imposed in many counties and in the city of Baltimore.

SALES TAX

A 5 percent sales and use tax is levied on the purchase of tangible personal property and certain services.

PROPERTY TAX

The range of property tax rates per $1,000 of assessed value varies from $1.23 to $5.85. Most, but not all, intangibles are exempt. These rates are composites of locally applicable city, county, and school district rates. There may be additional levies by special districts and improvement assessments not covered in the foregoing figures.

RANKING REPORT

Data published in *The Rating Guide to Life in America's Fifty States* in 1994 showed Maryland ranking 25th from the most favorable with regard to property taxes.

For more complete tax information contact the Comptroller of the Treasury/Revenue Administration, Revenue Administration Center, Annapolis, MD 21401, 410-974-3441, (fax) 410-974-3456.

Note: The above information is based on applicable tax law information available at the time of publication. Because such laws and tax rates are subject to change, professional assistance should be sought if tax implications are critical to a relocation decision.

HERITAGE HARBOUR

ANNAPOLIS, MARYLAND

2745 South Haven Rd.
Annapolis, MD 21401
301-261-8930
Fax: 301-261-8229

Developer: US Home Corporation

Year of initial property sales/rental: 1979

Approximate total land area: 953 acres

Average elevation: 95 feet

Location: Coastal Maryland; Anne Arundel County; 4 miles west of Annapolis; 30 miles east of Washington, D.C.; 25 miles south of Baltimore; about 10 miles southwest of the intersection of Interstate 97 and U.S. Highway 50.

Nearest airport with scheduled commercial service: Baltimore/Washington International (15 miles)

Current number of housing units with year-round occupants: 1,650

Projected number of housing units: 1,710 (1998)

Resident eligibility: At least one family member must be 55 years of age or older.

Community visit/tour incentive program: None

Suggested newspaper: *Capital Newspaper*, 2000 Capital Dr., Annapolis, MD 21401 (410-766-3700)

WHY HERITAGE HARBOUR?

To those for whom location is everything, it is hard to imagine a locale with more convenient access to two major U.S. metropolitan areas—less than 30 miles to **Washington, D.C.**, or **Baltimore**—and yet in a setting essentially outside the urban distress zones of congestion, crime, and pollution. The development is nestled on a rolling, heavily wooded peninsula formed by tributaries of the **Chesapeake Bay**. Approximately half of its 1,000 acres are reserved for natural terrain.

New Choices magazine, in its fifth annual survey of the 20 best retirement communities in the United States, published in the summer of 1996, named **Heritage Harbour** for the third successive year as one of the selected few such communities to be so distinguished.

WHO'S IN CHARGE?

In 1997, the community was in a transitional phase from developer control to homeowner control. This process was scheduled to be completed in early 1998 with the election of a new board of directors composed of elected resident representatives. Prior to that time, a "shadow board" has led what is known as the **Heritage Harbour Community Association.** This is the mechanism through which homeowners provide day-to-day management, sharing such responsibility with the professional management agent representing the developer.

Assessments paid by homeowners are $85 per month. Such funds provide the financial support for maintenance and operation of all community amenities, including a private bus service, security personnel and facilities, cable television, common grounds upkeep, etc. Condominium owners pay additional fees for additional services that vary among different housing configurations.

THE WEATHER REPORT

Annapolis lies in a region that is between the harsh weather patterns to the north and the more forgiving climates to the south. With the **Atlantic Ocean** and Chesapeake Bay on its coastal flank to the east and the looming **Appalachian Mountains** to the west, there are substantial moderating influences tending to obviate temperature extremes, making for more equable climatic conditions than those of other locations further inland at the same latitude. Bay breezes often relieve what might be described as a subtropical marine climate with considerable heat and humidity during the summer months.

The nearest official weather station is at the **Baltimore/Washington International Airport**, about 15 miles north at the southern outskirts of Baltimore. The following average high and low winter and summer temperatures are reported:

December: high 45/low 28	**January:** high 40/low 23
February: high 44/low 26	**June:** high 83/low 62
July: high 87/low 67	**August:** high 85/low 66

Average annual precipitation: 39 inches
Average annual snowfall: 14 inches

HOME SWEET HOME

Single-family detached resale homes range in price from the low $180s to under $280,000, with floor plans varying in size from 1,300 to 2,500 square feet. Townhouses on the resale market generally cost between $130,000 and $250,000 in sizes from 900 to 2,200 square feet. Condominiums, with a broader price spread of $99,000 to $300,000, are found in sizes ranging from 900 to 1,900 square feet. One- and two-story villas typically start in the $140s.

The most recent new construction is a series of three-story condominium buildings, each with 30 units of various sizes and layouts and each with basement parking and storage. These units are built with many of the U.S. Home features that characterize the company's long list of trademark advantages, including Andersen high-performance windows, careful insulation protection, insulated patio doors, intercom security system, and dependable warranties.

MONEY MATTERS

Comparative living expense survey data is available for Baltimore, the nearest location for such information. With 100 percent representing the average cost of living index for 315 metropolitan and nonmetropolitan areas included in the survey, the Baltimore Primary Metropolitan Statistical Area (PMSA) showed a composite index of 99.9, just a shade under precise average. Of six weighted cost categories, three were above average (groceries, 3.6 percent; utilities, 11.1 percent; transportation, 3.2 percent) and three were below average (housing, 2.4 percent; health care, 0.9 percent; miscellaneous goods and services, 3.5 percent). The relatively small below-average values of the miscellaneous and housing categories nevertheless substantially affected the overall average, because they are the most heavily weighted values (33 percent and 28 percent of the total, respectively).

Local property taxes levied by the county are based on 40 percent of the sale price multiplied by .0259. For a $130,000 home, that translates to $1,347 per year. Especially noteworthy is the fact that full equity golf and country club memberships are included with every new home purchase.

TAKE GOOD CARE OF YOURSELF

The **Anne Arundel General Hospital & Medical Center** in downtown **Annapolis**, less than 5 miles from Heritage Harbour, is a full-service facility with 303 beds. It has a long tradition of state-of-the-art medical services for women with a focus on the screening, diagnosis, and treatment of breast cancer. It is also a premiere maternity facility. An affiliated medical park has centers for oncology, outpatient surgery, and health education. A nonprofit alcohol and drug treatment program offers adult and adolescent inpatient and outpatient recovery services.

A second nearby large acute-care medical institution, about 15 miles north at **Glen Burnie**, just south of Baltimore and near the airport, is **North Arundel Hospital** with 330 beds. Specialties include orthopedic nursing and surgical units, modern endoscopy, and a comprehensive rehabilitation program. The county health department offers outpatient services at

21 locations. There are five nursing and convalescent homes serving the greater Annapolis area. Nearly 350 physicians, surgeons, and dentists maintain practices in the area.

PLACES TO GO. THINGS TO DO

Heritage Harbour has more than its share of pleasurable amenities. A private nine-hole executive golf course, with a clubhouse (including a pro shop and instruction program), caters only to members. A 32,000-square-foot lodge is the center of social and recreational activity. It features indoor and outdoor swimming pools with sauna and spa, nine tennis courts (two lighted), a billiards room, woodworking shop, craft shop, fitness center, an auditorium and conference center, library, a television production studio, and card and game rooms. Nearby are walking/cycling paths and parks and playgrounds, further contributing to recreational options. Clubs and interest groups include bridge, square dancing, chorus, ballroom dancing, bowling, drama, newsletter publishing, music, golf and tennis, billiards, bingo, computers, and group tours/trips.

It would be hard to imagine being located closer to a greater array of world-class leisure attractions than those enjoyed by people living in the Annapolis area. Within a 35-mile radius lie all the cultural, recreational, entertainment, and educational resources of the nation's capital. Its endless sources of appeal are unequaled. From the extravagant stage productions at the **Kennedy Center** and the extraordinary endowment of the **Library of Congress**, to priceless **Smithsonian Institution** treasures, the most prestigious of museums, hallowed monuments and memorials, the halls of national government, highly regarded universities, and countless other enticements, there is nowhere else in the country to compare. Professional and collegiate sports of every description are readily accessible.

Within the same short distance are the virtues of another great city— Baltimore, with its own distinguished character. Perhaps most reflective of this metropolis was the transformation of an inner harbor area from a neglected and decaying area to a model of urban redesign and vitality.

With Annapolis a mere 4 miles away, Heritage Harbour can look upon this distinctive city of almost 35,000 inhabitants as its primary off-site playground, shopping destination, and escape hatch. It is the Maryland state capital, but it derives equal notoriety as the "sailboat capital of the world." The entire downtown section is a registered National Historic Landmark, with more than 60 18th-century structures contributing to its unique historical legacy. Its most notable institutional citizen is the **United States Naval Academy. St. John's College**, the third-oldest institution of higher learning in the United States, is a private liberal arts college known for a curriculum based on the great books of western civilization.

Annapolis has its own symphony, opera, live theater, chorale, ballet, brass quintet, and children's theater, among other professional and amateur companies. Artists in residence offer classes in fine art, dance, music, and many other mediums. The **Maryland Renaissance Festival,** developed on a 23-acre wooded site in nearby **Crownsville,** is a re-creation of a 16th-century English village featuring a jousting arena, four pubs, and eight major stages, along with inviting food and crafts booths, period costumes, and a variety of interpretive English accents with a hint of southern drawl or Appalachian twang.

SAFE AND SECURE

County law enforcement and fire protection departments are the primary agencies responsible for police and emergency functions, including ambulance service. In addition, the community contracts with a private security service for supplementary neighborhood security patrols.

LET'S GO SHOPPING

A full-service food market is just 2 miles from the community entrance. Two miles further is one of two large regional malls in Annapolis. Together with several smaller shopping concentrations and the downtown section, there is little consumer need that goes unmet. The extent of commercial development is reflected in the fact that there are 19 banking and savings and loan institutions, each with several branches, serving metropolitan Annapolis.

LEISURE WORLD OF MARYLAND

SILVER SPRING, MARYLAND

14901 Pennfield Circle
Silver Spring, MD 20906
301-598-2100
Fax: 301-598-8950

Developer: International Developers, Inc. (IDI)

Year of initial property sales/rentals: 1964

Total land area: 620 acres

Average elevation: 450 feet

Location: Central Maryland; Montgomery County; approximately 20 miles north of downtown Washington, D.C.; about 8 miles west of Rockville and Interstate 270; near intersection of State Highways 28 and 97.

Nearest airport with scheduled commercial service: Washington National (20 miles)

Current number of housing units with year-round occupants: 6,000-plus

Projected number of housing units: 7,500 (2005)

Resident eligibility: At least one member of the household must be at least 55 years of age. No permanent resident may be under the age of 50.

Community visit/tour incentive program: None

Suggested newspaper: *The Washington Post,* 1150 15th St., NW, Washington, DC 20071 (202-334-6000)

WHY LEISURE WORLD OF MARYLAND?

Located on the outskirts of the nation's capital, **Leisure World of Maryland** is an active adult community offering advantages beyond compare. The community is the hallmark of adult-only developments in all of metropolitan **Washington, D.C.** By virtue of size alone (about 4,400 housing units and more than 7,000 residents), it's in a class by itself. It is minutes away from some of the greatest historical, cultural, recreational, and entertainment attractions in the world. It is a community surrounded by a huge "bedroom" population of government workers, corporate and national association offices, and others, who commute into the District of Columbia to work. Along with its neighboring northern suburbs, LW is part of an area that boasts an unusually well-educated population and an economy that is generally more stable than that of any major city in the nation. The Washington suburbs, throughout Maryland and Virginia, are brimming over with community events and ongoing activities—enough to satisfy the most resolute of leisure life styles.

For almost three decades, the redeveloper, IDI, has been the recipient of numerous awards, many of which have been won repeatedly as new sections of the community were completed. There were nine such honors bestowed in the 1970s, 13 in the 1980s, and eight more through the mid-1990s. These most recent awards included: five-time presentations for "Finest for Family Living," given by the **Washington Metropolitan Builders Council**; an "Outstanding Remodeler Achievement Award" from the **Northern Virginia Building Industry**; and an "Award of Excellence in Seniors Housing," by the **National Association of Home Builders**.

The community is served by its own "minibus" transportation system. Residents pay no fare for trips that are scheduled on an approximate hourly basis during much of each weekday and on a curtailed schedule on Saturdays. Trips include stops for shopping, and at professional offices, restaurants, etc., both inside and outside the community. Special "dial-a-ride" transportation for door-to-door service is also available during extended hours at a moderate cost.

WHO'S IN CHARGE?

The **Leisure World of Maryland Corporation** is a nonprofit entity headed by the **Community Council**, its governing body. The council is comprised of representatives from each of 21 "mutuals" (separate sections or neighborhoods within Leisure World), in which all property owners are automatically members. The council meets monthly to consider matters that affect the entire community. Each mutual is governed by its own board of directors, elected by residents in each such jurisdiction. Such bodies approve annual budgets for the care and upkeep of all commonly owned properties and community services, and also communicate and enforce policies and regulations regarding the use, occupancy and maintenance of such properties. All residents share equally in the operation of all community facilities, including the clubhouses and all recreational amenities. Several hundred residents serve voluntarily on the council, on the independent boards of directors, and on various standing and special committees. A semimonthly community newspaper and closed circuit television channel keep residents informed of activities and management developments as they affect property owners. Some mutuals distribute their own newsletters as well.

Undeveloped areas are owned and controlled by the developer, a private firm, which carries out the continuing physical expansion of the community. The developer is separate and distinct from the community corporation and is not involved with the administration of Leisure World recreational amenities or programs, common grounds or residential areas.

Current monthly condominium fees range from $285 to $404, depending on size. They cover water/sewer/trash services, common grounds and building maintenance, insurance, security, transportation services, clubhouse operations, medical center costs and reserves for future capital repairs and replacements. Some recreational activities are not covered and require modest user fees (golf, swimming, bowling, etc.). Electricity used for the common areas is also covered by the condo fee; living units are individually metered.

THE WEATHER REPORT

The middle latitude of the District of Columbia and surrounding suburbs create a west to east atmospheric flow that favors a continental climate with four well-defined seasons. Summers are quite warm and can be quite humid. The coldest temperatures can be expected during late January and the warmest during the last half of July. Precipitation is rather evenly distributed throughout the year, but thunderstorms are more likely during late spring and on through the summer. Damaging storms are unusual.

The following weather data are drawn from **Washington National Airport**, about 20 miles from Leisure World, and the nearest official weather station to the community:

December: high 47/low 32   **January:** high 42/low 27

February: high 46/low 29   **June:** high 85/low 66

July: high 88/low 71   **August:** high 87/low 70

Average annual precipitation: 39 inches
Average annual snowfall: 16 inches

HOME SWEET HOME

Leisure World has single-family homes, townhouses, apartments, and condominiums. New units currently on the market, however, are all condominiums in four five-story buildings, being offered in a large new section on a wooded knoll overlooking the golf course and landscaped courtyards. The new community, **Turnberry Courts,** offers one-, two-, and three-bedroom plans, ranging in size from 888 to 1,496 square feet, and priced from the mid-$130s to more than $270,000.

The resale market offers all types of living units, including a significant number of townhouses and single-family, primarily two-story homes.

MONEY MATTERS

It is well-established that the cost of living in the Washington, D.C. metropolitan area is considerably above the average for major U.S. urban centers. Research on living expenses for 315 metropolitan statistical areas, cities, and rural places shows that the District ranks fourth from the most expensive, behind San Francisco, New York City, and Boston. More specifically, the composite index for the six weighted categories of living costs was shown to be 24.3 percent above average. All but one category (utilities) reflected such high side figures. Housing was the singularly most dramatic influence on upward pricing pressures with a 58.8 percent above average reading. The remaining categories (groceries, transportation, health care, and miscellaneous goods and services) showed to be above average in ranges from 9 percent to 25.3 percent.

Property taxes are based on 40 percent of the gross purchase price of the dwelling at a tax rate of $2.7961 per $100 of value.

TAKE GOOD CARE OF YOURSELF

An on-site outpatient medical center is an integral part of the Leisure World community. The facility is staffed by more than 25 physicians and other health care professionals. Medical specialties include internal medicine, psychiatry, dermatology, podiatry, surgery, ophthalmology, and gynecology. The neighboring medical professional building is the site for dentists, registered nurses, pharmacists, and social workers. Fees for services are competitive or less than similar services outside the community, based on Medicare maximum allowable fees. An emergency nurse is available 24 hours a day, seven days a week, including holidays. A pharmacy owned by Leisure World is also located at the medical center, supplementing parallel services provided by a drug store in the shopping area.

Just 6 miles away, **Holy Cross Hospital** in **Silver Spring** is the closest full-service inpatient facility to the community. It is the largest single provider (with 442 beds) of primary and complex acute health care services in **Montgomery County,** and maintains teaching affiliations with the **Children's National Medical Center** and **George Washington University School of Medicine.** Areas of recognized special competence include departments of cardiovascular health, gastroenterology, oncology, orthopedics, and women and children's services. The hospital regularly offers free community health seminars and often participates in community health education activities, including health screenings and health fairs.

Montgomery General Hospital, with 229 beds, is located in nearby **Olney,** only 8 miles from Leisure World. It operates a notable addiction and mental health center, as well as an outpatient surgery program, a maternal and child health center and a radiation therapy cancer treatment facility. On-campus magnetic resonance imaging equipment and computer-enhanced imaging techniques are also distinguishing service features.

There are no fewer than 18 Health Maintenance Organizations (HMOs) in Montgomery County. Nearby multilevel care facilities include a large Marriott retirement operation (less than a mile from LW) with accommodations for

220 residents. An 80-bed nursing home with more intensive care levels is about 10 minutes away.

PLACES TO GO, THINGS TO DO

Two clubhouses, one with approximately 60,000 square feet of floor space, are the focus of recreational and social activities. Together they offer a broad range of leisure options, including restaurants, lounges, a 320-seat auditorium (venue for movies, concerts, lectures, and club meetings), a dining hall with patios, and special rooms for visual arts, ceramics, photography (dark room), sewing, billiards (five tables), and a complete woodworking shop. Other amenities found are a well-equipped fitness center, saunas, locker rooms, a four-lane duckpin bowling alley, and a travel office. Outside facilities include two outdoor asphalt surface tennis courts, shuffleboard, horseshoes, croquet, lawn bowling, an indoor swimming pool, and a lanai. A private (residents and guests only), 100-acre, 18-hole championship golf course, with a driving range and putting green, is the frosting on the cake. Hiking and nature trails also offer popular escapes. Classes are offered from time to time in everything from aerobics, bridge, and dancing to dramatics, sculpture, and foreign languages. More than 60 groups and organizations gather around such common interests as book reviews, mah jong, chess, genealogy, prayer and Bible study, music, or shared experience support groups.

A leisure activity for green thumbs in the community is the tending of personal gardens. Plots are provided for a fee of $7.50 a year which entitles the gardener to a 20-foot by 20-foot plot of ground and access to a complete assortment of tools and supplies. **The Leisure World Travel Club**, an enterprise owned and operated by the community, promotes an impressive agenda of group travel destinations. A recent announcement of 22 excursions described some as day trips, others from one- to three-nights' lodging, and some (cruises for example), planned as extended vacations. The number and variety of day trips are quite extraordinary, given the array of attractions, most within a 100-mile radius. Popular destinations include **Atlantic City, Williamsburg, Gettysburg, Luray Caverns, Chesapeake Bay, Baltimore Inner Harbor, Ocean City, Annapolis, Adventure World, Virginia Beach**, and a host of sporting events at such athletic coliseums as **RFK Stadium**, and any number of other professional and collegiate competitive sports arenas.

Museums, historical sites, art galleries, cathedrals, monuments and memorials, parks and government nerve centers in the Washington area are beyond counting. Visitors from around the world come to see the **Smithsonian Institute, U.S. Capitol, Washington, Lincoln,** and **Jefferson Memorials**, the **White House, Library of Congress, National Gallery of Art, Kennedy Center, National Archives, Mount Vernon, Ford's Theatre, Wolf Trap Farm Park for the Performing Arts, National Air

& **Space Museum**, and scores of other celebrated attractions. All are on the Leisure World doorstep, together representing an entire lifetime of exploration, enlightenment, and stimulation. The list of arts and crafts fairs and schedule of summer concert sites are too long to enumerate here.

More than 500 public and private nonprofit agencies offer, at any given time, around 2,000 opportunities for volunteer service. A dozen colleges and universities in the area make up some of the nation's most prestigious institutions of higher learning. Of special interest to mature adults is the Institute for Lifelong Learning at **Montgomery College**, with a campus in **Tacoma Park**, just minutes from the LW main gate. Credit and noncredit courses include various musical pursuits, computer literacy, interior and landscape design, history, personal finance, and writing.

SAFE AND SECURE

There are several staffed entry gates through which visitors to Leisure World must pass. The main gate operates automatically around the clock every day of the week. Secondary gates have guards on duty from early morning until late evening, after which entry is blocked to anyone who does not have an access identification card. In addition to gate guards, special, private police provide law enforcement and internal security. These officers are on constant patrol and take up stations at community functions at the clubhouses and elsewhere. When appropriate, they can request assistance from the **Montgomery County Police Department.** Fire protection is provided by the **Kensington Fire Department**, less than 2 miles away.

"Lifeline" is a personal emergency system, offered to all residents, enabling a caller to get assistance without having to get to a telephone. A small device worn or carried by the caller is activated with a push of a button. There is a minimal charge for the service. There is a 911 emergency phone system also in place for rescue, fire, or police assistance.

LET'S GO SHOPPING

A major business center, **Leisure World Plaza**, is located immediately outside the community's main gate. Among its 25 or so merchants are a major supermarket, three banks, eating places, and an assortment of specialty shops and service establishments, as well as a professional building. A free minibus operated by the community takes shoppers to this and several other nearby commercial areas.

Ten miles away, in **Rockville**, is **White Flint Mall**, fully enclosed with prominent department stores, along with some of the most exclusive shopping areas in the northern suburbs. Even closer is **Wheaton Plaza**, which also features notable department and specialty shopping.

NORTH CAROLINA TAX FACTS

INDIVIDUAL INCOME TAX

Graduated from 6% to 7.75% as follows:

- First $21,250 of income @ 6%
- Next $78,750 @ 7%
- Over $100,000 @ 7.75%

Exemptions/Deductions:

- Deduction allowed for Social Security and Railroad.
- Retirement Act benefits.
- Deductions for governmental and private retirement benefits.
- Qualifying widow(er) rate concession.
- Intangible taxes (on investment securities) are exempt.

SALES TAX

The state levies a general retail sales and use tax at the rate of 4 percent (reduced to 3 percent on sales of food for home consumption, effective January 1, 1997). A local rate of 2 percent is imposed by all counties.

PROPERTY TAX

Local property taxes are levied on real estate and tangible personal property other than household furnishings and personal belongings that are not used in business. There is no state tax on such property. Rates vary greatly among localities, but are in general moderate because most operating costs for public schools and for road construction and maintenance are borne by the state. The average combined rate (county, city, and district) on municipally located property in 1995-96 was $1.21 per $100 of appraised value (revalued every eight years). Household tangible personal property in the residence of an owner is exempt from property taxation.

RANKING REPORT

According to *State Government Finances*, among the 50 states, North Carolina ranks at precisely the midpoint, 25th from the most favorable in total state taxes per capita when only state levies are considered.

For more complete tax information contact the North Carolina Revenue Department, Public Information Division, P.O. Box 25000, Raleigh, NC 27640, 919-733-7211.

Note: The above information is based on applicable tax law data current at the time of publication. Because such laws and rates are subject to change, professional assistance should be sought if tax implications are critical to a relocation decision.

ALBEMARLE PLANTATION

HERTFORD, NORTH CAROLINA

One Plantation Dr.
Hertford, NC 27944
919-426-4653 / 800-523-5958
Fax: 919-426-7054

Developer: HPB Enterprises

Year of initial property sales/rentals: 1990

Total land area: 1,600 acres

Average elevation: 12 feet

Location: Far northeastern corner of North Carolina; Perquimans County; at the head of Perquimans Bay; an inlet off the north bank of Albemarle Sound; on U.S. Hwy. 17; 25 miles southwest of Elizabeth City; 65 to 70 miles south of the Virginia Beach/Norfolk/Newport News/ Portsmouth Tidewater area at the southeastern tip of Virginia.

Nearest airport with scheduled commercial service: Norfolk International (65 miles)

Current number of housing units with year-round occupants: 85

Projected number of housing units: 1,000 (2009)

Resident eligibility: There is no age restriction, but an estimated 95% of current residents are either retired or semiretired. Fewer than 5% of households have children under age 18 in permanent residence.

Community visit/tour incentive program: $139 a couple for three days/two nights in a condo on-site, with discounts on meals and pro shop; area and boat tour; free round of golf; other variations for "Plantation Getaway."

Suggested newspaper: *Daily Advance*, 216 Poindexter St., Elizabeth City, NC 27909 (919-335-0841)

WHY ALBEMERLE PLANTATION?

   Albemarle Plantation is still in the early stages of its development. While this directory is largely focused on communities with no fewer than 150 occupied homes, we have made an exception in this instance. There are strong indications that accelerated growth is likely to occur over the next few years.

   This is a community distinguished by its location and uncommon setting. It is perched on an inlet off the north bank of **Albemarle Sound**, the largest fresh water estuary in the United States, fed by the **Atlantic Ocean**. Easy access to the **Intracoastal Waterway**, to North Carolina's famous **Outer**

Banks beaches and the Atlantic Ocean, and to flourishing nearby cities of the **Tidewater**, offers a unique combination of geographical and topographical appeal. Much of the expansive site is endowed with pines, oaks, birch, and cypress, alongside stretches of wetlands inhabited by a variety of wildlife species.

The community's two sizable neighboring towns, **Edenton** and **Elizabeth City,** the former a short drive to the southwest and the latter to the northeast, both enjoy notable reputations. Each has been recognized as being among the best places to retire. Both are frequent destinations for all sorts of shopping junkets, entertainment, and family services.

WHO'S IN CHARGE?

Depending on the type of residence, homeowners pay an annual fee of between $400 and $600 annually for membership in the nonprofit **Albemarle Plantation Property Owners Association.** That income enables the community to pay for maintenance of interior roads, landscaping, and upkeep of the pool, tennis courts, and other recreational amenities. A regularly published newsletter keeps residents posted on the latest neighborhood developments, property improvements, home-building activity, profiles of family activities and leisure programs that are being planned or are underway.

THE WEATHER REPORT

The northeastern coast of North Carolina is described as having a moderate, four-season climate that offers a happy medium between the severe winters to the north and the tropical summers to the south. Reports are not uncommon of Floridians coming to these shores to escape the excessive heat that lingers for half the year and to enjoy the seasonal changes.

The maritime climate on the mid-Atlantic coast contends with a high humidity, but the summers are mild enough to avoid the most unpleasant consequences of that modality. It is rare for summer temperatures to rise into the 90s, as it is for winter lows to drop below 20. The closest weather reporting station is located at **Cape Hatteras**, about 75 miles to the southeast as the crow flies. Average high and low temperature readings for three winter months and three summer months are as follows:

December: high 57/low 41	**January:** high 52/low 37
February: high 53/low 37	**June:** high 81/low 67
July: high 85/low 72	**August:** high 85/low 72

Average annual precipitation: 56 inches
Average annual snowfall: 2 inches

HOME SWEET HOME

A "preferred builder" program features three residential construction companies that offer home buyers a range of choices in both single-family and luxury townhouse dwellings. Plans for single-family homes vary in size from 2,000 to 4,000 square feet with prices ranging from $175,000 to $500,000. About two-thirds of the individual homes built to date have been in this category. Townhouses are high-end properties with floor plans of from 2,200 to 2,800 square feet and price tags of between $375,000 and $425,000. Luxury condominiums, with 700 to 1,400 square feet, some overlooking the marina, sell for between the low $80s and the low $180s.

Condominiums and townhouses are generally available for long-term lease in a monthly rate range of between $800 and $1,500. Vacant homesites of between one-quarter and one acre sell from $40,000 to $275,000. A separate area is available for parking recreational vehicles.

Properties range from exceptional fairway locations and sites along Albemarle Sound, to private settings in pristine woodlands. Electric and telephone utility lines are under ground. The central sewage treatment facility is operated by Albemarle Plantation. The water supply comes from **Perquimans County**. Cable television is available.

MONEY MATTERS

Real property and certain personal property (boats, cars and other vehicles) are taxed locally at the very moderate rate of 78 cents per $100 of appraised value. That compares with a state-wide average combined local rate of $1.21. North Carolina, among the 50 states, ranks 12th from the lowest in property taxes per capita.

Dare County, another rural coastal area, less than 40 miles to the southeast of Albemarle Plantation, is the nearest location for which there is comprehensive cost of living data available. The composite index of the referenced report is 106.1, meaning that it is about 6 percent higher than the average of all places shown in the survey, including both metropolitan and nonmetropolitan locations. Among five specific components measured in the survey, utilities showed the highest relative cost (an index of 127.5), while housing (117) and groceries (105.5) showed lesser above-average ratios; transportation (95.2) and health care (81.9) were below average.

TAKE GOOD CARE OF YOURSELF

The two nearest hospitals are located in Edenton (just 13 miles away) and Elizabeth City (23 miles). They provide 111 and 180 beds, respectively. Both are accredited by the national commission responsible for standards regulation. Within these two towns, there are more than 25 general practice physicians and almost the same number of specialists. More than 20 dental offices are also within that same radius. Two extended care nursing and assisted living facilities are found in these two neighboring towns and another in **Hertford**, only 10 miles away.

Not much further up the coast (about 40 miles beyond Elizabeth City), in the Tidewater cluster of major cities on the Virginia side of the North Carolina border, is an almost limitless availability of traditional and specialized therapeutic, rehabilitative, and related services, with **Norfolk** considered the primary center of that area for such resources.

PLACES TO GO, THINGS TO DO

The centerpiece of the Plantation's leisure amenities is the Sound Golf Links and the 12,000 square foot clubhouse overlooking the 18th green and the waters of Albemarle Sound. Designed by **Dan Maples**, the course is more than 5,900 yards from forward tees and more than 6,500 yards' tournament distance. The waterfront clubhouse is complemented by a 25-meter swimming pool and lighted composition tennis courts. A $7,500 initiation fee for club membership is paid by the developer for all initial purchasers. A full golf membership costs $115 a month. More limited social memberships in the club are only $35 monthly.

The marina at Albemarle is a 212-slip facility. It is one of the largest private marinas on the east coast. Situated just 20 miles off the Intracoastal Waterway, ocean-going craft as large as 60 feet in length can be accommodated at its piers. Boating visitors can step off their decks and, in a matter of minutes, be swinging a golf club in the midst of beckoning greens and fairways. A swim and fitness center is close at hand whenever a change of pace is in order. Adjacent picnic tables and grills add to the leisure time options.

In the planning stages are walking and biking trails that will hug the shoreline and meander through the woods to allow the best in picturesque relaxation and enjoyable exercise. A community garden is intended to bring out green thumb inclinations that result in the cultivation of an enticing variety of flowers, shrubs, herbs, and fresh vegetables.

The northernmost coastal reaches of North Carolina's famous Outer Banks lie less than an hour's drive away. To the south is a 75-mile stretch of one of the nation's natural treasures—the **Cape Hatteras National Seashore**. Here are beaches and docks famous for bird-watching, beachcombing, sightseeing, and most especially surf and deep sea fishing. Here is the east coast home of some of the world's greatest sportfishing fleets. **Kitty Hawk**, site of the **Wright Brothers'** historic first flights of man by powered aircraft, is just 38 nautical miles east, near the mouth of Albemarle Sound. A monument, historical markers, and a visitor museum commemorate the heralded highlight of Americana.

There are countless historical landmarks within a 40-mile radius of Albemarle. Hertford, Edenton, and Elizabeth City all have historic districts featuring tours of 18th century sites and structures, audio-visual presentations and exhibits. There are heritage museums, ancient lighthouses, wildlife refuges, and Elizabethan gardens. **Greenville**, a city of approximately 45,000 about 75 miles southwest of Albemarle Plantation, is the home of **East Carolina University**. **Old Dominion University** at Norfolk is a bit closer, a 65-mile drive. Just 25 miles down the road is **Elizabeth City State University**. Each of these regional educational institutions supports a wide array of collegiate sports that draw fans from far and wide.

Beyond athletics, on each of these campuses and in their respective communities, can be found all sorts of entertainment and cultural attractions typical of any active university environment. Live theater, symphony, dance, and opera are part of the variety of touring and resident companies that appear regularly. With three such population centers so accessible, there is also a notable selection of museums, libraries, cinemas, fairs, and festivals. Continuing education for adults is liberally featured.

Churches of almost any denomination can be found within a 25-mile radius of the Plantation. Volunteer opportunities are found in area hospitals, museums, political organizations, and a youth service center. Resident clubs and organized activities include aerobics, crafts, swimming, bridge, and, of course, various golfing groups formed around levels of playing skill.

Cable service provides five television network stations and public TV. Ten AM and FM radio broadcasters are on the airwaves, along with a public radio station.

SAFE AND SECURE

The community has a unique security position in that the presently developed site plan is mostly bordered by water, much of it the broad expanse of Albemarle Sound and **Yoepim Creek**, with tributary streams and creeks extending the encirclement. The main entry is gated with a staffed guard house that is operated on a seven-day, 24-hour schedule. Security patrols are on duty during night hours. Regular police services are provided by the **Perquimans County Sheriff's Department**. Fire protection is provided by the volunteer fire department from the adjacent town of **Bethel**. The county also provides paramedic and emergency 911 telephone services. Community spokespersons report that there have been no crimes committed since the development was founded in 1990, a rather remarkable state of affairs for this day and time.

LET'S GO SHOPPING

There are no commercial or service establishments on site. It is 7 miles to the nearest full-service food market. Major retail mall shopping is in Elizabeth City (25 miles). Other smaller shopping concentrations are found within a 10-mile radius, in or near Hertford.

CAROLINA TRACE COUNTRY CLUB

SANFORD, NORTH CAROLINA

P.O. Box 2100
Sanford, NC 27331
919-499-5121 / 800-227-2699
Fax: 919-499-9498

Developer: Carolina Trace Corporation

Year of initial property sales/rental: 1973

Total land area: 2,500 acres

Average elevation: 400 feet

Location: Near the geographical center of North Carolina; Lee County; on State Highway 87 South; off U.S. Highway 421, southeast of Sanford; 45 miles south and southwest, respectively, of Chapel Hill and Raleigh, the state capital; 25 miles north of Pinehurst and Fort Bragg Military Reservation.

Nearest airport with scheduled commercial service: Raleigh-Durham International (50 miles)

Current number of housing units with year-round occupants: 970

Projected number of housing units: 2,000 (2015)

Resident eligibility: There are no age restrictions for living in the community, but an estimated 75% of current residents are either retired or semiretired. Not more than 10% of households have children under 18 years of age living permanently in the home.

Community visit/tour incentive program: On-site accommodations in single-family cottages are available for a maximum stay of three nights at $75/night, including a property tour.

Suggested newspaper: *Sanford Herald*, P.O. Box 100, Sanford, NC 27330 (919-708-9000)

WHY CAROLINA TRACE?

Carolina Trace Country Club, for the second consecutive year in 1996, was ranked as one of the nation's 20 best places to retire by *New Choices* magazine, a publication of the *Reader's Digest*. It was the publication's fifth such annual survey. Whether moderately priced or upscale developments, winners were judged to offer exceptional value, to have outstanding recreational facilities, proximity to social and cultural amenities and medical and educational resources, and to provide environmentally appealing landscapes, open to newcomers of all races.

Much of the property is heavily wooded with hardwoods dominating evergreens. Situated in the midst of a mecca for golfing addicts, The Trace makes no bones about the fact that golf is king among a substantial majority of residents. Its rolling terrain (with elevation changes of as much as 150 feet) and 325-acre **Lake Trace** (with miles of shoreline) provide an idyllic setting for the best of two championship, tournament-quality golf courses. The surrounding countryside includes the **Pinehurst/Southern Pines** area, acknowledged by many to be the "golf capital of the world."

The geographic location of the community in the state's south-central heartland is considered a primary asset. It's an easy 1½ hour drive to the **Atlantic Ocean** on the east, and less than 3 hours to the rise of the **Blue Ridge Mountains** in the west. And to the north, only 45 miles away, is the world-class cosmopolitan cluster of "The Triangle" cities of **Raleigh**, **Durham**, and **Chapel Hill**.

WHO'S IN CHARGE?

Unlike some of its peer communities toward which retirees are drawn, this development is not a resort. It has no time-shares or short-term lodging. Rather, it is a member-owned country club community, fully under the control of the property owners who live there. Day-to-day operations are theirs alone. There is no outside management company engaged to establish and carry out program decisions and to maintain facilities.

Responsibilities for self-governing are in the hands of 17 separate neighborhood property owners' associations (POAs). The presidents of each of these groups serve on the board of directors of the **Carolina Trace Association**, the umbrella entity with community-wide authority for issues that encompass some or all neighborhoods (for example, entry and security and other common properties and services). The individual property owners organizations exercise responsibility for those amenities (neighborhood swimming pools, tennis courts, etc.) and policies that relate to the individual subsectors. A separate board of directors is responsible for overseeing the country club, golf courses, central swimming pool, and tennis courts, etc.

Membership in the neighborhood and master POAs is mandatory. A single combined assessment for these two entities ranges from $175 to $325 per month. Country club membership is optional and is offered under eight different equity and dues schedules, determined by the extent of golf course access desired. Such monthly fees range from $70 to $190. Country club initiation fees, again based on the level of benefits, range from $500 to $5,000.

THE WEATHER REPORT

A four-season climate brings with it dramatic spring and fall displays of nature's blessings. The community is located on the North Carolina coastal plain, a short distance east of the **Piedmont Plateau**'s rising doorstep to the mountains in the west. While the highest mountain elevations are more than 200 miles away, they nevertheless provide a defense against the cold waves of air that chill the nation's midsection. Normal snowfall is light and seldom remains on the ground more than a day or so. Coastal humidities are part of the normal weather patterns. Average daily high and low temperature readings for the three winter months and the three summer months are reported by the U.S. National Oceanic and Atmospheric Administration as follows:

December: high 55/low 33	**January:** high 55/low 29
February: high 57/low 31	**June:** high 89/low 64
July: high 91/low 68	**August:** high 89/low 67

Average annual rainfall: 43 inches
Average annual snowfall: 6.9 inches

HOME SWEET HOME

Carolina Trace, with 17 separate and distinct subdivisions, does not characterize those neighborhoods by virtue of housing costs, size, or style. Each has a balanced representation but may differ in the type or extent of services provided (for example, level of exterior home maintenance, amenities upgrading, activities staffing, etc.). All utility lines are underground, including those for cable television. The community operates its own well-water supply system and sewage treatment plant. A separate parking area for mobile homes is provided.

More than 90 percent of the homes are single-family detached. They range in price from $90,000 to $1.25 million, with square footage ranging from 1,600 to around 6,000. Almost 10 percent of the current inventory consists of "golf cottages" (1,600 to 2,400 square feet of living space) designed to free the homeowner of all exterior maintenance. These homes cost from $250,000 to $300,000. There is also a very limited number of townhouses varying in size from 1,400 to 2,000 square feet and priced from $80,000 to $110,000.

Long-term rentals of various descriptions are generally available for $750 to $1,400 monthly and may range in size from 1,700 to 3,000 square feet. Homesites can be purchased in a wide cost spread beginning at $10,000 and running as high as $150,000. Such vacant lots are generally in the 1/3- to 1½-acre range.

MONEY MATTERS

The nearest comparable location with reliable living cost data available is **Fayetteville**, just 45 miles southeast of Carolina Trace's home town of **Sanford**. The ACCRA composite index for that area (an analysis that includes costs of grocery items, housing, utilities, transportation, health care, and miscellaneous goods and services) shows the combined cost for all measured elements to be 3.1 percent below the average for all participating places. Housing was shown to be the least expensive category (15.8 percent below average), followed by health care (at 9.3 percent below). Local residential real estate agents proclaim housing to be as much as 25 percent lower in cost than comparable properties found in the urbanized Triangle suburbs of **Cary** and Raleigh, just 40 to 45 miles to the north.

Utilities were found in the survey to be at the high end with an index of 15.3 percent above average, followed by miscellaneous goods and services at 3 percent higher than average. The county millage rate on real property is 66 cents per $100 of appraised value. Because the community is outside the limits of Sanford, residents pay no city taxes. There are no additional special assessments for police and fire protection.

TAKE GOOD CARE OF YOURSELF

Just 6 miles from the Trace is **Central Carolina Hospital** with 137 beds and a staff of almost 90 physicians. Affiliated with the **University of North Carolina Hospital** (in Chapel Hill), an expansion of emergency room and outpatient surgery services was completed in 1996. **Sandhills Regional Hospital** is a second noteworthy medical facility available to residents. Twenty-five miles away in Pinehurst, it is a bit larger (180 beds) than Central Carolina with a somewhat different mix of specialties and services. Both institutions are fully accredited by the Joint Commission on Accreditation of Hospitals.

There are within a 20-mile radius an estimated 200 doctors in private practice, with perhaps 100 in medical and surgical specialties. There are 28 dentists in the same general area. Two assisted living and/or long-term nursing care facilities are located in Sanford, 5 to 7 miles up the road. A larger extended care operation (150 residents) is found in Pinehurst.

Just beyond the local radius are the vast resources of the Triangle area, where the **Duke University Medical Center** (in Durham) and the **University of North Carolina Memorial Hospital** (in Chapel Hill) are two among many preeminent health care institutions that attract statewide and regional patients in need of the ultimate in diagnosis and treatment.

PLACES TO GO, THINGS TO DO

Two 18-hole signature golf courses, both designed by widely acclaimed golfscape architect **Robert Trent Jones, Sr.**, characterize the unhurried and uncrowded life style of Carolina Trace residents. A putting green and driving range complement the activity package. A staff of four pros and assistants offer clinics and lessons.

Lake Trace, visual highlight and a centerpiece of the community, stretches into every part of the property. Its sparkling waters are popular retreats for swimming, fishing, and boating (no power craft). Overlooking the lake is the strikingly modern CTCC clubhouse with a pro shop, lounge, snack bar, game and meeting rooms, and a grand dining room that seats up to 250. An Olympic-sized pool and four lighted, all-weather tennis courts share the clubhouse site. A playground and picnic area are adjacent. Satellite tennis courts and swimming pools are also found in many of the separate neighborhoods. Nature trails crisscross the community, ideal for biking, jogging, or just walking and enjoying of the unspoiled landscape.

Country club membership comes in six categories. Costs for resident members range from $500 to $5,000 in equity or initiation fees and monthly dues from $70 to $190. Other community activities, mostly run by volunteers and with little or no cost attached, include about 60 interest-centered clubs that bring residents together for volunteer assignments, gardening, amateur drama productions, fishing expeditions, arts and crafts creations, bowling, aerobics, travel, tennis, golf, dancing, table games, book reviews, etc. A full-time activities director coordinates programs.

For those who thrive on spectator sports, professional football **(Carolina Panthers)** and basketball **(Charlotte Hornets)** are just a bit more than 100 miles west in **Charlotte**, the state's largest city. Collegiate powerhouses in all major athletic competition are a North Carolina tradition led by **Duke** and **North Carolina** and **North Carolina State Universities**, all within less than an hour's drive from Sanford. In golf, U.S. Open Tournament country is around the corner (25 miles) in the Pinehurst/Southern Pines area, one of the largest concentrations of quality golf resorts and clubs anywhere in the world.

Completely remodeled in 1984, the 339-seat **Temple Theatre** in Sanford is a cultural center for **Lee County**, offering audiences professional, community, and children's theater, as well as touring musical and theatrical performances. **Central Carolina Community College**, also in Sanford, serves 17,000 students annually. Within a 55-mile radius that includes The Triangle cities, there is an endless variety of the best in educational, cultural, and entertainment attractions, some connected with the three major universities or smaller colleges, others independently endowed and managed, or supported with public funds through governmental programs. Included are symphony orchestras, dance and theater and opera companies, choral groups, prominent exhibitions, and museums.

SAFE AND SECURE

Carolina Trace maintains a guarded entry gate seven days a week, 24 hours a day. A security patrol covers the entire community on a four-hour rotation around the clock. Law enforcement is provided by the **Lee County**

Sheriff's Department and the **North Carolina State Patrol**. A volunteer fire department operates inside the development. The county operates emergency medical services, including a 911 emergency phone system.

Crime rates in the county are exceptionally low for a number of reasons, not the least of which is the very high local employment level.

LET'S GO SHOPPING

The nearest full-service food market is about two and a half miles toward the center of Sanford. A $3-million shopping center opened in late 1996 in **Tramway** (a small village less than 5 miles to the west), in anticipation of a housing boom in the near future. Sanford itself has three small strip centers with upwards of five retailers in each. A farmers market nearby is a popular outlet for locally grown produce. The neighboring town of **Cameron** boasts a National Register Historic District and is known for its antique and collectibles shops. The nearest major shopping mall is in Cary, a southwestern suburb of Raleigh, about 30 miles north of the CTCC gate.

CARRIAGE PARK

HENDERSONVILLE, NORTH CAROLINA

2827 Haywood Rd.
Hendersonville, NC 28791
704-697-7200 / 800-639-8721
Fax: 704-692-9986

Developer: Carriage Park Development Corporation

Year of initial property sales/rentals: 1992

Total land area: 377 acres

Average elevation: 2,700

Location: Far western region of North Carolina; Henderson County; situated on a high plateau of the Blue Ridge Mountains; on Interstate 26; less than 15 miles north of the South Carolina border; about 3 miles northwest of Hendersonville; approximately 25 miles south of Asheville; 40 miles north of Greenville (South Carolina).

Nearest airport with scheduled commercial service: Asheville Regional Airport (10 miles)

Current number of housing units with year-round occupants: 130

Projected number of housing units: 663 (2001)

Resident eligibility: There is no age restriction, but an estimated 95% of current residents are retired or semiretired. There are no children under age 18 in permanent residence.

Community visit/tour incentive program: None

Suggested newspaper: *Hendersonville Times-News*, P.O. Box 480, Hendersonville, NC 28793 (704-692-0505)

WHY CARRIAGE PARK?

Located along a sloping ridge, a part of the landscape known as **Long John Mountain, Carriage Park** is perched some 550 feet above a valley floor below. Magnificent vistas outline the **Blue Ridge Mountains** with their deep timbered hollows, skyward-reaching peaks, and vast acres of national and state forests. This western North Carolina scenic wonderland has been a place where, since the late 19th century, the rich and famous come to live and play. Today, it is a major tourist destination and home to artists, writers, and craftspeople of every description.

Carriage Park is original in its "community of small villages" concept. Its design is intended to facilitate neighborliness, provide architectural diversity, preserve and utilize the natural environment, and engender a sense of open space with habitat privacy and serenity. The plan incorporates such features as a parkway feeder road system (to which no residential driveways directly connect), 26 separate and distinctive neighborhoods (each with its own architectural style and flavor), and restricted street traffic flow that contributes to a more peaceful ambiance.

The town of **Hendersonville** has garnered much recognition as one of the top quality-of-life places in America. It was listed in *The 100 Best Small Towns in America*, based on population, per capita income, incidence of crime, educational level of residents, and local spending on education. *Money* magazine rated Hendersonville among the 20 best retirement places in the country. *America's Best Places to Retire* extolled the same virtue. The spring 1995 issue of *Where to Retire* magazine also praised the town as a retirement haven. Few towns in the land can claim more commendations.

Hendersonville forms one of the corners of a rectangle, with **Asheville** to the north, **Brevard** to the southwest, and **Waynesville** to the northwest, within which there has been a major influx of retirees. Most are attracted by a moderate climate, exceptional health care facilities, unexcelled scenic beauty, a relatively low cost of living, and rich recreational and cultural resources.

The developers of Carriage Park recently were recognized by the **North Carolina Home Builders Association** with an "Award of Excellence" for the quality of their community.

WHO'S IN CHARGE?

Responsibility for managing community affairs and developing policy is vested in the **Carriage Park Homeowners Association.** Among other things, their function includes operation of the entry gatehouse, private road maintenance, and meeting all upkeep expenses associated with the clubhouse, pool, and other recreational amenities and common areas. The Association is a nonprofit entity. Membership by residents is mandatory. Dues for all owners are $650 per year. Townhouse dwellers pay an additional $300 to cover complete lawn maintenance services.

THE WEATHER REPORT

Carriage Park is situated on a plateau that is cradled between the **Great Smoky** and Blue Ridge Mountains. The climate is described as moderate, with four seasons that bring pleasant summer temperatures and winters that are much further north. The area enjoys such weather moderation largely because the mountain ranges to the north and west provide protection from the frigid air from Canada and the U.S. northern plains that annually descends upon middle America. While winter nights will often drop below freezing, seldom will the thermometer remain that low during the afternoon. Snowfall, averaging about 15 inches for the year, usually remains on the ground for no more than a day or two. About 50 miles away, on the other hand, at the higher mountain elevations, there are snow-covered slopes where winter sports are in full swing. Spring and fall, of course, are times of the year when the best of Mother Nature in western North Carolina gives all earth's creatures a taste of pure outdoor enchantment.

Average high and low temperature readings for the three summer months and three winter months in nearby Asheville (the closest weather reporting station, just 22 miles away) are reported by the U.S. National Oceanic and Atmospheric Administration as follows:

December: high 50/low 29   **January:** high 46/low 25

February: high 50/low 27   **June:** high 80/low 58

July: high 83/low 63   **August:** high 82/low 62

Average annual precipitation: 48 inches
Average annual snowfall: 15 inches

HOME SWEET HOME

The first phase of the development featured contemporary homes. The second and most recent phase exemplifies a "yesteryear look," creating a showcase for Charleston-style construction adapted from the South Carolina city's widely recognized plantation facade.

Single-family detached homes range in size from 1,800 to 4,000 square feet, priced between $145,000 and $350,000. Duplex townhouses (featuring minimum exterior upkeep) run from 1,800 to 3,200 square feet with prices from $177,000 to $243,000. Upon completion of the development (projected for 2001), it is expected that detached single-family and duplex homes each will constitute about half the total inventory. Virtually all home purchases are custom built, allowing owner preferences to be incorporated in the final design. Less than 5 percent of property availability is for resale (because few families have been living in the development for very long). There are no rental properties offered.

Homesites vary in size from less than 1/5 of an acre to almost 1½ acres. Prices range from $35,900 to $89,900. Many are on secluded culs-de-sac. Electric and telephone utility lines are below ground. The water supply and sewer system are provided by the city of Hendersonville.

MONEY MATTERS

A healthy economy highlighted by tourism and retirement has resulted in **Henderson County's** having among the lowest property tax rates any-where. Local levies are pegged at approximately .5 percent of total assessed value (based on 100 percent of market value). For homeowners in Carriage Park, outside the city limits of Hendersonville, the current rate (as of January 1997) was 51.5 cents per $100 of valuation. There is an additional modest levy for the fire district. Henderson County adds 2 percent to the 4-percent state sales tax on purchases of tangible commodities, lodging, and certain services (standard for all counties in the state). The state portion of the sales tax, effective January 1, 1997, was reduced from 4 percent to 3 percent on food items purchased for home consumption.

There is no known comparative data available to reflect consumer cost of living elements for Henderson County. Such data is found in the *ACCRA Cost of Living Index* (2nd quarter, 1996); however, for neighboring and rural **McDowell County**, located just to the northeast. The report measures relative price levels in participating areas for six consumer products and services, including groceries, housing, utilities, transportation, health care, and miscellaneous. The composite index for all listed locations ranged from 16.8 percent below average (Little Rock, Arkansas) to 164.3 percent above (San Francisco). McDowell County was shown to be 7.7 percent below the average for all places included in the study and the lowest index among the 14 North Carolina locations.

TAKE GOOD CARE OF YOURSELF

Hendersonville has an array of health care resources that belies its size. It is a major medical center for western North Carolina. **Pardee Memorial Hospital** is a full-service, 222-bed community hospital and a 40-bed nursing facility. Its list of services and specialties is far too extensive to list here, but includes orthopedics, maternity, pediatrics, intensive and coronary care, psychiatry, pulmonary rehabilitation, a sleep disorder lab, oncology, and a large emergency department fully staffed around the clock. State-of-the-art equipment includes MRI, CT scan, echocardiogram, and advanced angiogram, plus facilities for endoscopy, mammography, ultrasound, kidney stone lithotripsy, and bone densitometry.

Henderson County's oldest medical facility, **Park Ridge Hospital**, is in nearby **Fletcher.** It is a modern 103-bed institution for general, acute, and surgical care with exclusively private rooms. A directory limited only to a listing of physicians and dentists affiliated with Pardee Hospital shows more than 150 doctors in 30 different categories of practice, a truly impressive roster of health care professionals. In addition to the two primary hospitals, there is a variety of community health care centers, clinics and specialized services that cater to any number of specific medical needs, from newborns to seniors.

PLACES TO GO, THINGS TO DO

With respect to recreational, cultural, and educational appeal, the Hendersonville area is endowed with far greater resources than one might expect to find outside a large city. **Opportunity House** is a unique nonprofit center for arts, crafts, and cultural activities, dances, receptions, seminars, and business meetings. Volunteers are drawn from its 2,000 members to carry out extensive programming. Three miles from Hendersonville is the **Flat Rock Playhouse**, the state theater of North Carolina, recognized as one of the top summer stock theaters in the nation. Nine shows are produced each year, ranging from world premiers to the latest stagecraft from Broadway and London. The **Hendersonville Little Theatre** has entertained patrons in the area since 1966, staging four shows annually from September to May. Several other theater and drama groups add to the performing arts mix, along with choral groups, concert bands, and chamber music ensembles.

The **Henderson Public Library**, recently doubled in size, offers a reference collection that includes genealogy resources, extensive business information, and online computer search capability. Musical programs, speakers, and book reviews are routinely featured on the library calendar of events. The **Johnson Farm**, listed in the National Registry of Historic Places, is a hands-on museum and a demonstration of farm life at the turn of the 19th century.

The 70-piece **Hendersonville Symphony Orchestra** celebrated its 25th anniversary in 1996. It performs five subscription concerts a year, featuring guest artists from around the country. Hendersonville is believed to be one of the smallest communities in the United States to support a full symphony. The **Brevard Music Center**, just 10 miles down the road, enjoys an international reputation as an educational and performance mecca, showcasing the talents of students, faculty members, and well-known guest artists during its seven-week summer season.

The **Four Seasons Arts Council** is a virtual fountain of cultural assets. The Council promotes art appreciation and education, sponsors a professional dance guild and various arts festivals, and sustains a volunteer-operated **Arts Center** featuring a central information service and a gallery for local and traveling art shows. **Blue Ridge Community College** enrolls approximately 2,500 students and serves about 12,000 adults, many in continuing education courses. Through its **Center for Lifelong Learning**, those 50 years of age or older can pursue current academic interests and explore new areas of learning alongside peers who share in their quest for intellectual growth and stimulation. The **University of North Carolina** campus at Asheville is the site of the **Center for Creative Retirement**, a nationally recognized program that provides educational opportunities for people of retirement age and fosters intergenerational learning.

The recreational bounty of the area leaves little to be desired. While an almost limitless variety of leisure attractions are outside the Carriage Park perimeter, there is within the community a 9,000-square-foot clubhouse with a 60-foot-long indoor lap pool and adjacent tennis courts, just a short stroll from neighborhood doorsteps. Walking trails connect to parks and neighborhoods. Within a 5- to 20 mile radius, one finds everything from superb fishing, boating, camping, hiking, hunting, public gardens, and breathtaking scenery to a 32-lane bowling center (the largest in western North Carolina) and a half-dozen outstanding golf courses open to the public. There are countless fully-appointed picnic areas nestled in nearby **Pisgah National Forest** and tourist attractions such as **Chimney Rock Park**, less than 20 minutes away, the site of the 26-story solid rock "chimney" platform from which are seen sensational views 75 miles into the distance. And there's **Connemara**, former home of internationally renowned author and Lincoln biographer, **Carl Sandburg**.

The annual **North Carolina Apple Festival** consists of four days of celebration over the Labor Day weekend. The one-of-a-kind **Blue Ridge Mountain Parkway**, designed exclusively for vacation travel, is accessible just 12 miles north of Hendersonville. Homegrown or homemade are the criteria for every item offered for sale at the **Henderson County Farmer's Curb Market**, for 60 years an all-season cornucopia of shoppers' treasures. The first Saturday in October is **Farm City Day**, a gigantic spectacle where you can ride a wagon, play a dulcimer, or milk a cow. Exhibits, demonstrations, square dancing, a petting zoo, a dog show, and sack races are just part of the fun.

SAFE AND SECURE

Carriage Park is a gated community. Entry to the property is controlled by security personnel seven days a week, 12 hours a day. Daily patrols around the neighborhoods are also conducted. The county sheriff's department provides police response. A 911 emergency phone system is operational and paramedic services are provided by Pardee Memorial Hospital, only 2½ miles away. Crime incidents are low.

LET'S GO SHOPPING

There are no commercial or service establishments on-site, but the development is only 3 miles from the heart of Hendersonville. Some 150 businesses make downtown a veritable open-air shopping mall, lined with planters full of flowers and shrubbery. Several major department stores, a major mall, hundreds of specialty shops, and a variety of outlet stores are located throughout the area. For special shopping needs, less than 25 miles away is the hub city of Asheville, offering the ultimate in metropolitan shopping.

CUMMINGS COVE GOLFING COMMUNITY

HENDERSONVILLE, NORTH CAROLINA

3000 Cummings Rd.
Hendersonville, NC 28739
704-891-9412
Fax: 704-891-5633

Developer: Maston G. O'Neal, Jr.

Year of initial property sales/rentals: 1986

Total land area: 537 acres

Average elevation: 2,300 feet

Location: Far western region of North Carolina; Henderson County; on a plateau between the Blue Ridge and Great Smoky Mountains; near the intersection of Interstate 26 and U.S. Highway 64; about 8 miles west of Hendersonville; 25 miles south of Asheville; 45 miles north of Greenville and Spartanburg (South Carolina).

Nearest airport with scheduled commercial service: Asheville Regional (12 miles)

Current number of housing units with year-round occupants: 140

Projected number of housing units: 400 (year of buildout undetermined)

Resident eligibility: There is no age restriction, but more than 95% of residents are estimated to be retired or semiretired. There are no children in permanent residence under the age of 18.

Community visit/tour incentive program: Free round of golf.

Suggested newspaper: *Hendersonville Times-News*, P.O. Box 490, Hendersonville, NC 28793 (704-692-0505)

WHY CUMMINGS COVE?

Upon coming through the entryway to **Cummings Cove**, a commanding view of a sprawling golf scene leaves little doubt about the community's recreational inclinations. The immediately visible greens and fairways form a bowl shape, with hillside and hilltop homes dotting the landscape. Silhouetted against the horizon are the outlines of the **Blue Ridge Mountains.**

The triangle formed by **Asheville**, **Hendersonville**, and **Brevard** (with Asheville at its northern apex), has become one of the nation's top vacation destinations and a major retirement enclave. Located on a 75-square-mile plateau, cradled between the **Great Smokies** and the Blue Ridge Mountains, and at an elevation of about 2,200 feet, it has long been a favorite

225

annual retreat for Georgia's, Florida's, and the Carolinas' coastal inhabitants eager to escape the summer heat and humidity. Hendersonville has a charm that is reflective of its mountain terrain and horticulturally friendly climate. Only 50 miles from **Mount Mitchell**, the highest peak in the eastern United States, it is a magnet not only for summer visitors, but for those drawn to winter sports as well.

When it comes to decorating public places with nature's bloom, downtown Hendersonville takes a back seat to no other. Tree-lined Main Street is a sight to behold when seasonal flowers overflow large planters that line the sidewalks. Shoppers can spend the day visiting the unique collection of merchants and specialty restaurants while enjoying an environment that pleases the senses and soothes the melancholy of an empty purse. There are even sidewalk benches for tired feet and restful diversion. Added to this pleasing milieu is the fact that a large portion of the downtown sector has been designated as a part of the National Register of Historic Places.

For some, Hendersonville's location at the epicenter of another geographical triangle formed by Asheville, **Greenville**, and **Spartanburg** (the latter two across the state line in **South Carolina** and about 45 freeway miles away), gives it unique access to three sizable metropolitan centers (all three in the 45,000 to 65,000 population range). By the same token, it also provides convenient access to two well-traveled airports, thereby extending the choice of schedules.

WHO'S IN CHARGE?

Private ownership and control of all land, capital improvements, and program operations lie with the developer. Unlike most communities of this type, there is no sharing of proprietary interests with those who own homes. A committee of the **Cummings Cove Home Owners Association (HOA)**, each representing a different neighborhood, meets with the developer on a monthly basis to facilitate open communication and to address concerns and propose actions for community improvement.

An association fee of $185 per quarter pays for a homeowner's share in the upkeep of common areas, road maintenance, security, and amenities. A monthly newsletter is produced by resident volunteers and includes an advertising program to help defray publication expenses.

THE WEATHER REPORT

Topographical features are credited with giving the Hendersonville area a good share of climatic moderation. The higher mountain ranges to the north and west block much of winter's severity when arctic storms and cold winds come eastward across the U.S. midsection. While temperatures do fall below freezing on more than half the nights during winter, temperatures usually rise well above that mark during afternoons, tending to melt rather quickly any ice or snow that may have accumulated.

Summer weather characteristics can generally be described as considerably cooler than readings found in the **Piedmont** area to the east, and even more so than those associated with the coastal lowlands. Ninety-degree weather in mid-summer is out of the ordinary. Almost invariably, summer evenings are comfortably cool and can even call for a light wrap.

Average winter and summer high/low readings for nearby Asheville (the closest official weather reporting station) are reported by the U.S. National Oceanic and Atmospheric Administration as follows:

December: high 50/low 29   **January:** high 46/low 25

February: high 50/low 27   **June:** high 80/low 58

July: high 83/low 63   **August:** high 82/low 62

Average annual precipitation: 48 inches
Average annual snowfall: 15 inches

HOME SWEET HOME

Approximately 80 percent of homes built on the property are single-family, detached, ranging in price from the $150s to more than $500,000, and in size from 1,400 to 4,000 square feet. The remaining units are two-story, two-family condominium townhouses ranging in size from 1,300 to 1,400 square feet and selling in the $110,000 to $130,000 range. A recent construction project called "The Cottages at Laurelridge" is located on an island in the middle of the golf course. It features a two-level, single-family home with 2,393 square feet of floor space (plus a garage and screened porch), built at a base unit cost as low as $149,900 ($72 a square foot). A variety of options available to the purchaser make construction planning very flexible, including lower level finishing to expand living space at a later date.

Undeveloped homesites ready for construction sell for between $25,000 and $60,000 for one-third acre to just under an acre and a half. All utilities are underground. A central water system is serviced by the city of Hendersonville. A private central sewer system is maintained by a state-regulated company.

MONEY MATTERS

A diversified and balanced economy enables **Henderson County** and local governments to maintain a relatively attractive tax structure. Property taxes are lower than in many other North Carolina jurisdictions.

Taxes are appraised every four years, based on a 100-percent valuation of appraised value. The county tax base is 58.5 cents per $100 of assessed valuation. The county levies a local option 2 percent sales tax, which is added to the 4 percent state sales tax for a total of 6 percent.

There are no known comparative data available to reflect consumer costs of living for Henderson County. Such data is available in the *ACCRA Cost of Living Index* (2nd quarter, 1996), however, for neighboring and rural **McDowell County**, located just to the northeast. The survey shows relative price levels in 315 participating metropolitan and nonmetropolitan areas for six consumer product and service categories, including groceries, housing, utilities, transportation, health care, and miscellaneous. The composite index for all listed locations ranged from 16.8 percent below average (Little Rock, Arkansas) to 164.3 percent above (San Francisco). McDowell County was shown to be 7.7 percent below the average for all places included in the study and the lowest index among the 14 North Carolina locations for which data was collected.

TAKE GOOD CARE OF YOURSELF

Health services are said to be unparalleled for a community the size of Hendersonville. **Pardee Memorial Hospital** is a full-service community facility, licensed for 222 beds plus a 40-bed nursing care unit. Located near the downtown area, Pardee main line departments include acute medical and surgical, orthopedic, maternal, pediatric, intensive and coronary care, and mental health. Specialties include sleep disorder treatment, magnetic resonance imaging, CT scan, echocardiograms, advanced angiogram procedures, nuclear medicine, endoscopy, mammography, ultrasound, kidney stone lithotripsy, and bone densitometry utilization. Its radiation oncology center was dedicated in 1993, making the first hospital in the county to provide radiation therapy for the treatment of cancer. A major expansion of surgical facilities was completed in 1996.

Park Ridge Hospital in **Fletcher**, is less than 15 minutes away. It is a modern, 103-bed, full-service institution with all private rooms.

PLACES TO GO, THINGS TO DO

Cummings Cove bills itself as "a golfing community." Its **Robert E. Cupp**-designed, 18-hole championship course is said to place a premium on precision play, rather than power. The Scottish-styled layout has no sand traps but has lots of grass bunkers, trees, streams, and water accents. Cummings Cove was named by *Golf Week* magazine as being among the top 50 "most distinctive golf courses in the southeast." There is no initiation fee for golf club membership. Residents pay $1,200 annual greens fees for singles and $1,400 for couples. An annual personal golf cart trail fee comes to $550. A "pay-as-you-go" golf fee for 18 holes is $25 per person with a cart or $15 for a walking game.

The clubhouse, perched atop a knoll near the entry road, offers a grand vista from its front door. Indoor features include an informal living room, an outside deck, card room, snack bar, and pro shop. Just outside are two hard-surface tennis courts and a swimming pool. The clubhouse serves as a gathering place for a variety of planned activities such as holiday cocktail parties, card games, hobby and craft groups, ping pong, tennis competitions, and men's and ladies' golf leagues. The building and sailing of miniature radio-controlled boats has taken hold as a popular summer hobby around the small man-made lake on the property. An enthusiastic group of bowling aficionados gather regularly at the 32-lane bowling center, just a couple of miles north of downtown.

Hendersonville, Brevard, and **Flat Rock**, all within minutes of one another, bring a rich kaleidoscope of leisure attractions to visitors and residents alike. One of the brightest jewels in the performing arts crown is the **Flat Rock Playhouse**, "where Broadway spends the summer." Designated as the state theater of North Carolina, it is recognized as one of the top summer theaters in the nation. The **Brevard Music Center** is renowned at home and abroad as an educational center for outstanding young musical talent. A seven-week summer camp showcases internationally famous guest artists. There is a long list of professional and amateur theater companies, chorale groups, community bands, and galleries that feature juried exhibitions.

The 70-piece **Hendersonville Symphony Orchestra** celebrated its 25th anniversary in 1996. The orchestra performs seven concerts each season, featuring prominent guest artists from all across the country. **The Four Seasons Arts Council** has served as advocate for the arts in Henderson County for more than 25 years.

Connemara, the last home of America's legendary Pulitzer prize-winning poet, author, and historian **Carl Sandburg**, is a national historic site in Flat Rock, 3 miles south of Hendersonville. The historic **Johnson Farm** is a 19th-century tobacco farm with a main house built in 1876 of handmade bricks. Restored and renovated, it serves today as a hands-on museum and a demonstration of farm life at the turn of the century. There's something for everyone at Hendersonville's **Opportunity House**. It is a unique 2,000-plus member community center offering a program of activities that includes many arts and crafts, lectures, workshops, special occasion lunches and dinners, dances and fellowship for newcomers, retirees, and hobbyists.

Nearby **Blue Ridge Community College**, through its **Center for Life-long Learning**, offers a series of programs for seniors who wish to explore new learning objectives or to resume past educational pursuits. The **University of North Carolina** campus in Asheville, less than 30 freeway minutes away, is the site of the North Carolina **Center for Creative Retirement**, a truly imaginative and highly regarded program providing for intergenerational learning and a wide-ranging series of educational and experimental research opportunities for retirees.

The **Pisgah National Forest** and the **Great Smoky Mountains National Park** invite incomparable hiking, mountain climbing, picnicking, camping, and wilderness escape. Asheville's crown jewel of international attraction is the historic **Biltmore Estate**, a 250-room mansion, filled with priceless art treasures, set in the midst of a spectacular 10-acre garden. **Chimney Rock Park** is the site of a giant granite, 26-story monolith, from the top of which visitors behold a breathtaking panoramic view overlooking **Hickory Nut Gorge** and **Lake Lure**, 1,200 vertical feet down.

SAFE AND SECURE

Entry into the community at its only access point is controlled by an electronic gate next to an unmanned guard house (which can be staffed at such future time as it is determined to be necessary). Residents use a handheld remote device or enter a numerical code on the control pad to raise the gate for access. Under current conditions, and for more than a decade since the development opened, the incidence of crime is said to be so minimal as to make staffing arrangements inappropriate in proportion to the added costs that would be incurred. A community watch program is in place, however, in which neighborhood volunteers serve as block captains to provide certain precautionary security measures for the benefit of all residents.

LET'S GO SHOPPING

Full-service grocery shopping is available in **Etowah**, just 3 miles from the front gate, where there is a strip mall anchored by a major chain food market, along with a number of satellite stores (drug, hardware, car wash, storage, etc.) and restaurants. For more extensive shopping needs, downtown Hendersonville is a haven for antiques, apparel, art galleries, books and cards, gifts, collectibles, banking, jewelry, flowers, and other specialties. Within blocks of the downtown area, the **Blue Ridge Mall** is a modern enclosed emporium with more than 40 retailers, restaurants, and theaters. Several mini-malls are scattered about the city outskirts, some featuring large home furnishings or home improvement centers, discount department stores, auto repair centers, etc.

On market days, the **Henderson County Farmer's Curb Market**, located downtown, is typically overrun with shoppers hauling bags and boxes of fresh fruits and vegetables, dairy products, flowers, baked and canned goods, and all sorts of handmade craft items. A giant specialty food market is a mecca for health-conscious and dieting customers.

FAIRFIELD MOUNTAINS

LAKE LURE, NORTH CAROLINA

201 Boulevard of the Mountains
Lake Lure, NC 28746
704-625-9111, ext. 2204
Fax: 704-625-2053

Developer: Fairfield Communities, Inc.

Year of initial property sales/rentals: 1977

Total land area: 2,500 acres

Average elevation: 1,000 feet

Location: Western North Carolina; Rutherford County; on the lower reaches of the Blue Ridge Mountains; on the northern shore of Lake Lure; on U.S. Highway 74-A at the intersection of State Highway 9; 45 miles southeast of Asheville; 23 miles northeast of Hendersonville.

Nearest airport with scheduled commercial service: Asheville Regional Airport (32 miles)

Current number of housing units with year-round occupants: 700

Projected number of housing units: 1,400 (2000)

Resident eligibility: There are no age restrictions for living in the community, but an estimated 90% of current residents are retired or semiretired. Approximately 10% of households have children under age 18 living permanently in the home.

Community visit/tour incentive program: Various visitation incentive packages are available with a range of charges, depending on desired accommodations and length of stay.

Suggested newspaper: *Asheville Citizen-Times*, P.O. Box 2090, Asheville, NC 28802 (800-800-4204)

WHY FAIRFIELD MOUNTAINS?

One of three Fairfield communities in North Carolina and 15 nationwide, **Fairfield Mountains** has more than its share of enticing amenities and scenic allure. Cradled in a pristine Alpine setting along the shores of 27-mile-long **Lake Lure**, the community offers all that can be expected of a leading vacation resort.

Of special appeal is the proximity of FM to a sizable city—**Asheville** (population of more than 61,000 and growing), only a 45-mile drive. And about 90 miles to the east is the state's largest city, **Charlotte**, considered by many to be one of the nation's most attractive metropolitan centers. Residents enjoy the sense of remoteness from urban tribulations, yet maintain the convenience of easy access to rich cultural, recreational, and educational resources. The location is further enhanced by the fact that two principal interstate highways, 40 and 26, pass within a 15- to 20- mile radius. The **Blue Ridge Parkway**, a top tourist attraction in itself (with its 250 miles of winding mountain ridge roads, magnificent overlooks, and famous national parks along its route), passes less than 30 miles away. The homes of two of America's most distinguished writers, **Thomas Wolfe** and **Carl Sandburg**, both within a 40-mile radius of Lake Lure, are preserved for public enjoyment.

As further evidence of the appeal of the Lake Lure area, Hollywood has come to town in recent years. *Dirty Dancing*, a blockbuster film when it was released, had several scenes on the **Fairfield Bald Mountain Golf Course** and at a nearby Lake Lure site. Other movies filmed on location here were *The Last of the Mohicans* (another major production), *A Breed Apart*, *Fire Starter*, and *Rutherford County Line*. Lake Lure resorts have hosted many luminaries, including Franklin D. Roosevelt, F. Scott Fitzgerald, and Emily Post.

The special qualities of Fairfield Mountains have been recognized repeatedly by resort industry peer organizations. **Resort Condominiums International** bestowed its 1997 Gold Crown Award on the community for outstanding time share and vacation condos, citing excellence in hospitality, housekeeping, maintenance, and amenities.

A Resort of International Distinction award has been presented by RCI every year from 1989 through 1996. A book published in 1992 by John Wiley & Sons identified Fairfield Mountains as one of the 99 best residential and recreational communities in America.

For those who would trade skyscraper skylines for mountain vistas, Fairfield is an irresistible choice.

WHO'S IN CHARGE?

Fairfield Mountains Property Owners Association is the nonprofit governing body responsible for developing policies that affect homeowners and for managing community affairs. It is responsible for upkeep of all recreational facilities, activity programs, and common areas. Dues are $696 a year. Membership by residents is mandatory. Thirteen neighborhood associations, some benefiting time share or vacation condo clusters, have separate fees to cover those services related to that part of the development. A quarterly newsletter is published by resident volunteers.

THE WEATHER REPORT

The community is located in an area of the state that has been referred to as "a gift of nature." In meteorological terminology, it lies within what is known as an *isothermal belt*. It is a rather unusual weather phenomenon that tends to bless a land area with more moderate temperatures, both winter and summer, than would otherwise be true for a given latitude, altitude, and related topographical features. The practical effect is to make for year-round outdoor activity.

The resort lies between the **Blue Ridge Mountains**, which rise more than 3,000 feet above mean sea level on the east, and the **Great Smoky Mountains** on the west, reaching to elevations of 5,000 to 6,000 feet. Consequently, the mountain valley in which Fairfield Mountains is located, is protected by imposing barriers that tend to hold back the flow of cold winter air coming eastward and southward. It is relatively uncommon in the midst of winter for temperature readings to remain below freezing throughout the entire day.

Average high and low temperature readings for the three summer months and three winter months in nearby Asheville (the closest official weather reporting station) are reported by the U.S. National Oceanic and Atmospheric Administration as follows:

December: high 50/low 29   **January:** high 46/low 25

February: high 50/low 27   **June:** high 80/low 58

July: high 83/low 63   **August:** high 82/low 62

Average annual precipitation: 48 inches
Average annual snowfall: 15 inches

HOME SWEET HOME

About 90 percent of the housing market within the community is resale property and the remainder is new construction. Options include traditional one- and two-level single-family dwellings, villas, townhouses, and condominiums. In keeping with the vacation-resort aspect of the development, there is a program called **FairShare Plus**, in which buyers can participate in a nationwide interchange network of such properties.

Typical residences are hidden away in wooded enclaves or overlook a golf fairway or lake shore. Architectural characteristics tend to blend well with the rustic setting.

Prices for single-family homes begin at about $100,000 for floor plans as small as 1,200 square feet and go up to as much as $400,000 for 4,000 square feet. Townhouses range in price from $90,000 to $250,000 (1,200 to 1,500 square feet) and condominiums from $85,000 to $100,000 in the same size options. For those who choose to rent, there are nightly, weekly, and monthly rates for a wide variety of condominiums, townhouses, and villas, all completely furnished and accessorized. Many have deluxe features such as whirlpool tubs, fireplaces, and boat docks, as well as magnificent views from party decks and screened porches. Monthly rates generally run from $500 to $1,000 and, in season, up to more than $3,000 for the largest and most elaborate accommodations. Vacant lots available and ready for construction are mostly in the quarter- to full-acre size range and sell for anywhere between $15,000 and $80,000.

Utility lines are below ground. Sewer facilities include both septic tanks and a central system.

MONEY MATTERS

Rutherford County, in which Fairfield Mountains is located, has no known comparative data to reflect cost of living figures. Such statistics are found in the *ACCRA Cost of Living Index* (2nd quarter, 1996), however, for **McDowell County**, immediately adjacent to the north. The referenced report measures relative price levels in participating areas for six consumer products and services, including groceries, housing, utilities, transportation, health care, and miscellaneous products and services. The composite index for all listed locations ranged from 16.8 percent below average (Little Rock, Arkansas) to 164.3 percent above average (San Francisco). Rural McDowell County, similar in demographics to **Rutherford County**, was shown to be 7.7 percent below average for all locations included in the study and the lowest index among the 14 North Carolina locations.

Local property taxes for the county are 55 cents per $100 valuation; city taxes are 30 cents per $100 valuation.

TAKE GOOD CARE OF YOURSELF

Rutherford Hospital, a private not-for-profit facility in **Rutherford**, serves the entire county and beyond, and is the most accessible institutional health care program in the Lake Lure area. It has a 145-bed capacity, all in private rooms, and a full complement of specializations, including cardiac and pulmonary rehabilitation, psychiatry, mammography, occupational medicine, and oncology. In addition, it operates a family medicine and urgent care clinic within the Fairfield compound itself. **Pardee Memorial Hospital** in **Hendersonville** is a full-service, 222-bed community hospital with an additional 40-bed extended care unit. It underwent a major expansion in 1996. A second medical facility a few miles north in **Fletcher** is the 103-bed **Park Ridge Hospital**, with a full range of general, acute, and surgical care components. Less than an hour away in Asheville, there are larger institutions and more specialized services to meet virtually any health care requirement.

PLACES TO GO, THINGS TO DO

It is a foregone conclusion that virtually every resort community will feature golf as the primary recreational attraction and as the centerpiece of environmental appeal. Fairfield Mountains has not one, but two, 18-hole championship courses to offer and full-service country clubs (Bald Mountain and **Apple Valley**) to go along with each of them. The course at Apple Valley was designed by **Dan Maples**, the celebrated golf architect. Much of the residential development is built on sites bordering the two fairways.

Lake Lure, sharing its shoreline with a portion of the FM perimeter, is a recreational playground of no small proportion. Everything from powerboats and sailboats to canoes and water skis can be rented at the 50-slip lakeside Fairfield marina. A private beach with cabana is just around the bend, with nearby amenities that include indoor and outdoor swimming pools, miniature golf, four lighted tennis courts, and two restaurants. The lake, along with the trout stream at its entrance, provides year-round enjoyment for avid anglers. Large and small mouth bass, rainbow trout, crappie, several varieties of catfish, and perch are among the prime prospects for catch of the day.

Walking, hiking, and horseback riding trails through peaceful woodlands and alongside mountain glades often lead to hidden waterfalls and magnificent overlooks. **Chimney Rock**, within hiking distance from Fairfield, is a giant 26-story-high monolith within a 1,000-acre park. Nature trails lead to a dramatic view of **Hickory Nut Falls**, one of the truly inspirational natural wonders of Western North Carolina. Less than an hour's drive to the north is the town of **Marion**, where one can discover **Little Switzerland** and **Emerald Village**, open to the public for mining precious and semiprecious gemstones.

Horse lovers can drive south just a few miles into neighboring **Polk County** to visit the **Foothills Equestrian Nature Center**. There they will behold a 210-acre complex with a steeplechase course, show rings, a carriage trail, and a busy calendar of horsemanship events.

Fairfield Mountains is near several highly attractive cultural, educational, and recreational centers—Asheville, less than 40 miles to the northwest, and the Hendersonville, **Flat Rock**, and **Brevard** cluster of towns to the southwest, within a 20- to 30-mile distance. Each of these areas has unique enticements, some of which draw national and international attention. Asheville is replete with folk art showcases, historical Civil War landmarks, first-rate museums, art galleries and exhibition halls, music, dance, and theater companies, and an especially notable farmer's market. The **Biltmore Estate** features a 250-room European chateau built in French-Renaissance style by **George Vanderbilt**, grandson of tycoon Cornelius Vanderbilt, and furnished with priceless antiques and art.

The University of North Carolina in Asheville is the focus of one of the nation's most innovative institutes dealing with the opportunities and challenges of older Americans—the **Center for Creative Retirement**. This nationally recognized program provides educational options for seniors and fosters intergenerational relationships and sharing experiences with UNCA students, among many other unique components.

For a town with a population of about 9,000, Hendersonville has a remarkable array of community resources. It is believed to be the smallest community in the country to support a full symphony orchestra. The **North Carolina Arboretum**, described as "the most beautiful natural setting of any American public garden," offers workshops and seminars to botanical aficionados from far and wide. Just outside the downtown core is a 32-lane bowling center. Huge municipal parks, miles of nature trails, and an impressively endowed YMCA complex all contribute to a wealth of recreational amenities. Nearby **Flat Rock Playhouse** is rated as one of the top 10 summer theaters in the United States. The **Henderson County Public Library** is considered one of the finest of its size in the state. The **Brevard Music Center,** just a few miles further down the road, enjoys an international reputation as an educational and performance mecca, showcasing the talents of students, faculty, and notable guest artists during a seven-week summer season.

SAFE AND SECURE

An entry control gate is operated 24 hours a day, seven days a week, staffed with security personnel. The Fairfield Mountains security staff also provides routine neighborhood patrols. The town of **Lake Lure** provides municipal police services. Two volunteer fire departments respond to prevention needs as well as firefighting. An emergency 911 phone system is in place. Paramedic services are under Rutherford County's jurisdiction.

LET'S GO SHOPPING

Limited convenience shopping is available on site. Three major food markets are found in Rutherford, an easy drive of less than 20 miles. Hendersonville, a few miles further away in the other direction, has a more developed shopping selection that includes the enclosed **Blue Ridge Mall**, housing more than 40 retail shops, restaurants and theaters. The **Henderson County Farmer's Curb Market**, in the downtown section, treats shoppers to fresh fruits and vegetables, dairy products, flowers, baked goods, and a variety of handmade craft items.

A bit further away to the northwest is Asheville, the largest city in far-western North Carolina, with extensive retail and service outlets. In this regional core city, one can find a wide assortment of merchandise, professional offices, and special services, comparable to that found in a larger metropolitan center.

FAIRFIELD SAPPHIRE VALLEY

SAPPHIRE, NORTH CAROLINA

4000 Highway 64 West
Sapphire, NC 28774
704-743-7121
Fax: 704-743-2169

Developer: Fairfield Communities, Inc.

Year of initial property sales/rentals: 1971

Total land area: 5,400 acres

Average elevation: 3,200 feet

Location: Immediately north of the state line separating southwestern North Carolina from the extreme northwest corner of South Carolina; overlapping Jackson and Transylvania Counties; in a valley of the Blue Ridge Mountains; lying both north and south of U.S. Highway 64 and between State Highways 107 and 281; about 60 miles southwest of Asheville; 40 miles southwest of Hendersonville.

Nearest airport with scheduled commercial service: Asheville Regional Airport (45 miles)

Current number of housing units with year-round occupants: 850

Projected number of housing units: Unknown

Resident eligibility: There are no age restrictions for living in the community, but an estimated 80% of current residents are retired or semiretired. About 10% of households have children under age 18 living permanently in the home.

Community visit/tour incentive program: Introduction to the community is facilitated with a substantially discounted rate for on-site accommodations: two nights/three days for a total of $49.95; personally conducted presentation/tour required.

Suggested newspaper: *Asheville Citizen-Times*, P.O. Box 2090, Asheville, NC 28802 (800-800-4204)

WHY FAIRFIELD SAPPHIRE VALLEY?

This community is one of 15 Fairfield properties in 11 southern and western states. **Fairfield Communities, Inc.**, founded in 1966 and headquartered in Little Rock, Arkansas, is one of the largest vacation ownership developers in the world. Fully furnished villas and condos with all the comforts of home are at the heart of their vacation ownership products.

Fairfield Sapphire Valley is one of several in this family of resort areas that also offers subdivision acreage for second homes and for year-round residency. Nestled in a rustic setting, many of its sprawling neighborhoods wrap around golf fairways, lakes, or pristine wilderness. Mountain vistas are everywhere. Many residents (including a substantial proportion of retirees) choose to make this recreational/resort environment, offered to vacationing families, their permanent home. It allows them to take advantage of leisure amenities and programs that are paid for, in part at least, by those who come to the property for short-term stays, paying premium vacation prices.

Sapphire Valley is perhaps most distinguished by its appeal to both summer and winter sports enthusiasts. It is perched on the site of a popular ski area which, during the 1995-96 season, scored a record season with more than 6,000 skiers and snow boarders on its slopes. It is also a warm weather haven for golfing, fishing, camping, and all sorts of outdoor activities. Its golf course, in 1985, was singled out by *Golf Magazine* for being one of the most scenic mountain playlands of its kind. On its borders are **Pisgah National Forest** and **Nantahala National Forest**, both vast acres of virgin woodlands along the **Appalachian Trail**, home of towering mountains, incomparable hiking trails, and unrivaled natural beauty.

WHO'S IN CHARGE?

The **Fairfield Sapphire Valley Master Association** is the nonprofit mechanism through which residents manage their interests in the community. Dues range from $405 to $655 a year, depending upon in which of four subdivisions owners live. These amounts cover expenses for both the master association (operation of all social/recreational programs, upkeep of common grounds, and community-wide amenities) and the obligations of the three neighborhood associations (responsible for street repair and other improvements within their individual areas).

THE WEATHER REPORT

Situated in the south-central mountain region of North Carolina, the community's climatic character can be described as surprisingly mild for such lofty altitudes. A moderate four-season weather pattern best characterizes this area, although winters do bring subfreezing nighttime temperatures much of the time. Summer days generally bring high readings in the upper 70s with lows in the upper 50s.

Recent average high and low temperatures reported at neighboring **Highlands** for the three winter months and the three summer months are as follows:

December: high 44/low 26	**January:** high 41/low 22
February: high 45/low 24	**June:** high 75/low 53
July: high 77/low 56	**August:** high 76/low 56

Average annual precipitation: 50 inches
Average annual snowfall: 15 inches

HOME SWEET HOME

The site-built housing market in the community consists of an estimated 95 percent resales, with only the small remaining percentage in new construction. A larger percentage of manufactured housing (about 30 percent) accounts for new product, with the substantial remaining number of such homes also available in resales. Previously occupied homes range in price from $115,000 to $500,000, with square footage in a very broad range of 1,500 to 10,000 square feet. New construction costs begin at $60 per square foot for turnkey heated and cooled living space.

Townhouses and condominiums are available at prices beginning at around $65,000 and extending up to $230,000, in sizes from 700 to 2,000 square feet.

Long-term rentals lease for $1,500 to $6,000 monthly, with floor space as small as 700 square feet and on up to large multi-storied custom homes of virtually any size. Lots of ½ to a full acre cost anywhere from $25,000 to $125,000. Utility lines are both below and above ground. Some properties are served by a central sewer system, while others depend on septic tanks. Water supply is also mixed, with some areas served by municipal sources and others by community wells.

MONEY MATTERS

Typical of rural areas relatively distant from urban concentrations, living costs in general are considerably lower than would be expected in more densely populated places. Many people drawn to this popular tourist destination have been won over by both its scenic charms and its affordability, deciding to make a move for permanent relocation.

Property taxes depend upon which of two overlapping counties the Fairfield residence is located. In **Jackson County** on the west side of the development, the tax rate is 53 mills ($53 per $1,000 valuation) based on 100 percent of value assessment, making the levy on a $100,000 home $530 a year. In **Transylvania County**, the rate is slightly higher—69 mills, but based on 80 percent of assessed value, thereby essentially equalizing the final result. The sales tax of 6 percent includes 2 percent levied by counties on purchases of tangible commodities, lodging, and certain services. Effective January 1, 1997, the state sales tax on food items purchased for home consumption was reduced from 4 percent to 3 percent (for a total of 5 percent).

There is no known comparative data on cost of living for the particular counties named here. There is, however, another rural county (McDowell) that is some 50 miles to the northeast, for which it can be reasonably assumed that a close parallel exists with regard to living costs. The *ACCRA Cost of Living Index* (2nd quarter, 1996) measuring price levels for six consumer products and services showed the county to be 7.7 percent below the average among all the places in the study and the lowest composite index among 14 North Carolina locations analyzed.

TAKE GOOD CARE OF YOURSELF

Highlands-Cashiers Hospital is an acute care, all private room facility, just 10 miles from **Sapphire**. Accredited by the Joint Commission for Accreditation of Health Care Organizations, it operates a 24-hour emergency room and offers a number of specialized departments, including radiology, CT scan, mammography, ultrasound, and physical/respiratory therapy. In **Brevard,** about 18 miles east and across the county line is 64-bed **Transylvania Community Hospital** with general surgery and a coronary intensive care unit. It accommodates helicopter transport to several **Asheville** hospitals when higher levels of care are needed. Yet another medical care facility is **Harris Regional Hospital** in **Sylva,** about 30 miles to the north. This 80-bed health care center serves a seven-county area and has a 60-bed nursing facility in conjunction with its acute-care program. Recent additions to the complex have included a birthing center, a medical office building, and a radiation therapy center.

PLACES TO GO, THINGS TO DO

Golf and skiing dominate both the summer and winter seasons. The championship, 18-hole, par 70 **Holly Forest Golf Course**, open all year, is 3,400 feet above sea level and is surrounded by the lofty **Blue Ridge Mountains**, with sensational rock formations and magnificent waterfalls punctuating the fairways. A driving range complements the facility. For winter visitors attracted to the snow slopes, there is a ski lodge complete with snack bar, ski shop, and an oversized fireplace for retreating from the elements. Private and group lessons are popular features.

Sapphire is in a part of the state that has long drawn vacationers from across the nation and from abroad. **Cashiers,** 10 miles to the west, and Highlands, another 10 miles beyond, are among America's most exclusive mountain resorts. Their populations explode during the summer season to as much as five to 10 times their year-round size. Part of the area is within the Nantahala National Forest, a place of splendid isolation and primitive wilderness. Here lies the **Joyce Kilmer Memorial Forest**, 3,800 acres of virgin woodland, named for the poet who wrote "Trees," and site of miles of carefully cut trails through the forest, unmatched camping, swimming, and picnicking, and spectacular native flora. Naturalists who come to Sapphire Valley are drawn to a place said to have more than 1,300 species of flowering plants and 131 different kinds of trees. (In all of Europe there are fewer than 90.)

Fairfield Sapphire Valley is the only resort in western North Carolina that has an indoor health facility with swimming pools, Jacuzzi, sauna, gameroom, weight room, locker facilities, and an activities room (pool, air hockey, ping-pong, video games, and large screen television).

Adjacent to the health center is a heated outdoor pool and a miniature golf course. Two of eight Har-Tru composition tennis courts are lighted for evening play. Paddle boats, canoes, and fishing boats are all available to rent for use in three stream-fed lakes on the property. A full-time activities director coordinates all programs and special events.

Nearby stables cater to those equestrians who relish exploring the miles of scenic trails through unspoiled mountains. There is no topographical feature more unique to the Highlands/ Cashiers/Sapphire area than its many glorious waterfalls. **Whitewater Falls**, higher than the mighty Niagara Falls (at 411 feet), is the tallest in the eastern United States. Dozens of others form exquisite cascading backdrops to the wilderness landscape.

Less than 40 miles north, near **Hendersonville**, is **Connemara**, a national historic site and the last home of America's Pulitzer Prize-winning biographer, novelist, and poet, **Carl Sandburg**. The 264-acre farm, open to the public for tours, is home to the **Vagabond Workshop Theatre**, performing during the summer season. Also nearby is **Oconaluftee Indian Village**, an authentic re-creation of an 18th-century Cherokee Indian community. *Unto These Hills*, performed in the **Mountainside Theatre** against a background of the **Great Smoky Mountains**, is a popular outdoor summer dramatic staging of the inspiring tragedy and triumph of the Cherokee people.

Summer theater, folk art collections, chamber music concerts, cabarets, gem mines, historical landmarks, museums, forums, botanical gardens, state parks, campgrounds, highway overlooks, and 17 cablevision channels—all contribute to an appealing environment for zesty life styles and leisure fulfillment.

Two notable universities are within a 50-mile radius, each generating athletic events in all major sports and bringing to the region an endless calendar of cultural and educational advantages. Nationally prominent **Clemson University** across the state line in South Carolina, is less than 50 miles away. **Western Carolina University** is just 20 miles away in **Cullowhee**.

SAFE AND SECURE

A Fairfield Sapphire security department operates on a 24-hour-a-day duty schedule. Trained emergency personnel are available around the clock, supplemented by a county rescue squad out of the neighboring town of Cashiers. Additional police protection is provided by the **Jackson County Sheriff's Department**. Firefighting and prevention services also respond from Cashiers.

LET'S GO SHOPPING

A full-service food market is just 3 miles from the Fairfield front gate. The Cashiers/Highlands area has its share of exclusive shops featuring antiques, gifts, arts and crafts, and other collectibles, housewares, jewelry, women's and children's apparel, books, pet products, and so on. An inviting array of restaurants cater to summer visitors, bringing on creative menus to tempt any appetite and satisfy most any pocketbook. High-volume department, discount, and specialty stores, some in enclosed malls, are about an hour away on the near side of Asheville.

FEARRINGTON VILLAGE

PITTSBORO, NORTH CAROLINA

2000 Fearrington Village Center
Pittsboro, NC 27312
919-542-4000 / 800-277-0130
Fax: 919-542-4020, E-mail: fci@interpath.com

Developer: Fitch Creations, Inc.

Year of initial property sales/rental: 1974

Total land area: 1,100 acres

Average elevation: 500 feet

Location: Near the geographical center of North Carolina; Chatham County; on U.S. Highway 15/501; 8 miles north of Pittsboro; just south of the cities of Raleigh, Durham, and Chapel Hill.

Nearest airport with scheduled commercial service: Raleigh-Durham International (25 miles)

Current number of housing units with year-round occupants: 800

Projected number of housing units: 1,600 (2010)

Resident eligibility: There is no age restriction, but an estimated 70% of current residents are either retired or semiretired. Not more than 20% of households have children under 18 years of age living permanently on the premises.

Community visit/tour incentive program: A reduced nightly rate of $95 at the Fearrington House Inn is available Monday through Thursday.

Suggested newspapers: *Chapel Hill News*, 505 W. Franklin, Chapel Hill, NC 27516 (919-932-2000); *The News & Observer*, 215 S. McDowell St., Raleigh, NC 27602 (919-829-4800)

WHY FEARRINGTON VILLAGE?

A dominant appeal of **Fearrington Village** is its proximity to an area that is considered to be one of the most intellectually stimulating and culturally rewarding places in the United States. The three cities of **Raleigh, Durham,** and **Chapel Hill** anchor **"The Triangle,"** a thriving, interconnected metropolitan community of educational and cultural treasures. Only 8 to 25 miles from the village entrance, each of these cities is the home of one of three major universities—**Duke, North Carolina,** and **North Carolina State.** In the center of this confluence of higher education is **Research Triangle Park.** The nation's largest-of-its-kind collection of research giants, it is home to almost 100 leading companies in such diverse fields as biotechnology, medicine, environmental science, semiconductors, pharmaceuticals, and telecommunications.

In the fall of 1994, the Triangle became the first southern metropolitan area to be recognized by *Money* magazine (in its eighth annual survey) as being among the best places to live in America.

The Fearrington community of today was originally a 640-acre family dairy farm dating back to 1786. After being passed from generation to generation for almost two centuries, the land was sold to its present owners in 1974. Soon after, a conversion was begun to create a country village, including an uncommon residential development that is expected to be home to 1,600 families by 2010.

A dairy barn and silo still dominate the landscape. Cows still graze in the meadows. Ostrich, emu, and llama farms are county neighbors. A quaint Village Center, clustered around a courtyard and overlooking a 10-acre park, is highlighted by the upscale **Fearrington House** restaurant and country inn next door. Both are among the relatively few select lodging and dining establishments in the country to earn the Five Diamond Award from the **American Automobile Association**. The Village Center also offers more than a dozen retail shops and service offices.

WHO'S IN CHARGE?

The **Fearrington Homeowners Association** has responsibility for those sections of the community that have been released by the developer, largely after completion of construction. Membership by residents is mandatory. Directors are elected from among property owners for two-year terms. Annual dues and assessments vary according to the type of housing and neighborhood location. The basic rate of $65 a year covers newsletter mailings, community directory listing, access to "The Gathering Place" (an activity center), and all social activities. Those who live in townhouses pay an additional $115 a month for fire insurance, exterior building and lawn maintenance, trash pickup, termite protection, and reserve fund contribution. Use of the swimming pool is based on an optional membership, for which dues range from $125 to $175 annually (single and family, respectively) with a corresponding initiation fee of $250 and $350.

The Association publishes a monthly newsletter, typically running 18 or 20 pages. It features all sorts of news items, meeting agendas and reports, services available, scheduled activities and events, etc.

THE WEATHER REPORT

The Triangle is located in a transitional zone between the coastal plain and the **Piedmont Plateau**. It is centrally located between the mountains at the state's westernmost reaches and the Atlantic shores to the south and east. While the mountains are more than 200 miles away, they provide a partial barrier to cold air masses that sweep across the nation's midsection. An occasional snowfall is usually melted in a day or so. Summer temperatures pass the 90 degree mark an average of 25 days during a season. Coastal humidities are a part of the normal weather patterns. Normal high and low temperature readings for the three winter months and three summer months are reported by the U.S. National Oceanic and Atmospheric Administration as follows:

December: high 53/low 32	**January:** high 49/low 29
February: high 53/low 31	**June:** high 85/low 64
July: high 88/low 68	**August:** high 87/low 67

Average annual rainfall: 41 inches
Average annual snowfall: 6.9 inches

HOME SWEET HOME

Residential development, by design, has been at a restrained pace over more than two decades. About 50 floor plans have been created and sold. Upscale single-family homes are mostly on wooded low-maintenance sites, some more open to accommodate gardening. Prices for these custom detached units range from $140,000 to $400,000, sized from 1,200 to 4,000 square feet. Townhouses, with exterior maintenance and yard work done by a service provider, are in the $160,000 to $275,000 spread for plans ranging from 1,400 to 2,500 square feet. About two-thirds of home purchases are new construction, the rest resales.

Homes for lease are generally available at monthly rates between $900 and $1,200 in sizes from 1,200 to 3,000 square feet. Vacant lots of ⅓ to 1⅓ acres, ready for construction, are priced from $40,000 to $70,000.

Utility lines are below ground. The sewer system is operated by the community and is mixed with central treatment and septic tank installations. The water supply comes from the county.

MONEY MATTERS

The *ACCRA Cost of Living Index* (2nd quarter, 1996) shows the Raleigh-Durham-Chapel Hill metropolitan statistical area to be just slightly above average (½ of 1 percent). Utilities, followed by housing, came in at the higher index levels, while transportation, groceries, and other miscellaneous goods and services were well below average. Monthly gas and electric bills at Fearrington average $150 to $180, based on a two-story, 2,300-square-foot home. Health care was a moderate 1.4 percent above the midpoint.

Real estate and personal property taxes for **Chatham County** are 66.5 cents per $100 of assessed value, which translates to a property tax of $1,330 on a $200,000 home (as of January 1996).

TAKE GOOD CARE OF YOURSELF

World-class medical care is part of the cutting edge research for which The Triangle is noted. The **University of North Carolina's Memorial Hospital** in Chapel Hill is a research and teaching hospital with 665 beds and more than 1,200 attending staff, interns, and residents. **Duke University Medical Center** in Durham, even larger with 1,125 beds, draws patients from all over the Southeast. It was recently rated by *U.S. News and World Report* as being number three in the country among the nation's top hospitals. Eight other hospitals serve the area. All of these health care institutions are minutes away from the Fearrington doorstep.

Within the Village itself, there are several interesting and innovative programs designed to help residents cope with unexpected illness or injury. **Stay Put For Now** is a nonprofit community help and information service offering various forms of personal assistance to any member confined to home on a temporary basis. Run by volunteers, it also sponsors educational lectures and workshops on health care issues. Dues for 1995 were $10 per household.

The **Home Care Connection**, also organized and supported by local residents, provides professional visiting nurse coordinator services and connections with many quality home health services throughout a two-county area. The **North Carolina University Hospital** maintains a medical office at Fearrington. Patients are seen there by UNC physicians five days a week. A physical therapist keeps regular appointments there, too. A pharmacy is also located at the **Village Center**.

County rescue squads have the highest level of paramedic emergency care certification.

PLACES TO GO, THINGS TO DO

Unlike most of its peer communities, Fearrington is not a resort or country club development unto itself. There is no golf course within its perimeter. Because it is so close to the heart of a sprawling recreational, entertainment, and cultural environment, residents can easily avail themselves of whatever attracts their interests. The three universities alone offer the public an array of amenities that truly defy imagination. Each of them offers an overflowing calendar of activities that would satisfy the patrons of enlightenment in any metropolitan area.

There is a passionate and nurturing climate for the arts in the Triangle that rivals major cities. There is so much going on, in fact, that deciding what to do can become a dilemma! On virtually any day or night of the week there is an abundance of quality performances and festivals in theater, dance, music, and the visual arts. There are Broadway-bound stage productions, world-known chamber music ensembles, brilliant art museum exhibitions, internationally acclaimed symphony orchestras, ballet and opera companies, and ethnic and folk troupes. There are also prominent art galleries and craft centers. **Artspace**, in Raleigh, houses 23 working studios where professional artists create, display, and sell their work. The **North Carolina Museum of Art,** also in Raleigh, with 181,000 square feet of exhibit space, boasts the work of some of the world's masters. The **Piedmont Council of Traditional Music** dedicates itself to preserving and promoting traditional music, dance, and other forms of performing folk art.

Collegiate athletics, especially basketball, spark some of the most intense competition and fanaticism to be found anywhere in the country. **The Carolina Panthers**, a recently added National Football League franchise, have ignited a blaze of spectator sports fury. Professional minor league baseball is a top summer attraction.

The **Duke Institute for Learning in Retirement** is a year-round program providing a place where villagers 50 years old or older can enjoy classes, intellectual stimulation, and peer companionship. Together with the two other area universities and eight private and community colleges, there is an incredibly rich educational and cultural environment to enjoy.

Fearrington golfers have many enticing options. FV golf association members choose from dozens of nearby courses. The outdoor pool is 75-feet long with three lap lanes, a separate wading pool, and a separate hot tub. Volleyball and badminton are favorite games year-round. Bocce (a type of lawn bowling) is a popular pastime on the grounds, as is croquet. Fall tournaments highlight the year of casual play. There are two hard-surface outdoor tennis courts, and indoor night tennis is available in the nearby town of **Carrboro**.

Jordan Lake, a major recreational feature attracting more than a million visitors annually, is 12 minutes from Fearrington's doorstep. Its 150 miles of shoreline is dotted with state parks offering beaches, picnic sites, camping, pedestrian and equestrian nature trails, boat ramps, and a marina. Often described as "a giant farm pond," the lake offers open-water and bank fishing for striped bass, bream, bluegill, redear sunfish, channel catfish, and crappie, among other varieties.

Dozens of Fearrington clubs and organizations sponsor activities on a daily basis all year-round. There are day trips and overnight jaunts to places of interest. Groups are engaged in everything from arts and crafts, aerobics, bird watching, and card games to gardening, quilting, tap dancing, and yoga. As might be expected, there is a myriad of churches of virtually every denomination.

SAFE AND SECURE

While the Village has no gated entry, there is only one road leading into the property. In 25 years of development, there has been only one known incident (a residential break-in) that anyone can remember. A 911 emergency system was upgraded in 1995 to recognize and display to the dispatcher the caller's address even when there is no voice available to provide information. The county sheriff's department provides law enforcement services. Fire protection is provided by a combination of county and volunteer resources. A fire station is located across the street from the Fearrington entrance.

LET'S GO SHOPPING

The **Fearrington Village Center** is a collection of about 14 convenient retail and service establishments. In addition to the country inn and restaurant, there is a bank, a meeting hall ("the Barn"), a travel agency, a pharmacy, and a busy country store, along with a variety of distinctive specialty shops. Once outside the Village, within a 5- to 10-mile stretch into Chapel Hill, there is an endless choice of full-service food markets, clothiers, restaurants, department stores, malls, and antique and specialty shops. A few miles beyond Chapel Hill is the merchandising abundance of two large cities— Raleigh and Durham.

KNOLLWOOD VILLAGE

PINEHURST, NORTH CAROLINA

c/o Pinehurst Area Realty, Inc.
P.O. Box 1511
Pinehurst, NC 28370
910-295-5011 / 800-633-8576
Fax: 910-295-6000

Developer: Pinehurst Area Realty, Inc.

Year of initial property sales/rentals: 1976

Total land area: 150 acres

Average elevation: 500 feet

Location: South-central North Carolina; Moore County; near the intersection of U.S. Highway 15/501 and State Highway 211; 71 miles south of Raleigh-Durham; 106 miles east of Charlotte; 41 miles west of Fayetteville.

Nearest airport with scheduled commercial service: Moore County Airport (5 miles)

Current number of housing units with year-round occupants: 200

Projected number of housing units: 240 (1998)

Resident eligibility: There are no age restrictions, but an estimated 95% of residents are retired or semiretired. There are virtually no households with young children in residence.

Community visit/tour incentive program: A "VIP" visit for two nights/three days includes accommodations and golf for a flat charge of $100.

Suggested newspaper: *The Pilot Newspaper* (semiweekly), 145 W. Pennsylvania Ave., Southern Pines, NC 28387 (910-692-7271)

WHY KNOLLWOOD VILLAGE?

Knollwood Village is one of two active adult communities in **Pinehurst** under the aegis of **Pinehurst Area Realty, Inc.** As such, residents have access to the amenities of two complete residential resort communities (the other being **Midland Country Club**), about a mile apart.

Pinehurst is the second largest town (population close to 8,000) in **Moore County,** heart of the "Sandhills Area." It lies at the westernmost apex of a triangle formed by the county's three principal communities, joining **Southern Pines** (population near 10,000) and **Aberdeen** (about 3,000 inhabitants) at the other two corners. All are within a 5-mile radius of each other. Together, they are known internationally as an unparalleled center of world-class golf. There are 40 championship-quality golf courses in the county, including those hosting the 1991 and 1992 PGA Tour Championships, the 1994 Senior Open, the 1995 LPGA Women's Championship, and the 1996 U.S. Women's Open. The U.S. Open is scheduled for 1999 and the U.S. Women's Open will return for an encore in 2001. Few of the nation's golf resorts can claim the distinction of such illustrious company.

While golf has been the catalyst for major tourist traffic in the Sandhills, there are many other lures that bring visitors in droves from all corners of the world. Not the least of these is the reputation of Moore County as a leading hub of equestrian activity. Polo matches and harness racing dominate the scene. The 52-acre **Pinehurst Race Track** is a standard-bred trotters and pacers training facility listed on the National Register of Historic Places. Racing thoroughbreds and steeplechasers train here for appearances at leading tracks throughout the eastern United States. Southern Pines is home to the **Moore County Hounds**, a lodestone for invited fox hunters and for those guests who enjoy watching the chase.

The small downtown sections of Pinehurst and Southern Pines have been described as unique New England-style walking villages. Much of the ambiance comes from those origins. Situated some distance from major metropolitan centers, the Pinehurst/Southern Pines district generates enough air traffic to support its own commercial airport. Regional connecting carriers representing four major airlines serve the terminal. An AMTRAK rail station is also nearby.

WHO'S IN CHARGE?

The golf course and common areas are owned, maintained, and regulated by the developer. The homeowners association has primary responsibility for private road maintenance and for initiating organized golfing and social activities. An annual fee of $40 is set aside for street repair and beautification projects. A separate membership in the golf club is mandatory and fees for that portion of ownership obligation cover all property and facility upkeep and clubhouse operations. Golf fees range from $94 to $115 a month, depending on whether it is for a single or couple membership and whether access to both Knollwood and its sister course at Midland are to be included.

Condominium owners have their own association. Fees under that arrangement range from $36 to $112 a month, depending on the size of the unit. These assessments cover building and exterior maintenance, fire insurance, common area lighting, water and sewer, and cablevision.

The homeowners association publishes a monthly newsletter reporting on meetings held, activities and events, neighborhood news, etc.

THE WEATHER REPORT

It is said that Moore County enjoys a milder and drier climate than much of the surrounding countryside, largely because of the ocean environment combined with the hills that rise as much as 600 feet above sea level. Like most of North Carolina, it is further sheltered by the **Appalachian Mountains**. The sandy soil warms and cools more rapidly than other land surfaces, resulting in warmer days and cooler nights.

Data provided by the Pinehurst Area Convention & Visitors Bureau shows the following maximum and minimum mean temperatures for the three winter months and the three summer months:

December: high 55/low 33   **January:** high 55/low 33

February: high 57/low 33   **June:** high 89/low 64

July: high 91/low 67   **August:** high 89/low 67

Average annual rainfall: 47 inches
Average annual snowfall: none

HOME SWEET HOME

Knollwood Village is an affordable townhouse and condominium community. Residential construction features a variety of open, roomy designs with brick exteriors, skylights, optional fireplaces, and "Carolina" rooms. Prices are turnkey, including allowances for flooring, wallpaper, and lighting fixtures. Townhouses are sold as single-family attached homes under a fee simple ownership and do not carry maintenance fees. There are nine choices of condominiums. Privacy is assured with eight-inch-thick double-stud walls, with air space insulation engineered for soundproofing. Each condominium has at least one balcony and each has a view of the golf course.

Townhouse prices range from $110,000 to $155,000 in floor plans that vary in size from 1,450 to 2,200 square feet. Customized features can be added to basic packages at additional cost. Condominiums, constituting about one-fourth of the current inventory of built and occupied units, are priced from $50,000 to $85,000 with from 850 to 1,722 square footage. About 5 percent of dwellings in both residential categories are normally on the resale market at any given time. Water and sewage disposal systems are provided by the town of Southern Pines.

Long-term unfurnished townhouses are available on a minimum 6-months lease. Rates, depending on size (from two-bedroom, one-bath to three-bedroom, two-bath), are between $800 and $950 a month. Smaller unfurnished condominiums, also with two or three bedrooms and one or two baths, run from $600 to $725 monthly. Furnished studios and efficiencies lease for $425 and $450 a month, respectively. Furnished golf and waterfront condominiums and townhouses, in a wide variety of sizes and prices, can be rented on a daily or weekly basis with moderate cost differentials for in- and out-of-season occupancy. All units (except efficiencies) come fully equipped with full kitchens and laundry appliances. Monthly rents include unlimited golf privileges on two walking courses, plus all utilities and cable television.

MONEY MATTERS

Living cost comparisons can be drawn from **Fayetteville**, about 40 miles to the east, the nearest location with related data available. The ACCRA composite index for that area (an analysis that includes costs of food consumed at home, housing, utilities, transportation, health care, and miscellaneous goods and services) shows the combined cost for all measured components to be 3.1 percent below the average for all 315 participating places. Housing was shown to be the least expensive category (15.8 percent below average), followed by health care (9.3 percent below). Utilities were found in the survey to be on the high side, with an index of 15.3 percent above average, followed by miscellaneous goods and services at 3 percent higher than average.

County and municipal government property taxes are 50 cents (Moore County) and 27 cents (Pinehurst) per $100 evaluation. The Pinehurst millage rate is among the lowest of the 11 county towns and villages (five are set at rates of 50 cents or higher).

TAKE GOOD CARE OF YOURSELF

The 1997 health directory, published by the **Sandhills Area Chamber of Commerce**, belies the size of the Moore County health care market. Indeed, the market extends well beyond the county boundaries. Incredibly, it lists more than 30 medical clinics, 161 physicians in 33 different categories of practice, 11 pharmacies, 35 dentists (including three specialists), 19 domiciliary homes, two adult day care centers, six health and fitness clubs, four home health agencies, and 23 support and recovery groups!

At the center of this impressive array of medical and health support services is Pinehurst's **Moore Regional Hospital**, a private, nonprofit, acute-care facility. With 400 beds, 140 physicians, more than 2,200 employees, and an army of some 500 volunteers, the hospital serves a six-county primary-care area and an additional eight-county secondary-service area. The institution was recently honored for being among the top 100 of nearly 4,000 hospitals across the country (in a third-annual independent evaluation of hospitals' ability to deliver high-quality medical care with efficient operations and financial stability). A fully equipped and staffed **Health and Fitness Center** reflects a commitment to wellness and prevention. The proactive program includes a physician-supervised cardiac rehabilitation regimen, a diabetes self-care program, and other activities designed to reduce the expense of health care by improving the total health of those it seeks to serve.

St. Joseph of the Pines, a member of the Sisters of Providence Health System, offers a continuity of care that includes home health services, hospice care, adult day care, nursing services, and retirement living counseling. One of the five largest eye surgery clinics in the United States is located in Southern Pines. A veritable galaxy of public and private agencies is devoted to rehabilitative and social services for older adults. The county has five intermediate-care facilities, along with four nursing homes for those who are unable to maintain independent living but who do not require the intensive care of a hospital.

PLACES TO GO, THINGS TO DO

A 12,000-square-foot clubhouse is the focal point for social and indoor recreational activity. Bridge and other table games, club meetings, and luncheons are frequent bookings on the reservation calendar. The community amenities include not only two golf courses and two swimming pools, but a 22-acre golf practice facility with a driving range, two putting greens, and a chipping and pitching area. A PGA professional staff is on hand to teach beginners, as well as to help hone the skills of more advanced players. Both **Knollwood Fairways** and **Midland Country Club** are semiprivate nine-hole courses and both offer some of the most reasonable green fees in the area. Both endorse the emerging trend of allowing walking on the fairways rather than requiring carts.

Sandhills recreational opportunities beyond golf are plentiful and diverse. Horseback riding, tennis and cycling, archery, water sports, trap and skeet shooting, even lawn bowling and croquet, are favorite diversions. The Pinehurst area has long been regarded as a premiere training ground for U.S. and foreign cycling teams. Annual cycling events include the **Tour de Moore**—a grueling 100-mile road race held in late April.

The Pinehurst area has 10 outdoor park retreats with playgrounds, picnic areas, and sports facilities. Just an hour's drive away in **Asheboro** is the **North Carolina Zoological Park,** a 300-acre environment, vastly larger than most zoos, that allows animals to behave as they would in the wild. Places of historical importance are noteworthy, including period farm houses, venerable public buildings, 18th-century restored cabins, manors and plantation homes, historic walking districts, antebellum farms, and Indian ceremonial sites. The **Performing Arts Center** in Southern Pines is the resident facility for the **Sandhills Little Theatre, Community Concerts International**, and the **Kiwanis of the Pines Travelogue Series,** among other notable programs. **AutumnFest** features racing events, craft displays and sales, music, and great food. The **Arts Council of Moore County** maintains three galleries at the **Campbell House**, where a different artist is featured each month from September through June. The **Weymouth Center for the Arts and Humanities** provides the best in musical, literary, and lecture programs, and is widely known for its writers-in-residence program attended by writers and composers pursuing their work.

The Pinehurst area resorts and villages are attractions in themselves. Every month of every season brings a crammed-full calendar of exciting events, shows, festivals, and tours. The **Fine Arts Festival** in July (highlighting local and regional artists) and candlelighting celebrations in December are among numerous headline happenings. Golf tournaments—minor and major—and polo matches never fail to attract large numbers of enthusiastic spectators.

SAFE AND SECURE

Police and firefighting services are provided by the respective public safety agencies of Pinehurst and Southern Pines. There is a county-run emergency medical service with eight rescue stations scattered around the principal population concentrations. A 911 emergency communication system is in place.

LET'S GO SHOPPING

The Pinehurst/Southern Pines/Aberdeen triangle, along with some of the outlying communities, has become recognized as a regional shopping area. Mass retailers and specialty shops have become a significant part of the growth and development that have accompanied accelerated tourism and retirement influences. A restaurant guide published by the convention and visitors bureau shows an incredible total of 140 eating places.

The nearest full-service grocery market is just 3 miles from the Knollwood entrance. Morganton Road, connecting Pinehurst and Southern Pines, has a major shopping mall and other retail and service concentrations, also about 3 miles away.

LAUREL RIDGE COUNTRY CLUB

WAYNESVILLE, NORTH CAROLINA

630 Eagles Nest Rd.
Waynesville, NC 28786
704-452-0545 / 800-433-7274
Fax: 704-452-0548

Developer: Piedmont Golf Development Corporation

Year of initial property sales/rentals: 1986

Total land area: 876 acres

Average elevation: 3,600 feet

Location: Far western North Carolina; Haywood County; within the town limits of Waynesville; on US Highways 23/74, between Interstate 40, a few miles to the northeast, and the Blue Ridge Parkway, a similar distance to the southwest; about 25 miles west of Asheville; less than 90 miles northwest of Greenville (South Carolina).

Nearest airport with scheduled commercial service: Asheville Regional Airport (35 miles)

Current number of housing units with year-round occupants: 150

Projected number of housing units: 320 (2000)

Resident eligibility: There are no age restrictions, but an estimated 90% of current residents are retired or semiretired. There is no significant number of children under 18 years of age in permanent residence.

Community visit/tour incentive program: Special introductory package for qualified guests of three days/two nights, including golf, for $199; lodging arrangements on-site in 1-bedroom condos.

Suggested newspapers: *The Mountaineer* (triweekly), 413 N. Main St., Waynesville, NC 28786 (704-452-0661); *The Asheville Citizen-Times*, 224 Montgomery St., Waynesville, NC 28786 (704-452-1467)

WHY LAUREL RIDGE?

Laurel Ridge is located in the town of **Waynesville** at the edge of the **Great Smoky Mountain National Park**, one of America's great national treasures and gateway to the **Great Smoky Mountains**. It is a region of abundant woodlands, craggy gorges, and splendid wilderness, embracing two national forests and a long stretch of one of the nation's premier scenic highways—the **Blue Ridge Parkway**. A sprawling 56,000-acre Cherokee Indian reservation, known as **Qualla Boundary**, is nearby. It is no surprise that the area has been an important retirement and tourism destination for many years.

255

Few private, member-owned residential communities in the country are nested so high up in the mountains. The site rests on one of a series of plateaus that are relatively flat at elevations well above 3,000 feet. In most parts of the development, the range of view provides commanding panoramic magnificence. Acres of wildflowers decorate the landscape.

WHO'S IN CHARGE?

The Laurel Ridge Club is devoted exclusively to maintaining the golf course and club grounds, along with the clubhouse serving as the site for member activities. Streets are part of the city of Waynesville, so there are no assessments levied on residents for such maintenance. Matters of architectural policy development and implementation and common grounds upkeep are in the hands of individual neighborhoods or "complexes," each with its own homeowners association and each responsible for determining and paying for the collective needs of the area.

Membership in the LR Club comes in several different packages. A full equity golf membership affords unlimited golf and access to all clubhouse facilities (pool, tennis courts, etc.). The cost is $12,500 for membership equity, plus $2,000 in annual dues. Social memberships, which include invitations to all club social events, require a $1,000 initiation fee with dues ranging from $200 to $450 annually, depending on the level of intended use of the swimming pool or tennis courts. Various user fees apply (driving range, swimming pool, etc.), depending upon membership options selected. An estimated 90 percent of the residents hold one of the membership options.

A newsletter, *The Eagle's Eye*, is published monthly from April through October, keeping residents posted on newsworthy developments of the month, with heavy attention given to golfing and bridge activities.

THE WEATHER REPORT

Western North Carolina is especially characterized by four distinct seasons. Spring, summer, and fall weather invite outdoor recreation. The mountain ranges to the southeast and northwest moderate much of the effect of severe storms and extreme temperatures associated with weather patterns that sweep across the nation's midsection from the Canadian tundra and from the Gulf of Mexico. For most people seeking to avoid harsh winters or scorching summers, this part of the country offers as pleasing a balance of seasons as can be found anywhere on the North American continent.

There was no reliable data available for monthly high and low temperatures specific to the Waynesville area. **Asheville,** only 25 miles to the east, presents the nearest comparable readings. Because Waynesville is at a notably higher elevation, however, it should be recognized that both summer and winter temperatures are likely to be somewhat lower than those in Asheville.

The following summary of climatic averages is drawn from *The Blue Book of Asheville Communities,* based on 1995 records:

December: high 50/low 29   **January:** high 46/low 25

February: high 50/low 27   **June:** high 80/low 58

July: high 83/low 63   **August:** high 82/low 62

Average annual precipitation: 48 inches
Average annual snowfall: 16 inches

HOME SWEET HOME

More than half the dwellings at Laurel Ridge are single-family detached. Among these units, none is less than 2,000 square feet and the largest can be as much as 12,000 square feet. The price range for such construction is generally from $229,000 to more than $1,000,000. The rest of the housing product consists of luxury townhouses and condominiums, the prices of which start in the high $120s and go up to $300,000, with size options from 1,300 square feet to as large as 3,000 square feet. Home sales are 90 percent or more new construction, with a relatively small market for resales.

Long-term lease units are available at costs that vary between $2,200 and $2,800 a month for units that range in size from 1,300 to 1,800 square feet. Homesites are available from one to 10 acres at costs from the mid-$30s to $125,000. Electric and telephone lines are underground. Some locations are served by a central sewer system, others by septic tank. The entire development is connected to the Waynesville municipal water supply system. Road maintenance inside the community is also provided by the Town of Waynesville.

MONEY MATTERS

Like so much of western North Carolina, the economy of the Waynesville area is a compatible mix of seasonal tourism, year-round retirement living, and arts and crafts. Areas such as this tend to have healthy revenues generated by visitors and, therefore, can afford to offer residents more favorable property taxes than might be found in less active neighboring counties. There is no known data reflecting living costs for this county, but we can draw comparisons with a nearby place where conditions may be somewhat different, but which is close and can provide a reasonable level of insight. We have chosen for that purpose **McDowell County** which, like **Haywood County** to the west, borders on Asheville (**Buncombe County**) to the east. Asheville was not itself selected because it is more urbanized and therefore considered less comparable.

The *ACCRA Cost of Living Index* measures relative price levels in participating areas for six consumer products and services, including groceries, housing, utilities, transportation, health care, and miscellaneous goods and services. The composite index for all six measured categories in McDowell County was shown to be 7.7 percent below the average for the 315 metropolitan and nonmetropolitan areas analyzed nationwide. Measurements for each of the six component categories were as follows: groceries, 6.3 percent below; housing, 8.3 percent below; utilities, 7.5 percent above; transportation, 16.8 percent below; health care, 18.2 percent below; and miscellaneous, 7.2 percent below.

The Laurel Ridge community guide shows the tax rate on real property for the town of Waynesville to be 44 cents per $100 valuation and for the county 69 cents per $100 valuation. The county levy includes school taxes and all other services except fire districts, which range from 5 to 10 cents more.

TAKE GOOD CARE OF YOURSELF

Haywood Regional Medical Center is about 6 miles from Laurel Ridge, just outside of Waynesville. This modern, full-service 200-bed facility is the largest hospital west of Asheville, serving a wide multicounty section of the state's westernmost populations. Some 65 medical professionals practice numerous specialties. An urgent care center, operated by the hospital, provides comprehensive seven-days-a-week, extended-hours outpatient treatment for most nonlife-threatening emergencies. Two major medical centers in Asheville are about 30 minutes away. Under urgent conditions, transportation is expedited by Air Mobile Ambulance.

There are approximately 20 dental offices within a 20-mile radius of Waynesville and at least that many family-practice physicians.

PLACES TO GO, THINGS TO DO

The **Robert Cupp**-designed golf course in this private, member-owned community was described by *Golf Week* magazine as "the course by which all other mountain courses will be judged." Its appeal goes beyond the game for which it was created. It is an aesthetically pleasing 150-acre garden in the center of an 876-acre residential development. Four different levels of optional membership, from equity to social, are available. The 8,500-square-foot clubhouse features an excellent restaurant and pub. Three tennis courts and a large swimming pool with generous decking enhance the site. Hiking and biking trails are nearby. A privately operated fitness center is within walking distance of the front entrance.

There is nothing quite like **Folkmoot USA**, the area's prestigious international celebration. Patterned after classic European festivals, it is the largest event of its kind in the entire United States. For 11 days in late July (1997 was its 14th year), more than 300 musicians and dancers from all around the globe come to western North Carolina to share their cultural heritage, performing in authentic, colorful native costumes and playing unusual musical instruments. It is a cultural exchange of momentous proportions.

There are literally dozens of fairs and festivals in Haywood County throughout the year. Celebrations center on everything from the famous North Carolina apple crop (the state ranks seventh in U.S. production) to the even-more famous arts and crafts that flourish in Blue Ridge country. There are auto shows, running races, touring ballet previews, golf and tennis tournaments, fashion shows, bike races, tours of homes, and holiday celebrations from New Year's Eve to the following Christmas. The **Cataloochee Ski Area** near neighboring **Maggie Valley,** at a top elevation of 5,400 feet, offers nine groomed slopes and natural trails designed to accommodate any skill level. The **Haywood Volunteer Action Center** recruits and matches volunteers to nearly 50 member organizations. A foster grandparent program is built on the natural bond between young and old—a bridge connecting the generations of need.

Haywood Community College offers continuing education courses in more than 70 subject areas, from oil painting, jewelry casting, needlecraft, and rug hooking to sign language, magazine writing, computer basics, and public speaking. Tuition is very affordable and classes for those more than 65 years of age are offered free of charge. The **Haywood County Arts Council** provides a wide array of opportunities for appreciation and participation in a year-round program that touches all aspects of visual and performing arts. The **Haywood Arts Repertory Theatre** in Waynesville opened its 1996-97 season in a new home with five plays and three musicals and has been on a whirlwind production schedule ever since.

From March through mid-November, whitewater rafting is a short distance away. About 10 miles west is Maggie Valley, home of the **Soco Gardens Zoo**, where exotic animals, reptile shows, and a feeding and petting park keep visitors enthralled. The town is also known for its **Thunder Ridge** music festival. Less than a half hour's drive from Waynesville is the **Cherokee Indian Reservation**, with a replica of an 18th-century Cherokee community and a powerful live drama in a 2,800-seat theater under the stars (with a cast of 130) depicting the tragic history of the Cherokee people. There's also a tribal casino, legendary Indian craft displays, a fun park, a gold and ruby mine, and a museum of ancestral homeland artifacts and exhibits.

The **Museum of North Carolina Handicrafts** is housed in Waynesville. It has a unique collection of creations by some of the state's most renowned artisans—hand-carved dulcimers, ingenious folk art wood carvings, and the work of master potters, along with Navajo rugs, baskets, jewelry, and other Native American artifacts. **The Great Smoky Mountains Railway,** dating back to the 1840s, takes passengers on a dozen different unforgettable steam- and diesel-driven excursions through gaps and gorges, across rivers, and through the scenic rural mountains.

Less than a half hour's drive east from Waynesville is the city of Asheville, with its endless diversions. The **Biltmore Estate**, a 250-room European chateau filled with treasures collected from all over the world, is hailed as the most spectacular private residence in America.

SAFE AND SECURE

Because Laurel Ridge is within the city limits of Waynesville, it enjoys all the municipal services extended to all other sections of town, including law enforcement and fire protection. The incidence of crime is said to be insignificant— so much so that no private security services have seen fit to set up shop in the area. A 911 emergency response system is in place. Also pertinent to security concerns is the fact that there is only one entrance to the property and, while not currently gated, it could easily be converted if the need ever arose.

LET'S GO SHOPPING

A full-service grocery store is less than a mile from Laurel Ridge. Downtown Waynesville has more than 100 retail shops, restaurants, galleries, professional services, and lodging. Strolling the tree-shaded streets on a buying spree can be combined with people-watching and just taking in the sweep of the Great Smoky Mountains from the comfort of a sidewalk bench.

For those occasions when a wider selection or special shopping is required, Asheville is just 25 miles away, offering a bounty of choices. It is a market center for a much larger region than its own population of more than 60,000 might suggest. Its downtown section is dominated by early 20th-century art deco architecture, and it features gallery, boutique, and antique districts. The **Western North Carolina Farmer's Market** can be described as a 36-acre roadside stand overflowing with farm-fresh fruits and vegetables, flowers and ornamentals, mountain crafts, and scores of gift items. More than a million people each year visit the market.

OREGON TAX FACTS

INDIVIDUAL INCOME TAX

For married couples filing jointly:

- First $4,200 of income @ 5%
- Next $6,300 @ 7%
- Over $10,500 @ 9%

A variety of credits are available. Quarterly estimated payments are generally required for, among others, those who expect to owe $500 or more on their state income tax return.

SALES TAX

Oregon is among the four states that impose no state or local sales tax.

PROPERTY TAX

Calculated by county assessors each year, based on levies of local taxing districts and total assessed value, subject to reduction to meet the constitutional requirement that taxes do not exceed $15 per $1,000 assessed value.

RANKING REPORT

According to *State Government Finances*, among the 50 states, Oregon ranks 12th (tied with Florida) from the most favorable in total state taxes per capita when only state levies are considered. For property taxes, *The Rating Guide to Life in America's Fifty States* ranks it 7th from the most costly with a per capita figure of $854.

For more complete and the most current tax information contact the Oregon Revenue Department, Tax Help, 955 Center St. NE, Salem, OR 97310, 503-945-8604, (fax) 503-945-8738.

Note: The above information is based on applicable tax law information available at the time research was conducted for this publication. Because such laws and tax rates are subject to change, professional guidance should be sought if tax implications are critical to a relocation decision.

CLAREMONT

PORTLAND, OREGON

P.O. Box 91010
Portland, OR 97291-0010
503-690-8512
Fax: 503-617-9433

Developer: Claremont Development

Year of initial property sales/rentals: 1991

Total land area: 200 acres

Average elevation: 200 to 500 feet

Location: Northwestern Oregon; in Washington County; 15 miles west of the center of Portland; near the intersection of U.S. Highway 26 and Bethany Blvd.

Nearest airport with scheduled commercial service: Portland International (20 miles)

Current number of housing units with year-round occupants: 390

Projected number of housing units: 575 (1998)

Resident eligibility: 80% of the households must have a permanent resident at least age 55; 20% are not required to meet the age restriction. No permanent residents under the age of 18 are permitted.

Community visit/tour incentive program: None

Suggested newspaper: *The Oregonian*, 1320 SW Broadway, Portland, OR 97201 (503-221-8240)

WHY CLAREMONT?

Claremont is an upscale community with property prices notably above the norm when making nationwide or metropolitan Portland area comparisons. Customization of home planning and construction, along with premium lot availability, and a multitude of appealing topographical accents (streams, waterfalls, ponds, fountains, and attractive brick and rock landscaping) make for top-of-the-line features. That the community is located just minutes from the heart of **Portland,** one of the most popular destinations on the west coast for both tourists and those relocating, contributes to premium quality. The pull upon the purse strings is accentuated by the fact that the **Washington County** suburb in which Claremont is located is one in which property values are among the highest in the metropolitan area.

Underscoring its prestige among like communities in the Portland area, Claremont was named the best new community of the year in 1993, soon after its marketing program got into full swing. The recognition came at the annual Marketing and Merchandising Excellence Awards Banquet that year, when independent judges graded such factors as landscaping, model homes, advertising, land planning, and signage. In 1996, the community was again distinguished with an award for "the best townhouses of the year."

It is the nature of the northwest Oregon character that accounts for its magnetic quality. Its year-round mild maritime climate appeals to those who would escape the temperature extremes found in much of the rest of the country to the east. Portland is seen by many as bold and trendy, giving the distinct impression that it is ready to take on the 21st century. Its bountiful physical beauty, quality-of-life attributes and recreational diversity readily attract new residents eager to live their retirement lives in or near this "City of Roses."

WHO'S IN CHARGE?

The governing mechanism for the community is the nonprofit **Claremont Civic Association**, formed in 1997. Membership is mandatory for residents. The organization is responsible for upkeep of the clubhouse, the croquet/lawn bowling court, swimming pool area, tennis courts, and entry monuments. A very moderate assessment of $15 a month covers those obligations and allows each resident full use of the clubhouse and its facilities. A **Townhouse Association** is a separate entity created to meet the special needs of townhouse residents. Such homes receive complete landscaping and exterior maintenance and contribute to the upkeep of common areas in their neighborhood. Their monthly assessment is $67, in addition to the $15 paid to the **Homeowners Civic Association**.

THE WEATHER REPORT

Portland, and the northwest coast of the United States in general, suffers a major flaw in reputation for ideal living conditions. Not without reason, the region is perceived to experience lots of rain. It happens, however, that Portland is drier than most surrounding areas. In fact, its annual rainfall of 37 inches is less than places such as New York City, Houston, Atlanta, or New Orleans. The perception problem lies in the fact that almost 90 percent of the precipitation falls from October through April. July and August get very little rain—on average about 3 percent of the total.

A measurable snowfall may occur on an average of five days a year, seldom more than a couple of inches and typically lasting no more than a day or two. While winters are mild by most standards, misty cloudiness and fog hang around for at least part of many days in the fall and on into the new year, with much of the rest of the time producing gentle but persistent rainfall. Severe storms are infrequent.

Average daily high and low temperature readings for the three winter months and the three summer months are as follows:

December: high 46/low 35   **January:** high 45/low 35

February: high 51/low 36   **June:** high 74/low 52

July: high 80/low 56   **August:** high 80/low 56

Average annual rainfall: 36 inches
Average annual snowfall: 6.5 inches

HOME SWEET HOME

Almost 90 percent of the homes built to date at Claremont are detached single-family. Model homes display layout options and features that can be incorporated or modified to fit individual preferences and budgets, or buyers can submit their own renderings. Ten or more floor plans are offered in prices that range from $237,000 to $338,000, in sizes from 1,404 to 3,200 square feet. Townhouses have been built in the 1,700 to 1,800 square foot range, costing between $225,000 and $255,000. Most of the remaining construction before project completion is expected to be in the townhouse configuration. A limited number of resale properties are generally on the market.

There is no housing available for lease, nor are there any vacant lots for purchase. Telephone and electric utility lines are below ground. Water and sanitary sewer systems are provided by the city of Portland.

MONEY MATTERS

According to a 1996 Prudential Realty Relocation report, the overall cost of living in Portland is 15.6 percent above the national average. A breakout of five categories shows housing to be by far the greatest differential at 47.3 percent higher cost. Transportation costs are 9 percent higher and services/miscellaneous costs show a moderate 3.9 percent level over average. On the lower cost side are utilities, at 23 percent, and consumables, at 2.4 percent under the norm. Local real estate market reviews reflect the sustained velocity of activity that has pushed demand and costs to record highs. Comparing a 12-month period ending in July 1996 with the same period a year earlier, residential properties in the metropolitan Portland area appreciated by a robust 9.4 percent.

Property taxes in Washington County come to $15 per $1,000 valuation. Oregon is one of just a handful of states that imposes no sales tax on consumer purchases.

TAKE GOOD CARE OF YOURSELF

The **Providence Health System** operates four hospitals in Portland. One, **Providence St. Vincent Medical Center,** is a 451-bed full-service facility, only 5 miles from Claremont. It also operates the **Tanasbourne Urgent Care Center** at a separate nearby location for treatment of minor illness or injury.

PLACES TO GO. THINGS TO DO

The 9,500-square-foot clubhouse at Claremont is the focal point for social and on-site recreational activities. It is for the exclusive use of homeowners and guests. It is not part of a vacation property in which such facilities are shared with short-term visitors. Features include a great hall to accommodate large gatherings; a catering kitchen; a well-stocked pro shop; an athletic workout center; a large adjacent outdoor swimming pool; tennis, lawn bowling, and croquet courts (official headquarters of the **Portland Croquet Club**); and "the Claremont room," a cozy living area with a fireplace and club room with wide screen television and a wet bar for creative happy hours.

Residents have a selection of more than a dozen clubs and interest groups. Bridge, book reviews, hiking, and Spanish classes, along with golf, tennis, aerobics, and other physical pursuits fill a busy calendar. Other activities include video and popcorn nights, arts and crafts, water exercise, golf and gym clinics, dances and dance lessons, theme parties, and excursions to area attractions. There is a rich variety of volunteer activity within the community, to say nothing of involvement with hospitals, social service agencies, libraries, and a host of other public entities in the community at large.

Portland is situated at the confluence of the **Willamette** and **Columbia Rivers** where the two major waterways join to flow on as one to the **Pacific Ocean**, 80 miles to the west. About 30 miles to the east rise the steep slopes of the **Cascades**, highlighted by imposing **Mount Hood**, soaring 11,000 feet into the clouds. It is in this setting of nature's bounty that resides a wonderland of every imaginable recreational activity.

The city itself, and its surrounding communities, can be described with some justification as one gigantic park. The downtown area scintillates with fountains, waterfalls, sculptures, and sidewalk cafes. A sprawling park system includes 10,000 acres of forests, gardens, natural areas, and open spaces. **Forest Park**, within walking distance of Claremont, is the largest forested municipal park in the country, with 70 miles of hiking and nature trails, supporting a variety of wildlife, including elk and black bears. There are no less than three public rose gardens, each with its own special flair. The **Japanese Garden** is proclaimed one of the most authentic outside Japan.

Portland is a top cultural center of the northwest. The **Portland Center for the Performing Arts** attracts more than a million visitors annually. The home of **Hillsboro Actor's Repertory Theater** is less than 3 miles from Claremont. Suburban Washington County has more than a dozen arts organizations of its own, along with countless special events. The Portland **Civic Auditorium** is the venue for national touring companies, including ballet and grand opera. **Portland Opera** is ranked among the top 20 of North America's 105 opera companies. The **Oregon Symphony**, the oldest orchestra on the West Coast, celebrated its centennial season in 1995-96. Other experiences here include repertory theater, chamber music, a youth philharmonic, Shakespearean productions, and an art museum that ranks among the best in the Pacific Northwest. The **Institute for Science, Engineering, and Public Policy** presents a series of lectures by world leaders in science and technology.

The annual **Portland Rose Festival** is a happening of more than 80 events. Its grand floral parade is the nation's second largest all-floral event of its kind. Spectator sports abound. The **Portland Trail Blazers** are perennial favorites in NBA professional basketball. Spirited minor league teams draw enthusiastic fan support in baseball, hockey, and soccer. Live thoroughbred and quarter horse racing, as well as greyhound and sports car track competition, are big seasonal events. The **Metro Washington Park Zoo** has a first-class program that includes breeding for rare and endangered species. Six downhill ski areas are located on towering **Mount Hood** (Oregon's highest peak), catering to a variety of ability levels.

There are 15 colleges and universities in the metropolitan area. Four are within a 10-mile radius of Claremont. Among them is **Reed College**, a small, independent school that has produced 30 Rhodes scholars since 1915, a feat met by only one other college in the country. Also a few minutes away is **The University of Portland**, affiliated with the Congregation of Holy Cross at Notre Dame, and ranking as one of the top regional educational institutions in the American West. Also within this nearby cluster of higher educational resources is **Lewis & Clark College**, founded in 1867 and one of the largest private liberal arts and sciences colleges in Oregon. Its curriculum features a graduate school of professional studies and the **Northwestern School of Law**. There are a variety of special programs of interest to older adults offered by several Portland area institutions of higher learning, including three community colleges.

SAFE AND SECURE

Because the community does not lie within a municipal jurisdiction, law enforcement responsibility rests with the **Washington County Sheriff's Department**. Fire protection and a paramedic emergency response program are provided under the **Tualatin Valley Fire and Rescue**.

LET'S GO SHOPPING

Given the fact that the community is located inside the Portland city limits, in an affluent and well-populated residential and commercial area, there is no dearth of shopping convenience of every description, just minutes away.

SOUTH CAROLINA TAX FACTS

In terms of overall annual per capita tax liability of residents, U.S. Census Bureau data reveals that South Carolina ranks among the lowest in the nation. According to analyses released in 1994, that figure for the state was $1,584. Neighboring state comparisons were: North Carolina at $1,814, Georgia at $1,856, and Florida at $1,922.

INDIVIDUAL INCOME TAX

Calculating state individual income tax liability is based on taxable income reported on federal returns. Rates are graduated from 2.5 percent on taxable income up to $2,250 to a maximum rate of 7 percent on taxable income exceeding $11,250. Individual income tax brackets are adjusted annually to help offset the effects of inflation.

There is no tax on social security income. A $10,000 per year deduction is allowed for retirees who have reached age 65. National Guard and Reserve pay is not taxable, nor is there any intangibles tax on bank accounts, interest, dividends, investments, or other assets.

SALES TAX

The sales and use tax rate is 5 percent, but certain counties can add a 1 percent local option to the 5 percent. Counties imposing a local option sales tax must use a portion of the revenue collected from the additional levy to reduce that county's property taxes. A maximum sales tax of $300 is imposed on the purchase of motor vehicles, including boats and airplanes.

PROPERTY TAX

South Carolina counties, cities, and school districts impose *ad valorem* taxes on real estate and personal property. Local governments assess and collect such taxes. The market value of a residence and up to five acres of surrounding land is assessed at 4 percent.

The tax liability on property is determined when local government applies its millage rate to the assessed value. County millage rates vary widely, but the state average is 255 mills. Under that formula, the owner of a $100,000 home would pay property taxes of $677 in Aiken and $548 in Hilton Head Island. There is a $20,000 exemption on the fair market value of a home for those owners who have reached their 65th birthday.

Taxes for public school operations are on the first $100,000 of home value exempt, the maximum benefit ranging from $200 to $800, depending on the tax district in which the home is located. Personal property tax is collected annually on cars, trucks, boats, motorcycles, recreational vehicles, and airplanes, assessed at 10.5 percent of market value. The tax on a vehicle worth $10,000, based on the average millage rate, would come to $268.

For more complete tax information contact the South Carolina Department of Revenue, Public Affairs Office, P.O. Box 125, Columbia, SC 29214, 803-737-4405.

Note: The above information is based on applicable tax law information available at the time of publication. Because such laws and tax rates are subject to change, professional guidance should be sought if tax implications are critical to a relocation decision.

DEL WEBB'S SUN CITY HILTON HEAD

BLUFFTON, SOUTH CAROLINA

P.O. Box 1869
Bluffton, SC 29910
803-757-8700 / 800-978-9781
Fax: 803-757-8535

Developer: Del Webb Corporation

Year of initial property sales/rentals: 1995

Total land area: 5,600 acres

Average elevation: 20 feet

Location: Extreme southeast corner of South Carolina; Beaufort and Jasper Counties; straddles U.S. Highway 278; 8 miles west of Bluffton; 6 miles east of Interstate 95 at exit 8; 13 miles west of coastal Hilton Head Island; 19 miles north of Savannah, Georgia.

Nearest airport with scheduled commercial service: Savannah International (20 miles)

Current number of housing units with year-round occupants: 650

Projected number of housing units: 8,000 (2010)

Resident eligibility: At least one person in each household must be 55 or more years of age. Home ownership, however, is not restricted by age. No one under age 19 can reside in the community for more than 90 days during a calendar year.

Community visit/tour incentive program: "Vacation Getaway" program offers qualified guests a well-appointed, fully equipped, one-bedroom villa with an optional round of golf and access to all facilities on the 45-acre recreation campus. Reservations are subject to availability. Packages offer a three-night/four-day stay ($79 without golf, $119 with golf), or a six-night/seven-day stay ($199 without golf, $239 with golf).

Suggested newspaper: *Carolina Morning News*, P.O. Box 486, Bluffton, SC 29910 (803-837-5255)

WHY SUN CITY HILTON HEAD?

Sun City Hilton Head (SCHH) is Del Webb Corporation's first project excursion east of the Mississippi River. Clearly, the location was chosen with care. It's a few minutes from **Hilton Head Island**, one of the world's premiere seaside resorts. It is less than a half-hour from enchanting **Savannah, Georgia**, a city of history and charm that has been called "the Florence of the South" and where southern hospitality is epitomized. The quaint seaside town of **Beaufort**, just 17 miles to the northeast, is a reflection of the classic South to the degree that its grand antebellum homes have become favorite Hollywood backdrops for major film productions (including *The Big Chill* and *Forrest Gump*). Even **Bluffton**, Sun City's post office address about 8 miles down the highway, has something of a national reputation for yielding the best-tasting, most succulent oysters to be found anywhere.

This is a naturalist's paradise, a habitat for deer, osprey, egrets, and blue herons. The property was formerly a tree farm where pine trees were grown and harvested alongside large stands of hardwood, including a sizable mature cypress forest. Marshes and woodland add character to this Carolina low-country setting.

Awards and citations are nothing new to Del Webb. At the end of the century, it will have been 40 years since this creator of the "active adult retirement community" concept first launched the prototype community in this field—Sun City—on the outskirts of Phoenix. Del Webb, the company's founder, was featured on the cover of *Time* magazine after creating Sun City in recognition of his dedication to giving a new dimension to those entering retirement. Since then, scores of honors have been given to this pioneer and his company.

Less than two years after its grand opening, Sun City Hilton Head received its own accolades when the **National Association of Home Builders** awarded the community its coveted "Best in Seniors Housing" for 1997. Once again, recognition was given to a leader among developers and builders for creating a satisfying environment for older adults seeking an active life style.

WHO'S IN CHARGE?

The **Sun City Hilton Head Community Association** is currently administered by a board of directors comprised of representatives of the developer. It will eventually be turned over to elected residents. The association is responsible for policy development and for overseeing the day-to-day management of community affairs. Each household pays a mandatory annual fee of $700 to cover operating expenses such as security, road maintenance, and common area upkeep. The fee entitles residents to full access to all recreational facilities other than golf. Separate fees applicable to the golf option include an annual greens fee permit costing $1,200, a $300 annual golf trail fee (for use of personal golf carts), and a $22 user's greens fee.

The Sun City Packet is a monthly community tabloid-size newspaper that typically carries 40 pages of features, a complete calendar of activities and events scheduled for the month, and an extensive descriptive summary of announcements, club meetings, planned activities, and community developments.

THE WEATHER REPORT

The Bluffton area, although several miles inland, is affected by the temperate marine climate that characterizes much of the southeastern Atlantic coastline. The sea and land breezes of barrier islands and coastal locations are not felt as much this far from the water, and thunderstorms and gale winds are less severe here. There is just enough change in year-round temperatures to define a four-season climate, generally producing about 200 days of sunshine each year. The nearest official weather station is in Savannah, about 20 miles to the south and situated about the same distance from the coast as is Sun City. Average high and low temperatures for the three winter and three summer months are reported by the U.S. National Oceanic and Atmospheric Administration as follows:

December: high 62/low 39   **January:** high 60/low 38

February: high 63/low 40   **June:** high 89/low 68

July: high 91/low 71   **August:** high 90/low 71

Average annual precipitation: 52 inches
Average annual snowfall: rare

HOME SWEET HOME

Homes and homesites are sold together at Sun City Hilton Head. The Del Webb Corporation acts as general contractor, building and delivering the finished product on a predetermined schedule. A model-homes village displays 12 different floor plans. A professionally staffed design center enables homeowners to individualize their new residences when selecting from more than 250 options of floor coverings, lighting fixtures, cabinetry, and appliances. Many features are specifically designed for the convenience of older adults who may at some time experience limited mobility. Large windows and skylight options add to more cheerful interiors.

Single-family detached homes constitute more than 80 percent of the total housing inventory. The rest are villas of various configurations. All are single story. Prices for the detached units range from the lower $100s to the mid-$200s, with floor plans from 1,151 to 2,856 square feet. Villas start at close to $100,000 to a high of about $135,000, with square footage from 1,039 to 1,437. Rental units are available through private agencies for $900 to $1,500 per month, in sizes from 1,100 to 2,800 square feet. Central water and sewer systems are provided by county resources.

MONEY MATTERS

It should come as no surprise that a world-class resort destination would have above-average living costs. Various studies have shown that the Hilton Head Island metropolitan area stands alone as the most expensive place to live in the Carolinas. Cost of living is comparable to other celebrated upscale vacation spots such as Palm Springs, California; Aspen, Colorado; and Santa Fe, New Mexico. It is the high cost of housing that has the most significant impact on the cost of living here, with daily household budget items (groceries, personal services, health care, etc.) being close to average. In view of the fact that Sun City Hilton Head offers a well-defined home purchase cost profile, it is not difficult to make comparisons and to conclude that SCHH pricing is considerably more affordable than living on the island.

Hilton Head Island is one of 315 metropolitan and nonmetropolitan areas in the United States included in a study of living costs conducted by ACCRA. In the ACCRA Cost of Living Index (2nd quarter, 1996), Hilton Head was shown to have an index reading of 116.7 percent, or 16.7 percent above the average for all places included in the analysis. Of six weighted cost categories, two were below average (groceries, 1.6 percent, and utilities, 7.8 percent). Four categories were above average (housing, 42.3 percent; transportation, 4.8 percent; health care, 4.8 percent; and miscellaneous goods/services, 15.1 percent).

The county tax assessor places an appraised value on real estate based on comparable sales, condition of the property, etc. This figure is multiplied by 4 percent (for a primary residence, 6 percent for a secondary home), to obtain the assessed value. The assessed value is then multiplied by the millage rate, which for Sun City Hilton Head is .1986.

TAKE GOOD CARE OF YOURSELF

The nearest hospital to Sun City is the 68-bed **Hilton Head Medical Center**, on the island, about 13 miles away. Under the ownership of a private partnership, the hospital's most recent additions are a 15-bed subacute skilled nursing unit, a physical rehabilitation clinic and a diagnostic cardiac catheterization lab. A "new perspectives center" is part of growing geriatric services program that centers on comprehensive psychoclinical care in treating older patients for disorders common to advancing age. The medical staff represents more than 30 specialties and subspecialties, far more than would normally be found in a community of little more than 30,000 residents. An impressive volunteer auxiliary program in a typical year logs more than 35,000 hours of devoted time, energy, and talent from volunteer workers performing tasks in more than 20 hospital departments.

A second principal health care facility convenient to SCHH is regional **Beaufort Memorial Hospital**, just 17 miles from the community entrance. This fully accredited not-for-profit institution is licensed for 170 beds.

PLACES TO GO, THINGS TO DO

The 18-hole **Okatie Creek Golf Club**, opened in late 1995, is the first of three championship courses and clubhouses to be built. Another 18-hole and a 27-hole course are planned. It is a Southern-style links course with five sets of tees per hole, making it a challenging layout for skilled golfers, yet enjoyable for high handicappers as well. The 10,000 square foot clubhouse now serving members offers a fully equipped pro shop and dining facilities. There is a driving range, a nine-hole natural greens putting course, and a regular practice putting green.

The fitness center at **Town Square** (the commercial and recreational heart of the community) features an indoor, heated, eight-lane pool with handicap access, locker rooms, an indoor therapy spa, and an outdoor recreation pool with sloped entry, resistance walking pool, bubble jet benches, and fountains. The top-drawer facility also features a swirling hot tub, a cushioned-floor aerobics studio, and a strength training room with exercise instructors and computerized equipment.

A social hall is the place where residents come together for a wide assortment of activities—from watching the stock ticker in the "Wall Street Room" to billiards tournaments, weekend dances, and concerts. Classes are regularly scheduled at the crafts center, where an oil painting, a ceramic masterpiece, or a computer Internet surfing lesson may be the subject. More than 30 clubs and interest groups meet regularly with more being formed on an ongoing basis. A multi-purpose ballroom seats up to 750. Just outside, there are four lighted bocce ball courts and another for grass croquet and horseshoes. Numerous lagoons have been stocked for fishing and the 20-acre on-site **Lake Somerset** offers a perfect dock for fishing or launching non-motorized boats.

A paved fitness trail with exercise stations encircles the 45-acre Town Square campus, with more such pathways planned for other areas of the community. Four lighted soft surface tennis courts are in use with two more in planning stages, along with an indoor tennis center to accommodate anticipated demand growth. A "tot lot" next to the fitness center provides playground equipment for visiting grandchildren.

A visit to Savannah, about 20 miles away, will enchant any visitor. It is a deep-south city that retains its history and southern gentility.

SAFE AND SECURE

Sun City Hilton Head is a controlled access gated community, with security personnel on duty 24 hours a day, seven days a week, providing roving vehicle patrols around the clock. The **Beaufort County Sheriff's Department** provides police protection and the county fire department/emergency medical team maintains an on-site station facilitating immediate response to urgent calls.

LET'S GO SHOPPING

Since Sun City Hilton Head broke ground in 1994, businesses and service establishments have blossomed steadily along roadways leading to the community. The **Okatie Center**, a 268-acre commercial development immediately adjacent to SCHH, is projected for completion in early 1998. The center will include a full-service food market and other retail outlets, restaurants, banks, motels, and various professional services, including medical facilities. A unique feature will be access to the center by golf cart. **Kittle's Crossing**, about 9 miles from Sun City, is anchored by a Food Lion market and has a number of mainstream and specialty shops.

Bluffton, the tiny community (population less than 1,000) nearest to SCHH, has a respectable share of shopping conveniences. The **Hilton Head Factory Stores**, just 10 miles from Sun City, represent one of the largest famous-brand discount centers in the state (with more than 75 shops). Just a few miles away, in Hilton Head, is **The Mall at Shelter Cove**, the only enclosed mall and food court on the island, boasting two department stores and some 50 fashion, jewelry, sporting goods, and specialty shops, and a half-dozen eating places.

Coligny Plaza, located on south island, was Hilton Head's first major shopping concentration, featuring more than 60 diversified shops and delectable eateries from which to choose. Oceanfront and beachside dining on the island provide succulent local seafood, harvested daily from nearby coastal waters.

HERITAGE PLANTATION

PAWLEYS ISLAND, SOUTH CAROLINA

P.O. Box 2010
Pawleys Island, SC 29585
803-237-9824 / 800-448-2010
Fax: 803-237-1096

Developer: Larry Young

Year of initial property sales/rental: 1990

Total land area: 637 acres

Average elevation: 10 to 20 feet

Location: Central-eastern South Carolina; Georgetown County; on the peninsula formed between "the Grand Strand" Atlantic Coast and the Waccamaw River; on U.S. Highway 17; 21 miles from Myrtle Beach; 12 miles to the northeast from Georgetown; 72 miles from Charleston; about 60 miles to the southwest from the North Carolina border.

Nearest airport with scheduled commercial service: Myrtle Beach Jetport (19 miles)

Current number of housing units with year-round occupants: 225

Projected number of housing units: 517

Resident eligibility: There is no age restriction or requirement, but more than 85% of residents are in retirement or semiretirement.

Community tour/visit incentive program: None

Suggested newspaper: *Sun News*, P.O. Box 406, Myrtle Beach, SC 29578 (803-626-8555)

WHY HERITAGE PLANTATION?

Pawleys Island is at the southern reach of the **Grand Strand**, of which **Myrtle Beach** is the center of activity. It is one of 10 communities that share this 65-mile-long northern third of the South Carolina Atlantic coastline. **Georgetown** (population just under 10,000), 12 miles to the south and the island closest sizable neighbor, was once part of a rice empire, where privileged plantation owners of great wealth guided the economy and developed the social order. It is a safe-harbor port of serenity and charm with a fabled history marked by ghost stories and folklore. In the opposite direction from Georgetown, a few miles north of Pawleys Island, is **Brookgreen Gardens**, designated a national historic landmark and scene of the nation's first public sculpture garden in which are displayed more than 500 works by more than 200 different artists.

This is an area where upscale residential communities have sprung up and where seashore vacation resorts indicate a growing prosperity. With its nine neighboring Grand Strand coastal towns, Pawleys Island nests on the **Intracoastal Waterway** with the **Atlantic Ocean** beaches at its doorstep. Such a setting, an enchanting natural environment, attracts an endless stream of visitors who never seem to tire of its shoreline virtues.

It is here that **Heritage Plantation** is located, by the waters of the **Waccamaw River**, at the widest and one of the most picturesque stretches of the Atlantic Intracoastal Waterway. Formerly the site of two sprawling plantations, the community is decorated with huge magnolias and live oak trees said to be up to 300 years old. With an ultimate buildout of 517 home-sites on 627 acres, its density of development is less than one home per acre, leaving residents with lots of elbow room and an extra measure of privacy. An architectural review board assures a high level of quality and consistency of residential construction and neighborhood appearance.

WHO'S IN CHARGE?

A nonprofit property owners association has been in place since the first stages of development. Homeowners pay $81 per month ($54 per month for vacant lot owners) in fees to cover clubhouse facilities and maintenance for common areas and roads and for 24-hour security. Marina and golf club memberships are separate options.

THE WEATHER REPORT

A generally mild, humid climate results from the area's latitude and the low elevations above sea level. Warm gulf stream currents and mountains to the north and west impact significantly on weather moderation. Spring starts in March with occasionally chilly days, and by mid-April the beaches are already alive with bathers and sun-worshippers. Summers can last into October, making for a six-month tourist season. Although generally mild, winters do sometimes invite below freezing temperatures—even snow on rare occasions. But most days from late November to early March are quite pleasant.

Charleston is the nearest official weather station, approximately 70 miles down the coast from Heritage Plantation. Average high and low temperatures there for three winter and three summer months are reported by the U.S. National Oceanic and Atmospheric Administration as follows:

December: high 62/low 41	**January:** high 58/low 38
February: high 61/low 40	**June:** high 88/low 69
July: high 90/low 73	**August:** high 89/low 72

Average annual precipitation: 52 inches
Average annual snowfall: less than 1 inch

HOME SWEET HOME

Only single-family homes are allowed. No condominiums, apartments, townhouses, or duplexes here. Many sites are purchased for future residential construction. There are no time limits within which homes must be built after lot purchase.

There are three types of homesites. In the estate category, typical lot sizes range from ½ to ¾ acre. Minimum square footage dwelling requirements vary from 2,000 to 3,000 square feet of living space, plus a two-car garage. In the custom category, sizes range from ⅓ to ½ acre with a minimum of 1,800 square feet of living area, with garage. The smallest grouping, called patio homesites, are typically from ⅕ to ¼ acre and accommodate floor plans with from 1,350 to 2,000 square feet, plus garage. Site prices range from $40,000 to $295,000, as determined by size and location. Only a limited number of lots remain unsold. Home prices start at $170,000 and extend upward virtually without any meaningful limit. The community has not been developed for a long enough period of time to have any significant resale market, but through the natural course of events, it can be expected to expand in time.

All utilities are run under ground. Water and sewer systems are provided by **Georgetown County**. There is space for boat storage but not for recreational vehicles.

MONEY MATTERS

Local real estate taxes on a home and lot amount to 1 percent of the assessed value. South Carolina has a homestead exemption of $20,000 on the fair market value of a home for residents who are age 65 or older.

Data on basic elements of living costs are found for the nearby Myrtle Beach area (21 miles north), the closest location for which such information is available. The composite index reported by the *ACCRA Cost of Living Index* (2nd quarter, 1996) is 98.9, slightly below average for the 315 towns and cities included in the survey. Among six specific components in the survey, groceries and utilities were the only two reflecting costs above average (0.6 percent and 3.9 percent, respectively), while each of the remaining four factors were below average (housing, 0.9 percent; transportation, 8.8 percent; health care, 0.9 percent; and miscellaneous goods and services, 1.3 percent).

For those residents who choose to become members of the **Heritage Golf Club**, there is an initiation fee of $7,000 and annual dues of $1,500 for an individual and $1,920 for a family.

TAKE GOOD CARE OF YOURSELF

There are two family health care clinics nearby, one in Pawleys Island and the other in neighboring **Litchfield**. A chiropractic clinic also operates in Pawleys Island. Some 50 or so physicians, including specialists, maintain offices within a 20-mile radius of Heritage Plantation, along with a substantial number of dentists and other health care professionals.

Georgetown Memorial Hospital, less than 15 minutes away, is a nonprofit, 142-bed acute-care facility, the sole provider of its kind in Georgetown County. Operating continuously since its opening in 1950, it has about 60 active medical staff members and a number of consulting physicians.

PLACES TO GO, THINGS TO DO

A truly breathtaking avenue of oaks leads to a 12,000-square-foot Southern colonial clubhouse graced with vintage antiques and elegant furnishings. Proclaimed to serve one of the top-ranked golf courses in the country, Heritage club members enjoy not only exclusive rights to their own course and clubhouse, but also have special privileges at the Grand Strand's other five courses built by the Heritage Plantation developer. A second clubhouse is the focal point for much of the other recreational activity and social life in the community. Its amenities include a 75-foot heated outdoor pool, Jacuzzi, four lighted Har-Tru tennis courts, fitness center, party, card and billiards rooms, a bar and kitchen, and a croquet green, all providing residents a wide selection of leisure options. Membership in this **Legendary Links Club** costs all of $30 a year!

A recently completed private marina and boat ramp on the Waccamaw River (Intracoastal Waterway) includes wet slips, dry storage, and a dockmaster's office. Boaters have easy access to **Gulf Stream** deep-sea fishing using the intracoastal channel to reach the open sea. Cruising to the Charleston harbor is a relatively short haul that promises the excitement of visiting one of America's most irresistible port cities.

There's a rather unique assortment of close recreational activities in this tidelands area of **Georgetown County**. Festivals, tournaments, or celebrations occur just about every month. Some recognize Canadian "snowbirds" who flock to the island for warmth and enchantment. Some celebrate the nesting of the Loggerhead Turtle. There are plantation tours, seafood feasts, tennis and fishing tournaments, blessings of the fleet, harborwalks, Fourth of July parade and fireworks, culinary and music festivals, and Christmas tours of homes. There are six top-flight golf courses just in and around Pawleys Island and its next-door neighbor, Litchfield. One is a **Jack Nicklaus** signature course. Others bears the names of **Dan Maples**, **William Byrd**, and **Tom Jackson**. There are photographic and biking excursions, historical tours, state park and nature center visits, and scuba diving trips, among other adventures.

For big-time live entertainment, of course, less than 30 minutes away, Myrtle Beach has become in recent years the east coast's answer to Las Vegas and Branson. Box office patrons there find more than 20,000 theater seats on sale nightly (in season), with some of the best known stars of country music and a variety of other performance favorites. The renowned **Gatlin Brothers'** new 40,000-square-foot theater at **Fantasy Harbor** regularly features the Grammy Award-winning trio, along with many other popular celebrities. **Broadway at the Beach** is a club district sporting a **Hard Rock Cafe**, a **Planet Hollywood**, and countless other "in-crowd" places to see and be seen. Added to the mix of country music venues, the **Carolina Opry, Dolly Parton's Dixie Stampede**, and the **Alabama Theatre**, all contribute to the excitement of the surging Grand Strand's bid as a nationally recognized pleasure capital.

Charleston, a metropolitan area of almost 300,000 population, little more than an hour's drive south, has more to offer, including noteworthy historical sites, cultural amenities, and educational opportunities.

SAFE AND SECURE

The community has enhanced security by virtue of controlled entry and exit staffed by internal security personnel. Law enforcement responsibility lies with Georgetown County police agencies, as does firefighting and mobile emergency services. There is a 911 emergency phone system in place.

LET'S GO SHOPPING

Pawleys Island and Litchfield enjoy a reputation for small, quaint shops with unusual wares. Particularly notable is something of a mystique that centers on handmade rope hammocks carried by more than a dozen shops. Custom jewelry and fine antiques also vie for recognition as products of special interest. Collectibles sometimes come with story telling or even food or games. Clocks and crafts, cross stitch, framing, yarns, and patterns—all clamor for patronage. Shops featuring clothing and accessories, gifts and jewelry, floral arrangements and home furnishings, and decorating, offer the relaxed shopping environment that can only be found away from the typical urban areas. There are clusters of a half-dozen or so shops here and there, but none would qualify as a regional mall!

On the more practical side of the shopping agenda, there are three large grocers in Pawleys Island, the nearest only about two miles from the Plantation entrance. For mainline shopping, there is a full-blown mall just 9 miles up the road at **Murrells Inlet** where several department stores, a food court, theater, and scads of specialty shops serve an extensive surrounding market area.

KEOWEE KEY

SALEM, SOUTH CAROLINA

1390 Stamp Creek Rd.
Salem, SC 29676-9684
864-944-2200 / 800-537-5253
Fax: 864-944-2807

Developer: Realtec, Inc.

Year of initial property sales/rentals: 1972

Total land area: 1,500 acres

Average elevation: 900 feet

Location: Far northwestern corner of South Carolina, known as "The Upcountry;" Oconee County; on the shores of Lake Keowee; at the junction of State Highways 183 and 130; about 10 miles from the North Carolina border; 40 miles west of Greenville; 35 miles northwest of Anderson.

Nearest airport with scheduled commercial service: Greenville-Spartanburg (45 miles)

Current number of housing units with year-round occupants: 900

Projected number of housing units: 2,200

Resident eligibility: There is no age restriction, but an estimated 85% of current residents are either retired or semiretired. Approximately 2% of households have children under 18 years of age in permanent residence.

Community visit/tour incentive program: "Getaway" packages can be arranged at rates from $99 to $201 for two people, depending on length of stay (two nights/three days or three nights/four days) and whether golf is included.

Suggested newspaper: *The Journal Tribune* (semiweekly), P.O. Box 547, Seneca, NC 29679 (864-882-2375)

WHY KEOWEE KEY?

Keowee Key is a residential and resort community with all the amenities one expects to find in a country club environment—fine golf and tennis facilities, swimming pools, country club, leisure trail, and marina. But the area has its own uniqueness. Nestled in the foothills of the **Blue Ridge Mountains**, it is a place of literally hundreds of waterfalls and highland enchantment. Old country inns, quaint restaurants, and antique shops abound. In its third annual selections (1994) of the top 20 retirement communities in the nation, *New Choices* magazine singled out Keowee Key to be among those so distinguished.

Lake Keowee, on the shores of which the Key is located, is no mill pond. It is an 18,500-acre water wonderland with 300 miles of shoreline and is part of a chain of lakes that stretches from the North Carolina border to near Augusta, Georgia. The community's nearest big neighbor is **Greenville**, only 40 miles away, named by *The Wall Street Journal* as one of the best six cities for business relocation and by *Money* magazine as being among the top 10 places to live in the United States. It is the state's second largest metropolitan area (population of about 325,000). **Atlanta,** prime metropolis of the southeast, has world-class leisure events and facilities and is a 2½-hour drive away.

There is no better way for an off-the-beaten-path community to enjoy an abundance of fulfilling activities and attractions than to be located near a major institution of higher learning. **Clemson University**, one of the most prestigious schools of the South, is a mere 14 miles down the road. Here, on its main campus, there is an array of sporting events, adult education programs, concerts, lectures, exhibits, and stage performances to satisfy any yearning for entertainment and enlightenment.

WHO'S IN CHARGE?

The **Lake Keowee Property Owners Association** is a nonprofit organization established in 1993. Membership by residents is mandatory. An annual fee of $887 from each homeowner provides operating revenues to support maintenance of all roads and common areas, as well as the round-the-clock security program. The organization produces a monthly newsletter for communicating with homeowners.

THE WEATHER REPORT

The nearest official weather observation station is in **Greer**, a short distance northeast of Greenville. It is here that the climatic conditions of the **Piedmont** section of the state (eastern slope of the **Southern Appalachian Mountains**) are recorded. Because Keowee Key in **Salem** is closer to the mountains (although at the same general elevation) and is close to large bodies of water, there are likely to be variations from the data shown, but they are not considered significant.

Nights are generally cool during the summer months, and winters are mild with temperatures rarely below freezing during daylight hours. Freezing rainstorms and snowstorms normally occur no more than two or three times a season.

Average high and low temperatures for three winter months and three summer months are reported by the U.S. National Oceanic and Atmospheric Administration as follows:

December: high 53/low 33   January: high 50/low 30

February: high 54/low 32   June: high 85/low 64

July: high 88/low 68   August: high 87/low 67

Average annual precipitation: 51 inches
Average annual snowfall: 5.9 inches

HOME SWEET HOME

Single-family detached homes are found in a wide spectrum of cost and size—from $100,000 to $700,000, and from 1,400 to 7,000 square feet. Town-houses, of which there are 65 on the property, range in cost from $119,000 to $225,000, with square footage from 1,200 to 2,000. There are almost 300 condominiums priced from $52,000 (1,000 square feet) to $175,000 (1,680 square feet). Golf, lake, and mountain views and secluded wooded sites are typical characteristics of vacant parcels ready for development. New construction is all custom-built by area builders of choice. Long-term rentals are available at monthly rates of between $850 and $1,750, in sizes from 1,300 to 4,500 square feet. Homesites from ½ to 2 acres can cost anywhere from $15,000 to $325,000.

Many single-family homes are custom-built by the developer's own construction company or by other private contractors. For those who prefer freedom from yard work and property maintenance, there is a great selection of sites for townhouses and condominiums, as well as resales, some located along the golf fairways, others near the lake and marinas. Electric and telephone lines are underground. The community is served by a central sewer system and water supply, both owned and operated by the Lake Keowee Property Owners Association.

MONEY MATTERS

The most reliable cost of living survey available includes the Greenville-**Spartanburg-Anderson** metropolitan statistical area. The *ACCRA Cost of Living Index* (2nd quarter, 1996) shows this area to be just slightly higher (101.0, with 100 representing average) than the average for the 315 places surveyed. Among the six categories measured (groceries, housing, utilities, transportation, health care, and miscellaneous goods and services), housing was rated at 4 percent, utilities at 4.3 percent, and miscellaneous goods and services at 1.5 percent over the norm. Of the remaining three groupings, health care was substantially below average (11.8 percent), while groceries were 1.6 percent and transportation .4 percent below. It should be pointed out, however, that Anderson, while part of the same general metropolitan area, is considerably less urbanized than the two larger cities with which it is linked and, if taken separately, would likely show significantly lower living costs. It is Anderson, just 35 miles from Keowee Key, that lays claim to having the 16th-lowest cost of living in the entire nation.

The community compiled a comparison of basic living costs based on data collected in December 1994. The local property tax picture was shown to have a rather favorable rate of .180 on an assessment of 4 percent of appraised value. Under the formula, a $200,000 home would have an annual real estate tax bill of $1,440. Electric bills for the same size home would average $80 a month, water and sewer at $36 a month, and telephone basic service at $23 a month.

TAKE GOOD CARE OF YOURSELF

It is estimated that more than 100 family practice physicians and specialists (including surgery) are within a 20-mile radius of Keowee Key. More than 65 doctors and dentists are on the active staff of **Oconee Memorial Hospital** in **Seneca**, only 10 miles to the south. This fully accredited medical center offers approximately 20 specializations, from anesthesiology and cardiology to radiology and urology. Preventive health services for the community are provided through its wellness center. The facility has 160 acute-care beds and 70 long-term care beds at its adjacent nursing home.

A hospital-based emergency medical service is staffed by certified paramedics and technicians. Ambulance and emergency field care is provided 24 hours a day. The hospital emergency department is staffed by specialists and a cadre of 20 nurses, all trained in emergency medicine. Two other area hospitals, **Easly Baptist** and **Anderson Medical Center**, are about 20 and 35 miles away, respectively. The latter is a 587-bed facility serving a broader population base and having additional state-of-the-art equipment and programs for more out-of-the-ordinary medical conditions.

PLACES TO GO, THINGS TO DO

Within the Keowee Key community there are generous amenities to keep fun-seekers close to home. The country club is a social center as well as a place to pamper golfers. A restaurant and bar and grill are favorite gathering spots for friends and neighbors to enjoy after-play relaxation. Lake Keowee is at the community's doorstep, with depths of up to 60 feet. It is a mecca for sailing, fishing, swimming, water-skiing, and any water sport a magnificent clear-water lake can inspire. The championship 18-hole golf course, designed by the eminent golf architect, **George Cobb**, is as near to fairway perfection as can be found. Five "pro-style" tennis courts have all-weather surfaces and lights for night play. A paved-surface, 2½-mile lakeside leisure trail takes walkers, joggers, and cyclists past two sand beaches, picnic grounds, and badminton and shuffleboard courts, as well as tranquil wooded surroundings.

Outside Keowee's gates lie more leisure attractions than can be experienced in a lifetime. Being close to a major institution of higher learning, such as Clemson University, invariably means having access to countless cultural, entertainment, and learning opportunities. The **Clemson University Tigers** sports teams lead the notoriety parade in drawing devoted fans. Its football stadium, long known as "Death Valley," seats more than 80,000, making it one of the 10 largest on-campus gridiron arenas in the United States. The National Football League's recently added franchise, the **Carolina Panthers**, played out their inaugural 1995 season there.

Clemson campus activities are by no means limited to football, basketball, or other sporting events. Of special interest to retirees is a senior adventure camp in which participants cram five days of trips, fishing, boating, tours, hay rides, nature walks, apple picking, and a host of other fun-filled activities. Evenings are devoted to campfires, entertainment, talent shows, and whatever diversions happen to surface. Lakeview lodges provide comfortable accommodations. Costs are surprisingly modest.

In the heart of the university is **Fort Hill,** the 1,100-acre plantation home of the eminent statesman, congressman, and U.S. vice president, **John C. Calhoun**. Built in the early 1800s, the house is open to the public. It is one of several historic Clemson landmarks. The university's modern **Brooks Center for the Performing Arts** has a full calendar of engaging stagecraft. The 200-acre **South Carolina Botanical Garden** has a seasonal calendar that includes a spring daffodil festival, a winter series of horticultural lectures, and a variety of other special events.

Beyond the university campus, there is an unending wealth of outdoor activity and natural beauty, all within sight of the Blue Ridge Mountains horizon. Extraordinary state parks in both **Oconee** and **Pickens Counties** are among the most appealing in the entire Appalachian region. **The Chattooga**, a wild and scenic river known nationally for its whitewater rafting and trout fishing, shares its prime stretches in the same county with Keowee Key. There are Shakespeare festivals and celebrations of local Indian heritage, the farming legacy, the coming of the railroad, and African-American literature and arts. Mountain crafts, music, square dancing, and flower festivals crowd community calendars. Seldom does a holiday fail to bring on a festive commemoration. **Whitewater Falls,** less than 15 miles from Keowee (near the North Carolina border), consists of two 400-foot cascades and is one of the most scenic spots in all the southeast. Just a few minutes from the Key gate is **Duke Power Company's** "World of Energy," a fascinating demonstration of how nuclear energy is generated.

Just outside Clemson is **Pendleton**, a 200-year-old community on the national register of historic places, replete with Revolutionary War and early 19-century landmarks. It is the home of the **Pendleton Playhouse**, where community and youth theater thrive, along with classic film showings and exhibits of local and visiting artists.

SAFE AND SECURE

The community has four controlled entrances. Two main gates are manned with security personnel. Two secondary access gates require entry pass cards. The homeowners association provides the supervision and funding for round-the-clock security patrols.

LET'S GO SHOPPING

For a town with a population of around 8,000, Seneca (just 10 miles from the Key) has a surprisingly well-developed commercial concentration. **Applewood Shopping Center** boast 24 stores. Fifty or more shops, restaurants, and service establishments are in the downtown area, and 30 or so more are scattered among several plazas. A multiscreen cinema shows current releases. Six financial institutions vie for customer favor. A full-service food market is on the near side of Seneca, about 8 miles from the Keowee Key entrance.

For more shopping choices just a few miles further on, Clemson and Pendleton offer their share of one-of-a-kind outlets and distinguished eating places. Clemson, with more than 700 lodging rooms and 60 restaurants, began operating a free campus/town bus system in 1996, a boon to shopping convenience. For those usually infrequent occasions when really serious shopping is called for, there is Greenville, where one can satisfy virtually any consumer need.

MYRTLE TRACE

MYRTLE BEACH, SOUTH CAROLINA

P.O. Box 3908
Myrtle Beach, SC 29578-3908
803-448-1045 / 800-227-0631
Fax: 803-347-1170

Developer: Hall Development, Inc.

Year of initial property sales/rentals: 1983

Total land area: 300 acres

Average elevation: 30 feet

Location: Far northeast corner of South Carolina; Horry County; 8 miles west of Myrtle Beach; near the intersection of U.S. Highways 17 Bypass and 501; 97 mile northeast of Charleston; 80 miles southwest of Wilmington (North Carolina).

Nearest airport with scheduled commercial service: Myrtle Beach International Airport (11 miles)

Current number of housing units with year-round occupants: 400

Projected number of housing units: 510 (1998)

Resident eligibility: At least one member of the household must be age 55 or older.

Community visit/tour incentive program: None

Suggested newspaper: *Sun News*, P.O. Box 406, Myrtle Beach, SC 29578 (803-626-0205)

WHY MYRTLE TRACE?

Closeness to Atlantic beaches and ocean recreation near one of America's premiere resort playgrounds with many big city amenities may be just your cup of retirement tea. **Myrtle Beach** and **North Myrtle Beach**, South Carolina's new entertainment magnet and one of the most popular group destinations on the east coast, have a combined year-round population of more than 35,000. **Myrtle Trace** residents are 10 minutes away from the vacation hub—near enough to join in the fun when the spirit moves them. White sandy public beaches stretch for about 65 miles along the **"Grand Strand"** area, the upper third of the South Carolina coastline, of which Myrtle Beach is the focal point.

The July/August 1994 issue of *New Choices* magazine, published by *Reader's Digest*, anointed Myrtle Trace as one of America's top 20 retirement communities. **Hall Development**, creators of Myrtle Trace, has 25 years of experience in the development, construction, and sale of residential communities. The company has completed major residential projects in Tennessee, North Carolina, and Georgia.

WHO'S IN CHARGE?

Membership in the nonprofit **Myrtle Trace Homeowner's Association** is required of all property owners. A monthly membership fee of $50 covers clubhouse and swimming pool operations, street lighting, and common grounds maintenance. A monthly newsletter keeps residents informed of community developments and activities. The association is governed by an elected board of directors, holds an annual business meeting, and has a number of committees appointed to handle various administrative and operational functions in accordance with established policies and regulations.

THE WEATHER REPORT

South Carolina coastal communities like Myrtle Beach enjoy a temperate climate, considerably due to proximity to the ocean. Prevailing winds are northerly in the fall and winter, southerly in the spring and summer. Summers are generally described as hot and humid, but temperatures rarely reach 100 degrees. Sea breezes tend to keep temperatures several degrees cooler than inland readings.

The late summer and early fall season brings the greatest threat of hurricanes and tropical storms. Some storminess can be expected in springtime as well. A winter snow flurry, most likely in January, would be a conversation piece at local lunch counters and worthy of front-page local newspaper coverage. On average, winter produces less than one cold wave or severe freeze. Temperatures under 20 degrees are very rare. The closest official weather station is in Charleston, also along the coast and less than 100 miles to the south. Average high and low temperature readings in Myrtle Beach for three winter and three summer months are reported by the U.S. National Oceanic and Atmospheric Administration as follows:

December: high 62/low 41	**January:** high 58/low 38
February: high 61/low 40	**June:** high 88/low 69
July: high: 90/low 73	**August:** high 89/low 72

Average annual precipitation: 52 inches
Average annual snowfall: .7 inches

HOME SWEET HOME

The marketing strategy for this development is somewhat distinctive in that the objective is to reach a very well-defined segment of the potential retirement relocation population. In contrast to developments that strive to be all things to all people, Myrtle Trace is aimed at buyers within a targeted home investment range of $120,000 to $180,000, for a living space of 1,400 to 2,000 square feet. There are no condominiums, duplexes, cottages, or apartments. All are custom-built single-family detached dwellings, all of which are constructed and sold by the developer from a choice of eight floor plans. As a result of very low turnover, resales are limited. Vacant residential sites range in price from $20,000 to $32,000. Long-term rental units are available at monthly rates of $700 to $1,100 for 1,000 to 2,000 square feet of living space.

Homes are planned in a configuration that allows most homesites to border a natural area—a golfing green, a wooded patch, or one of the many ponds scattered around the property. Utility lines are below ground, and a central water supply and sewage disposal system are provided by a local government authority.

MONEY MATTERS

The Myrtle Beach metropolitan statistical area shows a living cost index of just under the average for the 315 places identified in the *ACCRA Cost of Living Index* (2nd quarter, 1996). The composite index of the reference report is 98.9, meaning that it is 1.1 percent below the average of the towns and cities included in the survey. Among six specific components in the survey, groceries and utilities were the only two reflecting costs above the average (0.6 percent and 3.9 percent, respectively), while each of the remaining four factors were below average (housing at 0.9 percent below, transportation at 8.8 percent below, health care at 0.9 percent below, and miscellaneous goods and services at 1.3 percent below).

Based on an owner-occupied home with a $130,000 value, annual property taxes would come to $995 (millage rate of 191.4), or $842 if the resident owner is older than 65 years of age, with applicable exemption. Monthly expenses for the same home are estimated to be $205 (fire protection, electricity, water/sewer, trash collection, cable television). Homeowner's insurance would add another $460 annually. These are estimated costs and will vary on an individual household basis depending on utility consumption and insurance coverage.

TAKE GOOD CARE OF YOURSELF

There are two nearby hospitals. The 150-bed **Conway Hospital** is an easy walk from the Myrtle Trace entrance. It offers full service acute care programs in a variety of departments and has been serving the region for more than 65 years. The facility recently opened a new wellness/fitness center, two blocks from Myrtle Trace, with an impressive list of amenities that include an indoor swimming/lap pool, racquetball courts, indoor track, basketball court, exercise and weight training rooms, dressing rooms, sauna and a variety of classrooms for specialized instruction. The 180-bed **Columbia**

Grand Strand Hospital is about 18 miles away in the Myrtle Beach area. Both hospitals are accredited by the **Joint Commission on Accreditation of Hospitals**. A 50-bed nursing center is also just a few minutes away.

PLACES TO GO, THINGS TO DO

A monthly schedule of activities within the community, mostly taking place in the 2,000 square foot clubhouse, is posted in the newsletter distributed to Trace residents. Among the groups meeting regularly are a half dozen or more board game devotees, bingo enthusiasts, and those drawn to line dancing, craft creations, bowling, bird-watching, gardening, and other such leisurely activities. Special programs, tours, and celebrations are held throughout the year. Golf, of course, is one of the most popular leisure activities.

Stocked fishing ponds add charm to most neighborhoods. The community clubhouse has an assortment of amenities for residents and their guests, including a full kitchen, a meeting and game room, a library, and an adjacent swimming pool and picnic area.

The popularity of golf at the Trace mirrors the widespread fairway mania throughout the Myrtle Beach area. It is said that golf is practically a religion in these parts. There are approximately 90 championship courses in and around "the Strand," many designed by some of the game's legendary masters—**Nicklaus, Palmer,** and **Fazio,** among others.

Conspicuous in Myrtle Beach's prosperity is its rise to prominence as a major convention and vacation destination. There are now more than 20,000 theater seats for which, during the busier seasons, patrons often clamor at box office windows for scarce tickets. Many describe the scene as another Branson (Missouri), joining in the rivalry with Las Vegas and Atlantic City for spectacular live shows and extravagant stage productions. *Destination Magazine* dubbed Myrtle Beach "the hottest up-and-coming destination for 1996."

Just 38 miles south along the coast is the port city of **Georgetown,** once the heart of a rice production empire. Somewhat in contrast to Myrtle Beach, this historic town of genteel charm is a refuge of enchantment. A principal attraction is **Brookgreen Gardens**, a national historical landmark featuring the nation's first public sculpture garden. Also highlighting the gardens is a wildlife park that is home to foxes, alligators, deer, and other animals native to the region, as well as an aviary.

Coastal Carolina University, practically a next-door neighbor, offers a nine-week academic enrichment program that provides opportunities for continued intellectual, cultural, and social growth for men and women age 50 and older. Classes are taught by faculty as well as retired and semiretired professionals from the community. A recent course announcement included titles such as "Crisis in Bosnia," "Great Books Seminar," "The Holy Land,"

"Computers" (different sessions for introductory, intermediate, and advanced), "The Rise and Fall of the Big Bands," "A Spiritual Dialogue," "Classic Films" (review and discussion of vintage films from Hollywood's golden era), "Investing," and "Bird Watching/Ornithology."

SAFE AND SECURE

Law enforcement is the responsibility of the **Horry County** police agency. Firefighting services are provided by the city of **Conway**, only 5 miles away. Emergency paramedic response units are dispatched by Conway Hospital, immediately adjacent to Myrtle Trace.

LET'S GO SHOPPING

A brand-new full-service food market and pharmacy are about three blocks from the community entrance. Lodging, restaurants, and a bank are also clustered nearby. Less than halfway to Myrtle Beach, about three miles down the road, is a sizable shopping mall. The largest mall is **Myrtle Square** with a half-million square feet of retail space. Another, **Briarcliffe,** has 85 shops, 10 theaters, three restaurants, and a food court. Outlet stores play a dominant part in the retail landscape. The **Waccamaw Pottery** outlet is widely known for its bargains. **Barefoot Landing** is a collection of more than 100 shops and restaurants featuring a wide range of specialty products and culinary temptations.

SAVANNAH LAKES VILLAGE

MCCORMICK, SOUTH CAROLINA

101 Village Dr.
McCormick, SC 29835
864-391-2151 / 800-442-2829
Fax: 864-391-4124

Developer: Cooper Communities, Inc.

Year of initial property sales/rentals: 1989

Total land area: 3,987 acres

Average elevation: 400 feet

Location: Northwestern South Carolina; McCormick County; just north and east of the intersection of U.S. Highways 221 and 378; 25 miles south of Greenwood; 42 miles north of Augusta (Georgia).

Nearest airport with scheduled commercial service: Bush Field, Augusta (45 miles)

Current number of housing units with year-round occupants: 300

Projected number of housing units: 5,100 (2015)

Resident eligibility: There are no age restrictions for residency, but an estimated 75% of the current population is considered to be retired or semiretired. No more than an estimated 5% of resident families have children under 18 years of age living in the household.

Community visit/tour incentive program: Special lodging packages are available for up to three nights at the on-site resort lodge.

Suggested newspaper: *McCormick Messenger* (weekly), Main St., McCormick, SC 29835 (864-465-3311)

WHY SAVANNAH LAKES VILLAGE?

Cooper Communities, Inc. (CCI) has been building master-planned developments for active adults since 1954. They were among the first to recognize and respond to the fact that retirement life styles are constantly changing and that their success would depend on their adaptability to the marketplace. Five Cooper residential projects are located in four states (two in Arkansas and one each in Tennessee, South Carolina, and Missouri). They all have a land use design that preserves substantial portions of the property in natural, unspoiled common areas. Each homesite ensures optimal residential privacy by being connected to a common property green belt, whether a golf fairway, lake front, or untouched woodland. Evidence of the Cooper commitment to its land use conservation philosophy is reflected in the fact that among its many awards for outstanding achievement, none has been more gratifying than those received from organizations outside its industry, from groups not normally viewed as friendly toward developers such as the **Northwest Arkansas Audubon Society** (1990) and the **Arkansas Nature Conservancy** (1994). Honors from these organizations were presented to CCI for environmentally sound community development practices, well beyond the pale of economic return or aesthetic enhancement.

Savannah Lakes Village (SLV), just a few miles from the Georgia border, is situated on massive **Lake Thurmond** (70,000 acres), the largest of three lakes linked together by the **Savannah River,** and the second largest inland body of water in the Carolinas. The community occupies almost 20 miles of lake shoreline.

In something of a departure from features found at other CCI communities, there is a luxurious 80-room guest lodge at SLV, perched on a 14-acre peninsula, commanding a superb view of the lake. Complementing the lodge are a swimming pool, miniature golf, and tennis courts and a lakeside walking trail.

WHO'S IN CHARGE?

The **Savannah Lakes Property Owners Association** is a nonprofit corporation administered by a board of directors composed of five representatives of the developer and two community resident members. Homeowners pay $44 a month to support all administrative/staffing costs, security, and common area maintenance (including the golf course, activity center, and all recreational amenities). Unusually modest green fees ($3.25 for 18 holes!) help offset operating costs covered by the dues paid by all property owners.

There are two publications devoted to news and developments at SLV. *The Sun* is a monthly tabloid-size newspaper that goes to residents and absentee property owners, among others, giving readers current information on happenings of general interest. *The Villager* is a newsletter produced weekly, primarily for homeowners living in the community.

WEATHER OR NOT

Weather conditions in the McCormick area are comparable to those of **Augusta, Georgia**, approximately 42 miles to the south. Both lie near the boundary between the **Piedmont Plateau** and the **Coastal Plain**, known as the **Fall Line**. Both are located in the **Savannah River Valley** and share somewhat parallel topographical features regarding such elements as surface water, elevation, and latitude. Measurable snow is unusual. Severe cold, winter storms, and damaging high winds are rare.

Average high/low temperatures for the three winter months and three summer months for Augusta are reported by the U.S. National Oceanic and Atmospheric Administration as follows:

December: high 59/low 35   **January:** high 56/low 32

February: high 60/low 35   **June:** high 90/low 66

July: high 92/low 70   **August:** high 91/low 69

Average annual precipitation: 45 inches

Average annual snowfall: 1 inch

HOME SWEET HOME

Five of six planned subdivisions are now developed with more than 3,900 homesites served by utilities, telephone, and cable in place. Nearly 60 miles of paved roads have been completed. Construction of single-family and patio homes and townhouses is constantly in progress on both a custom and speculative basis. Home buyers may look to **Cooper Homes** (the CCI home building division) for any of more than 20 sets of unique floor plans (any of which can be modified), or they may have a completely customized home created by **Signatures**, the custom design team of Cooper Homes. Property buyers are free to engage builders of their choice.

Of some 350 existing housing units, almost 90 percent are single-family, detached dwellings. They range in price from the low $90s to close to a half-million dollars, with floor plans that run from 1,200 to as much as 5,000 square feet. Townhouses, some of which were built and occupied by second-home owners, account for the remaining inventory. Prices in that group generally begin in the low $100s and go up to the mid-$220s for square footage between 1,200 and 2,400. Vacant lots, ready for construction, from one-quarter to a full acre in size, can cost anywhere from around $8,000 to as much as $200,000 or more.

MONEY MATTERS

Rural America has always been looked upon as the place to be if you want to stretch dollars, live modestly, avoid debt, and keep a healthy bank balance. **McCormick County** is rural. Its county seat and largest town, **McCormick**, has a population of less than 1,700. Savannah Lakes has a population edging toward 600. Other county hamlets are mostly in the 100 to 200 residents category, The entire county population is less than 9,000.

Not surprisingly, there is no official cost of living research data available for McCormick County. There is, however, such information published for another largely rural area just a short distance to the south. The metropolitan area that includes **Aiken** (as well as Augusta, Georgia) serves as a useful parallel. For this area, the ACCRA Cost of Living Index (2nd quarter, 1996) reveals a composite index of 6.9 percent below the average for all places in the study. Five of the six items—groceries, housing, transportation (primarily the cost of operating a vehicle), health care, and miscellaneous goods and services (the most heavily weighted of the six groupings), were all shown to be moderately to sharply below the norm.

As for local property taxes, some would say they are unbelievably low. The formula is based on the full appraised value of the home, multiplied by 4 percent, and again multiplied by .225 mills. That calculation would bring the tax on a $150,000 home to $1,350, minus a state deduction of $400, for a total liability of $950.

TAKE GOOD CARE OF YOURSELF

Routine medical services are very conveniently accessible to SLV residents. **The Savannah Lakes Medical Center** is housed in a new building located inside the community perimeter. It is affiliated with two hospitals located within a 25-mile radius of SLV. Two physicians, a family nurse practitioner, and a licensed practical nurse constitute the normal professional staff makeup. Services include physical examinations, diagnosis, monitoring and treatment of common health problems such as diabetes and high blood pressure, medication prescriptions, surgical consultation and minor surgery, home health care, rehabilitative and physical therapy, and minor emergencies. A few minutes away, in downtown McCormick, there are private clinics for medical, dental, and chiropractic care. Also located inside Savannah Lakes is the **McCormick Health Care Center**, an 88-bed nursing home.

For more comprehensive or specialized care, there are two nearby hospitals. **Self Memorial** in **Greenwood**, and **Abbeville County Memorial** in **Abbeville**, are no more than 30 minutes away. Self Memorial is a nonprofit, 421-bed regional referral center serving a six-county area. More than 100 physicians on staff represent virtually every major medical and surgical specialty. The Abbeville facility is also a full-service hospital with a long list of departmental specialties that include intensive and cardiac care units, modern radiology services, physical, respiratory, and pain therapy, a wide variety of surgical procedures, and a comprehensive home health care program.

PLACES TO GO, THINGS TO DO

Like other Cooper communities around the country, Savannah Lakes Village reflects a recognition of contemporary retirement life style realities. That recognition revolves around the fact that today's more youthful, healthier retiree is likely to pursue a much broader range of leisure activities. For many, simply having access to a golf course, tennis club, and swimming pool will no longer suffice. Mechanisms and carefully planned activities designed to encourage and facilitate interpersonal relationships and to provide outlets for creativity have become essential ingredients to a well-rounded recreational retirement community.

This does not mean that golf, tennis, and other physical activities are of diminishing importance. The SLV 18-hole, 7,010 yard championship golf course and its graceful 9,000-square-foot **Tara Country Club**, take a back seat to no other. But the clubhouse rather subtly suggests that catering to golfers is not its primary reason for being. The pro shop, for instance, is connected to the main building by a covered deck, making it convenient for golfers, yet separate from the non-golf-related activities that make the facility a social center for the community.

Much more indicative of the Cooper philosophy in terms of diversity is the new 23,000-square-foot community and fitness center (opened in 1996). It is the place to gather for lectures, stage shows, dinners, and parties. The central ballroom will accommodate 350 for dinner or 500 for theater-style seating. Fitness facilities include a 25-meter pool, exercise areas, whirlpool and sauna, and a four-lane bowling alley. Outside are four lighted, pro-surfaced tennis courts and walking trails. A 42-slip marina offers a gas dock and ship's store, designed to eventually expand to accommodate 100 boats.

A glance at the activity calendar for any month of the year reveals a plethora of clubs and interest groups inviting all sorts of participation and challenge—from golf tournaments, tennis, bowling, biking, and bocce ball leagues, and water aerobics, to table games, crafting, computer learning, square dancing, discussion groups, wine tasting, bingo, pageant staging, and weight management. Key programs typically feature touring entertainment acts from various parts of the country and abroad.

Outside the community there are noteworthy leisure attractions. Among the most prominent of events in the area is the **Masters Golf Tournament**, held annually in Augusta and a premier international spectacle in the world of professional golf. For those who enjoy collegiate sport competition, the **University of South Carolina** in **Columbia** is about 70 miles away and **Clemson University** is about 80 miles away.

Four miles east of the Village, the town of McCormick is home to the **McCormick Arts Council at the Keturah**, a multipurpose arts center. First-rate live theater—from modern plays to Shakespeare—along with musical productions and museums are found in Abbeville and **Greenwood**, less than 25 miles away. The opera house in Abbeville is famous for having greeted such "golden age" stars as Jimmy Durante, Fanny Brice, and Groucho Marx. Augusta, about 15 miles away, is a source of further options in leisure and entertainment.

SAFE AND SECURE

A recently constructed on-site public safety building accommodates the Village's own uniformed security force and the volunteer fire department. The uniformed security unit is on duty around the clock, seven days a week. Their marked patrol trucks maintain constant surveillance of all the community subdivisions and assist residents with lost keys, lockouts, vacation house checks, emergency contact procedures, etc.

Law enforcement and emergency medical services are handled through the **McCormick County Sheriff's Department** and the **South Carolina Highway Patrol**, which stations several troopers in McCormick.

LET'S GO SHOPPING

Other than a convenience store and gas station in the Village, the closest shopping concentration is in downtown McCormick. This is a place that might be described as "down-home country," or "(very) small town America." Where else can you find a turn-of-the-century soda fountain that serves hand-packed ice cream cones and old-fashioned cherry sodas? However, a food supermarket and a small grocer are just minutes away, making shopping for necessities accessible. There are almost 40 retailers and service establishments, a smattering of professional and county offices, and several restaurants in McCormick, some with restored shop fronts that harken back to another era.

Easy-to-reach Greenwood (population 22,000) is a central shopping district serving residents within a 30-mile radius of its downtown section. This town lays claim to the "world's widest main street," with as many as 80 shops along broad sidewalks. It has a moderately sized enclosed mall with a good collection of retail business outlets and service establishments. Just 20 miles from the Village is Abbeville (population about 6,000), with its delightful town square, large National Historic Register District, and variety of good restaurants. Augusta, with a population of about 45,000, has a rich variety of shopping options. The **Augusta Artist Exchange** is a fine art gallery that promotes the best in local and regional art, along with large selections of limited edition prints, sculpture, pottery, carvings, blown glass, and other finely crafted decorative pieces. **Augusta Mall** is a regional shopping center with 150 specialty shops, four full department stores, and two food courts.

WILLBROOK PLANTATION

PAWLEYS ISLAND, SOUTH CAROLINA

P.O. Box 97
Pawleys Island, SC 29585
803-237-4000 / 800-476-2861
Fax: 803-237-9509

Developer: The Litchfield Company

Year of initial property sales/rentals: 1986

Total land area: 2,400 acres

Average elevation: 20 feet

Location: Just above the midpoint of the South Carolina coast; Georgetown County; near the southernmost portion of the "Grand Strand" between the Waccamaw River and the Atlantic Ocean; less than 2 miles west of U.S. Highway 17; about 10 miles north of Georgetown; 20 miles south of Myrtle Beach; 75 miles north of Charleston.

Nearest airport with scheduled commercial service: Myrtle Beach Jetport (20 miles)

Current number of housing units with year-round occupants: 190

Projected number of housing units: 2,000 (2010)

Resident eligibility: There are no age restrictions, but an estimated 75% of residents are retired or semiretired, with occupants under age 18 rare exceptions.

Community tour/visit incentive program: A "Stay on Us" program entitles qualified visitors to a two-night, three-day stay for a lodging cost of $199.

Suggested newspaper: *Sun News*, P.O. Box 406, Myrtle Beach, SC 29578 (803-626-8555)

WHY WILLBROOK PLANTATION?

If you love the beach, **Pawleys Island** will not disappoint you. If you love history, the tales of wealth, greatness, tragedy, and poverty growing out of the rice empire that flourished from the early 1700s until the time of the American Revolution can only whet your appetite to know more of this classic Americana heritage. **Waccamaw Neck** is a 25-mile slender finger of land along the **Atlantic Ocean** and at the convergence of four rivers. It is still endowed with marshes, moss, and majesty; a land of preserved plantation sites—imposing mansions, elegant gardens, and an air of graceful living. Many of these historic sites have been transformed into master-planned communities, recreational clubhouses, golf courses, boat ramps, garden homes, oceanfront villas, and sprawling wildlife preserves and conservation areas. It is a blend of rich legacy and modern amenities.

Willbrook Plantation, nestled on this southern stretch of the **Grand Strand** (South Carolina's vacation playland), occupies what was once three colonial rice plantations. Homesites have backdrops of towering cypress trees, giant magnolias, Carolina pines, and ancient oaks. The nearby beaches of **Litchfield** and Pawleys Island are among the widest and best preserved on the 60-mile-long South Carolina Grand Strand coast. Access to ocean and sand is just across the highway, within walking distance of the Plantation, at its sister development, **Litchfield By The Sea**. On its western flank is the **Waccamaw River**, a watercourse of the **Intracoastal Waterway**. Just minutes to the north, **Murrell's Inlet**, at the northernmost tip of Waccamaw Neck, is in the midst of a 10-year revitalization project that will put the scenic fishing village on the regional map of memorable family vacation destinations.

WHO'S IN CHARGE?

Willbrook Plantation presently consists of two master-planned golfing communities—**Willbrook Golf & Country Club** and **The Tradition**, each with its own governing body. The former includes **Allston Point**, a section of 57 garden homes and sites offering five different floor plans. The Tradition includes three sections, **Tuckers Grant, Hunters Preserve**, and **Weston Point**, each with specified home size restrictions.

Willbrook Community Association homeowner dues of $92/month for homesite only, and $119 a month for home and site (called "regime" fees), support common area and street maintenance, upkeep on recreational amenities, front and back gate and neighborhood security arrangements, administrative services, and contingency reserves. Fees also include an assessment that applies to access by Plantation residents to the beachfront community of Litchfield By The Sea, including tennis privileges at seven lighted courts. Homes located in Allston Point have a separate additional fee of $15 a month to cover various common area features exclusively applicable to that section of the Plantation. Residents in The Tradition pay a fee of $70 a month for similar benefits.

THE WEATHER REPORT

South Carolina's upper coast, by virtue of its sea level elevation and position of latitude, has a climate that can generally be described as mild but humid. Weather conditions are moderated by mountain ranges to the north and west that tend to protect the area from cold winter winds that would otherwise come from the midwestern plains and Canada. Spring starts in March with occasional chilly temperatures, and by the middle of April the beaches are already well-populated with sun-and-surf devotees. Summers can last into October, but winters, on rare occasion, can bring subfreezing weather—even snow in rare instances. But most days from late November until early March are quite pleasant. During the summer, there is an average of 46 days with temperatures of 90 degrees or more.

The **Myrtle Beach** Chamber of Commerce vacation guide, which covers as far south as Pawleys Island, summarizes average temperature highs and lows based on 30 years of data from an unspecified source:

December: high 58/low 36   **January:** high 59/low 38

February: high 60/low 37   **June:** high 86/low 68

July: high 88/low 72   **August:** high 88/low 70

Average annual precipitation: 52 inches (Charleston)
Average annual snowfall: less than 1 inch (Charleston)

HOME SWEET HOME

Centex Homes, the nation's largest builder of residential properties, operating in 44 major markets spread throughout more than 20 states, has been the exclusive builder of the homes at The Tradition. Custom builders have taken an active role in the development of other Willbrook neighborhoods. A resale market has developed, giving purchasers a broader range of choices.

All homesites provide easy access to the ocean, which is within walking distance of the community. But for those whose aesthetic tastes favor other vistas, there are options for creekside, lakeside, and marshview scenes to view from a bay window or an outside deck. The Tradition group of homes range in size from 1,332 to 2,580 square feet, with prices starting in the low $140s. Customized homes are open to almost unlimited size and price possibilities. Some have risen to as much as 4,500 square feet with a price tag around $650,000. Vacant lots ready for construction are generally in the .375- to .98-acre size and may cost anywhere between $42,000 and $150,000.

Water and sewer services are provided by the county. Underground electric and telephone utilities and street lights and rolled-edge curbing contribute to the area's appeal.

MONEY MATTERS

The ACCRA Cost of Living Index findings for the Myrtle Beach area (which is generally considered to include the "Strand" communities to the south, as far as 20 miles down the coast to Pawleys Island), reveal it to be slightly below the average for the 315 towns and cities included in the survey, reasonably equated with the national average. Among six specific components referenced, groceries and utilities were the only two reflecting costs above average (0.6 percent and 3.9 percent, respectively), while the remaining four factors were below average (housing, 0.9 percent below; transportation, 8.8

percent below; health care, 0.9 percent below; and miscellaneous goods and services, 1.3 percent below).

According to data published by the Myrtle Beach Area Chamber of Commerce, residential telephone bills average $20 a month for local access calls and the average energy bill (all electric) for an 1,800-square-foot living area is approximately $92 a month. Gasoline is taxed at 16 cents per gallon, included in the pump price. City and county property taxes for primary home, year-round residents, are determined by the assessed value of the home (typically 80 to 90 percent of the sale price), multiplied by the millage rate (currently at .2564), multiplied by 4 percent. Under that formula, a home purchased for $150,000 would have an annual tax obligation of $1,230. A homeowner over age 65, who has established one-year residency, is eligible for a homestead exemption of $20,000. The county imposes no additional local option levy above the 5 percent state sales tax.

TAKE GOOD CARE OF YOURSELF

Georgetown Memorial Hospital, 10 miles south of Willbrook, is a private, not-for-profit 142-bed facility, offering a full range of inpatient and outpatient services. It has tripled in size since its opening in 1950. Specialties include high technology nuclear medicine, oncology, cardiac catheterization, magnetic resonance imaging (MRI), lithotripsy, and surgical services. A full-service laboratory and diagnostic center are also available. A medical staff of 60 provides comprehensive patient care. Some 30 miles in the opposite direction is the larger **Columbia Grand Strand Regional Medical Center** in Myrtle Beach. A staff of 150 physicians represents more than 25 specialties in this 172-bed institution.

The **Waccamaw Public Health District** conducts programs throughout **Georgetown County** to help prevent health-threatening problems and to enhance early detection and treatment of disease or other unhealthy conditions that may affect the community.

PLACES TO GO, THINGS TO DO

On-site community amenities feature two 18-hole golf courses, one designed by **Don Maples,** the other by **Ron Garl.** Both are surrounded by distinctive residential properties. Golfers have their own clubhouse with a pro shop and grille. Membership requires approximately a $5,000 initiation fee, monthly dues of $150, and a monthly food expense minimum of $50. Two other clubhouses (2,000-square-foot **Willbrook Residents Club** and 1,650-square-foot **Tradition Residents Club**) are gathering places for neighborhood social and recreational activities. Seven outdoor tennis courts provide generous playing time for a relatively limited cadre of players. Private beach access adds great appeal to an already inviting ocean front resort atmosphere. On the drawing boards is a proposed marina to be built nearby.

The **Georgetown County Arts Commission** fosters and coordinates the cultural, economic, and social climate for the arts in Georgetown County. **Brookgreen Gardens**, located in Litchfield, about 2 miles from the Plantation, is considered by many to be the star feature of Georgetown's claim to distinction in civilized refinement. From its beginnings, Brookgreen has been a unique showcase for American figurative sculpture. Today, it is the largest permanent exhibition of its kind in the world. It is, as well, a place where plants and animals of the Low Country are preserved in their natural habitat. The **Bellefield Nature Center** is part of a 17,500-acre wildlife refuge called **Hobcaw Barony**. It boasts an ongoing research and education program about the area's rich natural history. A highlight of the facility tour is a saltwater touch tank where visitors can learn about sea life native to the area. Georgetown's **Rice Museum** presents a graphic display of the history of rice cultivation in the United States since the early 18th century. Local historic homes and churches, many of them restored to their past elegance, give the area character and charm.

The nine principal communities of the Grand Strand are collectively a land of festivals, Revolutionary War encampments, musical and storytelling events, plantation tours, fishing, golf, and tennis tournaments, boat racing, arts and crafts shows, street dances, and parades. Their clubs and organizations run the gamut from wood carving and homemaking to service clubs, stamp collecting, quilting, and adversity support groups. **Coastal Carolina University** in **Conway** (little more than a half-hour away), is a 242-acre campus with more than 4,000 students. The university's 26 degree programs and an active athletic program create a noteworthy influence on the region it serves.

Within a 20- to 30-mile stretch to the north lies the Myrtle Beach vacation and entertainment hub, where the attractions include modern shopping malls, unusual specialty shops, historical sights, along with the beach and water activities, about 100 golf courses, eight fishing piers, more than 200 tennis courts, and numerous campgrounds. Approximately 1,500 restaurants bring a variety of savory dishes to discriminating palates, including some of the world's best seafood. Myrtle Beach nightlife offers everything from glamorous, swinging cabarets and dinner clubs to quiet, romantic moonlit strolls along the beach, or out on a jutting ocean pier. Ten theaters spotlight headliners in country music, comedy, figure skating, and dinner shows. Names like **The Carolina Opry, The Dixie Stampede** (an 80,000-square-foot showhouse owned by **Dolly Parton's Dollywood Productions**), the **Alabama Theatre** (2,000 seats, top celebrity guests), **Fantasy Harbour** and the **Gatlin Brothers Theatre** (2,000 seats, home of country music's famous male trio), all shine brightly over the marquees announcing some of America's greatest stage personalities. The **Palace Theatre,** a 2,700 seat showplace opened in late 1995, is part of the new $250-million entertainment complex known as **Broadway at the Beach**. This competitor of Las Vegas

301

and Branson (Missouri), on a 350-acre tract in the heart of Myrtle Beach, combines 80 retail stores and 12 restaurants (including a Hard Rock Cafe), in addition to the Palace Theatre, where Broadway shows do indeed come to town and where the Radio City Rockettes might easily be the next booking. (They performed there during the 1996 Christmas holidays.)

SAFE AND SECURE

The community has a gated entry with security personnel on duty seven days a week from dusk to dawn. The **Georgetown County Sheriff's Department** provides police protection and fire protection services come from a nearby governmental department. A 911 emergency response system is in place.

LET'S GO SHOPPING

Just blocks from the Plantation entry is a full-service food market. When it comes to shopping for truly distinctive collectibles, antiques, gifts, home furnishings, and personal accessories, few places can match the retail clusters known as the **Planters Exchange** or the **Island Shops**. What's on *your* list for out-of-the-ordinary treasures? Antique clocks, weather instruments, hand-knit sweaters, island fashions, gourmet baskets, hand-thrown pottery, gold-encased sea shells, puppets, environmental T-shirts, fossils, sharks' teeth, hand-fashioned wind chimes, decorative carvings? You'll find them all at this shoppers' mecca. And then, of course, there is the one product for which Pawleys Island is most noted—the rope hammock, symbol of the Low Country life style. And for those traditionalists who cannot forego the anchor department stores in a weatherproofed enclosure, with the accompanying specialty shops, food courts, and theaters, there's **Inlet Square Mall** in Murrell's Inlet, only 8 miles down the road.

TENNESSEE TAX FACTS

INDIVIDUAL INCOME TAX

Taxable income, at a rate of 6 percent, is limited to dividends and interest from specified investments (stocks, bonds, investment trusts, mutual funds, etc.). Those taxpayers who are 65 years of age or older are exempt if income does not exceed $9,000 (if single) or $15,000 (if filing a joint return). Exclusions include: 1) interest and dividends from U.S. obligations (exempt under federal law); 2) interest on obligations of the state of Tennessee or its subdivisions; 3) interest on short-term commercial paper (under six months maturity); and 4) interest on passbook savings accounts and certificates of deposit.

Also excluded is the first $1,250 of taxable income if single or married filing separately; $2,500 if married and filing jointly. There are no provisions for: 1) dependency exemptions or credits; 2) deductions for business, nonbusiness, optional standard, or itemized; or 3) credit for income tax paid to another state.

SALES TAX

6 percent tax is imposed on retail sales, storage, use, rental, or consumption of personal property tangibles. Local jurisdictions (cities, counties, special districts) are authorized to levy an additional tax rate.

PROPERTY TAX

Property is assessed by actual value at a uniform statewide rate of 55 percent for realty and personal property.

RANKING REPORT

Data published in *The Rating Guide to Life in America's Fifty States* in 1994 showed Tennessee ranking 9th from the most favorable with regard to property taxes.

For more complete tax information, contact the Commissioner, Department of Revenue, Andrew Jackson State Office Building, 500 Deaderick St., Nashville, TN 37242, 615-741-2461, (fax) 615-532-2285.

Note: The above information is based on applicable tax law data current at the time of publication. Because such laws and rates are subject to change, professional assistance should be sought if tax implications are critical to a relocation decision.

FAIRFIELD GLADE

FAIRFIELD GLADE, TENNESSEE

P.O. Box 1500
Fairfield Glade, TN 38558
615-484-7521
Fax: 615-484-3764

Developer: Fairfield Communities, Inc.

Year of initial property sales/rentals: 1970

Total land area: 12,700 acres

Average elevation: 1,980 feet

Location: East-central Tennessee; Cumberland County; near the center of the Cumberland Plateau; 6 miles north of U.S. Interstate 40 at Crossville; 80 miles west of Knoxville; 90 miles north of Chattanooga; 125 miles east of Nashville.

Nearest airport with scheduled commercial service: McGhee-Tyson Airport, Knoxville/Maryville (75 miles)

Current number of housing units with year-round occupants: 3,100

Projected number of housing units: Unknown

Resident eligibility: There are no age restrictions for living in the community, but an estimated 70% of the population is retired or semiretired. An estimated 30% of households have resident family members under the age of 18.

Community visit/tour incentive program: Maximum three-day, two-night special promotional packages on request to director of marketing

Suggested newspaper: *Crossville Chronicle* (triweekly), 312 So. Main St., Crossville, TN 38555 (615-484-5145)

WHY FAIRFIELD GLADE?

The **Cumberland Plateau** in the **Cumberland Mountains** of eastern Tennessee, home of **Fairfield Glade**, has many enticing attributes. It is a region of uncommon scenic beauty, the largest wooded plateau in North America and site of one of the most varied species of plant life to be found anywhere in the world. Its topographical character with its high elevations makes for a close to ideal climate; an elevation of about 2,000 feet is not so high as to invite severe winters, but high enough to produce cool summer days. And the Fairfield Glade geographic location places it at an easy and almost equal distance from three of Tennessee's major cities—**Nashville**, **Knoxville**, and **Chattanooga**, all between 75 and 120 miles away. **Cumberland County**, home of "the Glade," has the fifth largest population of any county in the state, the largest in which there is no major urban center.

Crossville (1996 estimated population of more than 8,000), a few minutes from the Glade entrance, is the commercial nucleus for Fairfield residents looking to supplement their shopping, social, and recreational needs. **Crossville Municipal Airport** is touted as the best and most complete between Nashville and Knoxville.

Fairfield Communities is the developer of Fairfield Glade and approximately 14 other resort properties spread across the country in 11 states from California to Virginia. It is one of the nation's largest vacation ownership companies (timeshares). The Glade is among several such Fairfield developments that have become permanent residential communities with sizable retirement components, in combination with vacation resort operations. **Resort Communities International (RCI),** the dominant trade organization in that field, has bestowed on this community its "gold crown resort" designation every year since 1992, signifying the highest quality leadership in the industry for facilities and programs. In 1992 one of its golf courses, **Stonehenge**, was ranked by *Golf Digest* magazine as 14th best among America's top 75 resort courses, and in 1985, soon after it opened, it was ranked the best new resort course in the country. A full-service conference center with more than 7,000 square feet of floor space draws groups for meetings of every description from far and wide. There's a separate 3,000-foot crafts building where pottery and other artistic handiwork classes are held.

WHO'S IN CHARGE?

The **Fairfield Glade Community Club** is a nonprofit organization of elected community residents. Its charge is to conduct the management and fiscal affairs of the Glade's property owners' recreational and common area amenities. The FGCC board of directors meets monthly. Fairfield Communities, which operates time-share and other vacation properties, is represented on the board. All property owners are required to be members. An exceptionally moderate annual assessment of $216 (can be paid monthly) covers operating costs to support a sizable staff and to pay for maintenance and services in connection with recreation facilities and programs, security arrangements, the sanitary sewer system, and common areas. The fee entitles members to the use of clubhouses, pools, and many recreational amenities. Use of some facilities, including golf courses, tennis courts, and the marina, will require a very moderate additional charge from residents.

The *Glade Sun* is the community's own weekly newspaper, typically having a 40-page edition. It is largely supported by a strong display advertising program and is distributed without charge to Fairfield Glade residents. It has the look and professional quality of a commercial newspaper, offering readers comprehensive news reporting, and such features as classified ads, television program listings, crossword puzzles, a church directory, cartoons, editorial columns, and obituaries.

THE WEATHER REPORT

Fairfield Glade is located in the heart of the Cumberland Plateau, in the eastern third of Tennessee. This gives the region a relatively level mid-altitude mountain climate without the sometimes dramatic weather variables that can accompany the sharp elevation extremes of a typical mountainous region. In winter, the higher elevations of the nearby **Crab Orchard** and Cumberland Mountains tend to have a moderating influence on local weather conditions by retarding the flow of cold air from the north and west.

A local weather recording source in Crossville reported the following normal daily high and low temperatures for 1996:

June: high 81/low 59	**July:** high 84/low 62
August: high 84/low 61	**December:** high 40/low 26
January: high 43/low 24	**February:** high 46/low 26

Average annual precipitation: 54 inches
Average annual snowfall: 12 inches

HOME SWEET HOME

Housing at Fairfield Glade is considerably more affordable than it is in most resort communities with such a vast offering of recreational activities. The typical price range for single-family detached homes generally runs between $90,000 and $150,000 for living space between 1,400 and 2,800 square feet. Townhouses/duplexes are priced from $50,000 to $162,000 with floor plans varying from 1,200 to 1,900 square feet. There is one small neighborhood of manufactured homes. About 80 percent of the housing units are detached single-family. Lots available for home construction, in sizes from one-quarter to a full acre, cost anywhere from $10,000 to $200,000, depending upon the many variables that affect such purchases—size, location, utility access, etc.

There is no specific year for projected completion of development on all land available for development, but a total of more than 8,500 homes is forecast for some time before the year 2010. As might be expected in a community as large and mature as the Glade, there is always an active resale market, giving buyers a broad selection of price, size, and location from which to choose. Some neighborhoods are served by a central sanitary sewer system, others by septic tanks. Water supply is provided by a public utility district.

Fairfield Homes, a primary builder in the community, publishes a detailed summary of energy efficient designer/signature features and specifications applicable to its standard construction plans. New subdivisions and housing projects are continually being developed.

MONEY MATTERS

The property tax rate for **Cumberland County** is 75 cents per $100 value, based on a 25 percent ratio of assessment. The county also adds a 2.25 percent levy to the 6 percent state sales tax.

The nearest nonmetropolitan location to Fairfield Glade for which there is relatively comparable living cost information available is approximately 70 miles to the south—the city of Cleveland. Among the 315 U.S. locations presented in the *ACCRA Cost of Living Index* (2nd quarter, 1996), Cleveland came up 6.7 percent below average in the index combining six key weighted categories of family expenses. Its ratings in all six groupings were below average as follows: groceries: 2.1 percent; housing, 13.7 percent; transportation, 6.8 percent; health care, 8 percent; and miscellaneous goods and services (the heaviest weighted category accounting for ¹/₃ of the total impact), 1.6 percent. It is of some interest to note that of 10 Tennessee locations in the report, all were below the average in composite living costs, ranging from 88.9 to 96.3, with 100 being equal to the average of all places shown.

TAKE GOOD CARE OF YOURSELF

Ten miles from the community is the **Cumberland Medical Center,** a 186-bed acute care and 16-bed subacute care, not-for-profit hospital in Crossville. About 50 physicians serve on staff, supported by more than 700 employees. A regional cancer treatment center was recently established at the facility, along with mobile lithotripsy, cardiac catheterization lab, and dialysis services and a comprehensive wellness center. There's a 24-hour emergency room and same-day surgery suites. A state-of-the-art oncology department was incorporated in 1996. Cumberland Medical recently formed an alliance with two other of the largest hospitals in the region to form a health care network stretching from near Nashville to the west, to near Knoxville to the east. The three institutions together pursue joint activities ranging from managed care insurance products to home health care services. Other programs to improve the health status of area residents are in developmental stages.

Cumberland County, in addition to the regional hospital, has four full-time medical clinics (one of which is inside Fairfield Glade) and three nursing homes with a total of 305 patient beds. Three assisted living facilities are in the area offering a range of support services such as congregate meals, housekeeping, and other personal ministrations. There are about 20 dentists and more than 60 physicians in practice at these facilities.

PLACES TO GO, THINGS TO DO

Fairfield Glade offers an almost-unheard-of four private/resort golf courses. One, **Heatherhurst,** is a 27-hole course. Exclusive Stonehenge, as previously mentioned, was singled out for honors by *Golf Digest.* These, and the other two 18-hole courses, feature pro shops, bluegrass tees, and fairways and bentgrass greens. All are PGA-championship caliber. In a word, golf is king at Fairfield Glade. For tennis buffs, there are 10 indoor and outdoor courts with pro shops, ready for play day or night. There are no less than 11 lakes within community parameters for fishing and boating. One offers a private sandy beach and a 36-slip marina with boat rentals and fishing supplies. Another marina, with 28 slips, features more of the same. A recreation complex includes an outdoor swimming pool, miniature golf, horse shoes, a playground, and a refreshment cabana. A second recreation center features another outdoor pool and tennis courts. At the civic center there is a gymnasium, fitness room, video arcade, billiards, and a bicycle rental desk. Three asphalt walking/biking paths wind through woodland areas.

Dorchester Riding Stables offers complete supervised equestrian facilities, trail rides, and hiking. A 98-room guest lodge has an indoor swimming pool, saunas, and a cocktail lounge. Three restaurants, two at clubhouse locations and one open to the public, adjacent to the sales and information center, satisfy most appetites for food and ambiance. There are dozens of hobby and social clubs. Group tours bring residents together for one-day outings or trips of several days to more distant attractions. Holiday weekend jaunts to area fairs and festivals are especially popular. **Gatlinburg** and **Pigeon Forge**, both major entertainment centers, are less than 100 miles away, and the **Grand Ole Opry** in Nashville not much further. All are favorite destinations for group travel and enjoyment.

Beyond Fairfield's gates are scores of activities and nearby attractions. **Fall Creek Falls**, 90 feet higher than mighty Niagara Falls and the highest cascade east of the Rockies, is less than an hour's drive. Huge state and nation parks are close by, including **Cumberland Mountain State Rustic Park** on Crossville's doorstep, one of Tennessee's great natural treasures. The **Catoosa Wildlife Management Area** is a hunter's paradise where game harvests are carefully monitored to preserve the proper population ratios of deer, boar, wild turkeys, doves, grouse, quail, coyotes, foxes, and other protected species.

The **Cumberland County Playhouse** in Crossville is a tribute to local citizens who, more than three decades ago, launched a live theater program that has become a Tennessee legend. More than 300 performances, films, concerts, and classes are presented each season to an audience of more than 90,000 patrons. Scores of Tennessee artists are employed and hundreds of volunteers work in all areas of operation. **Oak Ridge**, home of the **American Museum of Atomic Energy**, is 50 miles east. Tours and international exhibits trace the history of energy and an extensive display of the **Apollo Space Mission** captures the imagination of visitors. Less than an hour and a half away is Knoxville, with 13 museums, a fine symphony orchestra, zoological park, and the main campus of the **University of Tennessee** with all the cultural and recreational assets of a major university, including some of the most exciting collegiate sports competition in the nation.

SAFE AND SECURE

Fairfield Glade has its own security personnel on duty around the clock. There is no gated main entrance, but several neighborhoods have automated access gates that are closed after prescribed after-dark hours. The crime rate is said to be negligible. The community also has its own volunteer fire department, including emergency paramedic response crews and equipment, supplemented by county volunteer departments in surrounding towns.

LET'S GO SHOPPING

At the nerve center of the Glade, along with the information and sales pavilion, guest lodge, restaurant, civic and convention halls, and duck pond, is the **Village Green Mall**. Stores include a sizable grocery store, pharmacy, post office, gift shop, book and collectibles store, beauty shop, professional offices, and a Cumberland Medical Center satellite clinic. Peavine Road, the highway connecting to Interstate 40 and a few miles beyond to Crossville, is home to a wide assortment of business establishments. Especially prominent are restaurants, interior decorators, realtors, health care services, bait and tackle shops, and banks.

Further along into Crossville, the choices increase substantially. Shoppers come from distant cities to hunt bargains at the **Factory Stores of America Outlet Mall**. The downtown area and nearby commercial concentrations have car dealerships, cinemas, specialty shops, and department stores. A general store, a trading company, a winery, and a cheese house are unique enough to develop a loyal following of local and visiting customers. Indoor and outdoor flea markets in Cumberland County are said to be the largest in the state.

TELLICO VILLAGE

LOUDON, TENNESSEE

100 Chota Center
Loudon, TN 37774
423-458-6822 / 800-646-LAKE
Fax: 423-458-5888

Developer: Cooper Communities, Inc.

Year of initial property sales/rentals: 1986

Total land area: 4,600 acres

Average elevation: 800 feet

Location: Eastern Tennessee; Louden and Monroe Counties; south entry on State Highway 72 near its intersection with U.S. Highway 11, just east of Interstate 75; north entry off U.S. Highway 321/State Highway 95; about 31 miles southwest of Knoxville.

Nearest airport with scheduled commercial service: McGee Tyson Field, Knoxville/Maryville (27 miles)

Current number of housing units with year-round occupants: 1,450

Projected number of housing units: 5,000 (2007)

Resident eligibility: There are no age restrictions for residency in the community, but an estimated 75% of residents are retired or semiretired, with fewer than 10% of households having children under 18 years of age as permanent residents.

Community visit/tour incentive program: A "Let's Get Acquainted" vacation package is available to qualified applicants interested in considering a move to the Village. Some restrictions apply. Visiting guests pay a very reasonable $85 for two-nights' lodging at an on-site, fully furnished townhouse. Participation in a sales orientation is required.

Suggested newspaper: *Knoxville News-Sentinel*, P.O. Box 59038, Knoxville, TN 37950-9038 (800-237-5821)

WHY TELLICO VILLAGE?

Tellico Village is one of five active-adult communities under development by **Cooper Communities, Inc.**—two of the earliest in Arkansas, one in Missouri, one in South Carolina, and this in Tennessee. Forty miles of **Tellico Lake** shoreline lie within the Village. No point on the site is more than a mile from water. Every homesite adjoins a golfing green or fairway, a body of water, or a preserved woodland, providing natural privacy buffers. About 25 percent of the total acreage is designated as wildlife habitat. It is a decidedly nonurban setting, but it is just about 30 miles from **Knoxville**, the center of a metropolitan area with a population of more than 400,000. The location gives Tellico residents easy access to all the conveniences and resources of a modern city.

Nearby are some of the country's most popular tourist destinations—the **Great Smoky Mountains National Park**, the mountain resort of **Gatlinburg**, and the burgeoning entertainment center at **Dollywood/Pigeon Forge**, all within 60 miles of the Village.

WHO'S IN CHARGE?

Tellico Village is a private community. It does not rely on local, state, or federal funding for operations. The **Tellico Village Property Owners Association (POA)** essentially serves as the local town governing body. It is an incorporated nonprofit entity in which membership by residents is mandatory. Its functions and responsibilities include maintenance of interior private roads, operation of water and sewer systems, police protection, and recreational amenities. It adopts and enforces regulations. It collects and spends revenues. It is administered by a staff of about 100 employees under the supervision of a general manager. A seven-member board of directors is composed of representatives of both the developer and the property owners. Oversight operations are carried out by nine board-appointed standing committees drawn from volunteer members of the association.

Most of the infrastructure in Tellico Village was built by the developer and then deeded, free of debt, to the POA. The POA, in turn, has full responsibility for setting and collecting the monthly assessment from each property owner, fixed at $58.25 at the time of publication.

User fees are very moderate for owners (nine and 18 holes of golf for $3.50 and $7 respectively, and $3 for tennis). Guest fees are sharply higher, as much as four times the amount paid by owners.

A **Tellico Village Homeowners Association (HOA)**, separate from the POA, is much less structured and functions as a communication link for addressing residents' concerns, sponsoring social activities, welcoming newcomers and promoting community improvement. Membership is voluntary for an annual fee of $5.

The Hawk is a monthly tabloid-size newspaper published exclusively for Tellico home and property owners, with production and advertising functions performed by a nearby commercial publisher.

THE WEATHER REPORT

The **Cumberland Mountains** to the northwest and the **Great Smoky Mountains** to the southeast substantially influence climatic conditions in the valley that lies between them and in which Tellico Village is situated. The Cumberland range tends to act as a barrier to the force of cold winter air masses that normally penetrate the open plains to the west. Heat extremes during summer are likewise moderated by these surrounding high elevations. The topographical conditions are such that there are seldom great temperature changes. Summer nights are almost invariably comfortable. An average 12- to 13-inch snowfall is typically well dispersed, usually falling in amounts of less than four inches at a time and remaining on the ground for a few days or not more than a week.

Average high/low temperatures for the three winter months and three summer months for Knoxville (the nearest official weather station) are reported by the U.S. National Oceanic and Atmospheric Administration as follows:

December: high 50/low 32   **January:** high 47/low 29

February: high 51/low 32   **June:** high 85/low 64

July: high 87/low 68   **August:** high 87/low 67

Average annual precipitation: 47 inches
Average annual snowfall: 12 inches

HOME SWEET HOME

Homesites are available in a wide range of prices and location characteristics. Lots average 1/3 of an acre. Interior sites begin at $8,000 to a high of about $15,000. Golf or lake view sites cost between $18,000 and $60,000. Golf frontage properties average $35,000 and lake fronts $120,000. Home construction plans must be approved by the POA architectural control committee. Home buyers have the choice of using Cooper Homes or any licensed builder to construct a residence.

Single-family, detached dwellings average 2,100 square feet in size at an average cost of $175,000. They may range from $120,000 to $750,000, with square footage from 1,000 to 6,000. Low-maintenance adjoining townhouses and patio homes (currently about 15 percent of the total inventory of built and occupied homes) also offer a broad selection with floor plans ranging from 1,200 to 5,000 square feet and prices from $100,000 to $500,000.

MONEY MATTERS

Tennessee ranks 47th in percentage of personal income paid in state and local taxes, in large measure because there is no state-earned income tax. (See state tax facts on page 303.) Other overall living costs for the Knoxville area are also well below the national average. The ACCRA Cost of Living Index (2nd quarter, 1996), in a recent study of 315 metropolitan and nonmetropolitan areas of the United States, revealed that Knoxville scored below average in five out of six categories measured, showing a composite index of -5.2 percent.

Property taxes in Tellico Village, depending upon in which of two counties the home is located, are either $2.35 **(Monroe County)** or $2.53 **(Loudon County)** per $100 of assessed value, with such assessments being levied at 25 percent of appraised value. Based on these two rates, the annual tax on a $175,000 home would be either $1,028 or $1,106. The combined average cost of all utility services (electricity, water, sewer, trash collection, and a basic telephone line) is estimated to be $155 per month. Electricity costs are especially reasonable because of the **Tennessee Valley Authority (TVA)** influence as the nation's largest utility provider. Adding the $58.25 monthly amenities fee, the total estimated fixed outlay is a modest $213.25. Actual costs will vary, of course, depending on the size of the home and the usage habits of its occupants.

TAKE GOOD CARE OF YOURSELF

Tellico has its own on-site health clinic at the village square staffed with a physician and nurse practitioner. It is affiliated with a nearby health care system. Knoxville, only 30 miles away, has become an increasingly important center for health care, medical education and research. **Fort Sanders Regional Medical Center** (575 beds) and the **University of Tennessee Memorial Research Center** (602 beds), the two Knoxville hospitals closest to the Village, are the largest of five general hospitals in the city, several of which are extending services and expanding facilities. The University Center is nationally known for its research programs in heart disease, cancer, birth defects, and mental retardation, as well as for its stature as a teaching hospital for physician continuing education. Fort Sanders hospital is widely known for the **Patricia Neal Rehabilitation Center** and its pioneering programs in community fitness.

PLACES TO GO, THINGS TO DO

Golfers can tee up on two of east Tennessee's finest courses, the second of which opened in 1996 (a third is scheduled for the year 2002). **Toqua Championship Golf Course**, opened in 1987, was nominated that year by *Golf Digest* for its "Best New Course of the Year Award." Two clubhouses and a $3.2-million yacht and country club are life style symbols in the community and principal gathering places for dining, club activities, and special events. One has an adjoining driving range, practice putting green, and a spacious veranda, pro shop, and choice of casual or formal dining. The other features a large wrap-around portico, along with another putting green, well-stocked pro shop, and food service.

The **Chota Recreation and Community Center**, a more than 17,000-square-foot fitness center, features a gymnasium, racquetball courts, weight and exercise rooms, a game room, sauna, locker rooms, a snack bar, and an all-purpose meeting hall. Outside are horseshoe pits, four tennis courts, a volleyball court, kiddie and Olympic-size adult pools. A nearby 1.6-mile, 8-foot wide nature and walking trail has marked native plants identified all along its course.

Tellico Lake, the centerpiece alongside which the Village was built, is 32 miles long, with 373 miles of shoreline, 40 miles of which form the eastern border of Tellico Village. Owned by the TVA, it accommodates 12 public boat launches, including two at Tellico. Sport fishing is at its best going after small and largemouth bass, crappie, bluegill, brown trout, white bass, and walleye.

The Village activity directory lists more than 70 clubs and programs, for everyone from antique car enthusiasts and armchair travelers to yoga fanatics and water exercise devotees. Few hobbies are missing from the Tellico roster. Among the more unusual—home beer brewing, rubber stamp art collecting, model ship building, and script/token collecting.

Within a 60-mile radius of the village by the lake is an awesome array of recreational/cultural attractions and entertainment options. The Great Smoky Mountains National Park draws more visitors than any other national park in the country. Sometimes referred to as "the playground of the Smokies," Pigeon Forge and Gatlinburg are prime resort areas to which some nine million visitors flock each year. There are more than 35 amusement attractions within a radius of less than 15 miles. Among them are Dollywood (country singer legend **Dolly Parton's** creation), **The Great Smoky Mountains Circus**, and the **Lee Greenwood Theater** (a 1,776-seat showplace of 200 performances annually). The winter season in these mountains of **Southern Appalachia**, which reach to elevations of more than 6,000 feet, makes it one of the most favored skiing resorts in the east.

Knoxville is the main campus home of the **University of Tennessee (UT)**, the hub of the state's higher learning resources. Fall is football mania time in eastern Tennessee. More than 100,000 fans going wild at the university's **Neyland Stadium** is nothing more than commonplace. UT basketball recently moved into a $30 million, 25,000-seat arena, the largest of its kind in the country. Women's basketball has produced eight straight years of NCAA tournament appearances (through 1996), four times as national champions.

More than a citadel of athletic prowess, the university offers a cultural atmosphere that is highlighted by an outstanding performing arts program. **Carousel Theater** presents theater in the round featuring musicals, comedy, drama, and dance. The **Clarence Brown Theater**, also on campus, is a professional repertory company in residence. Four plays a season attract many celebrated stars of stage and screen.

The university is by no means the sole source of a cultural milieu for the area. Knoxville has had its own symphony orchestra since 1935, now with more than 100 musicians. The **Knoxville Opera Company** regularly presents nationally and internationally known stars in guest appearances. **The Appalachian Ballet Company** offers a wide-ranging program and recently completed a European tour. Community and dinner theater utilize local talent and, along with the **Civic Center Series**, bring to the stage guest celebrities and productions by top Broadway touring companies.

The Knoxville library system, with 16 branches, boasts a recently built $2-million main building and an impressive circulating and reference collection, including more than 10,000 rare and out-of-print books on microfiche.

SAFE AND SECURE

The **Loudon County Sheriff's Department** provides police services to this open-access community. Internal security arrangements are provided by the Tellico Village Property Owners Association, which includes 24-hour on-site security personnel and patrol units. Firefighting/prevention and emergency medical unit responsibilities are handled by the **Tellico Village Fire Department** in conjunction with the **Fort Sanders Hospital Emergency Medical Service**, which operates five ambulances around the clock with life support equipment and paramedic crews on continuous duty. The Village provides 18 trained and certified volunteer "first responders," who are on call through the fire department.

LET'S GO SHOPPING

About 30 businesses are located at three different sites within the Tellico Village parameter. Most of them are clustered in an area near the visitor's center/administration building, including a gas station/convenience store, two banks, a cafe, travel agency, dentist, chiropractor, dry cleaner, beauty shop, and home decorating service. A major hardware/building supply store and garden center is located near the south entrance. **Lakeside Plaza**, not far from the south entry, features a food specialty market, two restaurants, and several other businesses.

Kingston Pike (U.S. Highway 11) runs parallel to Interstate 40, the main highway into Knoxville, readily accessed from the north entrance of Tellico Village. Beginning about 12 miles from that Village entrance is a stretch of commercial development that extends all the way into downtown Knoxville.

TEXAS TAX FACTS

INDIVIDUAL INCOME TAX

Texas is among the six states that impose no personal income tax.

SALES TAX

A "limited" 6.25 percent tax is levied on retail sales of in-state taxable items of personal property and certain services that are purchased, stored, consumed, or leased/rented. Local jurisdictions are authorized to levy an additional tax rate.

PROPERTY TAX

The range of property tax rates per $1,000 of assessed value varies from $5.44 to $22.10. Most, but not all, intangibles are exempt. These rates are composites of locally applicable city, county, and school district rates. There may be additional levies by special districts and improvement assessments not covered in the foregoing figures.

RANKING REPORT

Data published in *The Rating Guide to Life in America's Fifty States* in 1994 showed Texas ranking 30th from the most favorable with regard to property taxes.

For more complete tax information, contact the Comptroller of Public Accounts, LBJ State Office Building, Room 104, 111 E. 17th St., Austin, TX 78774, 512-463-4041, (fax) 512-463-4965.

Note: The above information is based on applicable tax law information available at the time of publication. Because such laws and tax rates are subject to change, professional guidance should be sought if tax implications are critical to a relocation decision.

DEL WEBB'S SUN CITY GEORGETOWN

GEORGETOWN, TEXAS

1 Texas Dr.
Georgetown, TX 78628
512-931-6900 / 800-833-5932
Fax: 512-931-6970

Developer: Del Webb Corporation

Year of initial property sales/rental: 1995

Total land area: 5,300 acres

Average elevation: 875 feet

Location: Central Texas; Williamson County; 5 miles northwest of Georgetown off Interstate 35 on Farm Market Road 2338; 30 miles north of Austin.

Nearest airport with scheduled commercial service: Robert Mueller International, Austin (30 miles)

Current number of housing unit with year-round occupants: 750

Projected number of housing units: 9,500 (2015)

Resident eligibility: One member of household must be at least 55 years of age and no one under age 19 may be a permanent resident.

Community visit/tour incentive program: "Vacation Getaway" arrangements for qualified prospective property buyers provide a two- or three-night package at a fully furnished home on the property, starting as low as $79 for two nights without golf. The package includes an optional round of golf, and use of the fitness center, swimming pools, and other recreational amenities.

Suggested newspaper: *Austin American Statesman*, 305 So. Congress St., Austin, TX 78704 (512-445-4040)

WHY SUN CITY GEORGETOWN?

The **Texas Hill Country** is a special place, not only for Texans who go there to escape urban congestion and to commune with nature, but for many sophisticated city folks from all parts of the country and beyond, who long for the wide open spaces. For many, it is the most appealing part of a state known for unparalleled diversity in its topography. A 150-mile chain of lakes winds through its heartland. Springtime bluebonnets and other wildflowers blanket this land. A diverse and abundant wildlife is part of the landscape. **Sun City Georgetown (SGC)** sits at the gateway to this fabled place of storybook campfires and cowboy traditions.

The Sun City location near the Texas capital city of **Austin** (about a half-hour drive down the interstate) is in itself a great source of appeal. It is a locale that has consistently won high praise in "the best places to live" sweepstakes created by some of the country's most popular magazines and ratings guides. It is the main campus home of the third largest state university in the United States—the **University of Texas**, with an enrollment of almost 50,000 students and a faculty of approximately 6,000. The Austin metropolitan area has passed the one million mark. The city is known for many things, not the least of which is its billing as the "live music capital of the world." It ranks first in Texas and sixth in the nation in the number of artists and musicians per capita. It is the birthplace of numerous Grammy-winning performers, including **Willie Nelson.**

The **Del Webb Corporation** brought the master-planned retirement community concept to public attention in 1960 with the opening of the first Sun City outside of Phoenix, Arizona. It was the launching of this pioneering vision for retirement living that prompted *Time* magazine to feature founder **Del Webb** on its cover for creating a new life style. Sun City Georgetown represents the company's first venture into Texas. The project has taken the state by storm. It was the best-selling community in the central Texas area in both 1995 and 1996, its first two years of operation, following which the Del Webb organization was named "builder of the year" by *Professional Builder Magazine.* In 1997 the community was recognized with the Texas Nature Conservancy Award for environmental responsibility. Nearly half of the SCG development acreage is dedicated to open space.

WHO'S IN CHARGE?

The **Del Webb's Sun City Georgetown Community Association (SCGCA)** is the incorporated nonprofit mainspring for involvement by residents in the operations of the development. Each SCG household contributes $680/year, which results in a share of ownership and entitlement to participation in more than $25 million of recreation, fitness, social and golf facilities. The organization, established soon after the first homeowners moved in, is free and clear of any debt and operates in close coordination with the developer. Its administration is under the supervision of a sizable paid staff. The first elected neighborhood representatives took office in May of 1997, each coming from a distinct neighborhood. Their function will include interacting with the Community Association board of directors.

Sun Rays is a lively monthly publication produced and distributed by SCGCA, chock-full of community happenings—past, present, and future. Each issue attracts a number of advertisers, helping keep the publication's budget balanced.

THE WEATHER REPORT

Sun City is more than 200 miles from the Gulf of Mexico. That's far enough inland to be safely beyond the wrath of any serious tropical storms, but close enough for the moist air from those waters to raise humidity levels and to generate some pretty unruly thunderstorms. Winter temperatures are relatively mild, but there can be a dramatic change from shirt-sleeve warmth at noon to windbreaker chill after sundown. During summer, temperatures higher than 90 degrees are the norm.

According to the National Weather Service, average Austin area daily high and low temperatures for three winter months and three summer months are as follows:

December: high 62/low 41   **January:** high 59/low 39

February: high 63/low 42   **June:** high 91/low 71

July: high 95/low 74   **August:** high 95/low 74

Average annual precipitation: 32 inches
Average annual snowfall: none

HOME SWEET HOME

Thirteen model homes in a landscaped mini-village present prospective buyers with the many home construction choices available in customizing each unit. Tall windows, stone exterior facing, porch variations, and sloped roofs reflect a Texas aura. All models have single-story, two-bedroom floor plans, some offering options for a third bedroom or den. Home sizes range from approximately 1,120 to 2,900 square feet. Prices range from the low $100,000s to the mid $200,000s. A design center in the sales pavilion is the place where homebuyers can examine, evaluate, and select from all the possible standard and upgrade feature alternatives, when formulating a home construction plan.

Utility lines are below ground. Water and sewer services are municipal systems supplied by the city of **Georgetown**.

MONEY MATTERS

Georgetown is one of 315 locations included in the ACCRA Cost of Living Index (2nd quarter, 1996). All but one of 25 Texas places (a suburb of Dallas) shown in the study revealed a composite result of cost measurement below average. With 100 percent representing the average cost of living index, Georgetown showed a comparative level of 95 percent. Of six weighted cost categories, only one was significantly above the norm—transportation (gasoline, car repair, etc.) at 6.2 percent over. The two most heavily weighted categories, housing and miscellaneous goods and services, were shown to be 6.5 percent and 2.5 percent below average, respectively. The remaining three headings were recorded as follows: groceries, 4.5 percent below; utilities, .1 percent above; and health care, 5 percent below.

Local ad valorem real property taxes are based on 100 percent of assessed value. The rate for the city is 37 cents, the county 33.78 cents, and the school district $1.44, for a total of $2.1478. The absence of any local or state income tax makes the total tax burden more beneficent than most. Cablevision costs include a $35 installation fee and a monthly fee of $21.99 (47 channels), according to recent pricing information.

TAKE GOOD CARE OF YOURSELF

The first phase of a comprehensive on-site health care clinic with programs geared toward seniors was opened in late 1996. It is operated by **Scott & White Health Plan** (an HMO) and affiliated with highly regarded **Scott & White Memorial Hospital & Clinic**, a major medical complex (634 beds) just 30 miles away in nearby **Temple**. Patients readily are accepted who are enrolled in other plans. The completed facility of some 34,000 square feet provides preventive, routine and acute primary care and is specifically developed for seniors. The clinic houses physician offices, a lab and x-ray unit, a special meeting area for wellness classes, and a telemedicine program to facilitate health care communications. It is the 17th Scott & White regional clinic.

Less than 10 minutes away is **Georgetown Hospital**, a community not-for-profit hospital licensed for 98 beds. Comprehensive diagnostic capabilities include CT scan, nuclear medicine, ultrasound, and mammography. Austin, the center of a vibrant metropolitan area, has five hospitals and about 850 office-based physicians, and lays claim to some of the finest medical institutions in the southwest.

PLACES TO GO, THINGS TO DO

The **Legacy Hills Golf Club** opened its fairways in November 1996, a **Billy Casper** signature course. Operated by **Del Webb Management**, it is owned by the **SCG Community Association**. The course is designed so that all levels of golfing proficiency can be appropriately challenged. The 10,500-square-foot clubhouse features a restaurant, grill, lounge, and pro shop. Practice putting greens and a driving range make it easy to work on raising skill levels. Three more golf courses are planned to be built on the property as housing expands and larger numbers of residents will require additional recreational space.

The **Village Center** is the social and recreational hub of Sun City Georgetown. It boasts a fully appointed state-of-the-art fitness center; a six-lane indoor swimming pool and an outdoor resort-type pool, four tennis courts, and a tournament-quality bocce court. For more relaxing pursuits, there are reading rooms, a lounge, a billiards parlor, and craft rooms for ceramics, art, and sewing. An open air pavilion on the banks of a creek features a cozy stone fireplace, nearby picnic tables, and a children's playscape for visiting grandchildren, all comfortably nestled on a 13-acre tract of parkland. Sun City's own dinner theater has become a favorite for fun and affordable entertainment right in the neighborhood.

There are clubs and special interest groups for bridge, arts and crafts, square and round dancing, sewing and quilting, nature, computers, various sports activities, and those interested in genealogy, investment planning, model planes/cars/trains, and for single folks. Other activities are getting underway or are in the works. Luncheon symposia and afternoon seminars may center on anything from "how to identify birds in your backyard" to arthritis pain management or fundamentals of estate planning. A "block buddies" SCG welcome wagon and a "helping hands" group to help neighbors out when in need are just two of many volunteer organizations offering opportunities for serving others. A community rose garden and a video production studio are recently established amenities that provide yet greater outlets for residents' creativity.

On-site educational and artistic classes are being organized all the time. Georgetown (population almost 15,000) is the home of **Southwestern University**, the oldest institution of higher learning in Texas. There, a flourishing schedule of collegiate sports, children's theater, quality "summer stage" productions, and a variety of lectures and other enlightening programs are on tap, and within a mere 10 minutes from the SCG entrance. **Lake Georgetown** is a 1,300-acre U.S. Army Corps of Engineers clear-water lake, surrounded by a huge, fully developed hill country park system. Its three parks offer fishing, boating, swimming, camping, picnicking, and numerous trails for hiking, drawing more than a million visitors each year. It is just minutes away from Sun City.

The Georgetown government/commercial square has a considerable antiquarian flavor, with three **National Register Historic Districts** and more than 180 official Texas historical markers. The town drew national attention in the early 1980s with its "Main Street Project," a restoration of the central business district. It was one of five national recipients of the Third Annual Great American Main Street Award, having been selected by a national jury from a pool of more than 90 applicants. The award recognizes economic revitalization in America's downtowns and honors overall achievement in civic renewal.

For those more inclined toward big-city attractions, Austin serves up a noteworthy lyric opera and ballet company, a chamber music center and nine major museums. **Zilker Park** and the **Botanical Gardens** offer the natural beauty of **Barton Springs**, where a 1,000-foot-long swimming pool gushes 27 million gallons of spring water daily. It is a favorite recreational fun spot for locals and visitors alike. The University of Texas has all the cultural and entertainment riches of a big city, most of it readily available to the public—a legendary collegiate sports program, public lectures, and seminars delivered by world-renowned personalities, professional-quality entertainment, and one of the greatest libraries to be found anywhere. Continuing education opportunities for mature adults are almost unlimited on the UT campus, as well as in programs offered by three private universities in the city and through an extensive community college system.

SAFE AND SECURE

A review of the 1996 crime data report for the city of Georgetown showed no homicides and what appeared to be exceptionally low incidences of violent felonies (rape and robbery). Most offenses were of the less serious variety— assaults, burglary, and theft. As for Sun City itself, it is said that the crime rate has been virtually nonexistent since the community opened, even though it is an open-access property.

Police and fire services are provided by the city of Georgetown. A 911 emergency call system is in place.

LET'S GO SHOPPING

Georgetown, less than a 10-minute drive away, has six significant shopping areas, including a sizable mall, offering a variety of merchandise and services. There are large retailers, some national chains, and a host of specialty shops. Professional offices include services from accounting, architecture, and attorneys to physicians and veterinarians. An antique mall and a candle factory draw their share of tourists and shoppers. Full-service grocery shopping is only 3 miles from the SCG entrance.

For those who choose to go the extra mile, Austin and its northern suburbs are not much farther. **Lakeline Mall**, opened in 1996, with a grand selection of department stores, specialty shops, and restaurants (including a food court), is about 25 miles away. Three other major malls punctuate the Austin shopping scene, along with several sprawling name-brand factory outlet malls on the south side of town.

VIRGINIA TAX FACTS

INDIVIDUAL INCOME TAX

Graduated from 2% to 5.75% as follows:

- ♦ First $3,000 of income @ 2%
- ♦ Next $2,000 @ $60 plus 3%
- ♦ Next $12,000 @ $120 plus 5%
- ♦ Over $17,000 @ $720 plus 5.75%

Exemptions/Deductions:

- ♦ No deduction for federal income tax paid.
- ♦ Federal, state, and private pensions *not* exempt.
- ♦ Social Security benefits are exempt.
- ♦ $800 personal exemption per person for over age 65.

SALES TAX

Retailers collect 4.5 percent with 1 percent of that amount returned to local jurisdictions where the tax is collected. Restaurants and lodging facilities collect additional levies at the discretion of the taxing authority in which they are located.

RANKING REPORT

According to *State Government Finances,* among the 50 states, Virginia ranks 18th from the most favorable in total state taxes per capita when all state levies were considered. In comparing property taxes per capita, *The Rating Guide to Life in America's Fifty States* ranks it 26th from the lowest amount.

For more complete tax information contact the Finance Office, Taxation Department, P.O. Box 1880, Richmond, VA 23282, 804-367-8005, (fax) 804-367-0971.

Note: The above information is based on applicable tax law data available at the time of publication. Because such laws and tax rates are subject to change, professional guidance should be sought if tax implications are critical to a relocation decision.

FORD'S COLONY AT WILLIAMSBURG

WILLIAMSBURG, VIRGINIA

One Ford's Colony Dr.
Williamsburg, VA 23188
757-258-4000 / 800-334-6033
Fax: 757-258-4248

Developer: Realtec Incorporated

Year of initial property sales/rental: 1985

Total land area: 2,500 acres

Average elevation: 70 feet

Location: Eastern Virginia; James City County; 7 miles west of Interstate Highway 64; just off the coastal waters of Chesapeake Bay; about half way between Richmond to the northwest (51 miles) and the center of the Norfolk/Newport News/Virginia Beach Tidewater area to the southeast (45 miles).

Nearest airport with scheduled commercial service: Newport News-Williamsburg International (15 miles)

Current number of housing units with year-round occupants: 885

Projected number of housing units: 2,800 (2002)

Resident eligibility: There are no age restrictions for living in the community, but an estimated 75% of current residents are either retired or semiretired. Approximately 30% of households have children under age 18 living permanently in the home.

Community visit/tour incentive program: Tour packages include four day/three night or three-day/two-night "vacation getaways" for two at a nearby hotel (adjacent to Colonial Williamsburg) at substantially discounted rates. Six arrangement combinations vary in price from $139 to $359. All include deluxe accommodations and complimentary breakfast, with optional add-ons for gourmet dinner and/or two rounds of golf.

Suggested newspaper: *Daily Press*, 7505 Warwick Blvd., Newport News, VA 23607 (757-247-4600)

WHY FORD'S COLONY AT WILLIAMSBURG?

The community is located at the threshold of one of the nation's most eminent historical places: **Colonial Williamsburg**. It is convenient to two principal metropolitan areas, the city of **Richmond** and the **Norfolk/Newport News/Virginia Beach** urban cluster, each less than an hour's drive away.

Ford's Colony (FC) is an upscale development that has garnered recognition from a long list of organizations and publications for outstanding achievement in property development and land use preservation. Commendations have come from the **American Resort Development Association,** the **U.S. Departments of Interior and Agriculture,** the **Commonwealth of Virginia,** the **College of William and Mary,** the **Colonial Soil and Water District,** the **Williamsburg Area Council of Garden Clubs,** and the **Colonial Williamsburg Foundation.** The community has been featured as a top retirement destination by *New Choices* and *Where to Retire* magazines, and by the authors of several books devoted to identifying the best in adult recreational living.

Accolades have been bestowed upon Ford's Colony golf courses and the clubhouse restaurant too. *Golf Week, Tee Time, Golf Digest,* and *Virginia Golfer* have all singled out the FC fairways as being among the best. The **American Automobile Association** gives "The Dining Room" a five-diamond award, one of only 35 such honors given to fine eating places in the United States. In its marketing program, the Colony has been recognized by the **American Resort Development Association** on 29 separate occasions, including its highest achievement award for excellence in advertising and promotion, making it number one in the country in that category among residential, resort, and timeshare entries. The same organization proclaimed Ford's Colony to be the top master-planned community in the United States.

More than half of Ford's Colony's 2,500 acres consist of woodlands and wetlands inhabited by various wildlife species. These acres have been permanently set aside to remain undeveloped.

WHO'S IN CHARGE?

The **Ford's Colony Homeowners Association,** a nonprofit corporation, currently conducts its business primarily through an elected advisory board. Residents serving on this body act as the principal communication link between property owners and the developer/management agent. This board researches issues and concerns raised by owners and discusses them with the management company **(Realtec)** for purposes of clarification and/or resolution. The board holds four "open house" meetings annually to update homeowners on the current status of community affairs. Subcommittees include finance, roads/maintenance/security, environmental control (neighborhood land use compliance, house plan approval etc.), and strategic planning. Membership in the homeowners association (HOA) is mandatory for all residents.

Eventually, when the development is near completion, the HOA will assume full ownership and responsibility from the developer for the private road system within the community as well as other aspects of community maintenance. The cost of maintaining these assets and providing security will be provided through the same arrangement of assessments against each lot or multifamily parcel as are currently in place. All association policy developments and activities, including determination of annual fees, will then be controlled solely by the members of the association.

A monthly newsletter called *Talk of the Colony* is published by the HOA with an assortment of articles, activity reports, and calendars designed to keep residents informed and involved.

THE WEATHER REPORT

Williamsburg is close enough to **Chesapeake Bay** and the **Atlantic Ocean** (and two of its major tributary rivers—the **James** and the **York**) to be characterized as having something of an ocean climate. The geographical location is south of principal storm tracks originating at the higher latitudes and north of the paths of typical tropical storms and hurricanes. Generally mild winters sometimes reach below freezing to single digit temperatures or even lower. Winters sometimes pass without measurable snowfall. Ideal spring seasons give way to long, warm summers. Temperatures do reach the upper 90s and higher on occasion, but northeasterly breezes off the ocean tend to cool things down before long.

Average daily high and low temperature readings in nearby Norfolk for the three winter months and the three summer months are reported by the U.S. National Oceanic and Atmospheric Administration as follows:

December: high 52/low 35   **January:** high 47/low 31

February: high 50/low 32   **June:** high 83/low 65

July: high 86/low 70   **August:** high 85/low 69

Average annual rainfall: 45 inches
Average annual snowfall: 7.4 inches

HOME SWEET HOME

The architectural theme at Ford's Colony maintains a colonial ambiance. In addition to traditional colonial styles, Georgian, Federal, and Greek Revival facades are also considered appropriate. All homes must adhere to strict preservation standards and require preconstruction review and approval.

About 75 percent of the Colony homes in early 1997 were single-family detached. They range in price from $200,000 to $2 million, with square footage from 1,500 to 8,000. Townhouses are priced from the $170s to the $250s in sizes ranging from 1,360 to 2,700 square feet. A small number of "courtyard homes" start at about $250,000. Almost 100 timeshare units are also available. An estimated 10 percent of home sales in early 1997 were new construction and 90 percent were resale.

Long-term rentals are typically available in the $975 to $1,875 per month for units that vary in size from 1,500 to 2,600 square feet. Vacant homesites ready for construction, 1/3 to a full acre, are priced from $40,000 to $750,000. On-site extra storage facilities are also available. All utilities are below ground. There is a central waste disposal system and a public water supply owned and maintained by the county.

MONEY MATTERS

The nearest comparable location with data available in the *ACCRA Cost of Living Index* (2nd quarter, 1996) is the Richmond metropolitan area, less than 50 miles away. The composite index for that area (an analysis that includes costs of groceries, housing, utilities, transportation, health care, and miscellaneous goods and services) shows the combined cost for all measured elements to be 2.8 percent above the national average among those places included in the survey. The grocery tab was the only category among the six groupings that fell below the average (2.7 percent), while the other five categories were higher. Housing and miscellaneous goods and services, the two most heavily weighted classifications, were only 1.2 and 1 percent higher than the norm, respectively, while utilities (16.3 percent), transportation (8.4 percent), and health care (8.6 percent) were substantially above.

Expenses connected to benefits derived from living at Ford's Colony include an $800 annual fee that covers all security operations, road, common area and recreational facility maintenance, and automatic membership in the swim and tennis clubs. For golfers who opt for country club membership benefits, the annual dues (with unlimited greens fees) come to $2,865. Unlimited golf cart usage adds another $1,980.

County real estate taxes are 87 cents per hundred dollars (100 percent of appraised value). Personal property tax (only motor vehicles and boats) is $4 per hundred dollar value.

TAKE GOOD CARE OF YOURSELF

Williamsburg Community Hospital is an acute-care institution just 4 miles from Ford's Colony. The 139-bed facility completed a $17-million upgrade in 1994, including new MRI equipment and services. Emergency trauma, pediatrics, cardiac care, orthopedics, home health services, and community health education are among its major programs. In conjunction with **Riverside Regional Medical Center**, it also operates a cancer treatment center. Riverside, in Newport News, a 20-mile run from the FC front gate, is a 576-bed facility offering comprehensive care in 29 specialties, including open-heart surgery, state-of-the-art radiation oncology, laser surgery, a hospice program, neonatal ICU, crisis intervention, substance abuse assistance, and a child-adolescent program.

The largest hospital within a 30-mile radius of the Colony is the **Veterans' Administration Medical Center** with 867 beds. It offers comprehensive mental health, hospice, and home nursing services, as well as dialysis therapy, substance abuse treatment, and specialized care for victims of spinal cord injuries. The professional staff maintains a strong affiliation with the faculty and students at the **Eastern Virginia Medical School**.

PLACES TO GO, THINGS TO DO

For those whose first love in recreation is golf, the Colony has two 18-hole, **Don Maples**-designed championship-caliber courses and a third one in development. An impressive number of feature articles and awards from prestigious publications and organizations in the golf world have recognized the special qualities of these properties. Eight tennis courts (four under lights) and a 25-meter lap pool are part of a separate recreation facility.

An activities committee provides residents with opportunities for social contacts and participation in a wide range of programs, most sponsored by established clubs and interest groups, meeting in the clubhouse. There are a dozen such groupings, ranging from bridge, bowling, and crafts to theater and travel. More than a score of other activities, with more informal organization, bring residents together for special events and for impromptu get-togethers centered around such mutual interests as biking, jogging (there are more than 6 miles of fitness trails), bird-watching, table games, dining out, and water aerobics. An expansive clubhouse sun deck is an especially inviting gathering place for casual social contact.

The Ford's Colony location is probably most distinguished by the fact that it is surrounded by some of America's richest historical treasures. Colonial Williamsburg, just 4 miles from the FC gate, is the world's largest outdoor museum, attracting history buffs from all over the world. It features 88 original 18th and 19th century buildings, some hundred acres of gardens, 225 exhibition rooms, and costumed actors depicting daily life in Colonial America. In the same area is the College of William and Mary, the second-oldest college in America, dating back to 1693, and alma mater to three U.S. presidents, including **Thomas Jefferson. Jamestown Settlement** and **Jamestown Island**, also within a 5-mile radius, reflect the environment of the first English-speaking settlers to the New World. Also just 15 miles away is **Yorktown Battlefield**, the hallowed Revolutionary War setting of the surrender by the British.

The area has attractions of virtually every description. **Busch Gardens**, less than a 15-minute drive, is a 17th-century European village theme park with heart-stopping rides and live-entertainment shows. **Water Country USA** has more than 13 attractions and features a huge water playground the size of five Olympic swimming pools.

More than a dozen nearby parks offer an abundance of outdoor activity including hiking, fishing, swimming, boating, and picnics. Chesapeake Bay is one of the country's great sailing waters where spinnakers grace the traditional summer racing extravaganzas. Three marinas are no more than 30 to

35 minutes from Ford's gate. **The Williamsburg Players** and the **Old Dominion Opry** deliver favorite stage performances in classical and contemporary drama, comedy, and live country music.

Six nearby colleges and universities, including top-ranked College of William and Mary, put FC in the midst of an especially lively scene for cultural, intellectual, and spectator sports activities. All are within a 45-minute radius of the Colony. Surrounding counties provide home bases for naval and other military installations, right alongside crabbers and oystermen coming home with their catches.

SAFE AND SECURE

Law enforcement services are provided by both the county police and sheriff's departments, including a modern computerized phone/address system for 911 emergencies. The community's own private security force involves roving guards on a 24-hour rotation and a house-check program for absent residents. Fire protection comes from the county fire department with four fire stations serving Ford's Colony, the nearest of which is but 1½ miles from the main entrance. A paid emergency paramedic squad is on duty around the clock.

LET'S GO SHOPPING

A wide variety of retail and service establishments are found in and around the Williamsburg area. Two convenience stores are within a mile of the FC entrance and several major food markets and full service pharmacies are within 4 miles. All manner of shops, department stores, malls, and specialty stores are in the Newport News/**Hampton** corridor.

Of special interest is a designer outlet mall representing more than 50 apparel, shoe, and home furnishing manufacturers. **Merchants Square** in Williamsburg is a mecca for shoppers looking for anything unusual. The **Williamsburg Pottery Factory** features domestic and imported pottery, china, glass, stemware, baskets, wines and cheeses, pictures, candles, and plants. The **Doll Factory** and the **Soap & Candle Factory**, both in Williamsburg, are one-of-a-kind enterprises that offer guided tours, making the creation of their products an educational experience.

WASHINGTON TAX FACTS

INDIVIDUAL INCOME TAX

Washington is among the six states that impose no broad-based personal income tax.

SALES TAX

A 6.5 percent general sales-use tax is levied on all purchases of tangible personal property and services, unless exempt. Taxable services include amusements, title insurance, auto parking, and credit bureau services.

PROPERTY TAX

The range of property tax rates per $1,000 of assessed value varies from $8.88 to $16.66. All intangibles are exempt. These rates are composites of locally applicable city, county, and school district rates. There may be additional levies by special districts and improvement assessments not covered in the foregoing figures.

RANKING REPORT

Data published in *The Rating Guide to Life in America's Fifty States* in 1994 showed Washington ranking 24th from the most favorable with regard to property taxes.

For more complete tax information contact the Washington Department of Revenue, Taxpayer Services Division, P.O. Box 47454, Olympia, WA 98504, 360-753-5516, (fax) 360-586-5543.

Note: The above information is based on applicable tax law information available at the time of publication. Because such laws and tax rates are subject to change, professional guidance should be sought if tax implications are critical to a relocation decision.

PROVIDENCE POINT

ISSAQUAH, WASHINGTON

4135 Providence Point Dr. SE
Issaquah, WA 98029
206-392-2300 / 800-648-1818
Fax: 206-392-2928

Developer: Swanson-Dean/Daewoo Partnership

Year of initial property sales/rentals: 1984

Total land area: 180 acres

Average elevation: 500 feet

Location: Central-Western Washington; King County; off Interstate Highway 90 just before entering the city of Issaquah; just east of the southeastern reaches of Lake Sammamish, across from Bellevue; approximately 15 miles east of Seattle.

Nearest airport with scheduled commercial service: Seattle-Tacoma International (18 miles)

Current number of housing units with year-round occupants: 710

Projected number of housing units: 1,100 (2000)

Resident eligibility: All residents must be at least 55 years of age.

Community visit/tour incentive program: None

Suggested newspaper: *Journal American*, 1705 132nd Ave. NE, Bellevue, WA 98005 (206-455-2222)

WHY PROVIDENCE POINT?

Few private planned retirement communities are located so close to one of America's premiere major cities. More often than not, the cost of land is too high to attract a large developer and to make such a project feasible. **Providence Point** is an example of the exception. The special qualities of the Pacific northwest, and the **Seattle** area in particular, give this community more than its share of appeal. Vistas of majestic mountain ranges, to the east as well as to the west, make for a glorious setting. For many residents who came from other parts of the country (or even from other countries), this is a land that combines climate, cultural richness, and scenic beauty in a way found in few other places. It has been an irresistible relocation destination for Californians as much as for New Yorkers, for Europeans as much as for Asians.

Bellevue, just a few minutes down the highway, is the cultural center of the east side of the Seattle metropolitan area. It is adorned with outstanding museums, a convention center that includes a 400-seat performing arts theater, a flagship regional library, and an extravagant mix of restaurants. More than 70 works of public art at 16 downtown locations play a special role in creating a rich sense of identity for local residents. Parks and open spaces add to the city's "livability index."

The Providence Point address city of **Issaquah**, at the base of the **Cascade Mountain range,** with a population of almost 10,000, is a growing upscale community. The greatest part of the housing inventory is well above average pricing for the state at large. More than 100 volunteer-based organizations reflect a devotion to the common good.

Amenities and programs at Providence Point won recognition in 1994 and 1995, having been named by *New Choices* magazine as one of the 20 best retirement communities in America.

WHO'S IN CHARGE?

The community consists of seven villages or neighborhoods. Each has its own homeowners association. An "umbrella board" is responsible for overall community policy development and implementation. Seven standing committees include membership, activities, buildings, asset management, grounds, and facilities. Membership is mandatory for all residents. Monthly fees range from $175 to $425, as determined by the size of the home and the level of services each community chooses to bring to its member homeowners. Such assessments cover property management, maintenance and repair of common properties, insurance coverage, security operations, community vehicles, educational programs, cable television, activities staffing, fire protection, water/sewer utilities, trash pickup (optional), taxes on common properties, auditing and legal expenses, etc.

To The Point is a monthly newsletter for residents of Providence Point that details the nature of activities and trips scheduled and publishes a variety of general interest news items, announcements, and personal messages.

THE WEATHER REPORT

Typical of the entire U.S. west coast, the climate here can be described as mild. The moderating air temperature effect of the vast Pacific waters is further tempered by the looming Cascade Mountains to the east, and to a lesser degree, the **Olympic Mountains** to the west. Both of these sentries protect the Seattle-**Tacoma** area from summer and winter temperature extremes that originate on the continental plains and in Canada.

The rainy season, which runs from October to March, brings most of the annual precipitation and considerable cloudiness. December typically qualifies as the wettest month; July the driest. While a normal winter will produce little more than a trace of snow, there have been a few unusual winters with more than 20 inches of snowfall. Average high and low temperatures, recorded at the nearest official weather-reporting station (Seattle-Tacoma Airport), show the following winter and summer readings:

December: high 45/low 36   **January:** high 45/low 35

February: high 49/low 37   **June:** high 70/low 52

July: high 75/low 55   **August:** high 75/low 56

Average annual precipitation: 38 inches

Average annual snowfall: 7 inches

HOME SWEET HOME

Providence Point is a community of townhouses (duplexes, triplexes, and larger combinations with one or more common exterior walls) and five condominium hotel-style three-story buildings. The latter units are all in Washington Village, one of the seven divisions on the property, which makes up a little more than one-third of the total housing configuration. The townhouses range in price from $125,000 to $325,000, with floor plans that range from 850 to 2,700 square feet. Condominium prices and sizes begin at $115,000 and 850 square feet, and go up to $260,000 and 1,600 square feet. Arrangements are available for contingent purchases pending sale of existing homes.

An estimated 90 percent of home purchases are for newly constructed units, with the remainder on the resale market. Long-term rental units are available for lease at monthly rates ranging from $950 to $1,150, offering from 850 to 1,100 square feet of floor space. Vacant lots for future construction are not available. Separate mobile home parking is available. Utility lines are below ground level.

MONEY MATTERS

The Seattle metropolitan area has historically been among the U.S. locations with living costs considerably above the national average in virtually every category. According to the **Economic Research Institute** of Redmond, Washington, Seattle is ranked at 131.1 percent above the national norm. Comparisons among selected cities published in *Where to Retire* magazine ("Chart of Living Costs: How 99 Cities Compare," Fall 1996; based on cost of living indices from ACCRA) showed Seattle to be at approximately the same composite index for primary living expenses as San Diego, Hilton Head (South Carolina), and Palm Springs (California).

Property taxes are levied by **King County**. The tax rate is based on 1.3 percent of the sale price of the property.

TAKE GOOD CARE OF YOURSELF

For anything short of inpatient admission to a hospital, a variety of basic health services are within walking distance of the Point. Adjacent **Marianwood**

Extended Healthcare Services, one of the top-rated facilities of its kind in the state, is more than a skilled nursing facility. It offers inpatient and outpatient physical, occupational, and speech rehabilitation programs. Nursing care may be short-, intermediate-, or long-term. It provides home health care specialists, medical social workers, rehabilitative therapists, and homemaker companions, as well as referral services to other resources. **Medalia HealthCare Pine Lake-Issaquah Clinic** is a medical and dental center at Providence Point's back gate. It is one of more than 40 such clinics under the Providence and Franciscan Health Systems.

Overlake Hospital Medical Center in Bellevue, with 275 beds, is a full-service advanced-care facility, 13 miles from the Providence Point gate. It encompasses a network of more than 550 physicians, including primary care and medical specialties. Being located in the shadow of Seattle, of course, means that any highly specialized medical diagnostic or treatment requirements are no more than 20 to 30 minutes away.

PLACES TO GO, THINGS TO DO

A two-building activity center covers 12,000 square feet of floor space. The clubhouse is the center of on-site recreational and social activity with an indoor swimming pool, exercise and game rooms, and a social area with complete kitchen facilities. The second building houses administrative offices for the homeowners association (HOA), a restaurant, and sales and partnership offices. A Providence Point brochure listing social and club activities describes approximately 30 different groups, including arts and crafts, card games, Kiwanis, ladies' breakfasts, residents' coffees, bible fellowship, book reviews, sports and exercise groups, computer users, and gardeners. A newcomers committee holds an informational social every month. A mutual support group called the "Care Bears" is for residents who care for spouses with health problems. Village socials within individual neighborhoods include potlucks, holiday parties, and barbecues. Chamber music concerts are presented at the clubhouse three times a year. There are monthly dances with live music. Seasonal social events run the gamut from grandchildren's Christmas parties to style shows and cookouts. The "Pea Patch" is a community garden where any resident can have a small plot of ground to call her/his own for planting, nurturing, and harvesting. A tennis court (and another in the planning stages) and a putting green draw their share of residents' attention. A full-time activities director coordinates all programs.

A truly unique educational offering at Providence Point is called **Communiversity Services**. Funded through homeowners' dues and operated by a governing board and a planning committee, small, informal classes are taught in an atmosphere in which students and faculty interact as peers. There are no tests and no grades. The curriculum is designed to include cultural programs and lectures on current issues. Classes generally meet once a week for eight weeks during each of three quarters during the year.

Greater Seattle probably has more different kinds of waterways in its environs than any other port city in the nation. From the open **Pacific Ocean** to countless lakes, rivers, sounds, bays, inlets, and canals, there is virtually no water-related recreation that is not accessible from every part of the metropolitan area. **Lake Sammamish** (about a mile from Providence Point) and **Lake Washington** (on the near side of downtown Seattle) are the closest water playgrounds for boating, fishing, and swimming. Nearby paved walking paths span approximately 75 miles of landscape near and beyond the community. Seven 18-hole public golf courses are within a 15-mile radius.

When it comes to describing the wealth of cultural, entertainment, and educational amenities in the Seattle area, of course, there is no limit to the scope of choices. Opera, symphony, museums of every type, theater, dance, collegiate and professional spectator sports, and parks galore are part of the leisure options. Fairs and exhibitions abound. It is a city at or near the top of almost every survey that professes to evaluate and recognize the best among the nation's places to live.

SAFE AND SECURE

Providence Point is discreetly protected by a hidden fence and guarded gates. Security personnel are on duty 24 hours a day. Law enforcement is provided by the county. The **Issaquah Fire Department** provides seven-minute response time. An emergency 911 phone system is in place. The community boasts a crime-free record in recent years, with the exception of minor theft of construction materials.

LET'S GO SHOPPING

A full-service grocery market is within a mile of the entry gate. Major retail shopping in and around Issaquah is within 3 miles. Providence Point operates its own minibus that makes regularly scheduled runs into Issaquah, to Bellevue, and to downtown Seattle, only 30 minutes away. Twice a month the bus is scheduled for a trip to a major shopping mall. Transportation is also provided for junkets to a host of entertainment and special events throughout the area, as occasions require.

One of the most fascinating shopping excursions anyone can contemplate is to **Pike Place Market**, on downtown Seattle's **Elliott Bay** waterfront. It is a conglomeration of fresh, exotic, and specialty foods, huge displays of cut flowers and plants, and some of the best seafood restaurants to be found anywhere. Crowds flock to the aromatic aisles of vendor stalls, many shoppers visiting from far corners of the world.

FOOD FOR THOUGHT

Here is a potpourri of opinions, suggestions, and reminders to help launch and conclude your search for a place to call your retirement home:

♦ A great retirement takes a spirit of adventure and even a willingness to take some calculated risk. There is no wisdom in relocating unless a new environment promises unique opportunities and rewards. It's all about change. The challenge is to "know thyself" well enough to catalog your interests and define your dreams. That done, go find that special place where it can all come together. It's out there!

♦ One good way to get to know a prospective destination area is to subscribe to the most prominent local newspaper over some reasonable period of time. A Sunday-only subscription may be quite satisfactory. There is no better way to get insights into virtually every facet of an unfamiliar locale.

♦ Are you a two-car family now? Will your daily routine change in ways that will enable you to get along quite well with one vehicle? You may find yourself trading the second car for a golf cart.

♦ When visiting a community to evaluate its promise as a retirement nesting place, there are some key issues to examine and questions to ask. Among them:

  ♦ The role of the homeowners' association, the manner in which it operates, the degree to which it facilitates resident participation, the leadership it has attracted.

  ♦ The condition of community finances.

  ♦ The nature and efficiency of community services provided (street maintenance, water supply/utilities, trash collection, etc.).

  ♦ The quality and availability of health resources.

  ♦ The nature, quality, and effectiveness of recreational programs.

  ♦ Nearby off-site conveniences and attractions (major shopping, entertainment, restaurants, cultural lures, points of interest, etc.).

  ♦ Perceptions of the nature and incidence of crime in the community.

  ♦ Availability of desired special services (housekeeping, landscaping, home repairs, interior decorating, etc.).

These and other questions and issues you may wish to explore can be drawn from any number of sources, including random residents you might meet or seek out, staff personnel, community volunteers (including board members), shopkeepers and clerks, etc. Most people approached for such information are more than willing to respond with candor to your inquiries.

One of the best ways to gain insights into community assets and liabilities is to ask: "What are the two or three things you like *most* about the community? What are the two or three things you like *least*?"

There is no more complex, confusing, or challenging subject than *taxes* when it comes to evaluating the cost of living impact on retirement relocation. Many people assign a disproportionate importance to the question of whether a state imposes an income tax. While that question is certainly one that deserves careful attention, it can easily be misleading. The fact is that few places offer any free lunch when it comes to providing governmental services. The taxpayer will feel the heavy hand of the revenue collectors one way or another. Typically, those states that impose no income tax have the highest levies on sales and/or property, or on other categories of public income.

This having been said, it is true that some states and localities do have enviable revenue sources that come from riches in natural resources (oil and gas particularly), which, in some cases, do lighten the tax load on individuals. But that is the exception and not a circumstance that can be expected to influence a relocation decision. The only valid way to draw meaningful conclusions about tax burdens is to examine the entire assessment picture—taxes and fees that apply to state and local income, real and personal property, sales and use, investments (so-called intangibles), pensions, estate, inheritance, and licensing, among others. It should be noted that not infrequently a tax is a tax by another name. Governments can find ways to disguise terms, avoiding the word "tax" and calling it something else (service fee, administrative charge, special assessment, etc.) to make it more palatable to the citizen taxpayer.

Most homeowners' associations are structured in such a way as to protect members from undue risk or disadvantage. It is well, however, to be aware of several key concerns:

♦ Does the association have unencumbered ownership and use of the clubhouse and other facilities? If it is under contract or lease from the developer or other third party, that means that the members are subject to an assortment of legal and contractual obligations. It is well to know in advance how such conditions affect membership.

♦ Is the association incorporated? It is of considerable importance that your personal liability be limited in the event of a claim against the association. Incorporation of such organizations is commonplace but not universal. It is the only way to protect your personal assets from attachment.

♦ Are the clubhouse and/or other tangible properties mortgaged to a first lein holder? If so, bear in mind that such mortgagees have prior claims and rights.

There is an endless list of precautions with regard to purchasing a residential property. Here are just a few:

♦ Be sure your lot drains well. Sites lower than the surrounding land could spell real trouble from flooding.

♦ Check out utility costs for your new destination. Electricity is normally a significantly more expensive way to heat a home and to provide hot water. Natural gas is preferable. Generously overhanging eaves, double-pane window glass, and a stand of sheltering trees will also contribute to reducing utility costs and enhancing comfort.

♦ Be sure to check insulation. Ceilings should have a minimum of R-30 and walls not less than R-11 ratings (more is better) in order to assure optimal savings for heating and cooling costs.

♦ Low maintenance exterior construction materials, while requiring somewhat greater initial outlay, can save money in the long run. Brick, vinyl siding, aluminum or concrete shingles, and such can keep maintenance expense to a minimum and sustain a more attractive appearance over the years.

Retirement communities that combine their use of facilities with resort/vacation features (time share, vacation rentals, on-site short-term lodging, and such) generally have to keep their recreational amenities in top condition or suffer the consequences of lost patronage. Restaurants in such communities also have to maintain quality and value standards sufficient to please temporary guests. Such considerations tend to benefit permanent residents/retirees who have also typically invested in and/or are users of the same facilities.

In addition, revenues derived from public access enable some communities to improve and expand their properties beyond the point that would otherwise be possible.

COMMUNITIES AT A GLANCE

Community Name and Location	Year Estab	Acreage	Age Limit?	# Housing Units 1997	# Housing Units at Buildout	Gated?
ALBEMARLE PLANTATION Hertford, North Carolina	1990	1,600	no	85	1,000	yes
BELLA VISTA VILLAGE Bella Vista, Arkansas	1965	36,000	no	7,600	17,000	no
CAROLINA TRACE COUNTRY CLUB Sanford, North Carolina	1973	2,500	no	970	2,000	yes
CARRIAGE PARK Hendersonville, North Carolina	1992	377	no	130	663	yes
CLAREMONT Portland, Oregon	1991	200	yes	390	575	no
THE COUNTRY CLUB OF MOUNT DORA Mount Dora, Florida	1991	440	no	325	745	no
CRESCENT OAKS Tarpon Springs, Florida	1989	850	no	310	434	yes
CUMMINGS COVE GOLFING COMMUNITY Hendersonville, North Carolina	1986	537	no	140	400	yes
DEL WEBB'S SUN CITY GEORGETOWN Georgetown, Texas	1995	5,300	yes	750	9,500	no
DEL WEBB'S SUN CITY GRAND Surprise, Arizona	1996	4,000	yes	175	9,500	no
DEL WEBB'S SUN CITY HILTON HEAD Bluffton, South Carolina	1995	5,600	yes	650	8,000	yes

Community Name and Location	Year Estab	Acreage	Age Limit?	# Housing Units 1997	# Housing Units at Buildout	Gated?
DEL WEBB'S SUN CITY ROSEVILLE Roseville, California	1994	1,200	yes	1,400	3,100	no
FAIRFIELD BAY Fairfield Bay, Arkansas	1968	10,155	no	1,000	1,400	no
FAIRFIELD GLADE Fairfield Glade, Tennessee	1970	12,700	no	3,100	n/a	partial
FAIRFIELD HOMES GREEN VALLEY Green Valley, Arizona	1972	18,000	yes	10,900	17,900	no
FAIRFIELD MOUNTAINS Lake Lure, North Carolina	1977	2,500	no	700	1,400	yes
FAIRFIELD SAPPHIRE VALLEY Sapphire, North Carolina	1971	5,400	no	850	n/a	no
FEARRINGTON VILLAGE Pittsboro, North Carolina	1974	1,100	no	800	1,600	no
FORD'S COLONY AT WILLIAMSBURG Williamsburg, Virginia	1985	2,500	no	885	2,800	no
FOUR LAKES GOLF CLUB Winter Haven, Florida	1995	500	yes	150	850	yes
HEATHER GARDENS Aurora, Colorado	1973	198	yes	2,426	2,426	no
HERITAGE HARBOUR Annapolis, Maryland	1979	953	yes	1,650	1,710	no
HERITAGE PLANTATION Pawleys Island, South Carolina	1990	637	no	225	517	yes
HOLIDAY ISLAND Holiday Island, Arkansas	1970	4,500	no	980	5,000	no

Community Name and Location	Year Estab	Acreage	Age Limit?	# Housing Units 1997	# Housing Units at Buildout	Gated?
HOT SPRINGS VILLAGE Hot Springs Village, Arkansas	1970	26,000	no	6,000	9,000	yes
KEOWEE KEY Salem, South Carolina	1972	1,500	no	900	2,200	yes
KINGS POINT IN TAMARAC Tamarac, Florida	1983	350	yes	2,650	5,471	yes
KNOLLWOOD VILLAGE Pinehurst, North Carolina	1976	150	no	200	240	no
LAUREL RIDGE COUNTRY CLUB Waynesville, North Carolina	1986	876	no	150	320	no
LEISURE WORLD LAGUNA HILLS Laguna Hills, California	1964	2,100	yes	12,736	12,736	yes
LEISURE WORLD OF MARYLAND Silver Spring, Maryland	1964	620	yes	6,000	7,500	yes
MYRTLE TRACE Myrtle Beach, South Carolina	1983	300	yes	400	510	no
OAKMONT VILLAGE Santa Rosa, California	1964	1,745	yes	2,800	2,950	no
PEBBLECREEK RESORT COMMUNITY Goodyear, Arizona	1993	760	yes	735	n/a	yes
PRESLEY'S SUN LAKES COUNTRY CLUB Banning, California	1987	963	yes	2,150	3,600	yes
PROVIDENCE POINT Issaquah, Washington	1984	180	yes	710	1,100	yes
ROYAL HIGHLANDS Leesburg, Florida	1996	779	yes	170	1,500	yes

Community Name and Location	Year Estab	Acreage	Age Limit?	# Housing Units 1997	# Housing Units at Buildout	Gated?
SADDLEBROOKE RESORT COMMUNITY Tucson, Arizona	1986	1,790	yes	1,650	4,000	no
SAVANNAH LAKES VILLAGE McCormick, South Carolina	1989	3,987	no	300	5,100	no
SONORA HILLS Sonora, California	1988	44	yes	190	235	yes
STILLWATERS RESORT Dadeville, Alabama	1971	2,200	no	260	950	yes
STONEYBROOK GOLF & COUNTRY CLUB Sarasota, Florida	1994	475	no	350	940	yes
STRAWBERRY RIDGE Valrico, Florida	1971	120	yes	525	865	yes
SUN LAKES RESORT COMMUNITY Sun Lakes, Arizona	1972	3,500	yes	7,200	10,000	partial
TELLICO VILLAGE Loudon, Tennessee	1986	4,600	no	1,450	5,000	no
TIMBER PINES Spring Hill, Florida	1982	1,420	yes	2,500	3,460	yes
THE VILLAGES OF CITRUS HILLS Hernando, Florida	1983	12,000	no	3,000	10,000	no
THE VILLAGES OF HIGHLANDS RIDGE Sebring, Florida	1991	453	yes	265	750	yes
THE VILLAGES OF LADY LAKE Lady Lake, Florida	1983	7,360	yes	8,000	23,549	yes
WILLBROOK PLANTATION Pawleys Island, South Carolina	1986	2,400	no	190	2,000	yes

STATE AND LOCAL COMBINED TAX RANKINGS

For states included in this directory*

PER CAPITA State/Rank**	Amount	PER WORKER State/Rank	Amount	PER $1,000 OF PERSONAL INCOME State/Rank	Amount
Maryland (8)	2,565	California (8)	4,858	Arizona (9)	120.51
Washington (10)	2,433	Washington (10)	4,758	Oregon (16)	114.25
California (12)	2,396	Maryland (11)	4,752	Washington (16)	113.32
Oregon (23)	2,169	Arizona (15)	4,607	California (22)	110.43
Arizona (27)	2,122	Florida (23)	4,260	Maryland (27)	108.89
Colorado (28)	2,092	Oregon (25)	4,194	No. Carolina (28)	108.74
Virginia (29)	2,073	Colorado (32)	4,015	So. Carolina (37)	105.16
Florida (31)	2,048	Virginia (34)	3,964	Texas (41)	104.04
No. Carolina (34)	1,975	No. Carolina (36)	3,862	Florida (42)	102.30
Texas (35)	1,932	Texas (37)	3,844	Arkansas (44)	101.36
So. Carolina (43)	1,736	Tennessee (44)	3,478	Colorado (45)	100.50
Tennessee (46)	1,684	So. Carolina (45)	3,471	Virginia (46)	97.70
Arkansas (48)	1,590	Arkansas (49)	3,329	Tennessee (47)	93.71
Alabama (49)	1,553	Alabama (50)	3,281	Alabama (49)	92.68
50-state median	**2,127**		**4,173**		**109.08**

* Source: Cal-Tex Research, "Taxing California," May 1996 (California Taxpayers Association).

** Number in parentheses indicates ranking among the 50 states, from the most to the least amount of tax imposition.

RESOURCES

ALABAMA

Alabama Department of Economic &
  Community Affairs
P.O. Box 5690
Montgomery, AL 36103
800-235-4757; Fax: 334-242-4203

Business Council of
  Alabama/Montgomery
2 N. Jackson, P.O. Box 76
Montgomery, AL 36101-0076
334-834-6000; Fax: 334-262-7371

ARIZONA

Arizona Chamber of Commerce
1221 E. Osborn #100
Phoenix, AZ 85014-5539
602-248-9172; Fax: 602-265-1262

Flagstaff Chamber of Commerce
  Information & Referral
101 W. Santa Fe Ave.
Flagstaff, AZ 86001
520-774-4505; Fax: 520-779-1209

Kingman Chamber of Commerce
P.O. Box 1150
Kingman, AZ 86402
520-753-6106; Fax: 520-753-1049

Phoenix Chamber of Commerce
Loraine La Morder, Info. Spec.
201 N. Central Ave., #2700
Phoenix, AZ 85073
602-254-5521; Fax: 602-495-8913

Prescott Chamber of Commerce
P.O. Box 1147
Prescott, AZ 86302
520-445-2000; 800-266-7534
Fax: 520-445-0068

State of Arizona, Administration Dept.
Information & Resources Management
  Division
1616 W. Adams
Phoenix, AZ 85007
602-542-5791; Fax: 602-542-2199

Tucson Metropolitan Chamber of
  Commerce
P.O. Box 991
Tucson, AZ 85702
520-792-2250; Fax: 520-882-5704

ARKANSAS

Fayetteville Chamber of Commerce
P.O. Box 4216
Fayetteville, AZ 72720
800-766-4626; 501-521-1710
Fax: 501-521-1791

Greater Hot Springs Chamber of
  Commerce
P.O. Box 6090
Hot Springs, AR 71902
800-467-4636; 501-321-1700
Fax: 501-321-3551

Greater Little Rock Chamber of
Commerce
101 S. Spring St. #200
Little Rock, AR 72201
501-374-4871; Fax: 501-374-6018

State of Arkansas, Secretary of State
Information Services (newcomers
guide)
State Capitol Bldg., Rm. 256
Little Rock, AR 72201
501-682-5160; Fax: 501-682-3510

CALIFORNIA

California State Chamber of
Commerce
P.O. Box 1736
Sacramento, CA 95812
916-444-6670; Fax: 916-444-6685

State of California, Trade & Commerce
Agency
Tourism Division
801 K St., #1600
Sacramento, CA 95814
916-322-2881; Fax: 916-322-3402

COLORADO

Colorado Association of Commerce &
Industry
1776 Lincoln St., #1200
Denver, CO 80203
303-831-7411; Fax: 303-860-1439

Colorado Springs Chamber of
Commerce
P.O. Drawer B
Colorado Springs, CO 80901
719-635-1551; Fax: 719-635-1571

Denver Metro Chamber of Commerce
1445 Market St.
Denver, CO 80202
303-534-8500; Fax: 303-534-3200

FLORIDA

Florida Chamber of Commerce
P.O. Box 11309
Tallahassee, FL 32302
904-425-1200; Fax: 904-425-1260

State of Florida, Community Affairs
Dept.
Information Systems & Services
2555 Shumard Oak Blvd.
Tallahassee, FL 32399
904-922-2289; Fax: 904-921-0781

MARYLAND

Maryland Chamber of Commerce
60 West St., #100
Annapolis, MD 21401
410-269-0642; Fax: 410-269-5247

State of Maryland, Business &
Economic Development Dept.
Tourism Promotion Division
217 E. Redwood St.
Baltimore, MD 21202
410-767-6266; Fax: 410-333-8628

NORTH CAROLINA

Asheville Chamber of Commerce
P.O. Box 1010
Asheville, NC 28802
704-258-6101; Fax: 704-251-0926

Charlotte Chamber of Commerce
P.O. Box 32785
Charlotte, NC 28232
704-378-1300; Fax: 704-374-1903

North Carolina Citizens for Business
& Industry
P.O. Box 2508
Raleigh, NC 27602
919-836-1400; Fax: 919-836-1425

State of North Carolina, Commerce
Dept.
Travel & Tourism Division
430 N. Salisbury St.
Raleigh, NC 27611
919-733-4171; Fax: 919-733-8582

State of North Carolina, Cultural
Resources Dept.
Public Affairs Office
109 E. Jones St.
Raleigh, NC 27601
919-733-5722; Fax: 919-733-1564

OREGON

Portland Metro Chamber of Commerce
221 NW 2nd Ave.
Portland, OR 97209
503-228-9411; Fax: 503-228-5126

State of Oregon, Economic
Development Dept./Tourism
Manager
775 Summer St. NE
Salem, OR 97310
503-373-1270; Fax: 503-581-5115

SOUTH CAROLINA

South Carolina State Chamber of
Commerce
1201 Main St., #1810
Columbia, SC 29201
803-799-4601; Fax: 803-779-6043

State of South Carolina,
Parks/Recreation & Tourism Dept.
Marketing Services Office
1205 Pendleton St., #248
Columbia, SC 29201
803-734-0135; Fax: 803-734-1409

TENNESSEE

Knoxville Convention & Visitors
Bureau
810 Clinch Ave.
Knoxville, TN 37902
423-523-7263; Fax: 423-673-4400

Memphis Area Chamber of
Commerce
P.O. Box 224
Memphis, TN 38101
901-543-5333; Fax: 901-575-3510

Nashville Chamber of Commerce
161 Fourth Ave. N
Nashville, TN 37219
619-259-4755

State of Tennessee, Economic &
Community Development Dept.
320 6th Ave. N, 8th Floor
Nashville, TN 37243
615-741-1888; Fax: 615-741-7306

TEXAS

Greater Dallas Chamber of Commerce
1201 Elm Street, #2000
Dallas, TX 75270
214-746-6600; Fax: 214-746-6799

Greater Houston Partnership
1200 Smith St., #700
Houston, TX 77002
713-651-2100; Fax: 713-651-2299

State of Texas, Commerce Dept.
Tourism Division
P.O. Box 12728
Austin, TX 78711
512-936-0100; Fax: 512-936-0303

Texas Association of Business &
  Chambers of Commerce
P.O. Box 2989
Austin, TX 78768
512-477-6721; Fax: 512-477-0836

VIRGINIA

Greater Richmond Chamber of
  Commerce
P.O. Box 12280
Richmond, VA 23241
804-648-1234; Fax: 804-780-0344

State of Virginia, Commerce Trade
  Office
Housing & Community Development
  Dept.
Jackson Center, 501 N. 2nd St.
Richmond, VA 23219
804-371-7025; Fax: 804-371-7090

Virginia Chamber of Commerce
9 S. Fifth St.
Richmond, VA 23219
804-644-1607; Fax: 804-783-0903

WASHINGTON

Association of Washington Business
P.O. Box 658
Olympia, WA 98507
360-943-1600; Fax: 360-943-5811

Greater Seattle Chamber of
  Commerce
1301 5th Ave., #2400
Seattle, WA 98101
206-389-7200; Fax: 206-389-7288

State of Washington, Community
  Trade & Economic Development,
  Tourism Division
P.O. Box 48300
Olympia, WA 98504
360-753-5795; Fax: 360-586-3582

State of Washington, State Parks
  & Recreation Commission
Public Affairs Division
P.O. Box 42650
Olympia, WA 98504
360-902-8501; Fax: 360-753-1594

BIBLIOGRAPHY

ACCRA Cost of Living Index (quarterly survey), ACCRA, Alexandria, VA

America's Best Neighborhoods for Active Retirees (special report), Vacation Publications, Houston, TX (1994)

America's Best Places to Retire, Richard L. Fox, Vacation Publications, Houston, TX (1995)

America's Most Affordable Retirement Towns (special report), William Schemmel, Vacation Publications, Houston, TX (1995)

Approaching Retirement, Durand C. Young, Avery Publishing Group, Garden City Park, NY (1995)

Commerce Clearing House State Tax Guide (1996)

Comparative Climatic Data for the United States Through 1995, National Oceanic and Atmospheric Administration National Climatic Data Center, Asheville, NC

Consumer Guide to the Best-Rated Retirement Communities and Towns, Norman D. Ford, Publications International, Lincolnwood, IL (1988)

50 Best Retirement Communities in America, Alice and Fred Lee, St. Martin's Press, New York (1994)

50 Fabulous Places to Retire in America, 2nd Ed., Lee Rosenberg and Saralee H. Rosenberg, Career Press, Franklin Lakes, NJ (1997)

Finding the Right Place for Retirement, Retirement Living Publishing Co., New York, NY (1996)

Intangibles Taxes (special report), Vacation Publications, Houston, TX (1996)

Modern Maturity (bimonthly magazine), American Association of Retired Persons, Lakewood, CA

New Choices (10 times/year magazine), The Reader's Digest Association, Pleasantville, NY

99 Best Residential & Recreational Communities in America, Lester J. Giese, L. Anne Thornton, and William Kinnaman, John Wiley & Sons, NY (1992)

Places Rated Almanac, David Savageau and Richard Boyer, Prentice Hall General Reference and Travel, NY (1993)

The Rating Guide to Life In America's Fifty States, G. Scott Thomas, Prometheus Books, Amherst, NY (1994)

Retirement Choices, John Howells, Gateway Books, San Rafael, CA (1987)

Retirement Living Communities, Deborah Freundlich, Macmillan Publishing USA, Indianapolis, IN (1995)

Selecting Retirement Housing, American Association of Retired Persons, Lakewood, CA (1991)

Tax Heaven or Hell—A Guide to the Tax Consequences of Retirement Relocation, Eve Evans and Alan Fox, Vacation Publications, Houston, TX (1996)

Weather Almanac, 6th Edition, Frank E. Blair, Gale Research, Detroit, MI (1992)

Weather of U.S. Cities, 4th Edition, Frank E. Blair, Gale Research, Detroit, MI (1992)

Where to Retire, 2nd Edition, John Howells, Gateway Books, Oakland, CA (1995)

Where to Retire (quarterly magazine), Vacation Publications, Houston, TX

INDEX BY COMMUNITY NAME